The Organ and Its Music in German-Jewish Culture

TINA FRÜHAUF

The Organ and Its Music in German-Jewish Culture

2009

OXFORD
UNIVERSITY PRESS

Oxford University Press, Inc., publishes works that further
Oxford University's objective of excellence
in research, scholarship, and education.

Oxford   New York
Auckland   Cape Town   Dar es Salaam   Hong Kong   Karachi
Kuala Lumpur   Madrid   Melbourne   Mexico City   Nairobi
New Delhi   Shanghai   Taipei   Toronto

With offices in
Argentina   Austria   Brazil   Chile   Czech Republic   France   Greece
Guatemala   Hungary   Italy   Japan   Poland   Portugal   Singapore
South Korea   Switzerland   Thailand   Turkey   Ukraine   Vietnam

Originally published in German as
Orgel und Orgelmusik in deutsch-jüdischer Kultur by Tina Frühauf
Copyright © 2005 by Georg Olms Verlag AG, Hildesheim—Zürich—New York

Copyright © 2009 English adaptation and translation by Oxford University Press, Inc.

Published by Oxford University Press, Inc.
198 Madison Avenue, New York, New York 10016

www.oup.com

Oxford is a registered trademark of Oxford University Press

Library of Congress Cataloging-in-Publication Data
Frühauf, Tina.
[Orgel und Orgelmusik in deutsch-jüdischer Kultur. English]
The organ and its music in German-Jewish culture / Tina Frühauf.
   p.   cm.
Includes bibliographical references and index.
ISBN 978-0-19-533706-8
1. Organ music—Germany—History and criticism.
2. Jews—Germany—Music—History and criticism. I. Title.
ML626.F7813   2008
786.5089′924043—dc22   2008011105

Visit the companion website online at
www.oup.com/us/theorgananditsmusic
Username: Music2
Password: Book4416

9   8   7   6   5   4   3   2   1
Printed in the United States of America
on acid-free paper

To Erhard,
who taught me to persevere,
and to Pryor,
who is teaching me patience
— I wish they had met

"I am not Stiller!" With this statement, Max Frisch's main character begins the novel *Stiller*, which centers on the identity of an individual torn between his specific and highly individualized self-image and society's expectations. While reading this novel, I realized that identity is always a matter of perspective, oscillating between the definition of the Other and the self. This thought serves as leitmotif for this study, which traces the changing identities of German Jews in the early nineteenth and twentieth centuries and treats the organ and organ music as representatives of Jewish identity.

The choice of the organ in Jewish culture as a research subject, especially for a scholar who is not Jewish, has raised others' questions about my own identity and motivations as well. How could a German not be interested in an important historical and religious aspect of her own country? As there is no simple answer or key event that would explain how I entered this world, perhaps the topic itself and some preliminary insights into my research will suffice: The subject matter—encountered when I discovered an old print of German-Jewish cantorial music with organ parts in the University Library of Bochum—piqued my curiosity not merely because of its eclecticism but also because of its apparent neglect by scholars of Jewish studies and musicologists alike. Choosing this subject was a combination of emotional, intellectual, and—most important—musical concerns and interests.

Although keyboard instruments have been present in Jewish communities around the world—from Europe and North America to remote communities in Argentina and Curaçao—the organ in Jewish culture has never been the subject of a comprehensive research study. One reason for this may lie in the fact that the organ was never elevated from its controversial status in Judaism. A rather marginal entity, the organ in the synagogue remained an oddity for Jews and non-Jews alike—a further motivation for and attestation to the necessity and urgency of this study.

As I perceived the position of the organ in contemporary global Jewish culture, which ranges from utter neglect to the very denial of its presence, it became my special concern as organist to preserve this part of Jewish musical culture and to present it to a diverse readership.

This study is neither an exhaustive discourse of the subject, nor does it present every work ever composed. Rather, it offers glimpses into German-Jewish musical life through representative compositions and selected communities. A comprehensive survey would be impossible, considering the extinction of Jewish culture, including the instruments installed in synagogues, as well as music in manuscripts and in print. In fact, the biggest challenge I encountered was to recover a musical culture systematically destroyed in the 1930s and 1940s by finding the repertoire and reconstructing the instruments.

Organ music that was written by composers of Jewish heritage or that did not meet the Nazis' requirements of "German music" was no longer allowed to be printed and published, reproduced, or even copied. Thus, a good part of the repertoire continued to exist only in manuscript form, and much did not survive the Holocaust and must be deemed lost. A number of public and private collections, as well as many individuals who were related in different ways to German-Jewish music culture, led to the resurfacing of a nearly forgotten body of work.

Through methodical research in nineteenth- and early twentieth-century organ journals and magazines, a mass mailing to the archives of German cities, and research in the records of various organ builders in Germany, I was able to recover most of the dispositions and other details of organs in synagogues that were destroyed by the Nazis. Ultimately, uncovering and grasping the richness of German-Jewish musical life led me to a deeper understanding of the magnitude of the Holocaust.

My research has yielded unforeseen gratifications and certainly a number of surprises, most notably the discovery of the life and work of Siegfried Würzburger (1877–1942), who was murdered in the concentration camp Lodz. All that apparently survived were references to his works in local Jewish newspapers of the 1930s, as neither biographical data nor compositions in print exist. Würzburger is representative of many lesser-known artists of Jewish origin whose work became extinct in the Holocaust. But this is also a story of success, perseverance, and friendship. With few leads to follow, I contacted the Stadtbibliothek in Frankfurt am Main to inquire about Würzburger's fate—the fact that he had such an eclectic Germanic name struck me as especially curious, making it even more worthwhile to pursue his life and work. The Stadtbibliothek provided me with the address of a certain Kenneth Ward (formerly Karl Robert Würzburger) in Wickford, England—the youngest son of Siegfried and Gertrud. Ward survived the Holocaust through the *Kindertransport* [refugee children relocation], the rescue mission for Jewish children that took place nine months prior to the outbreak of the Second World War. My fears that Kenneth Ward would reject my inquiry or perhaps not even answer because of the past proved to be unfounded. A lively reply was followed by an invitation to England, where, in addition to manuscripts, interviews, and correspondence, I received a gift even more priceless: a new friend.

Similarly curious and unforeseen was the research on Hermann Zivi (1867–1944), the chief cantor of the Jewish congregation in Wuppertal-Elberfeld and an avid composer of a diverse musical repertoire. Although I happened to find many of his works at the Jewish National and University Library in Jerusalem, his actual biography remained a mystery, especially with regard to what became of him and his family after 1938. Through an Internet search I was able to locate a distant relative in Brazil, where, in 1931, Zivi's son Paul founded the Hercules Company (Zivi Mundial), a cutlery manufacturing business with branches in Porto Alegre, Rio de Janeiro, and São Paolo. Although it had changed ownership, a relative still worked in the company and responded almost instantly to my inquiry. It came as a surprise that he then connected me to another relative who turned out to be an acquaintance of mine, the world-renowned first violinist of the LaSalle Quartet, Walter Levin— grandson of Hermann Zivi.

These are just two isolated stories out of many that made my research an extraordinary journey through time, life, and people. There are many more individuals who intellectually or ideationally supported my research or kindly provided materials: Samuel Adler, Haim Alexander, the late Herman Berlinski, the late Hans Hirschberg, Hagit Kochba, Hans Nadler, Maria Schlüsener, Martha Sommer Hirsch, Yuval Shaked, the late Fritz Steinmeyer, the late Werner Walcker-Mayer, Andreas Willscher, and Horst-Theodor Wuttke.

For their assistance with photographs I would like to thank Raymond Dittrich and the Bischöfliche Zentralbibliothek Regensburg, Thomas Leipnitz and the Österreichische Staatsbibliothek in Wien, Werner Hanak and the Jüdisches Museum Wien, Achim Seip, Gerhard Walcker-Mayer, and especially my husband, Pryor Dodge, for the hours he has spent on photo editing and restoration.

The research on which this book is based was funded by generous fellowships from the German Academic Exchange Service (1998) and the Cusanuswerk (1998–2001), the Organ Historical Society's Alan Laufman Research Grant (2006), and the Ruth and Clarence Mader Scholarship Fund (2006).

I am indebted to many authors and scholars who influenced my thinking about German Jewry and Jewish music, especially my mentor and friend of many years, Philip V. Bohlman. At Columbia University in New York I benefited greatly from the guidance and comments of Dieter Christensen and Aaron Fox. Horst Weber made many useful suggestions for the earlier German version of this book.

I am grateful for the many friends, acquaintances, and officials who facilitated my research in Israel: the staff at the Jewish National and University Library in Jerusalem, especially Gila Flam, and at the Archive of Israeli Music at Tel Aviv University, where Marina Ritzarev and Yohanan Ron kindly assisted me. The Music Department of Tel Aviv University supported my research in every way possible.

I would like to thank the archivists and librarians who helped with the extensive research I conducted in the United States: Eliott Kahn, who introduced me to the rich resources at the Jewish Theological Seminary in New York; the staff at the Center for Jewish History in New York and at the Hebrew Union College in New York and Cincinnati.

I greatly appreciate the continuous support of the Salomon Ludwig Steinheim-Institut in Duisburg, especially Michael Brocke, the series editor of the German edition, and Margret Heitmann, editor of the same. Both advised me on the contents of the English edition and helped with photo research.

Suzanne Ryan and the editorial staff at Oxford University Press made the birthing of the revised English edition possible through their efficiency, perseverance, and continuous support. Many thanks go especially to Norman Hirschy, who guided this project with great enthusiasm.

I wish to express my deep gratitude to David Bloom for being my right hand in editorial and translation matters, for his diligence and competence as linguist and editor, and for his dedication to my project. I would like to thank my friend Ben Epstein for his critical comments on earlier drafts of the English texts, his challenging questions, and abundant enthusiasm for my research.

Last but not least, I am grateful for the kindness of two strangers—John Pallotta and Christopher Steckel—the ones I shall never forget.

CONTENTS

CHAPTER ONE   The Organ, Jewish Music, and Identity:
               Preliminary Remarks   3

CHAPTER TWO   Jewish "Curiosities": *The Organ in Judaism
               before 1800*   11

CHAPTER THREE The Organ as a Jewish Religious Response
               to Modernity   27

INTERMEZZO   Sharing the Console: *The Synagogue Organist*   89

CHAPTER FOUR   Organ Music in Jewish Communities   101

CHAPTER FIVE   The Aftermath of Emigration   187

CHAPTER SIX   Between Assimilation and Dissimilation: *The Jewish
               Community in the Course of Modernity*   213

               Notes   221

               Bibliography   255

               Index   277

The Organ and Its Music in German-Jewish Culture

CHAPTER ONE | # The Organ, Jewish Music, and Identity
Preliminary Remarks

Due to its tradition in churches, the organ, originally a secular instrument, came to be regarded as emblematically Christian. But the Christian cultural world to which it is properly ascribed is only a limited one since instruments were rarely used in Coptic, Russian and Greek Orthodox, and Calvinist churches, for example. Until the Middle Ages, the organ was not officially permitted in any Christian liturgy inasmuch as instrumental music was associated with pagan rituals and with the Jewish services once held in the temple at Jerusalem.[1] As late as the eleventh century, the organ had much more of a secular function, was typically associated with court ceremonies, and was played in churches and monasteries only in isolated cases.[2]

The organ's introduction in the churches of Western Europe took place over an extended period. Between approximately 900 CE and 1100 CE it made its way into some churches, but was played only on extraliturgical occasions. Not until the mid-fifteenth century was it officially admitted for use in the worship service. Since the late Middle Ages, however, it has been an intrinsic part of the sacred architecture and the most important instrument of musical expression for most Western churches. During the same period, Jews began to see the organ as *ḥukkat ha-goi*, as an instrument belonging within the realm of Christianity.

As closely tied as the organ may be to the Christian church, a tie that dates back to pre-Christian times also exists between the organ and Jewish culture and deserves to be taken seriously. Like the church organ, the synagogue organ has not become a global Jewish phenomenon but is mostly limited to the Ashkenazic synagogues of Europe and the United States. In and of itself, the organ is neither Christian nor Jewish and belongs to both Western and Eastern cultures. As a musical component of religious worship, however, it belongs to the West.[3]

This study centers on the role of the organ and organ music in the lives of German Jews. It is important to note that German-Jewish culture extends beyond the current German border, as well as that of the Deutsches Reich. In actuality, it refers to the Jewish population of all German-speaking lands, including the Austro-Hungarian Empire, Alsace, and other regions that were involved in similar political and social developments.

The temporal focus runs from the nineteenth to the early twentieth centuries and is marked on either end by two key events: the introduction of the first organ into a synagogue in Germany in 1810 (beginning the evolution of a German-Jewish organ tradition) and the destruction of most synagogues and their organs in the Kristallnacht of 1938, which forced the end of the German-Jewish musical tradition. Between these two important dates, fundamental religious rulings and regulations substantially influenced the development of a Jewish organ tradition and legitimized it within the framework of the different interpretations of the *halakhah*, the collective corpus of Jewish religious law. At the same time, German-Jewish congregations evolved from a more strictly religious organization in the nineteenth century to a community of increasingly social and cultural functions in the early twentieth century.[4] The double function as a place of worship and a community center was one factor among many that influenced the role of the organ. In addition to becoming an integral part of Jewish Reform worship, it was increasingly used for secular events that took place in the synagogue, such as concerts, benefit performances, and events organized by the Jüdischer Kulturbund, an all-Jewish performing arts ensemble maintained by the Nazis between 1933 and 1941.

Taking a look at the organ in Jewish culture before and after the temporal limits of this book serves to contextualize German-Jewish developments. The early history of instruments in Judaism provides the scaffolding needed to understand the arguments and debates of the nineteenth-century Reform and the so-called organ quarrels. The continuation (or rather absence) of the German-Jewish musical tradition after the Holocaust focuses on two countries of immigration: the United States and Palestine/Israel, for both had been the main havens for the composers and musicians growing up in the German-Jewish tradition.

One of the key questions in this study has to do with how the musical culture of German Jews (specifically the way in which they introduced and used the organ in the synagogue) reflects Jewish identity. It is important to note that identity is always dependent on context and is thus both multidimensional and variable. Identity cannot be fixed, for it changes, takes different shapes, and refashions itself, thereby becoming a historical process in itself. A significant factor in the identity of German Jews is an indissoluble attachment to a core Jewish ethnicity as a minority in Diaspora.[5] This identity is manifest, among other things, in collectively established and recognized symbols. John Armstrong regards religious belief as the central and most important aspect of diasporic identity.[6] In fact, however, many practices can serve as such symbols "as the epitome of their peoplehood"[7]—one is music, another is tradition.

Although David Coplan argues that tradition is "a structure of historical culture fundamentally immune to history,"[8] Jewish tradition forms an exception. Rather, it has transformed over time into different Jewish customs through exile and migration, resulting in heterogeneous historical and cultural developments. These developments also apply to Jewish musical tradition, which has been subject to continuous and profound changes throughout history. Tradition is constructed history and, like identity, subject to change. It is a process of individual reinterpretation of the past,[9] a definition that applies well to "Jewish music," all the more so as there can be no homogenous tradition of Jewish music.[10] Tradition as a root and a constant in Jewish identity, with its varying interpretations and transformations, as we shall see, is closely tied to the introduction of the organ in synagogues.

As with every identity, Jewish identity is complex and based on many components, especially in Diaspora. Paul Mendes-Flohr states that German-Jewish identity is defined by an inherent duality: "Jews laid claim not only to German Kultur and thus identity but also to the right to maintain their Jewish identity (as either a subsidiary or a parallel identity, be it conceived in ethnic, religious, and cultural terms, or as a combination thereof)."[11] It seems as if the Jewish people consciously entered the dichotomy of a Jewish and a German identity. This duality refers to another crucial element: the variability and flexibility of identity. As music "provides means by which people recognise identities and places, and the boundaries which separate them,"[12] the organ and organ music of Jewish communities serve to illustrate the meaning of dual cultural and religious identity in the lives of German Jews.

Perhaps the most obvious marker of Jewish self-reflection is the search for a valid definition of "Jewish music" that took place at the peak of the development of German-Jewish organ music. In 1923 writer, musician, and painter Arno Nadel (1878–1944) wrote that there is only one true Jewish music—namely synagogue music.[13] Next to it exist Jewish secular music, folk song, and *zemirot* (Hebrew hymns chanted in the domestic circle), all of which can be deemed Jewish only to the extent that they are at least tangentially related to synagogue music. Nadel defines this "Jewish music"[14] as recitativic in character, consisting of a predominantly diatonic-melodious rather than homophonic form, and a rhythm resembling that of the Hebrew language. Additional characteristics include mixed tonalities, changing rhythms, and meditative expression.

Only a few years later, Viennese musicologist and critic Erwin Felber stated that the answer to the question "Is there a Jewish music?" (the title of his article published in *Anbruch*, an Austrian journal on contemporary music) is that there is only Western European music written by Jewish composers.[15] The reason for the absence of a Jewish musical culture, according to Felber, lies in the national-political situation, the dispersion of Jews to different countries of Diaspora.

Abraham Idelsohn, the father of Jewish musicology, was one of the first to attempt a universally valid definition of the concept of Jewish music. In the very first comprehensive history of Jewish music, published in 1929, he wrote the often-quoted statement that "Jewish music is the song of Judaism through the lips of a Jew. It is the tonal expression of Jewish life and development over a period of more than two thousand years."[16] At the end of the same monograph he qualifies his statement: "Music composed by Jews is not always Jewish music."[17]

Hermann Zivi, cantor of the Jewish Reform congregation in Wuppertal, Germany, theorist, and composer of nationalistic songs for the Deutsches Reich, dealt almost exclusively with one topic, the existence of which he himself had denied: Jewish music. Contrary to his beliefs, he composed Jewish liturgical music and wrote the first-ever symphony using Jewish themes. In his article "Is There a Jewish Music?" he provocatively states, "We find no trace throughout the ages of 'Jewish' music. Lacking a manner of musical notation and being dispersed throughout many countries, the Jewish people were unable to safeguard a tradition handed down from earlier days, much less to maintain and revitalize such a tradition."[18] In contrast, one of his earlier articles, titled "Jewish Music in Light of Verism," states that "the scope of the term 'Jewish music' merely encompasses the restricted realm of the religious."[19]

Under the National Socialists, music became part of the German Jews' struggle with an imposed identity. The National Socialists concerned themselves with Jewish music as an Other that had to be eliminated. Pamela Potter describes a paradox in the 1930s:

> At a Jewish Culture League conference in 1936, held in the presence of Music Chamber and Gestapo representatives, musicians, critics, educators, and scholars debated the parameters for defining Jewish music. They reached a consensus on synagogue cantillation and Jewish folk music, but as cultured bourgeois Germans, the Jews in the league felt that such music did not belong in a concert hall. In the end, the league's programs consisted mostly of art music from the nineteenth century, allowing for many hearings of the "racially" Jewish Mendelssohn, Meyerbeer, Offenbach, and Mahler, with some attention also to contemporary Jewish composers.[20]

Jewish music had become unequivocally defined by ideological (and in this case paradoxical) interests.

Among all of the attempts to define Jewish musical traditions and refer to them under one valid umbrella term, organs and organ music as part of Jewish tradition are almost never mentioned. The only exception is organist and composer Hans Samuel (1901–1976), who was the first to speak of "Jewish organ music" and to attempt to connect it to the existing definitions of Jewish music. Samuel believed that "Jewish organ music" must be recitativic in character and clearly demarcated from the repertoire used in Christian churches; thus it should convey deep religious expressions. He sought to differentiate between organ music for Jewish worship and that for Jewish secular culture, which he suggested be defined respectively as "synagogue organ music" and "Jewish organ music."[21] His detailed explanations on the style of this organ music are crucial for the development of the genre and the understanding of his oeuvre.[22]

Surveying the term *Jewish music* and its interpretation and application in the early twentieth century shows that it was both ideologized and individualized within the search for a new and clearly defined Jewish identity in music—obviously a pressing issue in the nineteenth and twentieth centuries—as that identity continually changed.

One singular attribute of Jewish music is the impossibility of a precise fixation—geographically and temporally. This idiosyncrasy is manifest in the music, more precisely in the insistent adherence to traditions for the preservation of identity on the one hand and on the other hand in the continuous dialectic between absorption and rejection of new, external, and non-Jewish elements. These practices can be understood as a creative process in itself. Thus, Jewish music represents both a historical and an ideological reality. In this book, the term *Jewish music* is used with the understanding that this concept can be easily subverted. For this reason, I use it merely as a linguistic and conceptual formula, for an explicitly Jewish music cannot exist, just as there is neither an explicitly German nor a specifically French music.[23] Behind the concepts of a national, an ethnic, or a religious music, however, lies the historical and cultural process of continuous influences by the Other—one of this book's key themes.

Jewish music is by no means monolithic but rather complex and multi-layered. Its main components stem from different traditions and sources: for one, characteristics commonly accepted by Jews as essential features of Jewish cultures and traditions; for another, the musical elements following or imitating Western music, especially in form and style. The scope of this study is the organ's role in the musical culture of Jewish communities in Western Europe, with strong emphasis on Germany. The German-Jewish organ tradition connects more than ever before two areas of life that have become an integral part of the identity and acculturation of Jewish people in the Western world since the Enlightenment: religion and art.

The Jews' adoption of Western cultural traditions (in other words, constituents of the "German environment") reflects their evolving dualistic self-understanding as Germans and Jews in a process that has been labeled variously as assimilation, acculturation, or amalgamation.[24] Musicologists use the different terms depending on the specific context: Bruno Nettl, for example, applies the concept of assimilation to the convergence of neighboring musical styles,[25] thus reducing it to stylistic developments. Margaret Kartomi criticizes the concept of acculturation for implying that a "closed" or isolated culture would be the norm, whereas in reality the synthesis of musical cultures is not an exception but the rule. Moreover, the term has a history of conflicting meanings that range from a development to the result of a process; further, acculturation is afflicted with ethnocentric and racist undertones; and last of all, it is often used literally and imprecisely as "adding cultures together."[26] Kartomi suggests "transcultural synthesis" or "transculturation" as alternatives.[27]

In Jewish studies, history, and other disciplines in the humanities, "acculturation" is typically the preferred term, especially when used in conjunction with Jewish Diasporic culture. Acculturation is used as an analytical and scholarly concept that refers to cultural change resulting from direct contact between different ethnicities or cultures. In contrast, assimilation often carries a political and an ideological component and implies the loss of culture. The debate about the terminology and what it entails is an ongoing process in Jewish studies that seems not yet fully resolved.[28]

In the case of German Jews, in the nineteenth century the term *assimilation* was often used in self-description and thus became an expression of their identity and an essential part of German-Jewish history. For many German Jews, especially during the Jewish emancipation (the abolition of discriminatory laws and the recognition of Jews as equal citizens) in the nineteenth century, the concepts of assimilation, amalgamation, melding, and convergence had positive valances. They implied refinement, improvement, completion, and *Bildung* (the latter encompassing cultivation, education, self-formation, and knowledge).[29] Later, after emancipation was achieved, assimilation designated the status and self-definition of most German Jews and, as a historical term, had become part of their identity: "The bulk of intellectuals, as well as of the urban middle classes, understood assimilation to mean the transformation of a corporate community subject to numerous disabilities into a religious community whose members enjoyed equal rights with non-Jews."[30] Although assimilation is linked to the *Bildungsbürgertum*, one needs to treat an equation of assimilation with embourgeoisement or secularization with care.[31]

In spite of the fact that assimilation is a complex and (historically) flexible term, I have chosen to use the concept in this book because it is a fundamental part and process of nineteenth-century German-Jewish culture and thus relates to the historical context of this work. Further, it offers greater analytical scope and is a broader term than acculturation, encompassing more than one culture and including different dimensions (social, cultural, and religious, the latter standing out as it granted the Jews the right to be different).[32] Finally, the concept of assimilation is understood as a historical umbrella term under which different processes operated at different paces, reached varying degrees of completeness, and also led to dialectic processes such as dissimilation.

The examination of German-Jewish organ culture is more than a mere stocktaking of musical and historical events in the nineteenth and twentieth centuries. Rather, it is a comprehensive treatment of the subject with regard to both the completeness of the material (several hundred dispositions of organs and illustrations are listed at http://www.oup.com/us/theorganandits music) and a consideration of the context of and coherencies between musicological, historical, religious, and cultural aspects.

Besides tracing the history and development of the synagogue organ in this contextual framework, I also discuss selected instruments in order to shed light on how synagogue organ building reflects upon Jewish identity. In addition to technical aspects and organ-building history, the architecture of synagogues and organ façades is another crucial factor considered.

Through the analysis of selected and representative compositions, this book examines the different expressive means and characteristics of organ music.

The study encompasses the various forms of compositions, as well as the motives and themes, which range from freestyle works to potpourris of Jewish vocal music integrated into instrumental music. Moreover, it investigates the relationship between the new repertoire and the organ compositions standing in the long-established tradition of Western church music (specifically, whether Jewish organ music followed its own path, emulated existing traditions, or combined both). The negotiation of identities among German Jews with their German and Jewish components is expressed in the stylistic evolution of organ music written for and performed in some synagogues for more than one hundred years. Rather than focusing on reception history and especially the effect of the organ repertoire, which may not allow for making universally valid statements, I trace the motives and intentions of composers of organ music, the interests and goals pursued in their works, and especially their compositional means. This implies that the individuals who were an integral part of the musical developments are at the heart of the study as well.

This book proposes a new approach to the study of music in which the dichotomy between musicology, understood as the study of Western music, and ethnomusicology, devoted to studying the music of the Other, is overcome by an integrated concept of music with pluralist methodology, research assumptions, and perspectives. The development of musicology and ethnomusicology as separate disciplines imposes unnecessary restrictions on the scope of the subject of Jewish music. Thus, the analysis of the notated organ music goes hand in hand with an examination of the musical behavior and social dimension associated with the Jewish organ culture. Indeed, the subject as a cultural phenomenon is connected to social and historical issues alike and is truly understood only when situated in a holistic approach to the forms of human expression. Finally, both judgment and critical encouragement of this interdisciplinary endeavor by members of Jewish communities served as an effective methodological tool in my effort to understand the past in light of the present.

CHAPTER TWO | # Jewish "Curiosities"
The Organ in Judaism before 1800

Although the history of organs in Judaism does not begin until the Middle Ages, the Hebrew Bible cites the *'uġav* four times and occasionally identifies it as a predecessor of the organ. However, controversy surrounds this designation. In extra-Israelite contexts, Genesis 4:21, Job 21:12, and Job 30:31 mention the *'uġav* as an instrument of mourning and a sacrilegious instrument played outside the temple, while Psalm 150:4 lists it as one of the instruments that serve to praise God.

Both the etymology of the *'uġav* and its identification are subjects of debate. At times the term denotes a musical instrument in general, while sometimes it is identified as a pipe, bagpipe, lute, harp, or even the ancient water organ—hydraulis (Jerusalem Talmud, Sukkah 55c)—but none of these can be supported on either historical or etymological grounds.[1] According to Joachim Braun, Curt Sachs offers what is currently the only plausible interpretation: "The onomatopoeic effect of the word (u-u), typical of flutes, and the connotations of love attached to the instrument suggest that it was a long end-blown flute of the kind found in neighboring cultures (the *ma't* of Egypt and the Sumerian TI.GI), and later distributed over a wide area of Israel/Palestine as the *nāy*."[2] In spite of the different interpretations of this biblical instrument, the term *'uġav* denotes the organ in modern Hebrew.

Another possible predecessor of the organ can be traced back to antiquity, when the tractate Tamid, the oldest treatise of the Mishnah (written soon after the destruction of the Second Temple by the Romans in 70 CE), describes the use and sound of the *magrepha* (literally, "to scoop") in the Second Temple (Tamid 3:8 and 5:6). Two passages from the Jerusalem Talmud (Sukkah 5:3 and 5:6) make similar statements. A tractate in the Talmud of Babylonia, Arakhin 10b–11a, portrays the magrepha as a bellows-operated pipe organ with ten different-sized reed pipes, each pierced with ten holes and having keys mounted to a reverberatory box. However, the accounts in the various rabbinical writings are fragmentary and contradictory (the term *magrepha* appears several more times in Talmud and Mishnah [e.g., Tamid 2:1–2, Shabbat 17:2; Shekalim 8:2], where it refers not to a musical instrument but to a shovel as part of the Temple instrumentarium). Even the rabbis of the Gemara suggest that the wild claims about the magrepha may be exaggerated.[3] Thus, the magrepha is described variously as a musical instrument similar to the organ, as a gong or drum, and as a nonmusical instrument (specifically a device for carrying ashes out of the temple).[4] What the significance, function, and origins of this ritual instrument may have been and whether it was indeed a predecessor of the organ have been subjects of debate since 200 CE. The possibility cannot be ruled out that the magrepha as a wind instrument might be a literary creation rather than an actual artifact.

After the destruction of the Second Temple in 70 CE, instrumental music was prohibited in synagogue services because it was considered a sign of mourning for the loss of temple and homeland. "Organ music" fell under this prohibition as well, to the extent that such music may have existed.

Nevertheless, the organ became a theme, if an isolated one, in Judaism. In fact, the instrument began to play a limited role in rabbinical thought and Jewish iconography and ultimately came to the synagogue itself. Over time, a progressive attitude toward and freedom from prejudice against the organ developed, as the sources cited here attest.

The Jewish Literature of Early Modernity

Early on, the organ was understood as a spiritual object, which is to say that it was present in the world of learned Jewish thought. Testimony to support this comes from a fifteenth-century treatise, the *Heshek Shelomoh* [Solomon's Desire][5] of Johanan ben Isaac Alemanno (Italy, 1435–1438 and after 1504), a philosopher and biblical exegete. In his philosophical commentaries on the Song of Songs, written at the request of Giovanni Pico della Mirandola, Alemanno reports the overwhelming experience of listening to a blind musician from Germany playing the organ at the Mantua court. Sources state that this blind organist must have been Konrad Paumann, who performed in 1470 at the court of Ludovico III of Gonzaga, where his skill earned him great honor.[6]

Another source in Hebrew,[7] one that dates back to the fifteenth century and almost certainly of southern French provenance, refers to that "dark chapter in the history of the organ"[8] when mixture stops first appeared. The manuscript is Judah ben Isaac's Hebrew adaptation of an anonymous Latin text on *musica plana*, which consists of five sections. An added sixth section in the translation (titled "Gateway to the Construction of Musical Instruments") describes the mensuration of monochords, organ pipes, and small cymbals and includes an appendix of medieval writings on music theory. The discussion on organ pipes distinguishes two different methods, the "old" and the "new" mensuration.[9]

Judah ben Joseph Moscato (Ossimo, ca. 1530–Mantua, 1590), one of the most important rabbis of sixteenth-century Italy, devoted one of his earliest sermons to music, the *Higgayon be-Kinnor* [Observations on the Playing of the Lyre], for the feast of Simhat Torah (the holiday of rejoicing in the law).[10] In a subsection titled "Comparison between Man and Instrument" (i.e., organ), he writes: "The breath of the spirit moves and impels me to compare him [man] with the *kinnor*,[11] the *organum*, which is so built in its relations and proportions as to give great beauty to its sound. Its potential sound does not enter into action, however, as long as it has not been given the implement of breath, through which the sound of its spirit may come out. Nor is this of any value until 'the player plays upon it,' for only then do his hands make music in planned art."[12]

Moscato's writing reflects the manifold meaning of the concept of *organum*. The term comes from the Greek ὄργανον [tool], whose first group of meanings incorporates musical instruments in general and the human voice, wind instruments, and the organ in particular.[13] In view of the organ's multiplicity of sounds, Moscato sees it as a worthy object for comparison to the human being, who is also composed of a multiplicity of elements. As the organ attains "value" through the player, so do a person's qualities come to fruition only in social interaction.

In order to have made use of such a comparison, Moscato must have had an idea of what the organ as an instrument was like—not merely an impression of its sound but also a notion of its technical construction, as is shown by the remark that the organ's potential sound comes into action only through the "implement of breath" (i.e., the bellows). Since the organ was not yet established in the synagogues of Moscato's time, his interest in the instrument is particularly noteworthy. It also suggests that the organ had a tangible presence in the minds of premodern Jews and that their interest was more natural than one would assume.

One of Moscato's pupils, Mantuan physicist Abraham ben David Portaleone (1542–1612), confronted the idea of music as part of a general attempt to rebuild the temple and its worship service in his *Shiltei ha-Gibborim* [Shields of Heroes] (Mantua, 1612).[14] Portaleone's speculations on the nature of Levitic singing and on the musical instruments of the temple are based on the practical music theory of his time and projected onto biblical antiquity. In the fifth through the tenth chapters of his treatise, he enumerates thirty-four instruments that, in his view, were used by the ancient Hebrews, then describes and categorizes them according to their functions. He devotes separate chapters to the *nebel* (interpreted as "lute"), kinnor (interpreted as "harp"), 'ugav (interpreted as viola da gamba), and *men* (plural *minnim*), which in chapter seven Portaleone interprets as both *clavicordo* and organ.[15] Since the eighteenth century, minnim has been commonly interpreted as a collective term for string instruments;[16] however, "organ" is also accepted as a proper translation.[17] In several chapters (notably 5, 10, and especially 6), he offers detailed descriptions of the magrepha based on sections in Tamid and Arakhin.

From the thirteenth to the seventeenth century the organ also appears in Yiddish Bible translations and prose. Instruments such as 'ugav and kinnor are often translated as *orgl* or *orgln*, the Yiddish words for organ.[18] Yiddish authors also emphasize the important role that portatives and pipe organs play in Solomon's thought, in Nebuchadnezzar's court orchestra, and in the Second Temple.[19] Organs, according to *Ayn shoyn Maysebukh* (Basel, 1602) and the Messiah song by Jacob ben Benjamin Taussig (Amsterdam, 1666), can be heard in the synagogue of the otherworld and will please the pious when the Messiah comes.

In Jewish thought, the transformation in the meaning and semantics of the organ proves that people's fascination with the instrument goes hand in hand with a certain kind of imagination, sometimes to the extent of fantasy. After considering the various interpretations of the organ in literature and especially its biblical history, one can conclude only that whether kinnor, 'ugav, and minnim indeed refer to the organ remains an open question.

Pictorial Sources of Different Cultural and Religious Provenance

Beyond the written sources, iconographic evidence provides information on the relationship between Judaism and the organ and may even confirm the existence of this instrument during the second and third centuries CE in ancient

Israel/Palestine. One of the apparently earliest sources is a group of terracotta oil lamps, discovered in ancient Palestine and now preserved in the kibbutz Ein ha-Shofet in Israel.[20] The front sides of these artifacts, all from the third or fourth century, feature relief depictions of a portable pneumatic table organ with seven pipes, always accompanied by two pairs of forked cymbals.[21] There is good reason to claim that these instruments were played during the music making of the local Samaritan community; however, a possible liturgical context for their use cannot be established.

The mosaic of Hama in Syria, excavated from the village of Mariamin in 1960, gives further evidence of the early use of the organ in the Middle East. Dating from the late fourth century, it depicts a group of female musicians with their instruments, among them an organ with remarkably developed features.[22]

Iconographical evidence of the magrepha appears for the first time in the *Second Kennicott Bible*,[23] copied in 1306 by the well-known Jewish scholar Joshua ben Abraham ibn Gaon in Soria (or one of his assistants) and decorated with brilliant colors, elaborate designs, and miniature pictures.[24]

Joachim Braun states that, starting in the thirteenth century, several Christian manuscripts depict King David playing an organ and call him *organista*.[25] In the Bible of Wenceslas IV, King of Bohemia[26] (before 1400), a miniature illustrates another Christian perspective on the organ in biblical times (see figure 2.1). It depicts a scene from the temple sacrifice in the Old Testament, musically accompanied by a portative. Featuring two ranks and sixteen pipes, the instrument is part of an ensemble that consists of other instruments: a triangle without rings, a fiddle, and wind instruments.

The Bible illustrations may have initiated the depiction of the organ in Hebrew manuscript illuminations, one of which appears in the *maḥzor* of the Heilbronn family of Germany (ca. 1370–1400).[27] The portative organ is part of a Gothic-style surrounding; above it appears this Hebrew prayer line: "I will sing of Thy power; indeed, I will sing aloud."

The *Farḥi Bible*,[28] copied in Spain between 1366 and 1382, contains drawings of the temple and its inventory, which features two trumpets, two *shofarot*, two lutes, two psalteries, and a portative organ with eight pipes.[29] Details even depict bellows and a tube, suggesting that this may have been a pneumatic organ.

Further sources attest to the organ as an ensemble instrument. A miniature from the so-called Kaufmann *Haggadah* of the late fourteenth century (Castile, between 1350 and 1360),[30] shows a portative organ accompanying Miriam and a female chorus in a nonreligious setting. The illustration reveals remarkable details of the instrument: It features a row of six pipes of even

FIGURE 2.1. The illuminated miniature from the Bible of King Wenceslas IV shows a two-rank positive (right of center). Reproduced by permission of the Österreichische Nationalbibliothek, Vienna.

height, enclosed by one Bourdon pipe of double height on each side. A Gothic-style pointed arch serves as a frame. Another miniature from the same manuscript contains an illumination that depicts instruments and dance scenes.[31] In the center, surrounded by fiddle and lute, is a portative organ. The fact that the player uses only his right hand suggests that he is simultaneously producing wind with his left hand.

One of the manuscript sources of the *Arba'ah Turim*,[32] the halakhah compendium of Jacob ben Asher (Spain, ca. 1270–1340), copied in Mantua in 1435, depicts a court scene with an organ player participating as part of a larger ensemble of musicians—the instrument itself is barely visible.

Most of the medieval Jewish iconography pertaining to the organ originated in Spain and represents it as either a secular or a temple instrument. In most cases the organ is small—a portative or a positive—and is used as part of a larger ensemble rather than a solo instrument.

From the Renaissance on, the organ appears almost exclusively in Jewish iconography of central Europe. A miniature in a *siddur* of German provenance (ca. 1471)[33] provides an example of the perception of the organ as a Western, possibly Christian, instrument. The portative organ is played by a young man, who appears among a group of musicians playing a variety of instruments. He is portrayed with blond curls and medieval headgear (apparently a fillet) that suggests a Western European origin. The miniature is of particular interest in that it shows musicians of different ethnicities and religions (Christians, Jews, and Muslims, clearly distinguishable by their physical features, attire, and instruments) in one composition.[34]

The first iconographic document depicting an organ being played in the synagogue is the siddur of the Bohemian family Lobkowicz (1494).[35] The illustration of the synagogue's interior shows a small organ, possibly a positive, being played in an ensemble with *neqqāra* [kettledrums] and a *Rauschpfeife*— an unusual combination.[36] The occasion appears to be of secular nature rather than a formal synagogue service.

For Joachim Braun, the transfer of the organ from Spain to central Europe and from the secular environment to the religious atmosphere of the synagogue in the fourteenth and fifteenth centuries is grounded in the organ's changing significance in visual arts and literature. Both the organ and the lute underwent a transformation in the musical history of the Jewish people,[37] and once the organ had been established as a theme in Jewish art and literature, it soon found its place in the synagogue.

The organ's move away from the Iberian Peninsula, however, may have taken place for principally historical reasons. With the persecution of the Jews beginning in 1391, their subjection to forced baptism, and finally their expulsion from Spain in 1492 and from Portugal in 1497, they settled in other areas of Europe, preferably in Venice, Amsterdam, London, and Hamburg. As a result of the displacement, the centers of Jewish economic and cultural life shifted to new locations, a fact that may explain the organ's position in the striving Jewish communities predominantly in central Europe.

———

Later iconographical sources from Prague attest to the early use of the organ in Jewish ceremonial life:[38] A 1716 copperplate engraving reveals that instruments were played in a public procession of Prague Jews honoring the birth of Prince Leopold I, imperial heir to the throne.[39] The celebration of the arrival of rulers and coronations with instrumental music may have been a common event, considering a 1741 copperplate engraving by Simon Franckel, which depicts a similar festive procession of Prague Jews with portable organs (see figure 2.2).[40] A detail of the illustration shows a small portative organ (figure 2.3).

The very early fascination with organs in Judaism was not at all inspired by the instrument's role and function in Christianity. Moreover, it seems that both religions independently developed an interest in the organ, a development that would take a new turn once the organ became an established instrument in Christian worship between 1100 and 1450. Later iconographical sources show that the role of organs in Jewish life was not limited to worship but was also used outside the synagogue and notably at processions.

Meshorerim as the Forerunners of Organ Accompaniment

In addition to the instruments described and depicted in written and visual sources, the use of *meshorerim* [singers] to assist the *hazzan* in leading the prayers during services is another musical tradition that provides a certain parallel to organ music.[41]

The practice of providing the prayer leader in Jewish liturgy with an accompaniment by one, two, or three assistants—*tomekhim, mesayim,* or *muznafim* (in non-Ashkenazi communities, *mezammerim, somekhim,* or *maftirim* —is said to date back to approximately 300 CE.[42] Over time, the increasing number of prayers necessitated the use of assistants. Since most prayers were transmitted orally until about the seventeenth century, the transmission became a ritual in its own right: To help the cantor recite them in the correct sequence during the liturgy, he was provided two helpers, and it soon became a requirement for one of these helpers to be present during the service. Eventually this innovation developed into a musical tradition. One of the earliest pieces of written evidence of meshorerim accompanying the cantor appears in a 1605 responsum composed by rabbi and scholar Leon Modena (1571–1648), who helped to bring about the recognition of the music of his day and introduced to the synagogue not only the choir but, if we trust the reports of his pupil Giulio Morosini (1612–1683), instrumental music as well.[43]

In general, the ḥazzan was accompanied by two meshorerim, one so-called *singerl* and one bass. The descant-singer part was usually sung by a boy soprano or falsetto since women were not permitted to participate musically in any way in the synagogue until the nineteenth century. It has been impossible so far to determine where and when meshorerim sang or what the precise purpose of accompanying the cantor was, nor is there any sound recording to provide an idea of what the singing sounded like. All that is known is that the singer and bass normally had free rein to improvise the harmonies of accompaniment. A clue to the nature of this plurivocal performance appears in the use of the German words *unterhalten* and *zuhalten*, implying that the bass improvised an accompaniment "under" the cantor.[44]

As Edith Gerson-Kiwi has described in summarizing old sources, the polyphonic singing of the meshorerim was bound by certain rules: The cantor recited the text, and the meshorerim accompanied him softly; at the end, all three voices sang with the same degree of loudness.[45] During the pauses both singer and bass were also allowed to come forward with solos, which they used for extended coloratura passages. In the seventeenth and eighteenth centuries this highly artistic vocal music flowered. Some congregations were even in a position to recruit a larger number of assistants who specialized in imitating the sounds of certain instruments. Meshorerim who used a falsetto range to imitate flute or clarinet were known, respectively, as *fletel* or *fistel* singers; those who imitated the bassoon were *fagottzinger*; similarly, a *sayt-bas* mimicked the sounds of the lower strings.[46]

Eliezer Ehrenreich interprets the task and function of the meshorerim as a first attempt to adopt the polyphony of Western art music into Jewish music: "In their endeavor to emulate the joyous splendor of music making introduced by Haydn (to which, however, all their means were insufficient), they came to the idea of bringing the beauty of instrumental music into the divine service. But since the rabbinical prohibitions stood in the way of this, they resorted to providing the cantor with helpers who accompanied his singing . . . after the fashion of instrumental music."[47]

Meshorerim represent a phenomenon that is of particular interest in several respects. If the playing of instruments in the synagogue was controversial or even forbidden, then the accompaniment of the ḥazzan by singers, even those who imitated instruments, offered a compromise solution. Nobody

FIGURE 2.2. On April 24, 1741, a procession was held in honor of the recent
birth of Maria Theresa's son, Joseph II, future Holy Roman emperor. Among other

instruments, a portable organ was played on this festive occasion. Reproduced by permission of the Jewish Museum, Prague.

FIGURE 2.3.
A detail of the engraving, under the number 13, shows the *Schulsinger* Sinaj Klaber, cantor at the Altschneuschul in Prague, with the organ positive that he frequently used in synagogue. Reproduced by permission of the Jewish Museum, Prague.

appears to have been disturbed by instrumental sounds when they were produced by human voices; thus, for the first time synagogue chant was accompanied and harmonized. In addition, in some cases the meshorerim themselves stepped forward during the ḥazzan's pauses.

It is far from clear whether the performances of the meshorerim should be interpreted as a conscious effort to substitute for the organ (or any other instrument) or simply reflected a strong tradition of vocal polyphony. What is certain, though, is that the practice in some way anticipated the developments of the nineteenth and twentieth centuries, when the organ began to provide harmonic support for the ḥazzan and make a bridge between his pauses by playing interludes. As Hermann Heymann Steinthal (1823–1899), professor at the Hochschule für die Wissenschaft des Judentums and one of the founders of social psychology, recalled at the end of the nineteenth century, "The organ sings what used to be sung by the meshorer and bass; and to the ḥazzan remains that which was always the ḥazzan's, the Word."[48]

The Synagogues of Prague and Venice

One of the first verifiable attempts in Europe to reform Jewish liturgical music and to admit instruments into the service began in the sixteenth century. Perhaps in response to the contemporaneous treatises dealing with instrumental music, a number of European communities—notably Frankfurt am Main, Vienna, and Königsberg (today Kaliningrad)—began introducing instruments into Jewish worship service.[49] In 1594 a synagogue was built for the congregation of the Prague ghetto by Mordecai ben Samuel Meisel (1528–1601), a celebrated Prague financier and philanthropist. He furnished it with an organ, which played every Friday evening, together with an authorized synagogue orchestra.[50] The earliest source to refer to this use of the organ is the siddur supplement of the first Jewish bibliography, *Siftei Yeshenim* (Amsterdam 1679–1680), by Shabbetai ben Joseph Bass (1641–1718). Bass, a singer at the Altneushul (Staronová Synagoga) in Prague, recalled that "A beautiful song was brought to listeners by Rabbi Shlomo Singer . . . [and was] sung in the Meisel Synagogue in Prague with the 'ugav [organ] and nebalim [string instruments]."[51]

Another early source is a report by Abraham Levi ben Menahem Tall (early eighteenth century). On a trip to Prague between 1718 and 1724 he observed the following on a Friday evening at the beginning of Sabbath services: "These cantors employ together with themselves other singers of music [presumably meshorerim] and organ pipes, as well as cymbals and violins."[52] Indeed, by the seventeenth century, the playing of string and wind instruments was permitted in nine different Prague synagogues. At least two of these (one of which was the Altneushul) were in fact outfitted with organs.[53] In 1683 Jewish builder Meir Mahler,[54] who constructed the portative organ at the Altneushul, is said to have lent the instrument to the Church of Our Lady in front of Týn in Prague.[55] Ethnographer and historian Johann Jacob Schudt (1664–1772) reports the following in his *Jüdische Merckwürdigkeiten*: "There is something else altogether strange / and probably not to be met with anywhere else in the world / that the Jews in the Alt-Neu Synagogue, as they themselves call it / have an organ / which however they make no further use of in the divine service / excepting only / when they sing the welcoming song for the Shabbos on Friday evenings / and at this time a Jew plays on the organ."[56]

Schudt's report suggests that the Altneushul allowed organ accompaniment for the introductory psalms on Friday evening during Kabbalat Shabbat. But once the Sabbath had formally begun with the recitation of Psalm 92, it was no longer used to comply with the halakhah. We also learn that the availability of an organ in the synagogue was not an everyday phenomenon and its rare occurrence was perceived as "strange." On the other hand, Schudt gives evidence of an extraordinarily progressive attitude when, after providing further details on the use of the organ in Jewish services, he remarks that this demonstrates that the organ is not to be considered a purely Christian instrument.[57] When he then notes that the Reformed Christians, "whose ancestors would suffer no organs in the churches / but today in many places / as I saw myself in Zerbst and Altena / use them in churches themselves,"[58] he is drawing a parallel between the introduction of the organ into the synagogue and its use within the Christian tradition. Schudt's remark addresses an aspect of the Protestant Reformation since the reforms initiated by Martin Luther (1483–1546) also concerned liturgical music in general and the organ in particular: The organ was rarely used in the Reformed liturgy in Luther's time because Luther himself regarded the organ as primitive.[59] It was only in the course of time, particularly during the seventeenth century, that the organ in the Protestant liturgy was fully reinstated.[60]

In 1745, only a short time after Schudt made his report on the organs of Bohemia, Empress Maria Theresa ordered the expulsion of all Jews from that region. Jewish religious life in Prague came to a halt—and the musical culture with it. Organs were not heard again in a Prague synagogue until the Old Shul was modernized in 1836 and regular services were introduced in April 1837.[61] Other synagogues in Prague followed in the course of the nineteenth-century Jewish Reform movement.

———

In Italy at the beginning of the seventeenth century, attempts were made to legitimize the organ as a synagogue instrument. In 1628, in the wake of Leon Modena's innovations, an organ was brought to the Spanish synagogue in Venice on Simḥat Torah to reinforce the vocal and instrumental ensemble. Because of the rabbinical prohibition,[62] however, a noisy protest arose during this extraordinary presentation, and the organ had to be taken away again.[63] Modena's pupil Giulio Morosini, who converted to Christianity in 1649, reported on the commotion: "Among the instruments, the organ was also brought into the synagogue, but the rabbis did not permit it to be played as an instrument that is ordinarily played in our churches."[64]

It was probably in the context of this incident that Nethanel ben Benjamin ben Azriel Trabotto (1576–1653), a rabbi in Modena who was recognized in his time as an authority among rabbis, discussed the confrontations that took place in the Adriatic coastal city of Senigallia over the question of liturgical music in Jewish worship and in particular over the awkward issue of the organ.[65] In a responsum addressed to Samuel Isaac Norzi of Ancona and dated November 9, 1645,[66] Trabotto granted permission for the organ to be used in the synagogue to accompany liturgical singing because it served to praise God.[67] The other rabbis involved in the dispute, Samuel ben Abraham Corcos and in particular Norzi, did not dispute Trabotto's pronouncement; in fact, they did not even acknowledge it. However, their passivity does not alter the fact that a rabbi had ruled, in a formal *psak halakhah*, in favor of the organ.

Furthermore, in a commentary on the *Shulḥan Arukh* (*Oraḥ Ḥayyim* 560:3), Abraham Joseph Solomon ben Mordecai Graziano (d. 1684), a rabbi in Modena and one of Trabotto's pupils, also held that Jewish musicians should not be forbidden to play the organ or sing songs and hymns of praise in honor of God.[68] The argument that the organ is a ḥukkat ha-goi was in his view irrelevant since no competent rabbi (only an ignorant one) would forbid organ playing.[69]

Nevertheless, owing to the resistance of the majority of rabbis, the organ did not become an official synagogue instrument, and toward the end of the seventeenth century its fate was sealed when anti-Jewish agitation began. New regulations were issued restricting the times and places when Jewish musicians were permitted to perform in concert; as a result, music in the Venetian ghetto was heard predominantly in the framework of liturgy.

It is no longer possible to ascertain what music was played on the synagogue organs of Prague and Venice and whether it included improvisation or "merely" provided accompaniment; the organ likely had a continuo function in connection with an orchestra and otherwise accompanied the chants.

The significance of organs and organ music in the synagogue before 1800 varied radically from place to place. In Prague, organs were played in synagogues and sparked no serious controversy; no sources suggest that it was regarded as an exclusively Christian instrument or that there was any debate on the issue in the Jewish community. The fact that at least one Jewish organ builder existed shows, moreover, that even if few organs were to be found in synagogues, the congregations took them for granted. The organ seems to have been perceived as an instrument whose remarkable sounds could beautify and enrich the divine service. Organs and organ music in Prague were dissociated from questions about and quarrels over adaptation to the overwhelmingly Christian environment. They did not lead to any questioning of accepted tradition and rather served to express a new musical identity in the community.

In the Jewish communities of Venice and Prague, the issues of organs and organ music were dealt with in entirely different ways: "Rabbinical means" such as the codex of the *Shulḥan Arukh* cited earlier were used as weapons in the struggle over whether the organ, as a Christian instrument, should be permitted in Jewish services. Although in the seventeenth century there was as yet no debate over emancipation and assimilation, the Jews of Venice evidently had no desire to totally assimilate to Christian models.

These isolated appearances of organ music in Jewish services had for the most part no impact on the development of the organ as a synagogue instrument in the nineteenth century; they were significant only insofar as they supplied organ opponents and advocates with arguments in the discussions that took place during the era of Reform. Thus, the organ's early presence helped pave the way for its eventual acceptance in Jewish life.

CHAPTER THREE | The Organ as a Jewish Religious
Response to Modernity

The Jewish Enlightenment, the *Haskalah*, which evolved from the work of philosopher Moses Mendelssohn (1729–1786), is generally considered to have played an important role in the development of modern Judaism. As an intellectual movement in Europe, the Haskalah originated as an effort to renew Judaism by restoring neglected textual traditions. It also called for secular learning and linguistic assimilation (especially in German-speaking countries) and in the late eighteenth century set in motion Jewish emancipation, which aimed at attaining legal and sociocultural equality for Jews.[1]

For the Jews themselves, the success of the movement, which lasted almost a century, was tied to the establishment of new forms of identity through cultural and educational institutions. In newly founded schools, Jewish children studied not only the Hebrew language and Jewish religion but also social studies, mathematics, and sciences. Many Jews of the late eighteenth century, whose beliefs and habits had been shaped by long-established traditions, resisted changes in the synagogue, but the younger generations, who would grow up under the ongoing emancipation, found it easier to adopt new styles. Thus, in the first decades of the nineteenth century, reform-minded Jews in Germany began developing ideas about a modernized worship service, which they introduced into schools and their own social circles rather than attempt to impose these innovations on the community as a whole. Importantly, the fathers of Reform did not regard changes in religious life as revolutionary: to the contrary; for them Reform was the "real" Judaism and not merely an affiliation or a sect. From their point of view Jewish practice had become ossified and lifeless, incapable of attracting modern Jews to their religion as Enlightenment entered the Jewish world. Their reforms applied especially to aesthetic aspects of the service: They shortened the liturgy, widely eliminated cantillation of the Bible, used both German and Hebrew, and presented speeches modeled on the Christian sermon. The musical aspect of the service also underwent radical changes designed to appeal more to a public that was increasingly educated in Western art music. These involved not only the option of congregational and choral singing in Hebrew or German but, even more important, the introduction of the organ.[2]

A new branch of Jewish music began as a result of these changes and marked the beginning of a new era of Judaism that would eventually divide the community; Orthodoxy emerged in response to Reform. Although the organ was not widespread in all Reform communities and was used by some congregations that did not consider themselves Reform, it nonetheless became a symbol of the division between Orthodox and Reform. This "emancipation of the organ" in the synagogue, however, was a long and gradual process. As such it was bound up in complex ways with the whole phenomenon of cultural change within the Jewish communities of the German-speaking world, for which it serves as a kind of paradigm.

From Liturgical Reforms to a New Musical Identity

During the first half of the nineteenth century the use of the organ in Jewish worship services was limited to only a few German synagogues. The first to set a path that would later be followed by many was a vehement advocate of Reform, banker Israel Jacobson (1769–1863). His principle concern, following Mendelssohn's ideals, was to improve the Jews' social position through education; thus, in 1801 he founded an educational institution for the Jewish children of poor families at Seesen, in Westphalia. Around 1803 he began taking the first steps toward the building of a synagogue in the school's courtyard, and from 1805 to 1810, despite public resistance, the plans were realized. The new synagogue's most striking novelty—"something hitherto unheard of"[3]—was an organ. Jacobson was finally able to conduct the first reformed Jewish worship service at the Jacobstempel synagogue at its consecration on July 17, 1810, the first recorded occasion on which organ music was heard in a German synagogue.[4] The performer was likely Gerson Rosenstein (1790–1851), the first Jewish organist of the so-called Jacobstempel.[5]

Rosenstein was closely connected to the Jacobstempel, first as a student and from 1810 to 1847 as the first music director; he later even published a collection of melodies performed in Seesen.[6]

Jacobson's task had undoubtedly been eased by the political events of 1807, when Westphalia became a French-dominated kingdom under Napoleon's brother Jérôme, and 1808, when Jérôme proclaimed the emancipation of Westphalia's Jews. After the reversals of 1813, when the French forces were expelled from Germany, the old regime and its legal restrictions on Jews were restored, and Jacobson moved to Berlin. There, within the confines of his house, he began holding Reform services in 1815, complete with organ music, choral singing, and German-language sermons. These services proved to be so popular (about a quarter of Berlin's Jewish population regularly attended) that a larger synagogue had to be set up, this time in the home of Jacob Herz Beer (father of composer Giacomo Meyerbeer), as we learn from a letter dated November 12, 1815, from Jewish religious and literary historian Leopold Zunz to his former teacher Samuel Meyer Ehrenberg, inspector of a Jewish school, the Samsonsche Freischule in Wolfenbüttel: "The rumor that the temple has been superseded is based on the following fact: The three rooms that Jacobson and Gumpertz arranged for the temple have become too cramped; moreover the organ is no better than a hurdy-gurdy. So the temple has been moved to the house of a local Croesus by the name of Beer, where they have even brought the organ from Seesen."[7]

The services on private initiative did not last long inasmuch as they aroused great indignation and opposition in the rest of the Jewish community. A successful appeal was made to Emperor Friedrich Wilhelm III to close the private synagogue on the assertion that the Reform schism was detrimental to the established rights of Judaism and was especially disturbing to Berlin's Jewish congregation. Because the Prussian government feared religious changes as much as political ones,[8] in December 1815 the government banned the services, claiming that Jews were not allowed to hold prayer meetings outside of community synagogues according to the existing regulations for Jews that dated back to 1750.[9]

Just two years later, however, as a result of the promptings of Eduard Kley, a rabbi who had moved from Berlin to Hamburg, the Neuer Israelitischer Tempelverein Hamburg [New Israelite Temple Association of Hamburg] was formed to conduct reformed services. The society was founded on December 11, 1817, and its synagogue, the First Temple on Brunnenstraße, was consecrated on October 18, 1818. The temple brought a completely new order to the worship service, including the official introduction of the sermon in German and choral singing with organ accompaniment for the first time in a synagogue open to the public (the Jacobstempel in Seesen had been used almost exclusively for school services); a loft was specially built for the organ and choir.

A musician named Bethuel (d. 1828)—of whom nothing further is known—served the Brunnenstraße synagogue as organist for ten years (1818–1828). According to the program for the consecration festivities, the organ, a gift from Hamburg banker and philanthropist Salomon Heine (1767–1844), uncle of poet Heinrich Heine, was used only for accompaniment. However, this instrument could not be installed in time for the consecration, so an "interim organ" had to be played. After the congregation's move to a new building on Poolstraße around 1844, an orchestra initially provided the accompaniment.[10] The reforms of the Hamburg Temple Association, including the introduction of German-language hymns and sermons but in particular the introduction of the organ, set off fierce controversy within the community.

The debate is reflected in two responsa advocating the organ (*Nogah ha-Zedek* [Brightness of Righteousness], published in 1818 in Arad [now in Romania], and *Or Nogah* [The Bright Light], published in 1818 in Dessau, Germany) and one rejecting it (*Eleh Divrei ha-Berit* [These Are the Words of the Covenant], published in 1819 in Altona, Germany).[11] The *Nogah ha-Zedek*, a collection of the views of different European rabbis, was published by Austrian Talmudist and agent of the First Temple's patrons, Eliezer Liebermann. Originally composed in response to inquiries by Jacob Herz Beer, the compilation is controversial in many respects. For one, Liebermann exaggerated the importance of certain rabbis; for another, he published only those views that permitted the organ without overly restricting its use.[12]

On the basis of *Shulḥan Arukh* (*Oraḥ Ḥayyim* 338:2), the organ's advocates argued that organ playing by a Gentile would be permitted for weddings and for the Sabbath. Although music in the synagogue had been prohibited after the Romans' destruction of Jerusalem's Second Temple in 70 CE, the organ's supporters argued that vocal music was allowed for religious purposes, and the Reformers merely wished to extend this compromise to instrumental music. In any case, Venice, Corfu, and Modena served as precedents for instrumental music in the synagogue. Finally, the views expressed in *Nogah ha-Zedek* characterize the organ as an instrument that is not explicitly Christian since it is not played in all churches.

Following the *Nogah ha-Zedek*, Liebermann wrote *Or Nogah*, in which he gives a lengthy and learned exposition of his own views in favor of Reform, claiming that organ playing had been the Jewish custom in the temple prior to the Christians' adoption of the instrument. In refutation of this book, the Hamburg rabbinate published the opinions of twenty-two prominent central

European rabbis. Titled *Eleh Divrei ha-Berit*, the collection also contained a declaration by Hungarian rabbi and pioneer of religious reform Aaron Chorin, who revoked his former opinion published in *Nogah ha-Ẓedek*. The rabbis maintained that a musical instrument may not be played on Sabbaths and holy days if only because it might require an adjustment or a repair, which would constitute forbidden work (*shevut*).

Although the argument that organ playing represented work continued to be a general concern, the subject of who should supply the organ wind by means of bellows pumping did not come up in the early debates. Until the mid-nineteenth century manpower was the only means of operating the blowers, and not until the latter half of the century did mechanical systems and later electricity replace human efforts. Because treading the bellows was not considered a devotional part of Jewish worship, it may have been performed by a non-Jewish person employed to perform activities forbidden to Jews on the Sabbath; thus, rabbis may never have had cause to address this issue.

Other concerns raised in *Eleh Divrei ha-Berit* were the general prohibitions on synagogue music as a sign of mourning for the destruction of the Second Temple and on imitating the worship of strange gods. The organ's opponents saw in its introduction a Christianization of the service and, with that, a loss of Jewish tradition and identity.

Perhaps because of these early debates, no other Jewish congregations in the subsequent three decades followed the Hamburg model. Meanwhile, the organ was also being used to accompany songs in school devotions (for example, from 1812 to 1853 in the Philantropin, the Jewish community's secondary school in Frankfurt am Main).[13] Beyond this, it also helped to introduce particularly important instructional lessons: "At the opening of the school all the boys and girls assemble in a hall where there is a song accompanied by the organ followed by discussion of a moral subject."[14] Was the organ meant here (much as a Christian model) to arouse a morally edifying mood, or was it simply a way to ensure that the students had musical support in their communal singing?

Evidence also exists that an organ at the University of Leipzig was used, according to the Hamburg model, to accompany Jewish services. At the opening of the annual Leipzig Fair in 1820, a Jewish service was held in one of the university's lecture halls and was attended by "the educated of all faiths." It featured the songs of German poets with organ accompaniment.[15] From both musical and literary standpoints, the event reflects the beginning of a new identity among the developing Jewish educated classes.

In some instances, efforts toward musical reform were only indirectly adopted at first. Thus at the Berlin synagogue on Heidereutergasse in 1837, violins were played at one service, and meshorerim imitated an orchestra. In this synagogue the installation of an organ was already being planned.[16] However, concrete plans did not materialize until several decades later, when the congregation expanded to the New Synagogue on Oranienburger Straße.

In the early 1840s several congregations were contemplating the acquisition of an organ, perhaps encouraged by Benedikt Levi's Reform contribution, *Beweis der Zulässigkeit des deutschen Chorgesanges mit Orgelbegleitung bei dem sabbathlichen Gottesdienste der Juden: Ein Beitrag zur jüdischen Liturgie.* As there was no Jewish newspaper at the time, the piece was first published in 1833 in a Christian journal for church law, the *Archiv des Kirchenrechts* 3.[17] Levi was especially concerned with the embellishment of liturgy and argued that it was vital to undertake anything that would enhance Jewish life. One of the aesthetic improvements he demanded was organ accompaniment of the liturgy. His argument for this is based on the Talmud, which, in Levi's view, neither fully proscribes music making on Sabbath as a violation of shevut nor fully prohibits the imitation of Christian traditions (only those that are immoral or idolatrous).[18]

Despite Levi's efforts to introduce the organ into the community of Gießen, where he served as rabbi, a lack of financial means forestalled his plans. Meanwhile, in 1841, an anonymous merchant's efforts to "have an organ built, on the occasion of the construction of a temple for the Israelite community of G—— [Gießen], in Electoral Hesse, toward the end of elevating the worship service and religious feeling" were quickly rejected.[19] In the late 1840s the Gießen synagogue was finally equipped with an organ, on which Levi's son Hermann, who later became Richard Wagner's longtime friend and favorite conductor, accompanied the services.[20]

Also during the early 1840s, the Jewish community in Bingen announced its intention to "see to the acquisition of an organ, after the example of some other congregations."[21] For this purpose the congregation requested both donations and the support of the rabbi in accordance with "the general desire."[22]

THE SECOND RABBINICAL CONFERENCE
AND THE STRUGGLE OVER RELIGIOUS REFORM

The proposals of the Bingen congregation inspired an official discussion at the Second Rabbinical Conference held at Frankfurt am Main, July 15–28, 1845, on the issues of whether the organ should be permitted in Jewish worship services at all and whether it should be played by Jewish or Gentile organists.[23] The first question, "whether organ playing in and of itself is allowed in the synagogue,"[24] was once again considered with regard to whether the organ was a neutral or a specifically Christian instrument and whether it should be disallowed on the basis of the traditional mourning for the loss of the Second Temple. The discussion closed with the comment that the organ was a foreign element in the Jewish liturgy and thus not strictly advisable.

Nevertheless, the conference consented to its use on the grounds that it was needed to encourage a mood of devotion. The conference participants also established a new order of service that would integrate the organ. As to the issue of whether the organ was a Christian instrument, they explained that the obligation of Jews was "to avoid imitating that which pertains to heathens only if . . . its heathenish aspect is an intrinsic part of the performance itself; but if it can be done in such a way as to be free of such aspects, nothing stands in its way."[25] The conference did not go so far as to assert positively that the organ was originally a Jewish instrument or a direct descendant of the ancient temple's magrepha since the sources provided only clues suggesting this, not actual proof.

With the unanimous decision at the 1845 Second Rabbinical Conference to permit organ playing in Jewish worship services—not only on weekdays but also on the Sabbath and holy days—the debates in the individual congregations came to a close, at least for the time being. However, later that year, a group of rabbis from Upper Silesia sent a statement opposing the organ to Zacharias Frankel (1801–1871), chief rabbi at Dresden, who had withdrawn from the conference on the grounds that its reforms were too radical. A notice in the *Allgemeine Zeitung des Judenthums* responded:

> We protest herewith against the address of these rabbis and state that the cities of Oppeln, Neisse, Neustadt, Zülz, Leobschütz, Hultschin, Katscher, Kosel, Krappitz, Tarnowitz, Ober-Glogau, Guttentag, Pless, Kreuzberg, and Gleiwitz, and indeed Ratibor, Rybnik, and Beuthen, as well, speak in an entirely different way from that which these rabbis try to paint before the public. . . The winds of Reform blow in most of the communities with health and strength. . . .
>
> What do these Upper Silesian rabbis hope to achieve with Dr. Frankel at all? Is he one of their group? Dr. Frankel, who brought the organ to Töplitz, who brought so many changes to the service in Dresden, who has a Christian cantor leading the synagogue choir.[26]

Despite the ongoing disagreement, many Jewish congregations now dared to acquire a pipe or reed organ. Among the earliest were those at Koblenz (1845), Heidelberg (reed organ, 1845), Berlin (in the prayer hall on Georgenstraße, 1846, and a private synagogue, 1848),[27] Hildesheim (1850), Mainz (1853), the Berlin Reform Congregation at 16 Johannisstraße (1854), Mannheim and Alzey (1855), and Leipzig (1856). In Buchau, the Jewish congregation undertook a rather unusual method of financing a new organ when it announced in 1846 that, on the basis of the Second Rabbinical Conference's rulings, "in future, when a child is called to the Torah, a voluntary contribution to the building of an organ in the synagogue here will be introduced."[28] In 1848 economic shortcomings led the new Jewish congregations in Bielefeld to appropriate the reed organ and sheet music from the wealthier second synagogue at Klosterplatz, which had acquired the instrument around 1847. However, the organ must have been returned since, on the second day of Passover that same year, another attempt was made to "borrow" the instrument.[29]

The introduction of the organ in synagogues was debated in other European countries as well. In France, the Consistoire Centrale, in a May 1846 ruling, assented to its use in synagogues for the celebration of all "religious" and "national" occasions.[30] In France, in part due to postrevolution attitudes, the church organ suffered a period of decline in performance, design, and importance in worship during much of the first half of the nineteenth century. After the 1846 ruling, however, organs and organ music began to recover. Thereafter, these instruments were acquired by the synagogues of Besançon, Lille, Lyons, Marseilles, Nancy, and Strasbourg. Austria-Hungary (with the exception of Vienna), Belgium, Denmark, Italy, Luxemburg, the Netherlands, and Sweden all followed suit, as did England, Poland, Switzerland, and the community of Odessa (South Russia, now Ukraine). Though not every congregation used the organ on Sabbath, it was at least played for weddings and paraliturgical occasions.

THE DISPUTE AT THE NEW SYNAGOGUE IN BERLIN

New debates began in 1861, coinciding with plans for the construction of an organ in Berlin's New Synagogue on Oranienburger Straße, which was then being built. The argument in this case is representative of the way the issue was more generally discussed in the nineteenth century. The congregation's board of directors collected various responses to the question "Is the presentation of an organ in the synagogues with a view to its being played in participation with the singing of the worship service, according to the Talmudic and rabbinical regulations . . . or possibly following the rituals sanctioned by custom . . . permissible or not?"[31] In two responsa by local rabbis, this usage was both rejected and condemned: On November 11, 1861, Elkan Rosenstein, assessor to the rabbinate, announced in a responsum that he was opposed to the organ because it was unsuitable for the liturgy.[32] Moreover, Rabbi Michael Sachs believed that the organ was alien to the character of the Jewish worship service and that it was ritually unacceptable to hire a non-Jewish organist for Sabbath and holy days.[33] The Berlin congregation then solicited the advice of a thirty-member committee that included music director Julius Stern, cantor Louis Lewandowski, and four well-known rabbis—Abraham Geiger (Breslau), Dr. Julius Landsberger (Darmstadt), Dr. Ludwig Phillipson (Magdeburg), and S. G. Löwe (Ratibor)—who approved the introduction of an organ.[34]

Concealed behind the problem of whether religious law permitted organs in synagogues were a number of issues that surpassed in scope and significance the purely musical concerns. This fact explains to some extent why most of the rabbinical responsa were published, while evaluations from a musical perspective fell into the background and can now be found only with difficulty, if at all. Of note was the quarrel over the introduction of an organ at the New Synagogue on Berlin's Oranienburger Straße, which was arbitrated not only by rabbinical responsa but also by the famous reformer of synagogue music, Louis Lewandowski (1821/23–1894).[35] The future music director and choirmaster of the Oranienburger Straße synagogue, Lewandowski was at that time still working as cantor at the synagogue on Heidereutergasse. The advisory opinion he contributed to the committee's findings was of decisive importance to his career as a composer and as one of the most significant cantors of the nineteenth century. It is also historically meaningful as the first of the only two reports on musical matters produced by a cantor (the other, by Salomon Sulzer, is discussed later). Here, for the first time, the argumentation is based on musical rather than halakhic premises.

In his response, *Gutachten betr. den Antrag wegen Bewilligung der Geldmittel zur Herstellung eines Orgelwerkes in der Neuen Synagoge*, dated January 13, 1862, Lewandowski says that the organ is the most appropriate support for the newly introduced congregational and choral singing because it alone is in a position to "control and to lead large masses in large spaces":

> The claim has been made on the subject of the introduction of the organ in the Jewish worship service that the organ cannot be brought into harmony with the peculiarities of the ancient Jewish style of singing. Such reservations, however, are based on a complete misunderstanding of the instrument, together with a lack of any musical understanding. The organ, in its magnificent sublimity and multiplicity, is capable of any nuance, and bringing it together with the old style of singing will inevitably have a marvelous effect.
>
> The necessity, in the almost immeasurably vast space of the new synagogue, of providing leadership through instruments to the choir

and most particularly to the congregation imposes itself on me so imperatively that I hardly think it possible to have a service in keeping with the times in this space without this leadership.

I make this assertion out of the deepest conviction and hope that the praiseworthy authorities of our congregation will soon succeed in bringing this question, of such vital importance to the natural evolution of the liturgy in the new synagogue, to a favorable final resolution.[36]

Lewandowski argues here as a musician; rather than alluding to the strict traditions in which he was raised, he speaks of dedicating himself to "keeping with the times." Nor does he enter into the discussion of whether the organ is a Christian instrument. He avoids a consideration of the organ as a solo instrument in the Jewish liturgy and instead limits himself to its vitally important function as an instrument of pure accompaniment. In both cases he would have had to argue against the rabbis.

Lewandowski's unambiguously positive attitude toward the organ as a synagogue instrument, as well as his strategically cunning arguments, may have had a key influence on the decision to introduce it to the Berlin congregation. At the same time, his relationship to the organ appears more ambivalent in Aron Ackermann's report of a conversation with the composer in 1892: "I remember his words precisely: 'See here,' he said, 'I, who organized the music of the whole worship service and organized it indeed with the organ, I am myself in my heart of hearts an opponent of the organ in the synagogue.'"[37] Ackermann explains Lewandowski's earlier arguments in favor of the organ as forced on him by his official position as cantor and goes on to say, "His Jewish sensibility compelled him to the side of the organ's opponents, and the fact that he expressed his opposition at the end of his life, after thirty years of observing the organ's effects, gives his opinion an altogether particular value."[38]

However authentic Ackermann's recollections may be, one must interpret them with caution; Lewandowski wrote all of his compositions for solo organ, as well as liturgical pieces for other keyboard instruments, in the last years of his life, and if he were adamantly opposed to the liturgical use of the organ at that time, he would hardly have written these works. On the other hand, there is reason to wonder about the relatively few pieces he created for organ, especially considering how old he was when he composed them and his decades of employment at a synagogue with an organ. For although he wrote not only a great deal of liturgical vocal music with organ accompaniment but also symphonies, cantatas, and lieder, liturgical pieces for solo keyboard instruments constitute only a tiny part of his oeuvre. Thus, even though Lewandowski was fully conscious of the organ's effectiveness as a synagogue instrument, he may not have been a wholly convinced advocate of its use. His motivation for composing any organ pieces at all may be viewed as the fulfillment of a sort of duty. Moreover, as the central figure in the renewal of synagogue music, he may have decided to complete his vision by including the organ as both an instrument of accompaniment and a solo instrument.

The representatives of the Berlin congregation continued to be uncertain as to whether they should authorize the building of an organ, as a communication of the *Allgemeine Zeitung des Judenthums* of January 11, 1863, indicates:

> The issue concerning the installation of an organ in the new house of God was not brought to a conclusion in today's representative session; a motion to dedicate funds to the building of an organ, reserving its use in the worship service, of course, according to the regulations as definitively provided by statutory authority, received 11 votes out of 19, that is less than two thirds of the members present, so that the question is not yet settled. It is certainly to be expected that the board of the congregation will prepare a new draft to be introduced at an early period, with clarifications to accommodate the wishes expressed by some of those present (according to which the board as well should provide a description of the use of the organ as a ritual matter, following the conclusions of the congregational authorities as strictly based on the relevant paragraphs of the congregation's statutes), and its acceptance through the required number of votes is hardly to be doubted.[39]

In fact, the congregation was divided on the question of the organ, and the debate echoed well beyond Berlin. Orthodox Rabbi David Deutsch (1810–1873) of Sohrau, for example, addressed it in a lengthy essay, "Die Orgel in der Synagoge," in which he offered his "opinion on these rabbinical reports, as on the organ question altogether, and indeed an opinion from an Orthodox-Talmudic standpoint, motivated strictly by scholarly intentions."[40] The proposed organ in the Oranienburger Straße synagogue was the object of particular sarcasm: "Indeed, the questioners solicited two advisory reports from professional musicians [Julius Stern and Louis Lewandowski], who asserted that the organ is indispensable. In my naiveté, I ask myself: If, as has been claimed, the extent of the proposed synagogue in Berlin is to be so great as to make it impossible for a whole choir of human voices to make itself adequately heard, how will the single voice of the preacher be able to do this—given that the sermon is surely as important an element of the service as the synagogue chants? Or will the organ be used to support the preacher as well?"[41]

On January 18, 1863, at any rate, the board approved the introduction of the organ by a vote of fifteen to four "and achieved yet another victory for the matter of progress."[42] After almost three years of prolonged deliberations, polemics, and rabbinical responsa, a decision had finally been reached. At the consecration of the Oranienburger Straße synagogue on September 5, 1866, the organ was officially inaugurated: "At about noon an organ prelude played by Schwantzer introduced the festive service, and the synagogue choir, accompanied by organ and orchestra, under the direction of the royal music director Lewandowski (who had also written the music for pieces that were sung) intoned the Hebrew opening blessing as the congregation entered."[43]

THE JEWISH SYNODS AND THE
FINAL QUEST FOR THE ORGAN

The introduction of the organ in the New Synagogue at Oranienburger Straße was the harbinger of a moment of change in the history of the Jewish community that was more fully expressed in June and July 1869 at the First Jewish Synod in Leipzig, where for the first time rabbis from throughout Europe, the United States, and even the West Indies assembled to discuss the views of an "enlightened" liberal Judaism. The sole representative of the cantors and synagogue musicians in the synod was Salomon Sulzer (1804–1890), one of the most outstanding hazzanim of his time and, from 1826 on, chief cantor at the newly built City Temple in Vienna's Seitenstettengasse, a position he held for fifty-six years. According to the official report of the deliberations, in a well-received speech Sulzer argued in favor of the introduction of the organ: "[A]n instrumental accompaniment for the singing in the worship service should be introduced everywhere, in order to ease the active participation of members of the congregation in the same. . . . To provide the requisite accompaniment to this end, the organ deserves to be recommended, and no religious reservations conflict with its use on the Sabbath and holy days."[44]

Sulzer's stance is surprising considering his role in developing the so-called Viennese rite together with the preacher Isaac Noah Mannheimer (1793–1865). This moderate revision of the liturgy and traditional synagogue music was characterized by what the Viennese congregation viewed as greater decorum and aesthetically pleasing music. Edifying sermons were delivered in the vernacular, while the Hebrew language and the traditional text of the prayers for the service were retained in a slightly abbreviated liturgy. Although it differed from prevalent customs, the new service balanced traditional and modernizing elements while adhering to Jewish law.

The most notable sign that Vienna's Jews eschewed significant reforms in their quest for modernity was the absence of an organ in their new synagogue. Originally, certain Jewish leaders announced that the organ was to be intro-

duced in Vienna, but resistance was fierce, and the decision was not carried out.
For some time it was as if the Viennese rite of Reform Judaism "progressed"
without the organ. Although the Viennese Jews rejected the ideological changes'
that were gaining popularity in German-Jewish communities, the question of
Reform was nevertheless continually being renewed. Though blocked at first,
the organ eventually made its way, beginning in 1887, as a synagogue instrument into the Turkish Temple and several Ashkenazic and Sephardic Viennese
temples (see figures 3.1 and 3.2), while the controversy continued.[45]

FIGURE 3.1. The Leopoldstadt Temple, Vienna's largest synagogue,
located at 5 Tempelgasse in the Second District, was one of the first congregations to consider building an organ; the occasion was its consecration
in 1858. However, opposition was intense, and it was not until the late
nineteenth century that the congregation purchased an instrument, a reed
organ built by one of the most prestigious instrument builders in Vienna,
T. Kotykiewicz. Its placement and use represent the concessions the congregation made: The reed organ was concealed behind the ark of the Torah
and played only on request during private celebrations not held on Sabbath. Photograph courtesy of the Jüdisches Museum Wien.

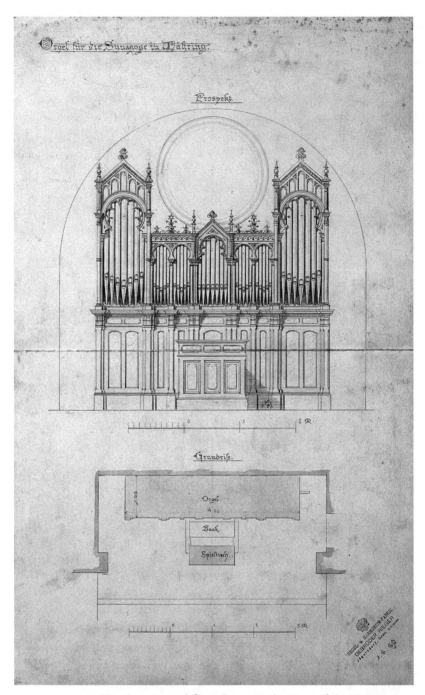

FIGURE 3.2. The elevation and floor plan are indications of the Viennese organ controversy. In 1889 the congregation of the Schopenhauerstraße synagogue in the Eighteenth District (Währing) had the organ-building firm Gebrüder Rieger draw up a proposal for an organ, but in the end, its opponents were victorious. Courtesy of the Jüdisches Museum Wien.

The synod accepted Sulzer's conclusions, and at the Second Jewish Synod in Augsburg in 1871, the decision was broadened with the addition that both Gentiles and Jews were permitted to officially play the organ on Sabbath and holy days.[46] Sulzer's own memorandum on reforms in the worship service at the Viennese synagogue goes still farther:

> Since it has been recognized by authoritative persons [i.e., by the First Jewish Synod in Leipzig] that no religious objections can prevail against the introduction of the organ in the synagogue and that there is no prohibition against organ playing on the Sabbath, from the musical point of view I can only speak in favor of the same. As a tested means of enhancing the devotional atmosphere, for the precision and purity of the sung parts and the support of the recitative, and finally to hold the singing in a large synagogue together and to direct it, the introduction of the organ seems frankly a necessity, not to be rejected, and indeed a good many evils could be avoided this way. It goes without saying that this would have to be done in the religious-national spirit of Israel and that preludes and accompaniments would need to be performed in the same serious style.[47]

Sulzer, in contrast to Lewandowski, refers to the organ as having a function as a solo instrument in the Jewish worship service, and for its use in accompaniment he values it above all other instruments:

> Only the organ is in a position to lead, to control, to cover dissonances, and it deserves to be reinstated in public worship in the place from which it has, to the detriment of religious edification, been excluded for far too long. The organ allows the ḥazzan to perform his priestly function independently of his personal artistic ability and at the same time protects him from that self-satisfied pseudo-artistry that often attacks aesthetic beauty as a mildew attacks a seedling crop and poisons it, protects him from those trivial vocal ornamentations misused by provincial cantors as a way of trying to appeal to the masses, or that weepy Polish virtuosity that drives the younger generation—most of whom have some musical training—to flee from the house of God.[48]

Lewandowski and Sulzer, both eminently qualified musicians, argue exclusively as such in their statements, recommending the introduction of the organ to synagogues on musical grounds but with different effect: In Lewandowski's congregation the organ was introduced, whereas in Sulzer's, despite his recommendation, it was blocked.[49] However, this did not prevent Sulzer from carrying on his ideas in his musical compositions. He provided optional organ accompaniments for the four-part mixed chorus arrangements of his monumental *Schir Zion*, a collection of prayers for the whole liturgical year,[50] and he wrote several organ preludes for liturgical use. Moreover, though he had been unable to achieve the introduction of the organ in the Vienna congregation, he donated a reed organ to the congregation of his hometown of Hohenems, where liturgical and musical reforms were more advanced.

EMBRACING ASHKENAZIC REFORMS: ORGANS IN SEPHARDIC SYNAGOGUES

Vienna finally obtained its first synagogue organ with the building of a new Sephardic synagogue in 1887: the Turkish Temple. This synagogue belonged to one of the very few Sephardic congregations to adopt the organ and organ music along the lines of the Ashkenazic model. Cellist and composer Joseph Sulzer (1850–1926), the youngest of Salomon Sulzer's sixteen children and brought up primarily in the Ashkenazic tradition, contributed to the synagogue's opening ceremony in September 1887. At the festival program he played one of his compositions, a prelude for organ.[51]

As in other Sephardic congregations, the introduction of the organ was a matter of disagreement; however, a serious conflict was apparently avoided when the younger members asserted themselves against the elders. The organ itself, a twelve-stop instrument by Viennese builder Franz Strommer, was used mainly for occasions on which the congregation agreed that the use of a musical instrument would not constitute a gross offense against Orthodoxy. Abraham M. Elias, a conservative board member, and Marco Russo, representing the younger generation, drew up special rules. Elias even offered to fund the organ's building and installation in the synagogue on condition of a notarized written agreement that it would never be played on a day when the use of an instrument in general is halakhically prohibited.[52] Therefore, the organ of the Sephardic community in Vienna was played only at weddings, and the music was assigned to four categories depending on the status of the families involved: A wedding of members of the first class was held with a large choir, an organ, and two harps; a second-class wedding, with a small choir and organ accompaniment; a third-class one, with unaccompanied men's chorus; while for poorly situated families a rabbi and cantor had to suffice.

The Turkish Temple in Vienna was no exception; in fact, the organ appeared in Sephardic synagogues as early as 1841, when the originally Orthodox congregation Kahal Kadosh Beth Elohim in Charleston, South Carolina, acquired an instrument. Not only was it the first synagogue in the United

States to install an organ (albeit in spite of great objection), but Kahal Kadosh became the first Reform Jewish congregation in the United States.[53] In contrast to Vienna, here the organ was used during all liturgical celebrations, in the same fashion as in the Ashkenazic congregations. The disputes that arose from this and other innovations eventually led to the permanent breakup of the congregation.[54] Further Sephardic congregations that adopted the organ (always with controversy) were those of London, New York,[55] and Bayonne, France.[56]

THE PEAK AND THE DISSOLUTION OF THE ORGELSTREIT

The organ controversy reached its peak and final resolution in intense discussions in the Cologne Jewish community, where negotiations over the introduction of an organ in the Roonstraße synagogue began in 1902. The squabbles in Cologne were different from all previous ones in that they were led by a unique coalition of the traditionally oriented devotional society Adass Jeschurun (founded in 1863) and a Zionist organization. The coalition's spokesman was David Wolffsohn, a member of the congregation's leadership and later the second president of the World Zionist Organization after the death of Theodor Herzl in 1904: "Wolffsohn opposed the introduction of the organ with all his strength. Conviction and political calculations may have played equal roles. He used the traditional argument in which the organ was seen as a sign of assimilation and imitation of Christian worship, which would inevitably lead to a split in the community."[57]

In the end, the Zionists and the Orthodox faction were defeated, and on April 4, 1906, the organ was played for the first time at the Roonstraße synagogue.[58] At its general meeting on June 20, 1906, the Adass Jeshurun society voted unanimously to leave the Roonstraße synagogue and to reconstitute itself as a new, independent congregation, thus representing the most obvious split of the community into Orthodox and Reform branches. Incidentally, after this point, debates over the introduction of pipe and reed organs in Germany's Reform synagogues came to an end. Indeed, a substantial number of Jewish communities decided to replace the instruments they had with larger, better ones.

One of the last synagogues to be furnished with an organ was that on Prinzregentenstraße in Berlin (the very last synagogue organ in Germany prior to the Second World War was built in 1931 for the Oberstraße synagogue in Hamburg). In February 1929 the board of the Berlin Jewish community invited the Steinmeyer firm Oettingen to "submit an offer and proposed disposition for an instrument appropriate to this space," and just a week later Steinmeyer presented them with a ten-page cost estimate for a 75-stop organ. For financial reasons, this plan had to be scaled down to 52 stops. A third proposal for concept and disposition was provided by a team of experts consisting of Wolfgang Reimann, professor at the Staatliche Hochschule für Kirchenmusik in Berlin-Charlottenburg and later director of the Hochschule für Musik in Berlin and of the Staatschor and cathedral choir there, as well as organists Arthur Zepke and Ludwig Altman (born Altmann, the latter altered his name upon emigration to the United States). At the end of August 1929, Alexander Weinbaum, the synagogue's choir director, announced that "the issue of the organ will not be resolved for some time yet." Some months later, the order was at last given to Steinmeyer for an organ with 65 stops and three transmissions. In the inspection report of September 7, 1930, Reimann praised the result:

> Acoustically, this three-manual instrument, with its 68 sounding stops, is one of the loveliest organs in Berlin. . . . The full organ fills the space well, even though high pressure is not used in any of the registers. This is all the more important in that the placement of the organ cannot be called very favorable for the full effect of its sound volume. With an altogether adroit and spacious organization of the main manual and the excellent room acoustics, the danger of a dull overall sound has happily been overcome. The intonation of the individual voices has been carried out with palpable affection by a master hand. . . . This organ is an outstandingly successful instrument, particularly well adapted to serve as an accompanying instrument for solo and choral singing.[59]

The Steinmeyer organ, one of the largest and most significant not only in Berlin but also in all of Germany, was to exist for only eight years before it was destroyed, together with almost all of central Europe's synagogue organs, in the so-called *Reichspogromnacht*—Kristallnacht—of November 9–10, 1938.

THE DESTRUCTION OF SYNAGOGUE ORGANS IN THE KRISTALLNACHT AND ITS AFTERMATH

The annihilation of organs in the November 1938 pogrom was carried out in different ways. In some cases the entire synagogue was burned down with the organ inside it; in others, parts of the synagogue were set on fire one at a time (the organ was a particularly popular object to destroy in this fashion).[60] Samuel Adler, son of cantor and composer Hugo Adler, was ten years old at the time and has left an eyewitness description of how the storm troopers dealt with the Mannheim synagogue, which was not a freestanding building but incorporated into a block of apartments and business premises and therefore could not be completely demolished: "So they set two explosive charges; one in the ark which by the way contained the 122 Torah scrolls of all sizes, the other under the organ. The first explosion blew out the entire front walk, the second blew a huge hole in the choir loft floor, destroyed the balcony and blew the organ over the side so that it hung from a cable over the balcony about fifty feet from the main floor."[61]

When Adler and his father arrived at the synagogue in the hope of saving at least part of the music library, the collection had not yet been damaged. Their plan, however, proved to be a perilous enterprise since the men of the *Sturmabteilung* [Storm Division, or SA] were guarding the building. It was the organ that quite dramatically saved their lives: "Just then, since there was so much dust, I sneezed. Immediately we heard one of the officers downstairs command a man to go upstairs and to shoot anyone there on sight. He had hardly finished shouting when the cable of the organ gave way and the console crashed to the floor barring the entrance to the door leading upstairs. Confusion reigned down there while my father and I weighed down with books rushed down the stairs into the secret passage and safely reached the house across the street, and miraculously all in one piece we had accomplished an impossible deed."[62]

Another witness recalls the events at the Königsberg synagogue before it was demolished: "The windows of the neighboring synagogue had been smashed in; inside a riot of thugs was busy systematically wrecking the benches, ripping the Torah scrolls from the Aron Kodesh, tearing the prayer books apart, and stacking everything in a great pile in the middle of the synagogue, while someone was playing the *Horst Wessel Song*. After the work of destruction inside the synagogue was finished the pile in the middle was set alight, to the horrible sounds of the organ as it went up in flames."[63] Evidently, the organ as a synagogue instrument was abused by playing anti-Jewish and even National Socialist repertoire—a blasphemous desecration that took place before the synagogue was reduced to rubble.

The organ of the Munich synagogue, built in 1929 by the firm of G. F. Steinmeyer, was insulted in an especially cynical way, as reported in the *Stürmer* of October 19, 1938:

IT IS A DISGRACE!

THE JEW ORGAN IN THE CHURCH OF ST. KORBINIAN IN MUNICH

It is reported to us by a trustworthy source from Munich that the organ of the former Jewish synagogue in Munich has been acquired through purchase by the Bishop's Office from the Jewish religious community.

Shortly before the demolition of the synagogue, the organ was moved by the transport firm A. Frank and Sons at 160 Westendstraße, Munich, to the church of St. Korbinian on Gotzingerplatz. The organ case is said to have been bought through the Steinmeyer firm in Oettingen in Bavaria and installed in the church of St. Korbinian by the same company. Now when the faithful arrive for worship in the church of St. Korbinian, they will have the peculiar pleasure of hearing music from an organ that has stood in a synagogue for years. The very organ that once accompanied the Jews' songs of hatred for non-Jews now adorns a Christian church. It is a disgrace![64]

Inasmuch as this sarcasm incites Christians against Jews, the idea of the organ as a Christian instrument is legitimized. Organs and organ music are now stripped of their legitimate significance in Jewish culture. This involves not only the synagogue as a place but also the organ itself, which is regarded as an instrument that, above all, represents Germanness in Hitler's sense and is thus used to accompany the National Socialists' political functions.[65]

Some organs were not destroyed in the pogroms, but almost none of them escaped the war's devastation. The New Synagogue on Oranienburger Straße in Berlin survived the Kristallnacht, as did its organ, when a German police officer, Wilhelm Krützfeld, noticed that a commando of SA men wearing disguises had set a fire in the synagogue's lobby and chased them off before calling the fire department. His was a unique reaction to the National Socialists' destructive rage, which most Germans merely watched and few fire departments opposed.[66] Six months after the pogroms, a service with organ music was once again held—on the eve of the first Passover seder—in Oranienburger Straße. The cantor, Siegmund Hirschberg, reported in a letter to his son Hans, who had already emigrated to Palestine, that "the solemn full organ roared, in powerful chords, above the deeply shaken crowd, in a well played classical prelude—in grand style."[67] However, only a few months later, the *Wehrmacht* appropriated the synagogue for use as a quartermaster's store, Heeresbekleidungsamt III. During the night of November 22–23, 1943, a British air attack completely leveled the structure and with it the largest existing organ in a German synagogue.

Before the Dortmund synagogue was torn down in October 1938, the organ, or at least parts of it, had been sold to the Catholic Gertrudis congregation on Hackländerplatz in the city for about 10,000 reichsmark (quite a bargain since the equivalent today would be about US$50,000). There it was consumed by flames after the church was bombed during the Second World

War. Similarly, the organ of the Munich synagogue, transferred to the church of St. Korbinian in 1938, was obliterated in a bombing raid in 1944.

The Aachen synagogue housed an exception. Its organ, built in 1865 by Ibach und Söhne of Barmen was bought in 1906 by the Roman Catholic parish of Fleckenberg in Sauerland; between 1955 and 1958 the instrument was restored by the Breil firm of Dorsten and is now installed in the Trennstätt church in Lippstadt.[68] The synagogue organs of Augsburg and Konstanz, which had similarly been sold to Catholic parishes, were also saved from destruction.

At least some of the pipes of the Kronenstraße synagogue organ in Karlsruhe have survived at the Erfatal Museum in Hardheim (on permanent loan from the Vleugels firm of Hardheim). The synagogue from which they came was built between 1872 and 1875; its organ was built in 1875 by the firm H. Voit und Söhne of Karlsruhe-Durlach. This organ must have been disassembled before the 1938 demolition of the synagogue because the pipes ended up by undetermined means in the Catholic church of Karlsruhe-Rüpper, where the Vleugels firm found them when it was restoring the organ. Vleugels subsequently transplanted the Kronenstraße pipework to the instrument at the Erfatal Museum.

Given the pogroms' extensive depredations, the destruction of the organs and organ music of the Jewish communities in the German-speaking world was complete. Today there are again, even if only few in number, organs in German synagogues in Aachen, Berlin, Dresden, and Frankfurt am Main. The organ in the Frankfurt synagogue is not used during worship services as the congregation follows the Orthodox rite; it is sometimes played during weddings. The same is true of the reed organ in the Aachen synagogue. Despite the few remnants of the German-Jewish organ tradition, the historically significant instruments have been annihilated, and the tradition of organ music in synagogues no longer exists in Germany.

THE DYNAMICS IN THE DEVELOPMENT OF SYNAGOGUE ORGANS: FACTORS AND FACTS

Organs in German synagogues followed a dynamism of their own. After hesitant beginnings, a breakthrough occurred in the wake of the 1869 Leipzig Synod and the beginning of the *Gründerjahre* of German industrialization (around 1870), when there were ten times as many organs in German synagogues as there had been twenty years earlier. This trend continued throughout the following decades. Some congregations decided on a more economical alternative and used a reed organ to accompany their services.

It was perhaps not only the resolutions of the rabbinical conferences and synods that led to the increased building of organs. The urbanization of the Jewish population in the mid-nineteenth century was as much a factor as its economic and social rise in the years between 1848 and 1871. The unprecedented economic successes of Jews in this period are tied to the liberalizing economic policies of the German government. In the first years after the founding of the unified German state and the end of the Franco-Prussian War, an extraordinary economic upturn took place in the newly emerging German Reich, and the Jewish population took part in this growth.[69] These developments were triggered especially by the payment of five billion francs in French war damages and also by the economic space attained by the founding of the empire, which allowed a reduction in internal tariffs; the unification of business law, coinage, and the system of weights and measures; and the establishment of the Reichsbank. Nevertheless, as early as 1873, when a worldwide economic crisis caused the stock exchange to crash and the collapse of banks and a number of new companies, a depression that lasted for several years replaced the boom of the Gründerjahre.

Jakob Thon's statistical research at the beginning of the twentieth century provides a broad yet precise picture.[70] Thon not only provides lists of the provinces where synagogue organs were to be found but also correlates the arrival of organs with community size and establishes the proportions between pipe and reed organs. Thus he is able to conclude that the smallest congregations—those with fewer than one hundred members—almost never possessed an organ due to their lack of financial means; out of 762 such congregations in the whole of the German Empire, only three—one in the duchy of Oldenburg and two in Saxony—possessed pipe organs.

On the other hand, an impressive number of smaller Jewish congregations owned a reed organ: five synagogues in Westphalia, two in Braunschweig, two in Württemberg, one in Saxony, and one in the grand duchy of Hesse. The number of keyboard instruments grew with the size of the congregation; in synagogues having 100–300 members, about a tenth had an organ, and only 3.3 percent a reed organ. Out of 77 German congregations of 300–500 members, almost a third possessed an organ (31.2 percent); more than half of those with 500–1000 members did (51.6 percent), while only four of these had a reed organ, all in Prussia. Of the big-city synagogues with more than a thousand members, organs were the norm (21 out of 30 congregations in Prussia and 17 out of 21 elsewhere), while only one of these used a reed organ.

The quantitative picture of the organ's increase in German synagogues shows that it was no isolated phenomenon. Rather, from its original position as a "Jewish curiosity," the instrument became a symbol of the changes in

Jewish culture beginning with the Reform movement and an integral part of liberal Judaism in the twentieth century.

The Synagogue Organ in the Context of Organ-Building Traditions

Organ building for the synagogue never followed its own independent path; one might suppose that liturgical requirements would have led to the development of a typically "Jewish" type of organ alongside "Protestant" and "Catholic" types in the nineteenth and early twentieth centuries, but this did not happen.

Walter Kwasnik first discussed the idea that organ building has certain characteristics related to a particular religion or denomination. He argued that small and medium-sized instruments intended for Protestant churches tended to have a fully developed foundation chorus and a reduced proportion of string stops, mainly because of the importance of polyphonic preludes. In contrast, the lesser-developed foundation chorus and orchestral timbres of the Romantic style were favored by the more homophonically arranged, largely improvised music of the Catholic Church, together with its emphasis on the *Grundtönigkeit*[71] in the accompaniment of congregational singing.[72] However, Reichling, in a detailed consideration of factors such as the purpose for which the organ was intended, its sound aesthetic, disposition, registration, and physical placement, found no such pattern: No global differences on a strictly denominational or ritual basis can be established since "each individual case . . . must be seen in the interconnections of many different relationships; reducing the question to the confessional aspect alone would inevitably lead to a distorted interpretation."[73]

The approaches of both scholars must be considered with care. Reichling has ignored characteristics of the different physical placement of organs. One obvious and classic difference is that organs in Catholic churches are traditionally placed in the rear gallery to support the organ interludes between Latin chants, whereas organs in Protestant churches are more often found in the front to accompany the choirs. Kwasnik's general remarks on the disposition of organs can be disproved with the example of French Romantic organs for Catholic churches, which featured full-sounding foundation choruses in all divisions when resources allowed. Thus, extending Kwasnik's argument to a hypothetical third type—the synagogue organ—would be equally problematic.

A number of considerations support the argument that a characteristically Jewish organ did not exist. The status of the synagogue organ began to develop in the first place as a result of a function imposed from the "outside"—by rabbinical conferences, congregations, and organists, not to mention the various written discussions. To what extent did the instrument take on a subordinate position (accompanying the cantor and congregation), and to what extent a leading (solo performance) role? To what degree did it differ in these respects from a church organ?

Organ building evolved predominately in the context of the instrument's use in churches, which led to the development of traditions that would have to integrate future innovations. Nonetheless, some organ builders advocated changes in organ technology and therefore influenced the usage of organs, often not in response to the church's requests. Since organ building in Jewish congregations did not begin to develop until 1810 and grew only very slowly during the nineteenth century, the synagogue, with its particular advantages and disadvantages, likely provided a context for experimentation. Did the special characteristics of organs (especially technical innovations) built for synagogues reflect their unique functions?

The possibilities of deploying an organ in the Jewish worship service are strongly connected to its disposition. Were the disposition and timbre of an organ in the synagogue different from those of organs in churches? In 1908 Rafael Frank claimed, "The organ, the supremely religious church instrument, can—with the necessary change in registration—successfully transform itself into a synagogue instrument, and has already done it."[74] How true is this assertion?

In the following sections I examine selected aspects of the synagogue organ on the basis of representative instruments and dispositions, the ways in which the existing traditions of organ building were applied, and how the music was played.

SPLENDID NEW INVENTIONS

As was the case in most churches that could afford organs, the aspect that dominated the synagogue organ at first was its almost exclusive use in the accompaniment of congregational singing. The express demand was for the "introduction of organ accompaniment, indispensable for the adequate production of choral singing."[75] The dispositions of the early synagogue organs, as far as the surviving documentation shows, reflect this limitation. Apart from a few exceptions, instruments built before about 1860 used ten or twenty stops in two or at most three departments (generally *Hauptwerk* and pedal with an occasional second manual). The purpose of pure accompaniment is evident from the dispositions of the smaller organs, which emphasize fundamental pitches to an extreme degree. In the first half of the nineteenth century, deeper stops such as the 8′ and 16′ were preferred, a tendency that grew considerably during the second half of the century. Examples are the organs of the synagogues in Bayreuth (early nineteenth century, builder unknown), Hildesheim (1850, Schaper of Hildesheim), and the Reform Congregation on Johannisstraße in Berlin (1854, Buchholz of Berlin; table 3.1).[76]

During the nineteenth century, when the organ began to lose its sovereign status to the modern orchestra, a change came about in organ building. In the context of a general process of secularization, interest in liturgy and the organization of life around worship diminished, and the organ itself began moving from church to concert hall and other public places almost simultaneously with its introduction in synagogues.

At the same time, in nearly every part of the German-speaking world, organ building was influenced by a new class of professional experts (*Orgelsachverständige*), usually chosen by civil or church authorities. Whenever a new instrument was to be built or an old one restored or renovated, these experts were required to review the plans. It was their responsibility to revise the proposed disposition and establish both the number of stops and the

TABLE 3.1. Disposition of the Organ at the Berlin Reform Congregation on Johannisstraße, Built by Carl August Buchholz in 1854

Manual 1		Manual 2		Pedal	
Bourdon	16′	Salicional	8′	Violon	16′
Gamba	8′	Gedeckt	8′	Subbaß	16′
Principal	8′	Flûte	4′	Violon	8′
Rohrflöte	8′			Cello	8′
Octav	4′				
Gemshorn	4′				
Quinte	2⅔′				
Octav	2′				
Mixtur	4fach				
Trompete	8′				

number and type of the *Spielhilfen* [registration aids].[77] Lively discussions took place in the congregations over the experts' qualifications and the criteria they used to make their decisions. Thus, the building of church organs was supervised and regulated by a committee that made technically detailed plans on the basis of fixed rules.

In the synagogue, by contrast, these responsibilities tended to fall to an undefined commission that was neither strictly organized nor subject to regulations. The members of these groups belonged to different faiths and varied extensively in their knowledge of organ building. In Munich, the first organ built at the synagogue on Westernriederstraße (1876, Maerz und Sohn) was reviewed by Prof. Dr. Carl Emil von Schafhäutl, a well-known organ expert and acoustician of the time; Catholic organist Joseph Rheinberger; and Prof. Friedrich Riegel, who prepared the purchase report.[78] The composite of the respective committees shows that Jewish musicians were clearly underrepresented and played only a marginal role in determining the scope of the instrument. But perhaps the lack of Jewish musicians on the panels reflects the simple fact that they may not have had sufficient knowledge of organ building and that the congregations needed to rely on outside experts. Given that established organ specialists exerted great control, in many cases it must have been easy for the organ builder or commission members to implement technical innovations or unusual construction designs instead of catering to the needs of the Jewish congregations.

The organs of the Mannheim and Frankfurt synagogues, both by E. F. Walcker et Cie. of Ludwigsburg, provide examples of the way in which Eberhard Friedrich Walcker influenced the development of the Romantic organ when his pupils and other builders applied his ideas. Possibly the most significant of these innovations was Walcker's introduction and dissemination of the *Kegellade*, or cone chest. This new windchest system appeared in the first phase of development (1840–1844), Walcker's op. 28 in Stuttgart (1834–1845), op. 35 in Ludwigsburg (1840), op. 36 in Frauenzimmern (1839–1842), and Kegel[79] (1838–1842).

Zagreb's op. 127 (1855), which has a foot-operated combination and the crescendo in all stops, is an example of the registration aids made possible by this development. None of these, however, were synagogue organs. In his instruments for Mannheim and Frankfurt am Main, on the other hand, Walcker used new ideas of a still more experimental nature.

The Mannheim synagogue organ (table 3.2), also denominated op. 127, was built in 1855. As a contemporary report by Eberhard Kuhn suggests, the nineteenth-century method of dividing the stops among the keyboards according to their volume was applied to this instrument: "The tone color of

TABLE 3.2.
Disposition of the Mannheim Synagogue Organ, built by
E. F. Walcker et Cie. in 1855

Manual I		Manual II		Pedal	
Prinzipal	8'	Prinzipal	8'	Subbaß	16'
Viola di Gamba	8'	Salicional	8'	Violonbaß	16'
Copula	8'	Gedeckt	double lipped 8'	Posaunenbaß	16'
Flauto	8'	Clarinette	inward striking 8'	Violoncell	8'
Trompete	8'	Fagott	inward striking 8'	Oktavbaß	8'
Oktav	4'	Physharmonika	8'		
Oktav	2'	Dolce	8'		
Quinte	2⅔'	Flöte	4'		
Mixtur	4fach				

the secondary manual, compared with that of the main manual . . . is delicate
and noble."[80] Moreover, Kuhn notes that the organ used a spring chest for the
tone-channel chest. Although the spring chest is equal to the slider chest in
sound quality, it is rarely built because of its complexity and susceptibility to
damage. If it was indeed a spring chest rather than a cone chest (note 79 suggests the interchangeability of the terms at least in the mid-nineteenth century), it would seem to represent an experiment on Walcker's part since he
had never before used a spring chest in an organ intended for continual use.[81]
In addition, the organ was equipped with a swell.[82]

Architectonically, the instrument was well suited to the synagogue in that
Walcker divided the pipe works into two sections in order not to hide the rose
window of the front façade and allow sufficient space for the choir. This space-
saving solution was yet another of Walcker's devices.[83]

The organ for the Frankfurt synagogue (table 3.3) was built just four years
later, in 1859, as op. 168. From Walcker's bid document of April 28, 1857,
the instrument was clearly conceived with a view to its use in the Jewish wor-

TABLE 3.3. Disposition of the Synagogue Organ in Frankfurt am Main, Built by E. F. Walcker et Cie. in 1859

Manual I		Manual II		Manual III		Pedal	
Prinzipal	8'	Prinzipal	8'	Aeoline	8'	Prinzipalbaß	16'
Bourdon	16'	Fagott	8'	Gedeckt	8'	Subbaß	16'
Viola di Gamba	8'	Klarinette	8'	Fis harmonica	8'	Violonbaß	16'
Kopula	8'	Gedeckt	8'	Flöte	4'	Posaunenbaß	16'
Flauto	8'	Dolce	8'			Oktavbaß	8'
Trompete	8'	Rohrflöte	4'			Violoncello	8'
Salizional	8'	Fugara	4'			Fagott	8'
Quinte	5⅓'	Flautino	2'				
Oktave	4'	Nassard	2⅔'				
Kleingedeckt	4'	Kornett	8' 4fach				
Traversflöte	4'						
Quinte	2⅔'						
Mixtur	2' 5fach						
Scharff	1' 3fach						

ship service. Walcker recommended the incorporation of a pneumatic lever, which facilitates the key action when manuals are coupled, on the grounds that the synagogue service requires the organist to make especially rapid changes in registration.[84] Of course, salesmanship may have been an important factor in his praise of his new invention as particularly suited to Jewish needs; still, this indicates that he had taken those needs into consideration.

Other devices used in the Frankfurt organ include a crescendo pedal for a seldom-built single register, the Physharmonika,[85] and the widely favored foot-operated crescendo. In addition to the two manuals (each disposed so as to enable playing with all of the stops out), the swell box contained a third "harmonic," or *Farbwerk* division. The first manual is based on a comprehensive set of principals, while the second lacks principals in the 4' and 2' ranges. The instrument used a mechanical cone chest and a Barker lever (the Frankfurt organ is only the second instrument in which Walcker used the latter). Surprisingly, he equipped this middle-sized organ with a Barker lever, which he otherwise employed only in very large instruments, such as that of Münster cathedral (op. 122, 1856, IV/100), in all of the key and stop actions; the organ of the Marktkirche in Wiesbaden (op. 190, 1862, III/53), only in the first manual; and the concert organ at the Boston Music Hall (op. 191, 1863, IV/89), in all manuals.

The Grundtönigkeit of the Mannheim and Frankfurt synagogue organs, as well as their free-reed stops and Physharmonika, are by no means exceptional in Walcker's output. He had already used the Physharmonika, for example, in the organ of the Frankfurt Paulskirche (1827–1833), St. Michael's in Schwäbisch Hall (1832–1837), St. Peter's in Saint Petersburg (1836–1840), and the Protestant church in Lambsheim (1845–1848). Similarly, a disposition oriented to fundamental pitches and free-reed stops are not novelties but were present in earlier Walcker organs.[86] What is particularly unusual in the Physharmonika stop in the Frankfurt synagogue is the way it is constructed in its own division, with dedicated swell, something that occurred only in isolated cases in nineteenth-century organs.[87] One might reasonably suppose that the Frankfurt synagogue organ at least provided Walcker with an opportunity to experiment in building the Physharmonika as a swell stop.

All the same, Walcker did not incorporate his most forward-looking innovations in organ building into his first two synagogue organs. The sound ideal he had in mind, as well as the principle of combination tones—*additive Klangverschmelzung*[88] (discovered by Georg Andreas Sorge and Giuseppe Tartini, treasured by Abbé Georg Joseph Vogler, and frequently used in Walcker's instruments)—are not found in these two organs even though they were probably features of the Frankfurt Paulskirche organ (completed in 1833).[89]

THE ALSATIAN ORGAN REFORM

Later in the nineteenth century, the use of the organ in the Jewish worship service underwent a far-reaching change. Hermann Ehrlich, a cantor at the synagogue of Berkach bei Meiningen and editor of the *Liturgische Zeitschrift zur Veredelung des Synagogengesangs mit Berücksichtigung des ganzen Synagogenwesens*, reported that the organist no longer merely accompanied the congregational singing and the recitative of the prayer leader but had gradually taken on a solo role in the observances as well: "Interludes arose only at a later time, and only the basic melodies were accompanied by the organist in the earliest period. For the reason, however, that the later organists wished to make their artistry heard in the ongoing chants, and therefore filled in between the overly long stanzas and verses with all sorts of lovely tones and chords as rest pauses for the congregation, and then tried to lead them back to the correct starting note, a great variety of interludes evolved."[90]

For Ehrlich, organ playing in the Jewish service fulfilled a number of functions: The prelude arouses a feeling of devotion and thus leads worshippers into the mood of the service that is to follow; the playing of the chorale "must be simple, leading, supporting, uplifting, natural, and flowing" and should include the interlude; the accompaniment of the preacher's or choir leader's recitative should be based on no more than a few chords; and in the postlude (e.g., fugues, fantasias), organists can demonstrate their abilities.[91] Furthermore, they promote the use of church music principles, that is, a precise knowledge of figured bass.

The orientation toward Christian music is obvious in the use of concepts such as "church music" and "chorale." Beyond this, Ehrlich's detailed account of the organ's functions in the synagogue shows their remarkable quantitative and qualitative development throughout the nineteenth century. This is also confirmed by Viennese cantor Josef Singer, who provided another definition of the organ's tasks and significance in Jewish services in the 1880s. Singer stated that the synagogue organ has "a function to fulfill that is of the utmost importance in three ways, namely as an instrument of accompaniment for the choral and congregational singing, as an instrument of accompaniment for the solos of the cantor, and as a solo instrument."[92]

An undated pamphlet from approximately the same period states that the cantor should avoid working with the organ to the extent possible; the instrument should not play during the recitative, and even brief preludes, interludes, and postludes added to chants (not to mention key transpositions) would disrupt their unity and thereby disturb the devotional mood.[93] Furthermore, according to the pamphlet, the organ "should serve the arousal, support, and deepening of prayerfulness."[94] In the performance of preludes and postludes during the service, organ playing should "provide meaningful transitions in mood between the sections of the service, for example between the Hallel and the taking out of the Torah scrolls, or between the return of the scrolls and the Musaf . . . and [accompany] the cantor's large pieces and the congregational singing."[95]

Finally, during the late nineteenth century, the organ's specific functions in the Jewish worship service and the closely connected issue of the instrument's registration were both established. According to the *Oesterreichisch-ungarische Cantoren-Zeitung* of January 11, 1892, the registration in the accompaniment of monophonic congregational chant should be done so as not to fatigue the congregants. It further stresses that children's choirs are made possible only through the use of an organ because the instrument provides support for the youngsters' thin-sounding voices and fills in the missing lower tones with its own deeper register. The accompaniment should in general not drown out the singing but rather be "gentle and harmonic." Thus, at the close of the nineteenth century, the organ was seen as having a double function—on the one hand helping and supporting, and on the other, independent and free: "Both tasks are of equal importance, for both are in the service of the Lord."[96]

The diversification in the use of the organ during services was reflected in the size of the instruments. Between 1860 and 1930 many organs continued to be built with relatively small dispositions,[97] but very large instruments (in no way characterized as ordinary instruments for accompaniment) also began to appear. Around the turn of the century a number of synagogue organs boasted four departments and a disposition of as many as seventy stops.[98] From the 1870s on, the general pattern of larger organs reflects the fact that the organ was more often used as a solo instrument in the Jewish service.

At the same time, organs took on warmer sounds with relatively strong differentiations of sound quality. Further characteristics of the disposition are the use of strings, fundamental-based particular timbres, and free reeds (not only the Clarinet but even the Trombone and Trumpet stops were frequently made with free reeds). By about 1900, the characteristic late Romantic organ, with its *grundtönig* disposition and orchestral effect, made its appearance; these instruments, as Wolfgang Adelung sums it up, were "at a dead end, with their over-refined timbral capacities, no longer susceptible to any further improvement, so that a radical reaction was inevitable."[99]

———

In the wider world of the concert hall and the church, critical voices began to make themselves heard around the mid-nineteenth century, pointing out the shortcomings of contemporary organs and their limited use in the performance of early organ music, in particular the works of Johann Sebastian Bach. The need for a new path in organ building led to the Alsatian organ reform movement, which took the classic French organ as its model. The integration of French and German elements of 1871 was undoubtedly influenced by the political situation following the Franco-Prussian War, in which France was forced to cede the territories of Alsace and Lorraine to the German Empire.

The modernization of organ building was echoed in the construction of synagogue organs. In Berlin's Oranienburger Straße synagogue, the organ's disposition showed that clearly recognizable "features of the Alsatian organ reform led by Albert Schweitzer, Emile Rupp, et al. at the turn of the century [had been] successfully applied."[100] This organ (built in 1910 by the Walcker firm as op. 1526) provides an especially apt illustration of how up-to-date or indeed ahead of its time organ building for the synagogue could be, as, for instance, in the demand for many soft mixtures that would be available in all departments. Albert Schweitzer's suggestion that the pedal's relative weakness in comparison to the manual should be offset by the use of mixture, as well as 4′ and 2′ stops, was not incorporated into the Walcker organ for the New Synagogue.[101] On the other hand, the organ uses a greatly expanded number of mutation stops, as well as the rare, high-pressure stop Synthematophon, a Walcker invention that was essentially a principal that develops a tone four or five times stronger than a normal principal. Walcker employed this stop for the Hamburg Musikhalle (1907), the Reinoldkirche in Dortmund (1909), and the Michaeliskirche in Hamburg (1912), and other organs.

Schweitzer also called for improvements in the system of accessory stops and registration aids. The obligatory principles he laid down for these were innovative for the time. Bringing together French and German traditions of organ building, he envisioned a medium-sized organ using pedal couplers, manual couplers, super- and suboctave couplers, free combinations with dual use for each department (including the pedal), and a stop-crescendo pedal.[102] The organ in the Oranienburger Straße synagogue (table 3.4) is a large instrument, and its accessory stops are disposed on the grand scale. Although it did not realize the ideal of the stop-crescendo pedal, it did use general crescendo and decrescendo and had an automatic piano pedal.

Schweitzer aimed at a fusion of German and French elements in the console and the organization of the registration aids. He proposed having main couplers and combination devices that would be workable by both push-buttons and pedals so that each button would correspond to a pedal.[103] The console of the Oranienburger Straße organ illustrates this blending of French and German elements: Together with the four free combinations (which could not in fact be switched on independently for each manual and the pedal as the reformers recommended), fixed combinations that could be operated independently were installed for each department. The builder devised this particular configuration so that the organist could match the sound volume to the needs of the music in question, not the timbre—which ideally has priority from the standpoint of the Alsatian organ reform. The matching of the volume was wholly adequate for the requirements of the reformers and many organists as well; as Emile Rupp says, "Namely in the instruments planned for the Catholic and Israelite rituals, a restricted range of free combinations would no longer be up to date, a principle which for example the Walcker firm, in its more recent works—among them the instruments of the synagogues of Berlin-Charlottenburg[104] and Berlin Oranienburger Straße (with 63 and 91 stops respectively)—has constantly taken to heart and implemented. . . . For the present we must reckon with the fact that most of the newer German organs have no more than one or two free combinations, and these often without the optional hand controls."[105] Even though the ideal of mechanical action was also missing from the instrument, it did have "the electropneumatic action which is the only one, apart from the mechanical, that is worthy of a reform organ."[106]

The organ of the Oranienburger Straße synagogue can thus be classified as an organ of the "transitional" style insofar as it implemented elements of the nineteenth-century orchestral organ together with those of the Alsatian organ reform movement. In the contemporary press it was treated as a progressive instrument. A report in the *Zeitschrift für Instrumentenbau* states the following:

> Organist Rabe from Berlin has set up the disposition of the instrument, designed according to the new principles, and has been lingering here over the past days to subject the organ to a comprehensive examination and to put a few particular wishes into prompt effect. He and all of the visitors, among whom we would like to name Herr Prof. Lang of Stuttgart, Herr Prof. Hegele of Nürtigen, Herr Musikdirektor Nagel of Eßlingen, the Herren Organisten Keller and Binder of Stuttgart, and Herr Fischer of Schorndorf, are in agreement that the new organ, with its rich overtone registers, radiates with a glorious, seldom heard tonal sparkle, and there is no doubt that with the new organ further progress has been made toward the new type of organ for which many young organists have especially been striving.[107]

The organs of the Strasbourg synagogue are another example of the realization of various elements of the Alsatian organ reform movement that were tied to the attempt to develop a type of organ suitable for use expressly in Jewish services. The first organ of the Strasbourg consistorial synagogue (table 3.5) was built by the E. F. Walcker firm and finished in 1898.

Over time, the disposition came under severe criticism from Emile Rupp, a representative of the Alsatian organ reform movement who in 1914 became

TABLE 3.4. Disposition of the Organ at the New Synagogue on Oranienburger Straße in Berlin, Built by E. F. Walcker et Cie. in 1910

Manual I		Manual II		Manual III		Manual IV (Fernwerk)		Pedal		Schwellpedal	
Prinzipal	16'	Lieblich gedeckt	16'	Bourdon	16'	Quintatön	16'	Prinzipalbaß	32'	Gedecktbaß	16'
Bourdon	16'	Geigenprinzipal	8'	Viola di Gamba	8'	Prinzipal	8'	Prinzipalbaß	16'	Gambabaß	16'
Prinzipal	8'	Fugara	8'	Hornprinzipal	8'	Echo Gamba	8'	Subbaß	16'	Flötenbaß	8'
Synthematophon	8'	Salicional	8'	Violoncello	8'	Hohlflöte	8'	Kontrabaß	16'	Sanftbaß	8'
Viola di Gamba	8'	Konzertflöte	8'	Quintatön	8'	Bourdon doux	8'	Harmonikabaß	16'	Cello	8'
Doppelflöte	8'	Lieblich gedeckt	8'	Flute harmonique	8'	Voix céleste	8'	Quintbaß	10⅔'	Basson	16'
Gemshorn	8'	Aeoline	8'	Rohrflöte	8'	Nachthorn	8'	Oktavbaß	8'		
Bourdon	8'	Voix céleste	8'	Dulciana	8'	Spitzflöte	4'	Flötenbaß	4'		
Flauto dolce	8'	Prinzipal	4'	Geigenprinzipal	4'	Prinzipal	4'	Terzbaß	6⅖'		
Quinte	5⅓'	Flauto dolce	4'	Viola d'amour	4'	Oktave	2'	Oktavbaß	4'		
Oktave	4'	Fugara	4'	Flute octave	4'	Mixtur	2⅔' 5fach	Kornettbaß	8' 3fach		
Gemshorn	2'	Flautino	2'	Piccolo	2'	Quinte	2⅔'	Posaune	32'		

Rohrflöte 4'	Mixtur 2⅔' 4fach	Scharf 2' 5fach	Trompete 8'	Posaune 16'
Quinte 2⅔'	Trompete 8'	Sesquialtera 2⅔' u. 1⅗'	Vox humana 8'	Trompete 8'
Oktave 2'	Clarinette 2'	Groß Kornett 8' 3–5fach	Glockenspiel	Clairon 4'
Mixtur 2⅔' 4–6fach		Bombarde 16'	Tremolo	
Kornett 8' 3–5fach		Trompette harm. 8'		
Cymbel 1⅓' 4fach		Orchester Oboe 8'		
Trompete 16'		Clairon harm. 4'		
Trompete 8'				
Clairon 4'				

TABLE 3.5. Disposition of the Organ at the Consistorial Synagogue in Strasbourg, Built by E. F. Walcker et Cie. in 1898

Manual I		Manual II		Pedal	
Principal	16′	Lieblich gedeckt	16′	Principalbaß	16′
Bourdon	16′	Geigenprincipal	8′	Subbaß	16′
Principal	8′	Konzertflöte	8′	Violonbaß	16′
Viola di Gamba	8′	Quintatön	8′	Posaunenbaß	16′
Gedeckt	8′	Salicional	8′	Bourdon doux	16′
Bifra	8′	Aeoline	8′	Quintbaß	10⅔′
Doppelflöte	8′	Vox coelestis	8′	Octavbaß	8′
Gemshorn	8′	Klarinette	8′	Violon	8′
Dolce	8′	Stentorgamba	8′	Octav	4′
Trompete	8′	Flauto dolce	4′		
Stentorflöte	8′	Fugara	4′		
Prästant	4′	Doublette	2′		
Clairon	4′	Kornett	8′		
Rohrflöte	4′				
Piccolo	2′				
Mixtur	2⅔′				

the synagogue's organist. Rupp stated that the instrument did not satisfy his reformist expectations, partly because of his belief that organ building should relate to a religion or denomination in certain characteristics; thus, he regarded the disposition of this instrument for synagogue use as a failure:

> In spite of the temple's outstanding acoustics (we find here the organ's niche in parabolic form, and the central cupola, gathering and distributing the sound, of *Abbé Vogler!*) and the first-class quality of the material and work, which were equivalent to those of the best products, one could only describe the practical value of this instrument for the Israelite ritual, which places such elevated requirements on the music,

as a very relative success. It was disposed by a Protestant musical academic from the Palatinate, and directly calculated for the chorale singing of a very large Protestant congregation. It would be as ill adapted to a Catholic service as the Israelite one.[108]

In his notes on the instrument, Rupp marked the Doppelflöte, Bifra, and Stentor Flute in the first manual, the Stentor Gamba of the second, and the Violon of the pedal with exclamation points, as he also did with the Hauptwerk's fifty-four notes and the pedal's twenty-seven notes. The Doppelflöte is generally built with open (or covered), double-mouthed, wooden pipes and double flue, which give it a brighter sound than a single-mouthed flute. The Bifra stop—a bright flute voice—is double mouthed (that is, each pipe has two mouths, one of which is set slightly higher than the other, normally with vibrato tremulant). The high-pressure Stentor Gamba stop, which was equipped with extra-strong wind pressure (250 water column, in this case, as opposed to the usual 50–80), would later be used by Walcker in his op. 1000 for the Johanniskirche in Danzig (1900) and an organ for the Protestant church in Warsaw (1902). The Violon was mostly built as a kind of substitute for the excessively piercing 8′ Violoncello, had broader scale, and generally produced a clearer, round tone.[109]

Moreover, this organ was furnished with four preset, foot-operated combinations (labeled Piano, Mezzoforte, Forte, and Tutti), *Walze* (a swell in the form of a cylinder rolled by the foot), a swell pedal, a manual coupler, and two pedal couplers. Even with these registration aids, however, the instrument proved to be wholly unsuitable for the accompaniment of the choir and the soloists, according to Rupp: "[It has] no free combinations, no usable stop crescendo, no octave coupler. In the frequent transitions from *pp* to *mf*, *f*, or even *ff* of the modern choral literature of a *Naumbourg*, *Lewandowski*, *Kirschner*, *Sulzer*, etc., which have to be taken at lightning speed, and the exceedingly great dynamic animation of these choral and solo compositions, directly connected to the meanings of the words, in which the organist's right foot can leave the swell shade only for brief moments, the author, at the beginning of his engagement, found himself in continual conflict with this genuinely bureaucratic-boring 'expert' disposition."[110]

The concrete views on the disposition of an organ in the synagogue developed by Rupp agreed with the principles of the Alsatian organ reform. Thus he strictly opposed a grundtönig disposition on the grounds that this was maximally unsuited to the choral and solo singing: "Namely, in the use of woodwind stops (flutes and Gedackts, some still with semicircular cut-up!) a sinking in pitch is noted, both on the parts of the cantor and of the choir, especially in piano passages."[111] In Rupp's opinion, mutation stops and mixtures (that is, a disposition on the whole bright and with an emphasis on overtones) would come closer to the desire for a "new organ, up to date and up to its task, which would be capable of carrying out any requirement whatever of Jewish worship."[112] As a consequence, in 1923 the Alsace-based firm of Edmond Alexandre Roethinger[113] was finally assigned to rebuild the old organ on the basis of the principles set forth by Gottfried Silbermann and Aristide Cavaillé-Coll (see table 3.6). By mutual agreement with the organist and the choir-master, it was suggested that wood pipes be used only sparingly (except in the pedal and the bass octave of the Bourdon) and that the flutes be built as "overblowing" (or harmonic) stops and the Bourdons as Chimney Flutes in order to brighten the sound of the foundation stops. Another plan was for a complete series of mutation stops.

To compensate for the old Walcker organ's failure to provide flexibility in registration, numerous registration aids were proposed, such as manual, pedal, and octave couplers; free combinations operated by both stop knobs and foot pistons; fixed combinations labeled Piano, Mezzoforte, Forte I, Forte II, Plein Jeu, Reed Voices, Trumpet Choir (operated by knobs in both pedal and man-ual), an off switch for 32' and 16'; and various hand registers, pedal pistons, tutti pistons, tremolos, and swells in second and third manuals and pedal. In close connection with Rupp's conception of the registration aids are his other ideas for the console, which aimed at building a unified console (*Einheits-spieltisch*) on ergonomic principles, meaning that the most important and fre-quently used registration aids should be built as pistons.[114] Rupp built two unified consoles himself: one at the Protestant garrison church of St. Paul in Strasbourg (1907) and the other at the Strasbourg synagogue (1925). Kwas-nik regards both of these efforts as not fully matured in conception.[115]

In the organ of the consistorial synagogue of Strasbourg, at long last the innovations and ideas of the founder of the Alsatian organ reform were real-ized, simultaneously with the requirements for a specifically confessional organ building.[116] Nevertheless, it should be critically noted that the reform proto-type had already been applied to quite a few organs.[117]

THE GERMAN ORGAN REVIVAL

If the use of the synagogue organ in the nineteenth century was liturgical, it gradually took on the additional tasks and status of a concert instrument after the turn of the century. The process reached its zenith between 1933 and 1938, when the National Socialist regime forbade Jews to attend public functions, including, of course, concerts; at the initiative of the Jüdischer Kultur-bund numerous concerts were held in synagogues, and these opened or closed with organ music.

The largest synagogue organs were built at the beginning of the twentieth century. Various reasons have been advanced for the enormous scale the dispositions attained, and it is likely that a number of factors played a role in this development. The Jews of Germany had received full civil rights with the founding of the empire in 1871. As a consequence of the general economic boom, Jewish congregations in the large cities were, by the turn of the twentieth century, among the wealthiest religious organizations in the land. These congregations made use of the competitive architectural environment of the 1890s to build new houses of worship, in which the architects were even given, for the most part, a free hand.[118] Since the building plans normally took up to fifteen years to realize, one would logically expect that large synagogues began to appear at the beginning of the twentieth century and that organ building underwent a comparable development.

Theodor Wohnhaas has argued (using the grandly scaled Berlin organs as examples) that these instruments were built only because no Jewish congregation wished to be outdone,[119] but this is not borne out in the cases of individual congregations since none of them ordered a large organ purely on the basis of prestige. They generally took the advice of an expert consultant, who was in turn motivated mostly by artistic considerations. Had the congregation wished to acquire an organ merely for display, it could simply have furnished the wall with an appropriate façade without going to the length of having a large instrument built. Moreover, the congregants understood that the attainment of an impressive sound requires not only the requisite instrument but also a skilled performer and worthy music.

Not all congregations were in a position to invest their budgets in an organ, as is evident in the following excerpt of a response from the Steinmeyer firm, dated November 26, 1912, to the Jewish Reform Congregation on Johannisstraße, Berlin, on the subject of a synagogue organ that was to be completed in 1913:

> Therefore, we expressly declare that any reduction in the number of stops for the organ could only be at the cost of the unconditionally necessary sonic effect of the instrument, which is certainly to be regarded as a major error and would be deeply regrettable in the interest of the project. We thus request that the needed number of stops be retained as in the proposed disposition.

TABLE 3.6. Disposition of the Organ at the Consistorial Synagogue in Strasbourg, Built by Edmond Alexandre Roethinger between 1923 and 1925

Grand-Orgue I		Positif Expressif		Récit Expressif		Pédale	
Montre-Violon	16'	Bourdon à cheminée	16'	Quintaton	16'	Basse acoustique	32'
Bourdon	16'	Cor de chamois	8'	Diapason	8'	Grosse-Flûte	16'
Montre	8'	Flûte à cheminée	8'	Cor de nuit	8'	Basse de Viole	16'
Bourdon	8'	Quintaton	8'	Flûte traversière	8'	Flûte	8'
Flûte harmonique	8'	Salicional	8'	Viole de Gambe	8'	Flûte	4'
Violoncelle	8'	Unda maris	8'	Harpe éolienne	8'	Grosse-Quinte	10⅔'
Prestant	4'	Fugara	4'	Voix céleste	8'	Bombarde	16'
Flûte à cheminée	4'	Flûte pastorale	4'	Prestant de Viole	4'	Bourdon-Basse	16'
Nazard	2⅔'	Cor de daim	4'	Flûte octaviante	4'	Soubasse	16'
Doublette	2'	Quinte pastorale	2⅔'	Viole d'amour	4'	Bourdon	8'
Tierce	1⅗'	Flageolet	2'	Quinte conique	2⅔'	Violoncelle	8'

Grand-Cornet	3–5fach	Tierce conique	1³⁄₅'	Octavin	2'
Plein-Jeu	4fach	Larigot	1¹⁄₇'	Tierce	1³⁄₅'
Trompette	8'	Piccolo	1'	Septième	1¹⁄₇'
Clairon	4'	Clarinette	8'	Plein-jeu	4fach
		Basson	8'	Basson	16'
		Trémolo		Trompette harmonique	8'
				Basson-Hautbois	8'
				Voix humaine	8'
				Clairon harmonique	4'
				Trémolo	

We are unfortunately unable to consider any reduction in the costs, as we have really already quoted the lowest prices in view of the use of only first-class materials under the supervision of qualified artists.[120]

The congregation had obviously asked whether an organ with a smaller disposition could be built as a way of reducing costs. The reply shows that the organ builder not only felt a personal obligation to build the disposition as originally planned but had also recommended it.

For Hans Hirschberg, it was not so much issues of prestige and economy that dominated; more important were musicological (especially organological and acoustic) standpoints. On the construction of large organs in Berlin's synagogues, Hirschberg notes "that the congregation turned to important experts in organ building in order to obtain the design of a good instrument, appropriate to the space."[121] These experts may have advocated an instrument with a large disposition because they had acoustics foremost in mind. The Steinmeyer firm corroborates this in the following response:

> The disposition we agreed upon for an organ of 28 stops is so arranged, with consideration of the spatial characteristics of the house of worship and a careful selection of the characters of the individual voices, that the instrument will, with the proper voicing, really achieve what is wanted from it.
>
> In view of the very large interior, the high dome, and the ca. 1200 seats in the house of worship, and with a regard to the fact that when it is fully occupied it will detract noticeably from the power of the organ's sound (since as is known the clothes of those present absorb a great deal of sound), an urgent warning must be made against canceling even *one* stop from the distribution.[122]

An important criterion is undoubtedly the architecture of the synagogue: The new buildings, with their Moorish, Egyptian, Gothic, and neo-Romanesque features, were conceived with very large spaces and cathedral-like acoustics, which favored the planning of large organs.[123]

The change in the synagogue organ with respect to size, as well as the development from its original main function as an accompanying instrument to solo instrument and ultimately concert instrument, is also tied to the history of organ building. The German *Orgelbewegung*,[124] which eventually led to a comprehensive new orientation in organ construction during the 1920s, returned to the voicing and scaling of the Baroque organ. In addition, the proponents of the Orgelbewegung took academic and practical account of Baroque principles[125] (e.g., use of the principal chorus as the foundation of all the other stops; application of the *Werkprinzip* to every department; note channel with mechanical action; enclosed casework). Moreover, the Baroque organ's sound was associated with the idea of a "true German" music.[126] This gave the organ movement a nationalistic impact, which was adopted into the national political trends of the time and perverted into National Socialism.

The 1930 organ of the Berlin synagogue on Prinzregentenstraße (table 3.7), built by the Steinmeyer firm of Oettingen, op. 1525, "participated," according to Hans Hirschberg, "in the further development of the modern organ movement in German organ building."[127] But contrary to Hirschberg's view, the ideals of this movement, developed under the influence of Hans Henny Jahnn, Wilibald Gurlitt, and Christhard Mahrenholz, are less than fully incorporated into this instrument—with its pouch chest and electric action, two swell departments, and individual swells for the Zartgedeckt and Vox Humana stops. Nevertheless, the influence of the Orgelbewegung is evident not so much in its technical as in its sound conception. True, the Baroque traditions, such as the use of the principal register as the foundation for the other stops and the North German Werkprinzip, are not fully incorporated; on the other hand, there is a balanced proportion between 8′ and 4′ stops, "purposely hard-voiced mixtures,"[128] and reed stops deployed in each department. A swell box was also provided as "the organ's ideal medium of dynamic expression."[129] Moreover, the swell departments were equipped with stops of all types and sizes.

Surprisingly, the organ made use of a transmission system, which is a complex arrangement of doubled pallets, grooves, and sliders that allowed individual stops to be coupled from one division to another, often from manual to pedal but also from manual to manual. The reformers regarded the transmission system as a makeshift to be used only in smaller organs and an "exception that must be justified for every case."

Erwin Jospe, who served as organist at the Prinzregentenstraße synagogue from 1928 to 1934, recalled the following: "Liturgical music was predominantly homophonic, and the disposition of the organs was suited to the circumstances. The sound was to be 'expressive.' Whole manuals were built into the swell boxes. Each synagogue organ had at least one stop-crescendo pedal for general crescendo. The sound ideal was 'Romantic.' Frequently used and well liked accompaniment stops included Gamba, Salicional, Aeoline, and Unda Maris, played if possible with Tremolo. Mixtures and other stops that brighten the sound were rarely available and used sparingly."[130]

Initially an assistant organist at the same synagogue and principal organist from 1934 to 1938, Werner Baer interpreted the Prinzregentenstraße organ's disposition along similar lines: "Part of the instrument consisted of

TABLE 3.7. Disposition of the Organ at Berlin's Prinzregentenstraße Synagogue, Built by G. F. Steinmeyer in 1930

Manual I		Manual II		Manual III		Schwellkasten		Pedal		Transmissionen	
Großprincipal	16'	Bourdon	16'	Stillgedeckt	16'	Zartgedeckt	8'	Majorbaß	16'	Echobaß 16'	16'
Principal major	16'	Principal	8'	Hornprincipal	8'	Vox humana	8'	Kontrabaß	16'	Flötenbaß 16'	4'
Violoncello	8'	Gamba	8'	Spitzflöte	8'			Harmonikabaß	16'	Fagottbaß 16'	16'
Gemshorn	8'	Gambe celeste	8'	Quintatön	8'			Subbaß	16'		
Harmonieflöte	8'	Dulciana	8'	Salicional	8'			Großnassat	10⅔'		
Gedeckt	8'	Konzertflöte	8'	Unda maris	8'			Principal	8'		
Octave	4'	Nachthorn	4'	Praestant	8'			Gedecktbaß	8'		
Rohrflöte	4'	Kleinprincipal	4'	Flauto amabile	4'			Violon	8'		
Superoktave	2'	Blockflöte	4'	Koppelflöte	4'			Choralbaß	4'		
Quinte	2⅔'	Salicet	2'	Flautino	2'			Waldflöte	2'		
Cornett	8' 3–5 fach	Schwiegel	2'	Larigot	2'			Rauschpfeife	2⅔' 4fach		
								Kontrabombarde	32'		

Mixtur	2' 4fach	Rohrquinte	2⅔'
Cymbel	1' 4fach	Terz	1⅗'
Trompete	16'	Sifflöte	1'
Tuba	8'	Großmixtur	2⅔' 4–5 fach
Clairon	4'	Scharf	1⅓' 3–4 fach
		Basson	16'
		Trompete	8'
		Euphone	4'
Echomixtur	2⅔' 3–4 fach	Posaune	16'
Oboe	8'	Baßtuba	8'
		Trompete	4'

stops that were very rich in overtones (mutations) and mixtures, which were especially appropriate for the playing of Baroque organ music, but were almost never used in our Jewish synagogue music, with its exclusively Romantic emotional charge. Whenever I tried to use one of these stops, expressions of misgiving and disapproval were heard."[131]

Evidently the listeners in the synagogue congregations (and many organists as well) had developed a conception of the sound of the organ and organ music that was associated with their own religious music but did not unconditionally correspond to the sound ideals of the organ at the time. Presumably these very different notions reflected the very dissimilar tastes in contemporary organ building. Overtone-rich stops were available but were not used because the performers fell back on the Romantic repertoire, as happened with the disposition of the organ at the Prinzregentenstraße synagogue.

Like the organ of the Oranienburger Straße synagogue, the Prinzregentenstraße instrument can be characterized as a "transitional organ," in which Romantic principles are united with the Baroque principles put forward by the German Orgelbewegung. Above all, the aesthetic conception of the sound of this organ (as probably in many others as well) was not formed on the basis of religious-liturgical criteria. This impression is corroborated by organs of the nineteenth and early twentieth centuries in general, in which more purely musical criteria dominated, whether the instruments were to be used in worship services or concert halls.

The experimental ideas applied in the building of some synagogue organs may appear remarkable at first, but church organs also provided at least as extensive a field for experimentation. In this sense the synagogue organ—its use in the Jewish service, its disposition, and its incorporation of unusual features—does not represent a special case. No disposition specialized for synagogue use was realized in Germany, or at any rate I found no source that indicated that such a venture was contemplated. In this sense the synagogue organ is not in general any different from "conventional" church organs of the period. While there may have been various types of organ construction, individually marked by features associated with time, geography, and religious orientation, it is nevertheless possible to speak of a "transconfessional" style that existed, like the builders themselves, over and above the boundaries of nationality and faith. The consequence for the organ music of the Jewish congregations is that, if it was influenced by the organ at all, it was only by the sheer fact of the instrument's presence in the synagogue and not by any special characteristics of the instrument itself.

As far as the sound conception of the organ is concerned, the synagogue organ and the church organ are more or less equivalent. However, this statement must be qualified, at least initially, by a consideration of the façade as a part of the synagogue's architecture and art.

Even though we have no sources that provide a representative picture, we can ascertain some general tendencies in the positioning of the organ in the prayer sanctuary. Saskia Rhode finds an "approximately equal proportion of organs on the west side and by the choir, with a slight preference for the choir organ, more or less integrated with the ark and the reader's platform."[132] This discovery seems startling at first, as one would expect the synagogue organ to be built more often on the western wall than the eastern (in the direction of Jerusalem, toward which traditional congregations pray), where it could be heard but not seen (only when the direction of prayer changes temporarily with Lekha Dodi, a prayer that worshippers recite while turned toward the entrance to the synagogue, Friday at dusk to welcome Sabbath).

German Catholic churches of the nineteenth and twentieth centuries show an unambiguous preference for positioning the organ in the western gallery, however, and Rhode sees the placement of the organ in the synagogue as a consciously chosen way of distinguishing it from Christian practice: "Jewish congregations and architects did not feel free to use stylistic trends, motives, and emblems from civil and church architecture unless they were precisely those that were out of fashion in church building and church art. Why should it be any different in the case of the organ? Putting it in a different place, possibly giving it a different face, shows the choice of a building style for synagogues that is in opposition to that of churches."[133]

In spite of Rhode's speculations, there may be some practical points involved in the placement of organs at the front of the synagogue. Considering that the cantor's place should be as close as possible to the *bimah* and ark up front, this would also be the place for the choir. Thus, it would be awkward to have the organ in the rear when close collaboration with and accompaniment of the cantor are required. In contrast, the Catholic worship before the Second Vatican Council called for a detached role of the organ for responsive congregational support and interludes—hence its western position.

In the end, practices have differed from country to country and from congregation to congregation, especially since the early twentieth century. Certain Jewish congregations place both choir and organ behind a screen (e.g., West London Synagogue) or hide it behind the ark (e.g., Berlin's Fasanenstraße synagogue; Budapest's Great Synagogue at Dohány Street, which survived the Second World War) (see figure 3.3). Other congregations chose placements at the front, on the side, or in the back (see figures 3.4–3.6). The reasons for the varying placements differ as well, ranging from practical and aesthetic to devotional considerations.

Michael Meyer maintains that the organ was the element least susceptible to Judaization.[134] In spite of this, it was the Jewish congregations themselves who sought to "Judaize" the instrument, an aim that, if it could not be accomplished on a musical basis, could at least be partly realized architecturally. Unusual features in the positioning of the organ and the way the façade is built are depicted in some sources.[135] A railing, for example, sometimes separates the organ from the prayer room; the pipes, especially in an unenclosed façade, may be bundled into a form resembling the ark of the Torah or the Torah scrolls (figures 3.7a and 3.7b). Similarly, numerous organs are decorated with Jewish symbols such as the Star of David (figures 3.8–3.10) or the Tables of the Law, as on the organ of the Szekszárd synagogue in Hungary (built by Josef Angster in 1911) or on the still-existing instrument by Charles Wetzel in the Benfeld synagogue in Alsace (see http://www.oup.com/us/theorgananditsmusic). Many instruments, on the other hand, are furnished with a façade in conformity with Moorish, Gothic, or classic style (i.e., an established element of church architecture).

The organ, often designated as a traditionally Christian instrument, became an integral component of liberal Jewish identity; it was not adopted, however, by way of creating a "synagogue organ" as a counterpart to the "church organ" but by binding the instrument into the sacred space even if it had to be combined with elements of Jewish life that were considered traditional. This integration, which is reflected in the architectural form of the organ façade, is manifested visually; internal, auditory qualities (aside from the abundance of string and soft accompanimental stops that can be ascribed to the Jewish worship service) are not found in synagogue organs.

In this way, the organ was definitively not an expression of tradition within the Jewish community in the nineteenth century but rather a symbol of the process of social and cultural assimilation of Germany's Jewish population. The organ, as the main instrument of Christian churches, became the only possible medium for expressing the community's "progress" with regard to the synagogue's liturgical music. Within the framework of this assimilation process, religious life took on features of the surrounding culture, with its Christian orientation. Supported by the fact that, in the age of secularization, religion came to be a private concern, "the disparities between Christians and Jews gradually lost significance."[136] Religious assimilation was one

FIGURE 3.3. The first organ for Budapest's Great Synagogue on Dohány Street was built in 1859. Franz Liszt and Camille Saint-Saëns were likely the most famous musicians to play on this remarkable instrument built by J. F. Schulze und Söhne. In 1930 the original was replaced with a large, four-manual organ with seventy stops, built by Gebrüder Rieger (op. 2485). Jehmlich Orgelbau rebuilt the organ in 1996 (op. 1121). It still consists of four manuals and sports sixty-four stops. Photograph courtesy of Achim Seip.

FIGURE 3.4. The organ at the synagogue in Essen was placed in the front. Built in 1914 by E. F. Walcker et Cie. (op. 1761), the instrument had fifty-one stops on three manuals. Photograph courtesy of the Gidal-Bildarchiv im Salomon-Ludwig-Steinheim Institut, Duisburg.

FIGURE 3.5. The first organ at the synagogue in Stettin (now Szczecin, Poland) was built around 1877 by local builders Friedrich and Emil Kaltschmidt. Nothing further is known about this instrument. In 1913 E. F. Walcker et Cie. built a new three-manual, forty-two-stop organ (op. 1821), which was placed at the back of the synagogue. Photograph courtesy of Gerhard Walcker-Mayer.

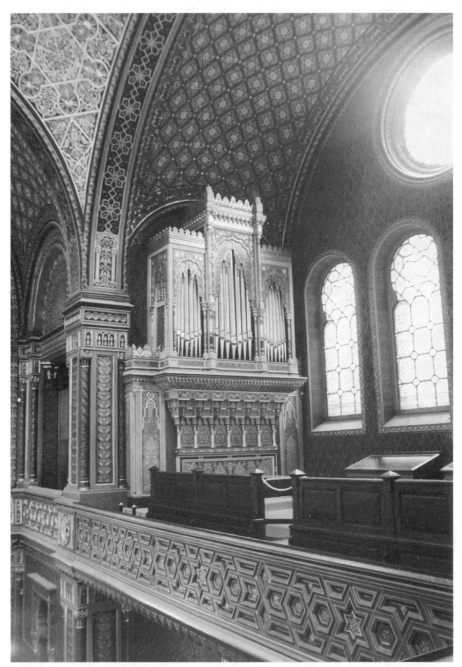

FIGURE 3.6. The Spanish Synagogue, built in 1868 on the site of Prague's oldest Jewish house of prayer (the Old Shul), was equipped with an organ in 1881. The tracker organ, built by Karl Schiffner, was replaced in 1935 with a pneumatic instrument (two manuals, twenty stops) built by Josef Melzer of Kuttenberg (now Kutná Hora, Czech Republic), who reused the old organ case. The organ is situated in a niche on the upper side balcony, and both are covered in the Mudejar-style horseshoe designs. Photograph courtesy of Hans Nadler.

FIGURE 3.7A. The organ for the Dortmund synagogue was built by the Walcker firm in 1899 (op. 883). With three manuals and forty stops, it was one of the larger synagogue organs. Nonetheless, only seven years later, the Jewish congregation commissioned an echo manual to expand the organ, and several other changes were made as well. Most significant, the organ prospect was located high above the ark of the Torah and almost appears to be a copy of the actual ark. The façade further shows that the pipes in the front were organized to resemble the shape of the Torah scrolls. Photo in the author's possession.

FIGURE 3.7B. The most crucial addition to the organ at the Dortmund synagogue is apparent only upon closer scrutiny of the console.
Above the keyboard is a peculiar opening that houses a light-colored roll.
Apparently the organ was complemented by a mechanical self-playing
device, in this case an organola, which was one of the major innovations
of the time.

of the most significant components of social acculturation since it was from
there that new Jewish traditions evolved.

THEORETICAL PROPOSITIONS FOR A "JEWISH ORGAN"

While no project of a dedicated "Jewish organ" was ever realized, this does
not mean that no attempts were ever made to establish what such a project
might entail. Organist-composers such as Hans Samuel and Herman Berlinski formulated ideas for a synagogue disposition while in Germany and, in
later years, in emigration.

Orgel- und Harmoniumfabrik GEBRÜDER RIEGER in Jägerndorf.

Synagoge in Teplitz.

FIGURE 3.8. Built by the Rieger firm in 1885 as op. 143, the small organ at the synagogue in Teplitz (now Teplice, Czech Republic) has two manuals, a pedal, and fourteen stops. Reprinted from *Orgel-Katalog* (1890).

A vukovári izr. templomban. — Im isr. Tempel zu Vukovár.

FIGURE 3.9. The organ for the synagogue in Vukovar (now in Croatia) is another example of the integration of the Star of David. Built in 1890 by Josef Angster of Pécs, Hungary, it is a smaller instrument with only eight stops on one manual. Reprinted from *Orgona-Katalogus Angster József* (1896).

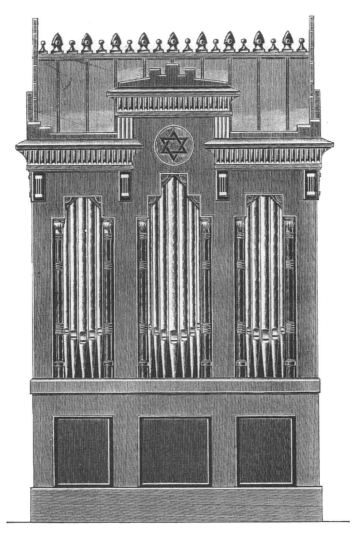

FIGURE 3.10. The one-manual organ at the synagogue in Königgrätz (now Hradec Králové, Czech Republic) was built by Jan Tuček, Kuttenberg, Czech Republic, in 1905. The disposition is unknown. Reprinted from *Orgel-Catalog Jan Tuček* (n.d.).

For Hans Samuel, the electropneumatic organ provided ideal conditions for organ music in Jewish congregations. He believed that a "modern" organ "would have to encounter the essence of Jewish music in a totally different way, as it lingers in his memory from prayers, table songs, and Torah reading, if played by a Jewish person filled with the spirit of the traditional melodies."[137] Therefore he preferred the electropneumatic organ, because of its greater maneuverability. Furthermore, the swell technology would allow dynamic differentiations, and, not least, ensure easy playability and a differentiated use of pianistic attack forms. In this way one can "produce any kind of accent, and through good phrasing it is possible to give a living expression to precisely the syncopated, rhapsodic element that plays an essential role in ḥazzanic recitative, corresponding to the mostly syncopated word stress of the Hebrew language."[138]

At a much later point, Berlinski worked out the principles of an obligatory "synagogue organ disposition."[139] His conception of a synagogue organ is based on the organ's religious neutrality and, at the same time, its anchoring in Christian tradition, which for Berlinski is a contradiction only in appearance:

> The organ consists of zinc, tin, copper, wood, leather, ivory, and a hundred other things that are neither Jewish nor Christian. It is the creative spirit that composes and the hand that plays that are moved by the Christian or Jewish spirit.
>
> The organ was probably invented by pagans but developed further within the church because it was rich and powerful enough to serve her needs. We liberal Jews gladly take the organ as a gift from the church to the synagogue, but we do not come into this relationship empty-handed. Because when someone folds his hands and prays in churches, when someone says and sings "Amen" and "Hallelujah," then that person is using the Hebrew language. And that is very far from all that we have in common.[140]

Berlinski lists ten criteria for the disposition of a synagogue organ, which can be summarized and evaluated as follows:

1. The "biblical sounds" concept

> This refers to the carrying over of biblical elements (reconstructed from texts of the Bible) into the sound of the organ. Several groups of instruments have been identified from these texts: plucked strings (kinnor), woodwinds (halil, abuv, 'uġav), metal trumpets, and shofar, all of which the organ pipes imitate. It is doubtful, however, that a reconstruction of this sort can be achieved since the instruments named are ancient ones, and there is not enough evidence to replicate their sound qualities. Furthermore, in the case of the kinnor, it is not even clear whether this instrument was a harp or a lyre,[141] and similar interpretation problems exist for the flutelike instruments halil,[142] abuv,[143] and 'uġav.[144]

2. Psalmody

Psalmody is a musical domain that appears in both Greek Orthodox and Roman Catholic practice. Berlinski clearly takes his
point of departure from Hebrew psalmody, which is performed
very freely (almost improvisationally) and is closely connected
to the intonation of the Hebrew language.[145] In the disposition
of an organ, psalmody should be taken into consideration insofar as the organ plays an accompanying role. Berlinski suggests
a register with a "plucked" sound as that of a harpsichord so that
the accompaniment will not take on too much of the character
of functional harmony.

3. The historical prayer modes and the cantor's free improvisation

"Historical prayer modes" are the broad musical models generally known by the Yiddish term *shtayger*. Each of these bears the
name of the prayer to which it was originally sung (e.g., Magen
Avot, Ahavah Rabbah, Adonai Malakh). The shtayger are built
on different modal systems; Ahavah Rabbah, for example, de-
rives from three modal systems; Adonai Malakh from just one.
As in the case of Hebrew psalmody, the organ disposition must
be arranged to avoid the effect of functional harmony. However,
it is questionable whether historical prayer modes and the cantorial improvisation can be enhanced or even supported through
a specific disposition or registration. Much more important in the
accompaniment of psalmody and improvised chant is the style of
the accompaniment itself, whether improvised or composed.

4. The traditional melodies of the Jewish religion

Among the traditional, mostly orally transmitted melodies of
the Jews are the *Mi-Sinai* melodies.[146] These are late medieval
tunes and recitatives sung mainly on High Holidays and are thus
seasonal. Berlinski holds that they must be accompanied by a full
organ, with the support of solid principals and mixtures.[147]

5. The mystic world of the Kabbalah and the music of the ḥasidim

The Jews of Poland and Ukraine created a special type of music
that is generally known as ḥasidic chant and is usually tied to
elements of Jewish mysticism in kabbalistic songs. Its "un-
bounded sound dimensions" should be registered with mutation

stops.[148] Here too, the disposition of the organ seems not to be of primary importance. All fairly large organs have mixtures, principals, mutation stops, and the like. The organist's skill in registration is more at issue than the disposition itself.

6. The compositions of the early Reform period

Important features of the music of nineteenth-century Reform Judaism are the absence of improvisatory elements and the reliance on Western art music. The choral works, moreover, are frequently set to German texts. Probably because of these aspects, Berlinski does not propose any particular requirements for the "synagogue organ disposition" in regard to this music.

7. The music of the Jewish-folkloric school in Russia at the end of the nineteenth century

Compositions from the Jewish Nation School were, owing to the political circumstances and the general lack of an organ tradition in secular and sacred spaces in Russia, normally not written for organ. In fact, the few organ compositions that came out of this school were based more on intellectual concepts than on instrumental reality. Because of the quality of the works, however, they could, in transcription, "be played on the large organ with a truly astounding power. No instrument seems better suited than the organ to save this music from its impending disappearance."[149] For the realization of this music, Berlinski especially recommends stops of the string family; for the solo stops, suitable possibilities include Konzertflöte, Oboe or Clarinet, or Spanish Trumpets.

8. The renaissance of Jewish liturgical music in the United States

As in the case of the "through-composed music of the early Reform," a repertoire of Jewish liturgical music developed in North America during the nineteenth century. An important feature is that the words were sung at first in German, then (and ultimately almost exclusively) in English.

9. The new organ music of contemporary Jewish composers

According to Berlinski, the Jewish music of the twentieth century contains two new elements: the twelve-tone technique introduced by Arnold Schoenberg and a related "new" polyphony. Both can be implemented on the organ only through an individual tone color (timbre) for each particular stop.

10. The role of the great, common organ literature in the synagogue from the early Baroque to the present

These compositions, which at first seem to have no affinity to Judaism, must be considered in the design of a disposition since, given the small number of works for an exclusively Jewish worship service, it will be necessary to fall back on the common literature for organ.

This multitude of musical requirements for a synagogue organ could scarcely have been realized in a single instrument. For Berlinski, the question is less one of implementing all of the possibilities and more of a compromise: "There is no one organ on which all this music could be played. But one should beware of using this as an excuse for designing an instrument on which almost nothing can be played. . . . The organ too, as a servant of the synagogue, is imaginable only as a product of creative compromise, [and therefore one can only] try to create an instrument that can do, if not everything, as much as possible in the service of liturgical music."[150]

As the sound ideal for his notion of a synagogue organ, Berlinski favors the Baroque organ because, given its overtone-poor Blockflöten, narrowly bored principals and mixtures, and silvery reed stops, it comes closest to the biblical instruments. He further recommends Harp or Unda Maris stops to represent the sound of the ancient plucked instruments. Finally, the concept of a typical "synagogue organ" should be underscored by the use of stop names such as Ḥaẓoẓerah (or *ḥassrah*, presumably temple trumpets) and Shofar.

Berlinski's theory or model is unambiguously historical in character. It is unclear, all the same, what kind of "Baroque organ" he had in mind (i.e., either the "Baroque" ideal of the 1920s' musical classicism or that which has spread from the new tendencies in historically informed performance practice since the 1950s); the two are fundamentally different. Considering that Berlinski began to study organs and organ building only after his immigration to the United States, one must keep in mind not only the historical but also the regional aspect of organ building in this country. Between 1930 and 1960 organ building in the United States was oriented heavily toward historical-Baroque elements.[151] In addition to the sound aspect, other factors such as mechanical action, wind system, and casework were strictly founded on the Baroque model, typically aiming at the ideal of fully mechanical organs and copies of historical instruments. At the same time, a new eclecticism began to develop in organ building, one that combined Renaissance, Baroque, French classical, and Romantic elements and is often referred to as the "American classic" style of organ construction. Both trends in American organ building are explicitly reflected in Berlinski's concept of organ building for the synagogue. He formulated the ideal of a historical Baroque organ, but it was one whose disposition would integrate elements of the Renaissance and Romanticism in equal measure. In spite of his vehement advocacy of an individual style in synagogue organ building, Berlinski emphasized that the instrument itself cannot create a connection to a religious faith; only the creative musician can do so.

INTERMEZZO | # Sharing the Console
The Synagogue Organist

The initial controversy over the introduction of organs into Jewish worship services eventually subsided, but debate continued over whether the halakhah allowed organs to be played on Sabbath and holy days and, if so, whether Jewish or non-Jewish musicians should play them. These issues were discussed in congregations, rabbinical conferences, and written polemics. As with the question of the organ itself, discussions of the organist's religious identification continued well into the twentieth century. Those who opposed the hiring of organists of Jewish faith but supported the idea of Christian musicians playing in the synagogue argued that it is halakhically forbidden for a Jew to work on Sabbath (and even to engage a Gentile to play for Jews on Sabbath can be considered a shevut, or disturbance of the Sabbath rest). However, others held that, according to the halakhah, music making would not be not considered work. Heinrich Lemle, who was the youth rabbi in the Frankfurt Jewish community and belonged to the Jewish Reform movement, correctly states that "ultimately it cannot be established whether the halakhah prohibits the organ as a ḥukkat ha-goi, and this is why it is so difficult to say to what extent one can make music on Sabbath. Thus, hiring a Christian organist may offer a solution."[1]

For the time being (or at least until the rabbinical conferences ruled on the matter), Christian musicians did play the organ. That Christian musicians, of all people, took over playing the instrument during Jewish liturgy was, according to Lemle, even supported by the halakhah: Because organ playing in

Jewish worship is considered a mitzvah, it is halakhically permitted to hire a Gentile for that and other Sabbath services.[2] Hiring a Christian musician to serve in Jewish worship, and justifying this on halakhic grounds, is certainly surprising considering that organs and organ music in the synagogue had been resented as "Christianizing elements."

In 1845, rabbis attempted to find a general and binding solution for all congregations. In the official and conclusive report of the Second Rabbinical Conference of Frankfurt, the question of the legality of the organ in Jewish worship is broken down into two parts: "1) whether organ playing in the synagogue in itself may be permitted, and 2) whether it is allowed to be carried out by an Israelite on Sabbath."[3] The rabbis voted unequivocally for the organist's being of Jewish origin, arguing that the Talmud does not consider music making work but rather a display of art. They corrected the resolution published twenty-five years earlier in *Or Nogah* and *Nogah ha-Ẓedek*,[4] which ordered that a non-Jew should play the organ. In fact, they explicitly recommended that a Jewish musician play the organ. They also defied the argument that a Jewish musician would violate the halakhah by repairing the organ if necessary since the organ builder—not the musician—was considered responsible for the instrument. They emphasized that the organ "is such an artfully built instrument that any improvement [tuning and conservation] cannot be executed instantly anyway, and this would not be the task of the organist, but of the organ builder."[5]

The rabbinical decision was based on the assumption that only a Jewish artist is familiar with the Hebrew language and its "musical representation" and that only a Jewish artist is capable of creating a fitting musical program for Jewish worship. Furthermore, an organist of Jewish faith would understand how to use the organ's registration to maintain the character of the ancient Jewish music. Designating organ playing as forbidden work was inappropriate, moreover, for in a purely quantitative sense, on Yom Kippur the ḥazzan already had a great deal more to do than an organist would.[6]

Other reasons for hiring a Jewish organist were based on the proposition that organ playing is a mitzvah; thus, the organist should have the same working conditions and opportunities as the cantor or ḥazzan. The idea that only an organist of Jewish faith is familiar with Jewish music was also further developed by Oskar Guttmann, for example, a musicologist and former choir director at Berlin's New Synagogue on Oranienburger Straße: "The organist, of course, must be familiar with the mentality of the Hebrew language, with its musical construction, and with the character of Jewish music. Therefore, he also has to know a great deal about Chazanuth [the solo singer's specific melodies and musical style]. The organist must be a Jew by all means."[7]

Many congregation members and rabbis as well were strongly opposed to hiring a non-Jewish organist—no matter how talented—as they were convinced the musician would not be able to develop a sensibility for Jewish music: "The non-Jewish organist—be it a Joh. Seb. Bach—is a foreign element in our flesh, is a foreigner in the praying Jewish community. His genius, often his musical instinct, may permit him to feel much empathy, and to meet the mood fortuitously. . . . The non-Jewish organist—'Judaized' by years of practice though he may be—will never be a Jewish musician."[8] A more practical argument against hiring a church musician was that the person would often work full-time in church and only part-time in the synagogue. If Jewish holidays coincided with Christian ones, the organist had to give priority to the church's requirements.[9] In addition, the rules that some church musicians were obliged to follow posed a problem: Organists who worked for the Catholic Church were not allowed to actively participate in non-Catholic liturgy. Even if they accepted a part-time position as synagogue organists, the church administration would often force them to give it up.

The fact that non-Jewish musicians were employed as organists in the synagogue was a unique phenomenon. If it had heretofore been the Reform Jews that aimed at assimilation, now it was non-Jews who were establishing a relationship with Jewish *Kultus*.[10] Here, assimilation is no longer understood as a process in which the Jewish people adapt but rather as one in which the minority has an important part in redefining the "majority" culture.[11] The reasons and motivations for their assimilation, in spite of the differences, nevertheless show a similar incentive: Both were driven by economic factors. The assimilation of German Jews also aimed at social integration and economic stability. Working for synagogues enabled church musicians to increase their salary through a well-paid, part-time job that, in addition, often provided a new and much better instrument to practice on.

Naturally, a position at a synagogue led organists to engage with Jewish liturgy and music and to assimilate musically to some extent as a result of accompanying the cantor and the synagogue choir. Their relationship to Jewish Kultus was, however, subconscious and passive. The church organists were not so much concerned with musical assimilation as with the need to acquire the necessary knowledge of Jewish music and liturgy, and in this way their connection to Judaism remained confined to professional boundaries.

Although temporarily resolved, the debate on organists and their role in worship had still not been completely settled. Rabbi Israel Schwarz of Cologne doubted whether the organ should be heard at all on Sabbath and religious holidays, regardless of who was playing it. On December 20, 1864, he wrote the following: "Besides, the use of musical instruments on Sabbath and holy days is forbidden for Jews; according to Talmudic principles it cannot even be permitted for a non-Jew for liturgical purposes."[12] Addressing the question of organ music at Berlin's New Synagogue, Michael Sachs, a rabbi who took the conservative side against the Reform, also found it ritually inadmissible to hire even a non-Jewish organist for Sabbath and religious holidays.[13] He so strongly opposed the introduction of the organ into the synagogue that he retired from the rabbinate rather than acquiesce.

Despite the discussions and the rabbis' official pronouncements, debates concerning the origin or faith of synagogue organists did not lead to a consistent and enforceable solution. Each congregation independently decided whether it wanted to hire an organist of Jewish or Christian faith. Many congregations had, in principal, no objection to organ playing in Jewish worship so long as the organ was not played by a Jewish musician on Sabbath and holy days. Consequently, church musicians were initially hired for the position of synagogue organist. This compromise was reached not only because the general desire was to avoid conflicts with the different interpretations of the halakhah but also because the Jewish congregations had little other choice, for until the late nineteenth century very few Jewish musicians were as familiar with the organ as church musicians were. Without any tradition of organs and organ music in Jewish culture, there were virtually no trained organists of Jewish faith. An early awareness of this problem led to a call for the professional training of synagogue organists of Jewish origin, as this example from 1846 shows: "We believe that the time has come when we must modestly propose two special programs whose effects will be evident only in the future, and therefore cannot be implemented too soon: the integration into the curriculum of Jewish seminarists of a practical course in the delivery of religious prayers and sermons, and instruction in organ playing (which is already an urgent necessity for the teachers of choral singing)."[14]

Although state-supervised training of ḥazzanim in Germany and other parts of Western Europe began in the early nineteenth century, the education of synagogue organists remained unregulated. Only later in the century did organ playing become a requirement in some seminaries, most notably in Würzburg and Esslingen. In Esslingen, organ proficiency required the playing of chorale accompaniments and literature, as well as improvisations; basic knowledge of the instrument's construction; and composition of simple accompaniments.[15]

By the turn of the century, the first generation of Jewish organists had been trained and placed in various synagogues, marking a turning point. As of 1932 it was possible to speak of a "number of excellent Jewish organists."[16] The sudden growth in the number of organists of Jewish origin was also a result of the changing political situation in Germany, when the National Socialist laws prohibited Jews from employing Germans. For example, it became common to hire Jewish pianists to serve as organists, as Ludwig Altman reports: "In 1933, with the advent of the Nazis, it became clear to a number of us young musicians in our middle twenties that our careers would be truncated because of the anti-Jewish laws which started to be given out right away. A number of us switched over to become organists because there were always synagogues in Germany that needed organ players."[17]

Due to the lack of Jewish organists, well-trained pianists capable of playing the organ's manual keyboards were a welcome alternative. Other kinds of musicians turned to the organ as well: When Werner Baer was unable to continue his promising career as an opera conductor as a result of racial discrimination, he decided to work as a substitute organist at various synagogues in Berlin in order to continue his vocation.[18] Many Jewish musicians decided to learn to play the organ in the hope of immigrating to the United States, where many Jewish communities were in dire need of an organist and would offer positions to immigrants looking for work.

The Synagogue Organist in the Framework of Christian Traditions

Because of the church's long tradition and its practice of organs and organ music, church musicians who began working as organists in synagogues brought with them a wealth of experience and a repertoire that made up for those that Jewish musicians had not yet established. Therefore, the choice of organist—Christian or Jewish—played a role in shaping the instrument's liturgical use. A comparison of the church organist's occupation with that of the synagogue organist illustrates this contention.

Traditionally, music in the Ashkenazic synagogue was represented mainly by the recitation of the cantor or the ḥazzan, while the congregation had only a small role. Its function expanded in the course of the nineteenth-century Reform movement, when congregational singing was introduced so that the community could actively and musically participate in worship. As in Christian congregations, monophonic congregational chants were often performed with the cantor in the form of alternate singing (in either Hebrew or German). Originally, the synagogue chants were predominantly in the form of free recitatives. During the reforms, they were adapted to the fixed rhythm and meter of Western music, and the congregation was introduced to the novelty of choral singing. In this new situation, the organist was "indispensable in leading and covering the synagogue chant"[19] and was charged with giving support to the congregation in the hope of bringing order to the "chaotic singing of thousands . . . [in] the most muddled sing-song."[20]

The synagogue organist set the singing tempo and led the congregation from one mood to the next in the worship service by means of brief interludes (e.g., between the recitation of Hallel and the taking out of the Torah scrolls; during the Musaf prayer).[21] In addition, the organist accompanied the cantor and the multipart singing of the synagogue choir by playing both *colla parte* and independently, especially in the cantor's solo sections and in preludes, interludes, and postludes. Organists often improvised during the silent prayers, thus musically creating an atmosphere of devotion. However, until the early twentieth century, it was only in the preludes and postludes, if at all, that the synagogue organist as virtuoso and soloist could "develop his art and fully do justice to his organ."[22] Martha Sommer Hirsch recalls from her time as organist at the synagogues in Wiesbaden and Frankfurt am Main that some organists would begin playing a quarter of an hour before the service began. The long prelude served to create an appropriate atmosphere for worship.

Although organists were predominantly accompanists, they were expected to be highly skilled. In reminiscences of his own career as organist, Erwin Jospe describes a competitive selection procedure that was in place around 1928:

> Shortly after finishing my organ studies with Professor Heitmann, organist at the Kaiser-Wilhelm-Gedächtniskirche and at the Akademie für Kirchen- und Schulmusik, I became organist at the new synagogue in the Prinzregentenstraße. Built by Steinmeyer according to specifications by Professor Wolfgang Reimann, the organ was an impressive, great, richly equipped instrument. For the competition for the organist position, the committee invited ca. 40 applicants. Around 15 of these were invited for a second audition. Three candidates were invited to the third and final round, where they had to play the following works: Bach (Toccata and Fugue in D Minor), a piece of their own choice, improvisation on a given theme, and the accompaniment of a cantorial solo by ear. At the end of the competition, Professor Reimann came up to the organ loft to tell me that the examination panel had chosen me, though owing to my youth—I was only 21—grave reservations had been expressed.[23]

Emile Rupp, organist at the consistorial synagogue in Strasbourg from 1914 to 1939, saw the requirements imposed upon the synagogue organist as a stimulus to improving the art of accompaniment. Comparing the skills of organists at Catholic and Protestant churches as well as synagogues, he states: "Without a doubt, the Catholic organist is in many ways ahead of his Protestant colleague due to the liturgical necessities of his Kultus, namely with regard to transposing and free improvisation. Nevertheless, we believe that a minimum of ten years activity in a large synagogue will lead, even for the most significant organist, to an invaluable improvement of the art of accompaniment, giving him the ability to remain calm and collected even in the most unforeseen musical circumstances."[24]

Moreover, during the first half of the nineteenth century, the development of organ music was no more significant in churches, Protestant or Catholic, than it was in synagogues, principally because of the order of worship. The Catholic Church clearly defined the tasks, such as "organ playing during the entrance of an apostolic legate, cardinal, bishop . . . playing alternatim with a large choir in Mass and Office . . . limitation to strict accompaniment on most Sundays in Advent and Lent."[25] Only in the latter half of the nineteenth century did the organ regain an important role in both the Catholic and the Protestant Church, thanks to the renaissance of old forms and genres combined with new harmonic idioms, as well as the use of chant as a unifying element in vocal and instrumental music. Somewhat later, around the turn of the century, a similar process began in the synagogue, where it reached its peak in the synagogue concerts of the 1930s, which opened or ended with organ music, although concerts in which the organ was the featured instrument throughout were seldom given.

As far as their repertoire is concerned, synagogue organists, perhaps surprisingly, often performed works that had been associated with Christian liturgical tradition for centuries, such as preludes by Johann Sebastian Bach and Dietrich Buxtehude. The choice of an obviously non-Jewish repertoire was a consequence of the early practice of hiring only church musicians who had naturally chosen familiar and available works, which thus became part of synagogue music as well. In addition, until the end of the nineteenth century, very little organ music had been composed for specific use in the synagogue, and the few Jewish-inspired organ works that had been created posed little artistic or technical challenge to the well-trained organist.[26] During the early twentieth century, Jewish composers finally began writing art music for the organ based on Jewish liturgical, paraliturgical, or folkloristic-traditional melodies. Combining Western European styles with Jewish melodies, they created a repertory that could be performed not only in concert but in Jewish liturgy as well. In a parallel development, Jewish organists increasingly sought out distinctly Jewish organ music, intentionally conceived to be different from that of churches. By composing organ music with themes based on synagogue melodies, they consciously attempted to distance themselves from Christian models. Many musicians, among them Ludwig Altman, Herbert Fromm, and Arno Nadel, contributed to the new organ repertory (discussed in detail in the following chapter).

The responsibilities of synagogue organists and church musicians appear to have been relatively similar, suggesting an answer to the question of whether the Christian service served as a model for the use of the organ in the synagogue and consequently for the synagogue organists' duties. The training that the synagogue and church musicians underwent and the repertoire they performed indicate that a relationship did indeed exist; in fact, there appears to have been something of a convergence from both sides, Jewish and Christian. A survey of the educational background of four generations of organists at the New Synagogue in Berlin and a brief look at their repertoire serve as case studies that illustrate this point.

Organists at the New Synagogue in Berlin

The first organist at the New Synagogue was Hugo Schwantzer (1829–1886), who grew up in Prussia, where he learned to play the organ in his youth and later became organist at the church adjacent to his school in Neiße (now Nysa, Poland). Later, Schwantzer studied at the Königliches Kirchenmusik-institut in Berlin and the Akademie der Künste and eventually became a music teacher. Between 1852 and 1866 Schwantzer worked as organist for the Berlin Jewish Reform Congregation, and on July 1, 1866, he became the first organist at the New Synagogue. This part-time position supplemented his other occupations as pianist, composer, and teacher. For the synagogue's official consecration festivities on September 5, 1866, Schwantzer even composed an organ piece, the *Praeludium für die Orgel zur Einweihung der neuen Synagoge zu Berlin*, op. 19,[27] which he himself premiered at the consecration as an introduction to the ceremonies.

Arthur Zepke (1892–1973), another church musician in the Christian tradition, studied at the Staatliche Hochschule für Musik in Berlin and was the main organist at the cathedral of Gnesen (now Gniezno, in the Polish province of Posen/Poznán). He played the organ for more than ten years at the New Synagogue and was known as a musician who "quickly and confidently became familiar with synagogue music and could adapt as fast as lightning to the unforeseen musical situation in worship."[28] In fact, he was more than just the synagogue's organist. Zepke also collaborated with the cantor and the choir and trained the first generation of Jewish organists. He bonded with not only the other synagogue musicians but also the Jewish repertoire that was part of this congregation's tradition. Further, as Hans Hirschberg recalls, Zepke "knew by heart the musically complicated Jewish liturgy for the whole year, including all the holidays. . . . He loved this music."[29]

The relationship of both of these church musicians to their work at the synagogue suggests that Jewish liturgy and music served as a source of inspiration for them. Both were influenced and stimulated by Jewish culture.

Because of the National Socialist laws on the employment of Gentiles by Jews, Arthur Zepke had to leave his position at the synagogue in December 1935[30] and was succeeded by Ludwig Altman (1910–1990). Altman had studied German literature and musicology in Breslau (now Wrocław, Poland) and then continued at the Staatliche Akademie für Kirchen- und Schulmusik in Berlin from 1929 to 1933. Besides singing, choral conducting, and organ and piano playing, theory and composition were also part of the curriculum. Altman seems to have first discovered his enthusiasm for the organ at the academy, at least in part because of the quality of the available instruments: "The most valuable instrument was the organ in the 'Koenigin Louise Kapelle,' also called the 'Easander Kapelle.' It housed a very famous organ built by Arp Schnitger shortly after 1700. . . . The lessons took place there."[31] One of his teachers there was Arthur Zepke.

At the age of twenty-three, Altman was appointed organist at a Berlin movie theater used by the Jewish community as a prayer room. Describing his first job and the expectations he had to fulfill as organist, he shares the following details: "My choir director made me play loud because he said Berlin people only like music that is loud. That was very strange to me, and whenever I rehearsed, he said, 'Altman, play louder!' And after, I pulled stop after stop until there weren't any stops left, he still said, 'Can't you play louder?' I said, 'Herr Vogel, the only thing left now is thunder and lightning.' Well, he was suspicious, and he said: 'You know what we'll do? Whenever I give you a special signal with my left hand, you play thunder and lightning.' So whenever he did that, I kicked the air, and he was happy!"[32] Evidently the instrument was a theater organ as no other would have offered registration options such as thunder and lightning. Years later, the cantor of the prayer room explained why the choir director had demanded such a loud volume from the organ. It was not, as Altman had supposed, the choir director's deafness but rather his dislike of cantors: The organ's exceedingly high volume was simply a means to drown out the cantor.[33]

A year later, in 1934, Altman accompanied services in the Philharmonie—a position he saw as a challenge. He was faced with the prospect of accompanying (in a single service) two cantors, who shared the very long solo parts by singing them alternately. For the first cantor Altman had to transpose to a higher key; for the other, to a lower key. Altman jocularly called the playing of the liturgy in two unrelated keys a "tremendous improvement" of the music.

In 1935 Altman finally became the organist at an "ordinary" synagogue, and in 1936 he was appointed principal organist at the New Synagogue; however, he stayed for only a short period of time as he emigrated to the United States later that year to settle in San Francisco. As principal organist at the New Synagogue, Altman gave private organ lessons to both Jews and Christians who were interested in playing the instrument in a synagogue. In addition, he made a name for himself by playing the organ in many concerts held in Berlin's synagogues. Altman was enthusiastic about his work at the New Synagogue, and in an article published in the *Gemeindeblatt der Jüdischen Gemeinde zu Berlin*, he praised the "unlimited possibilities of the sound combination" that the organ there offered.[34] In a letter of recommendation, the Jewish community of Berlin describes him as a well-versed, all-round musician:

> Equipped with a healthy understanding of music and supported by a sound training in the organ, Mr. Altman has raised the musical standard of the service with his artistic qualities; and through a good capacity for understanding Jewish liturgical music he has created an atmosphere for solemn devotion. His gift for adapting has enabled him to present the cantorial parts of the service in a musically well-rounded form. Mr. Altman, who with the organ at the New Synagogue was entrusted one of the largest organs of Berlin, has proven himself to be a reliable and well-versed organist—not only in worship but also in a truly excellent fashion in the synagogue concerts that we have organized, where he performed difficult organ compositions with considerable artistic ability.[35]

Paul Lichtenstern (1903–1991), the last organist at the New Synagogue, was also trained by Arthur Zepke. Formerly a professional pianist, he switched to the organ after just a few lessons to learn pedal technique and organ registration. Altman's and Lichtenstern's training is representative of that of most Jewish organists in German-speaking Europe. Because of the lack of educational alternatives, they had no other choice but to take lessons at institutions of a Christian stamp and with Christian teachers. Usually Jewish organists studied organ (or even church music as a major) at church music academies or conservatories that specialized in the training of church musicians. Felix Saul, cantor and music critic in Stockholm, described the problem: "And if the organ is to be used in Jewish worship in a sensible and tasteful way and really express in its own way what the Jewish heart feels, then we must educate Jewish organists. But where?"[36] Saul demanded a comprehensive education in all aspects of the musical style of Jewish liturgy, including the "instrumental element." He suggested entrusting the program to the German-Jewish umbrella organization Preußischer Landesverband jüdischer Gemeinden [Prussian Association of Jewish Communities], with support from other individuals and institutions interested in such training. However, the plans he proposed were never realized inasmuch as the education of Jewish musicians was abruptly ended in 1933. Lisel Lewin-Kassewitz, organist at the Heidelberg synagogue from 1931 to 1938, describes this dramatic change in an autobiographical article: "My exam at the Karlsruhe conservatory took place on April 1, 1933. However, I could not finish it. The examiner brought with him liturgical music—Protestant and Catholic—for the prelude test. When he became 'aware' that neither one nor the other stack of music was suitable for me, he made a pointed show of disdain and made it clear that under no circumstances would I pass the exam."[37]

The Impact of the Organist Question

The appointment of an organist in the late nineteenth and early twentieth centuries posed a new challenge for many Jews: Once they had given up their resistance to the introduction of the organ, they faced the presence of a non-Jewish musician using it to play non-Jewish music, thus creating a new area of conflict between the traditionalists and the Reform oriented. It was only when some of these church musicians, later followed by cantors, composed suitable synagogue music for organ, that a first step was taken toward improving the musical situation and calming the critical voices in the Jewish communities. Another step toward independence from Christian influences was the training of Jewish organists. Nonetheless, those influences were still noticeable since the organ teachers were Christians and inevitably taught the general and non-Jewish repertoire.

However, the perception of the organ as an alien element in Jewish worship paradoxically changed when it came to the question of the organist. Although the organ in the synagogue was initially controversial, Jewish congregations sooner or later realized that it was not the instrument that led to the loss of traditional Jewish music and identity but rather the compositions performed during the service or at other synagogue functions and, in the end, the organist who chose the repertoire.

Quite different from the problem of the organist or the organist's faith was the vexed question of the bellows blower (beginning in the mid-nineteenth century, the organ wind was first produced by alternative systems and later electricity). Although treading the bellows required substantial physical effort—in other words, work (without the reward the organist received in producing art)—and should thus have been forbidden to Jews on the Sabbath, this problem is not discussed in the sources, and how it was resolved remains unknown. One tradition, however, was observed in the Jewish community of Witten on the Ruhr, where especially "spiritual" means were used to lighten the physical burden for a Jewish member of the congregation. In his reminiscences, Jewish teacher and cantor Jacob Ostwald (1863–1910) reported:

> Now, in closing, I would like to show that despite sorrows and hard work I did not lose my sense of humor. What follows is a letter that I drafted in the name of our wind maker at the organ, the drunkard Samuel Pels [Jewish merchant, 1833–1920]. I recently found this copy, which is regrettably undated.
>
> Esteemed parish council, you may know that all functionaries of empire, state, and county, from the highest to the lowest, aim at higher salaries. Although my official services take place in the darkest corner of the synagogue—the organ case—they are nonetheless of great importance. I am like a violet blooming in obscurity. The element to which I dedicate my strength, the wind, is an element of high rank in the order of nature, in the life of the human being, and in our holy religion—especially in our new prayer book. While according to the old book the *Mashiv ha-Ru'aḥ* [a formula for expressing God's omnipotence: "He causes the wind to blow and the rain to fall."] is only sung in wintertime, now we are praising God all year long as the great power that reigns over the winds. How useful is your well-educated organist, if I do not support him? If my powers fail, the organ collapses and our wonderful choir is confused.[38]

The bellows blower, who was neither seen nor heard, had never been a topic in the discussions of modernizing the Kultus. Organ and organist, however, became the insignia of the renewal of Jewish liturgical music. The struggles surrounding the selection of organists according to their religious heritage—Jewish versus Christian—are emblematic of the complexity of assimilation. Modernization was the ultimate goal of going beyond tradition but nonetheless remaining recognizably Jewish.

CHAPTER FOUR | Organ Music in Jewish
Communities

As with the integration of the organ into Jewish worship, the development of
specifically Jewish organ music was a long and difficult process. Beginning in
the early nineteenth century, serious attempts were undertaken to create a
solo repertoire specifically designed for the newly introduced synagogue organs. Nonetheless, it took almost one hundred years for Jewish composers to
begin finding their own voices in organ music. By the time this process had
peaked (the 1930s), most of the newly composed repertoire could no longer
be published and distributed. Then, around 1933, as Jewish composers and
organists were increasingly emigrating or being sent to concentration camps,
the development of a German-Jewish organ repertoire came to an end.

    In this chapter I trace the main phases of the origin and development of
organ music in Jewish communities. I make no attempt to define the problematic and ambivalent concept of "Jewish music" (see chapter 1). Rather, I
base the discussion on an examination of repertoire that represents the different stages, and I focus on two kinds of compositions: those that fulfill a
specific function in Jewish worship and those that are based on Jewish themes
(table 4.1). The boundary between these two categories is somewhat fluid
inasmuch as some pieces are created specifically for the synagogue and at the
same time based on Jewish themes.

    The first group of organ compositions comprises works that were expressly
composed for Jewish congregations and events. This functional relation is

TABLE 4.1. Selected Compositions

Date	Composer	Title of Composition	Theme	Cultural Specification
1820	Anonymous	*Introduction zur Thodenfeier*	independent motive and theme	None
1864	Moritz Deutsch	*Zwölf Präludien für Orgel oder Pianoforte zum gottes-dienstlichen und häuslichen Gebrauch nach alten Synagogen-Intonationen*, Prelude no. 12	Yaḥbi'enu Selaḥ Na	Ashkenazi
1889	Louis Lewandowski	*Fünf Fest-Präludien für die Orgel*, op. 37, Prelude no. 4	Ha'El, Akdamut Millin	Ashkenazi
1933	Heinrich Schalit	*Eine Freitagabend Liturgie für Kantor, einstimmigen und gemischten Chor und Orgel*, op. 29, "Nachspiel"	variety of different motives	Ashkenazi, Sephardi, Middle Eastern
1933	Arno Nadel	*Passacaglia für Orgel über "Wadonaj pakad es ssarah"* (*Toravorlesung am Neujahrsfest*)	cantillation, te'amim	Ashkenazi, eastern Europe
ca. 1934	Siegfried Würzburger	*Passacaglia und Fuge über "Kol Nidre"*	Kol Nidrei	Ashkenazi
ca. 1930s–1940s	Hans Samuel	*Variations in Canonic Style on a Hebrew-Oriental Prayer Cantillation ("Aḥot ketanah") for New Years Day acc. to the Yemenite Minhag*	Aḥot Ketannah	Yemenite

often revealed in the title of the work or in the composer's intention as expressed in letters, conversations, and other sources.[1] Although much organ music of the "classical repertoire," such as preludes and fugues by Johann Sebastian Bach, Dietrich Buxtehude, and others, was performed in Jewish secular and sacred contexts, I mention it only in regard to its use but do not incorporate it into the musical analysis.

The second group, organ compositions built on a Jewish theme, is more complex by far since the "theme" might be anything from Jewish historical or religious matters to motivic-thematic topics. One train of thematic material that has been used in organ music of a devotional character is that of Jewish liturgical, vocal music such as psalmody, biblical cantillation, modal improvisations of prayers, and nineteenth-century synagogue songs (mostly based on texts from the siddur), as well as seasonal songs. Moreover, secular melodies derived from folk songs and vocal music for everyday life, domestic festivities, and ceremonies that are part of Jewish life also serve as source material. Examples include love and wedding songs, lullabies, and dance tunes.

Finally, there are paraliturgical and extraliturgical songs that are, according to Amnon Shiloah, "Hebrew devotional texts relating to religious precepts that are binding on the individual, even though they are not part of either the prescribed or expanded liturgy. Thus verses dealing with circumcision or bar mitzvah, for example, are included in the paraliturgy."[2] Unlike purely secular or devotional music, paraliturgical song extends to religious music transferred to an extraliturgical context, such as the celebration of life-cycle events or expression of commitment to the return to Israel. Paraliturgical music in Sephardic tradition extends to *pizmonim*, *coplas*, and strophic songs for birthdays, weddings, and lamentations for the dead, as well as contrafacta. In this way, organ music containing motivic-thematic content based on Jewish music can theoretically be divided into three major parts: the devotional, the secular in the celebratory framework of weddings and bar mitzvahs, and the paraliturgical.

Identifying Jewish themes is a difficult undertaking, especially considering the complexity of a coherent definition of Jewish music. The problem of identifying a melody as authentically Jewish lies in the possibility that it may have absorbed extra-Jewish musical elements acculturated into the different Jewish Diaspora communities. This is especially true for Ashkenazic synagogue song (in German, *Synagogengesang*), which emphasizes commonality and processes of exchange that are key elements of the nineteenth-century Reform.

It is common knowledge that synagogue song, plainchant, and medieval German folk song share certain parallels in their melodic and rhythmic formation. Eric Werner suggests that synagogue song had absorbed elements of style and repertoire from the surrounding environment, an assimilationist process that, in his view, is evident in the process of borrowing from non-Jewish melodies for metrical *piyyutim* (Jewish liturgical poems).[3] Thus, many synagogue melodies (almost exclusively orally transmitted until 1800) count as having been adapted from Christian or Western music culture. Werner's explanation for the similarities between synagogue song and Christian chant needs to be treated with care, considering the lack of convincing source material. The fact that often only the initial motive of synagogue song, church music, and folk songs is similar could also imply that these melodies share a common origin, with a different further development in each culture.

Another possibility is a correlative influence of Jewish and non-Jewish music. Several processes of a possible exchange lead to different explanations of this phenomenon, and the theory of the diffusion of a melodic formula is a more likely development than a polygenesis in two or more different communities.[4] Considering the extensive migrations of the Jewish people, diffusion, indeed, is the most commonsense way to account for these similarities. Nonetheless, a full and credible explanation of the origins of the correlations among secular, Christian, and Jewish melodies is ultimately not possible due to the poor transmission (handing down) of sources and the fact that, until around 1800, Jewish music was generally an oral tradition. Regardless of where the genesis of Jewish melodies lies, sociocultural reception is a reliable indication of their Jewishness: What for generations (on the part of Jewish communities and congregations) has been deemed an integral part of "Jewish music" constitutes relevant material for this analysis.

Abraham Idelsohn's comprehensive systematic codification of around four thousand (partly orally transmitted) melodies listed in his *Hebräisch-orientalischer Melodienschatz* (Leipzig: Breitkopf und Härtel, 1914–1933; henceforth *HOM*) serves as a guide for Jewish vocal music. In this chapter I not only consider the collections of liturgical vocal music by composers of organ music but also (whenever applicable) point out parallels among Jewish, secular, and Christian melodies and uncover their possible origins.

Given the difficulty of defining Jewish music in an unambiguous manner, the problem of establishing the Jewishness of any particular piece is almost as thorny. However, a discourse on Jewish identity in organ music should not and, indeed, cannot avoid this task. Various people have attempted to establish a method by which to analyze Jewishness in music. Most notable among them is Zecharia Plavin, who made a comparative analysis of Bloch's Jewish-titled and general compositions. Through the titles he gives his pieces, Bloch himself distinguishes between those with Jewish content and those of a universal character. Plavin, however, is convinced that all of Bloch's works contain Jewish elements and tries to prove this with a microanalysis of sonority that includes several parameters and is represented on a scale of Plavin's own devising.[5]

Plavin's method cannot be applied to Jewish organ music, however, especially since his study does not aim at finding overlapping areas in "Jewish" and "universal" music—a special concern of this study—but at defining Bloch's complete oeuvre as Jewish. What one can learn from his method is the importance of qualities Plavin himself largely ignores: sociocultural and contextual aspects of compositions, such as the composers' background, their environment and individual style, and, most important, their own statements about their music.

This analysis of organ pieces seeks musical characteristics that are generally deemed "Jewish" by both scholars and Jewish people themselves by considering how organ compositions negotiate the preeminence of vocal music over instrumental music. The study explores whether the preference for improvisation according to set rules, motives, and modes affects the construction of the pieces; whether the correspondence of a mode with a certain ethos is prevalent in organ music; how the constant relationship between words and music is somehow preserved; and whether some types of melodic ornaments (e.g., melismas) that are similar to Middle Eastern prototypes are prevalent. These elements, commonly regarded as *Urformen* of Jewish music, serve as the main thread for analyzing organ music based on Jewish vocal music. Finally, the analysis scrutinizes the manifestation of Jewish identity in this music.

Beside its focus on these "Jewish" elements, the study also looks at the general compositional style of organ pieces as shown in their form, texture, melody, rhythm, and harmony and examines the composers' use of Jewish and general elements of Western music.

At the center of the analysis is the use of Jewish liturgical melodies and the ways in which different composers made them a basis for their organ compositions. Moreover, I discuss the recognizability of these melodies and their affects in the respective settings: Can they be easily heard and identified? Regarding melody and modality, do they maintain the melodic-diatonic character that is inherent to Jewish music? How are the basic elements of synagogue chant realized in organ music, especially psalmody and cantillation? And how does organ music that draws upon these musical genres as thematic material differ from the vocal music that it absorbs? In short, I examine the transformation of traditional Jewish melodies within instrumental music.

One characteristic of traditional Jewish music is a nonlinear concept of time, which disappears upon notation of the music and the rhythm.[6] A kind of transfiguration of the rhythm is noticeable in the organ music that is based on Jewish music with free or irregular rhythms. I address the ways in which composers attempted to avoid distorting original rhythms and how they nonetheless occasionally did so.

On the basis of Bruno Nettl's assertion that the application of functional harmony reveals a composition's affinity with Western music,[7] I have analyzed the integration and development of harmony from modal elements[8] to chromaticism in Jewish organ music. Harmony affects the most traditional elements of Jewish music, such as musical modes (shtayger) and their realization in and adaptation to organ music. I also discuss how composers sometimes transformed these elements by embedding them in functional harmony and the resulting effect on their inherent harmony. A further factor is the way in which the syntax of Jewish music is maintained in organ compositions, especially the recitative-like, improvisatory element with its changing rhythms and mixed tonalities.

If a composition is indeed based on vocal music, one needs to consider the liturgical context and the relationship between text and music as well, and especially the interpretation of the text through word painting and other compositional methods. Naturally, the question arises as to whether these melodies, even without text, convey the spirit and musical atmosphere of Jewish holidays. Finally, one must ask how far the composition manifests the improvisatory character of Jewish music, especially the imitation of the rich coloraturas and melismatic improvisation prevalent in some ḥazzanut.

A more general section of the analysis traces the compositional development of the pieces in the context of contemporaneous secular or Christian organ music. These reference points will help us to discern whether Jewish organ music was oriented toward preexisting models.

From Lewandowski to Schalit: The Stylistic Development of Jewish Organ Music

The nineteenth-century Jewish Reform movement not only revolutionized synagogue music by introducing organs and organ music to the synagogues but extended to other musical areas as well: Although mostly orally transmitted up to the nineteenth century, vocal music was now being written down and was thus forced into the "novel" scheme of notation and regular meter.

The inevitable orientation toward Western European models had profound consequences for the overall music of the synagogues: Stylistic elements of classical and Romantic music began to influence the structure and expression of music used in Jewish worship of the Reform. The cantors' improvisations slowly vanished and were replaced by a rhythmically and structurally firm melody with harmonic support from the organ, reed organ, or piano. The ḥazzan, with his excellent knowledge of liturgy, was succeeded by the cantor, who had a more profound knowledge of music. In addition, congregational singing in unison with keyboard accompaniment became a central part of Jewish worship.

These changes and their implementation were a lengthy process that included the development of an organ repertoire for Jewish worship that, in its motives and themes, was different from the selections performed in churches.

FIRST ATTEMPTS AT A NEW REPERTOIRE

Although organ music composed specifically for use in the synagogue existed in the early nineteenth century, these first works were exceptional cases. As a genre, organ music for the synagogue grew more gradually over the next several decades. The development began with what may be called a precursor of solo organ music, *Orgelbücher* [organ books] or compilations of organ accompaniments for congregational singing, written mostly by church musicians for Jewish congregations.[9] Some of these included a few short pieces for organ solo.

The earliest example of such an organ book is the 1820 *Choralbuch* [chorale book], folder Ia, "for the organ by C. Götter Senior, Frank[furter] Street no. 1."[10] This book functioned as "musical accompanist" to the hymnal for the Hamburg temple compiled by Rabbi Eduard Kley and contains predominantly Protestant hymns arranged for organ, with a new text underlain in German or Hebrew with Sephardic pronunciation. Götter, whose name appears at the end of page Ia, was the compiler, copyist, and owner of the volume. One of the arrangements (no. 45) was done by Leipzig Thomaskantor Johann Gottfried Schicht (1753–1823). Number 47, an *Introduction zur Thodenfeier*, is the only composition for organ solo in this compilation.

Analysis of the Introduction zur Thodenfeier

The *Introduction zur Thodenfeier* is a short prelude (largo con moto) in E minor comprising fifty-three measures for left and right hands only; no independent part for the pedal is notated, which suggests that the piece was composed either for an organ without pedal or for an organist who was not sufficiently trained in using it.

The *Introduction* is not based on any Jewish musical theme but was composed specifically for a Jewish funeral service. The prelude is freely conceived in form and can be divided into two separate parts (measures 1–18 and measures 19–53). The first five measures introduce the musical material of the piece (indeed, they do not in the least echo synagogue music: an ascending, broken E-minor chord in forte, each time introduced by an upbeat sixteenth note and followed by a descending line of second steps in unison). These first five measures are then repeated in the dominant. The upbeat sixteenth note remains a central rhythmic motive that is further developed in measures 11–13; in measures 13–14 it is part of a sighing motive that appears three times. The following four measures continuously use the sixteenth-note rhythm in varied forms, followed by multiple repetitions of the note B in quarter notes, thus ending the first part on the dominant.

The second part of the piece repeats the descending line of measures 4–5, albeit in figured form (measures 19–20). The upper part presents this two-measure motive solo, and after only one measure the lower voice imitates the motive in the lower octave; this interplay between the two voices is then repeated. In measure 23 a series of broken chords in the upper part (reminiscent of the prelude's beginning) is presented in B major and C major; this time, however, the rhythm (dotted) and accompaniment (chordal in the lower part) varies slightly. Beginning with measure 27, new motives are introduced: first a linear melody (measures 27–30) and then a sighing motive (measure 31). At the same time, the repetition of B, which first appeared in measure 17, recurs beginning with measure 31 (first lower parts, then upper parts), followed by a new short motive in measure 36. The following section draws upon this motive, repeating it at different pitch levels, combining it with the sixteenth-note upbeat, and slightly varying its rhythm. After a short transition of two measures (41–42), a homophonic passage follows that is reminiscent of measures 23–27 and begins with broken chords. Sighing motives and broken chords dominate the last twelve measures of the prelude, which ends in a fivefold repetition of E, thus emphasizing the E-minor tonality of the piece. Although the prelude is rather short, it ends in a long diminuendo, which underlines its solemn character for the occasion of a funeral.

The texture of the *Introduction zur Thodenfeier* is very simple: Only seldom does the homophonic construction dissolve into polyphonic parts, and a strong polarization between melody and accompaniment (mostly chordal) dominates. The melody of the upper part above the basso continuo, and the alternation of piano and tutti sections (measures 1–12) are characteristic of the *style galant*.

The harmonic construction of the piece is also simple, with a stiff tonic-dominant relation. At most we find a ninth chord (as in measure 8), and sometimes the tonic-dominant relation is interrupted by the secondary dominant

F-sharp major (measures 12–14, followed by a passage in B major), F-sharp minor, A minor, G major, and the minor dominant B minor (measure 35).

One of the most significant characteristics of the prelude is its rhythm, which is used almost as a theme in its own right. The rhythm is diminished in the course of three consecutive phrases (beginning with the first measure, then from measure 23, and again from measure 35) and serves to create suspense.

The compositional technique of the *Introduction zur Thodenfeier* does not meet the standards of the music of its time. Its triadic melodies and suspended notes are reminiscent of melodic structures of the late eighteenth century, while the melodic and harmonic simplicity reflects the ideals of rococo rather than of the early nineteenth century. In idiom, texture, and harmony, it seems displaced from the style of its period, suggesting that the author was probably a church musician and not a professional composer.

It does, however, exhibit parallels to the repertoire of liturgical *Gebrauchsmusik* by contemporary composers of church music such as Johann Christian Heinrich Rinck (1770–1846), Michael Gottard Fischer (1773–1829), Adolf Friedrich Hesse (1809–1863), and Immanuel Gottlieb Friedrich Faisst (1823–1894), whose works have been collected in chorale books of accompaniments for choral music, together with interludes and short introductory pieces for organ solo. An example is Rinck's *Allgemeines Choralbuch mit Zwischenspielen* (1829).[11] Rinck's liturgical compositions in *gebundene Spielart* [chorale based]—contrary to *freie Spielart* [free style]—are by no means virtuoso pieces,[12] but their compositional technique is solid. Having studied with one of Bach's students and as a contemporary of Mozart and Beethoven, Rinck combined Baroque counterpoint with the harmonies and melodies of the late classical idiom.[13] The free-style organ pieces for liturgy in this repertoire, in contrast, are often short and simple and can be played without pedal.[14] Embellished harmony, chordal style, and a long pedal point at the end that leads into a stereotypical cadence are further characteristics of liturgical organ music in the early nineteenth century.[15] Frequent suggestions for *Klangschattierung* [sound differentiation] by changing manuals and dynamic differentiation are also prevalent in the scores.

Almost all of these style elements can be carried over to the *Introduction zur Thodenfeier*, suggesting that the piece represents a "universal" composition that by no means draws upon elements of Jewish liturgy or music. Rather, because of its composition and expression, the piece could just as easily be played in a church.

The early compositions for Jewish worship were generally not oriented toward Jewish cultural elements. The *Introduction zur Thodenfeier* exemplifies the way in which they were at least sometimes directly inspired by (or even copied from) church music—primarily preludes in free style rather than chorale preludes based on Christian hymns, which would have been more difficult for the congregation to accept. Such compositions were among the first organ pieces to be played in synagogues. Church music was often borrowed, and church musicians were frequently commissioned to write pieces for the synagogue to create new repertoire for worship, a practice that continued well into the twentieth century; the most prominent example of this is *L'année liturgique israélite* (1938) by Jehain Alain. In addition, even if these organ compositions have an apparent relation to Jewish culture, many of them are nevertheless Western art music in structure and style. In any event, for the time being, the Jewish music tradition was abandoned and replaced by the already existing and only slightly adapted musical traditions of the Protestant and Roman Catholic churches.

In the years to come, more of these organ books (with and without pieces for organ solo) were conceived. The Eduard Birnbaum Collection in Cincinnati holds *Melodieen zum neuen israelitischen Gesangbuche verfasst und eingerichtet von F. F. Schwenke* (1833), a volume containing 130 chorale accompaniments written by the organist of St. Nicolai in Hamburg;[16] the organ accompaniment book of the Israelitische Gemeinde Braunschweig, dated September 1855;[17] another Braunschweig volume, undated, *Für den Organisten, Braunschweig, ein Orgelbuch, eingerichtet von A. Massmann*, which, besides chorale settings, also contains an organ prelude for Ḥanukkah;[18] and the organ accompaniment book of the Jewish congregation in Stuttgart, *Stuttgarter Choralbuch für die israelitische Gemeinde bearbeitet von Immanuel Faisst*.[19]

Organ books for Jewish worship can be regarded as predecessors of a more original organ repertoire with a uniquely Jewish identity that had yet to be conceived. Their simplicity and proximity to Christian models correlate with the status of the organ in Jewish culture, still only very recently established. Nonetheless, these books represent the first attempt to create an organ repertoire specifically for the synagogue and eventually led to more distinctive developments in the course of change in the identity of the German Jews.

"MUSICAL EMANCIPATION"

In the early and mid-nineteenth century the vital question among German Jews was how the community's integration into European society could best be accomplished. For the most part the debate was between the traditionalists and the liberals, who had just begun to form the Reform movement. "Emancipation" was a keyword for German Jewry because it expressed their wish for civic acceptance, equality, and social and societal improvement.[20] To be recognized as equal citizens and integrated into German culture were among their most desired goals; the first was realized with the attainment of full civic equality in the Imperial Constitution of 1871. This historical milestone initiated a profound change in direction among the German Jews. Although the degrees of Jewishness began to vary along a wide spectrum from Orthodoxy to residual elements, perhaps with the exception of the Orthodox German Jews, who formed a Jewish identity "that was non-Jewish in content but nonetheless marked them as Jews regardless of their closeness or distances from Judaism."[21] In spite of fierce differences within the community on reform in rite and liturgy, a collective Jewish identity prevailed within German society and even promoted various degrees of actual interconnection of the Jews and the Germans.[22]

Parallel to these developments, more and more composers took up the challenge of creating organ music for Jewish worship. In the course of the First Jewish Synod at Leipzig (1869) and the second at Augsburg (1871), the establishment of the organ as an officially permitted instrument in the synagogue contributed significantly to this process. Among the earliest composers of organ music were cantors, whose training was basically in performance but had in many cases included composition, harmony, and counterpoint. One of these was Moritz Deutsch (1818–1892) of Nikolsburg (today Mikulov, Moravia, Czech Republic), who served as cantor at the Breslau synagogue from 1844 until his death in 1892. One of Deutsch's contributions to the organ music genre is the collection titled *Zwölf Präludien für Orgel oder Pianoforte zum gottesdienstlichen und häuslichen Gebrauch nach alten Synagogen-Intonationen* (ca. 1864).[23] Inspired by his teacher, the famous Salomon Sulzer (Deutsch had spent the years 1842–1844 with him and worked under Sulzer as second cantor at the Seitenstettengasse Temple in Vienna), Deutsch wrote an introductory organ prelude for each Jewish holiday.[24]

Around the same time, Salomon Sulzer had composed some organ pieces as well. His major collection, *Schir Zion, gottesdienstliche Gesänge der Israeliten, zweiter Theil*, prepared for publication around 1859 but not printed until 1866, contains three short organ preludes dedicated to different feasts, as the subtitle of each one attests. Each piece is based on an Ashkenazic sacred song that served as a motto theme (Eric Werner uses the term *leitmotif*) for the musical repertoire according to its respective holiday: The prelude for Passover contains a motive from Yomar Na Yisrael and is intended to be played during the praying of Psalms 118:1–4; the prelude for Shavuot contains the traditional melody of Akdamut Millin. The prelude for Sukkot uses a motive from Hodu and Ana (Hallel). It is important to note that Sulzer never received any training as an organist, nor did his congregation use an instrument. The composition of the three short preludes reflects this, as these pieces do not have an independent pedal part and are structurally simple.

Deutsch, on the other hand, had a more developed background and more extensive experience: In addition to his training as a cantor, he had studied organ with August Gottfried Ritter (1811–1885), cathedral organist in Magdeburg. Perhaps Sulzer assigned the task of creating an organ repertoire for the synagogue to his more broadly trained student, Deutsch (and perhaps other cantors as well), because he was aware of his own shortcomings. Whatever the situation, the contemporary press praised Sulzer's efforts: "Instead of being inspired by Sulzer's example of arranging Al Ha-Rishonim- or Ze'enah U-Re'enah-motives for organ as in *Schir Zion II*, the synagogue had to remain a testing ground for 'Reform desires in the style of church singing' and had to digest all these arduous, but unfortunately impractical and soon forgotten works, which appear in the form of preludes, postludes, and interludes."[25] This newspaper excerpt illustrates the transitional state of organ music that persisted at the end of the nineteenth century: Although a few original organ works for Jewish worship had been conceived, obviously, most were still oriented toward Christian models, a situation that would change only slowly.

With his *Zwölf Präludien für Orgel oder Pianoforte zum gottesdienstlichen und häuslichen Gebrauch nach alten Synagogen-Intonationen*, Moritz Deutsch continued in the direction set by Salomon Sulzer. After a dedication to the board members of the Breslau synagogue in appreciation of their support of Reform worship, he added the following in his preface to the collection: "These preludes are intended in the first place for organ. I have used as a basis old characteristic synagogue intonations, whose *Volkstümlichkeit*[26] has survived into our times and which are therefore best suited to lend the preludes, and consequently the liturgy, an imprint of the respective feast or holiday. May they succeed in opening the way to a more intimate and religious relationship for the organ with our worship, and in consoling the still hesitant feelings of so many of our pious fellow believers with their dear old sounds."[27]

Rather than creating organ works full of novelty and originality, Deutsch intended to create simple preludes for practical use that could fulfill different functions in synagogue worship or in the Jewish home. He wanted to compose works that would introduce the character of the different Jewish services. Deutsch consciously aimed at Judaizing organ music and giving the repertoire its own space and role within Jewish liturgy. In this way he hoped to overcome the resentment of those who did not approve of the organ's being part of Jewish culture. The twelve preludes are composed for different occasions: two for Sabbath, two for Passover, two for Shavuot, one for Sukkot, one for Ḥanukkah and Tishah Be-Av, two for Rosh Ha-Shanah, and two for Yom Kippur.[28]

Although all are based on synagogue song, they are nonetheless quite different from each other in length (ranging from 24 to 119 measures) and character. The chants used in the preludes are Addir Hu, Al Ha-Rishonim, Hodu and Ana, Ki Mi Ẓion, Maʻoz Ẓur, Barekhu, Shema, Yaḥbiʼenu, and Selaḥ Na. The last prelude deserves special attention as it draws upon two different synagogue songs and even combines them. Intended for Yom Kippur, it uses musical motives associated with the sung prayers of Yaḥbiʼenu and Selaḥ Na, each of which is central to a different section of the Yom Kippur service. The poem Yaḥbiʼenu is a pizmon, written around 1140 by Isaac ben Samuel of Dampierre. Its verses form one of the main responsories in the Seliḥot prayers for the fifth day before Rosh Ha-Shanah in the Polish rite[29] and in the Neʻilah (the extra service unique to Yom Kippur; it centers on praying for the Torah, the Shema, God's redeeming help, and shelter during the night). Deutsch later singled out Yaḥbiʼenu (figure 4.1) for inclusion in his 1871 collection of synagogue music, *Vorbeterschule: Vollständige Sammlung der alten Synagogen-Intonationen*, where it can be found—in a version that reflects his deep knowledge of the old intonations—among the Seliḥot melodies.

Selaḥ Na is based on two biblical verses (Numbers 14:19–20) that, according to the Polish rite, are recited on the evening of Yom Kippur following the Kol Nidrei. In some Ashkenazic congregations, these verses are sometimes omitted or are not at all part of the rite; in Sephardic liturgy they are absent altogether. Selaḥ Na is also a prayer in the Neʻilah service. Commonly, the first verse is recited by the cantor, while the congregation answers with the second verse three times and fortissimo. After that, the cantor repeats the second verse three times. Moritz Deutsch's collection contains a musical arrangement (figure 4.2) of the first verse of Selaḥ Na (after Kol Nidrei and Venislaḥ Lekhol).

Analysis of Prelude No. 12

The prelude consists of two parts that are distinct in tonality, tempo, and meter. The first part (measures 1–18, in C minor) is based on the melody of Yaḥbiʼenu; the second (measures 19–119, in C major) draws upon the beginning of Selaḥ Na and is conceived as a free polyphonic arrangement. Like many other composers, Deutsch may have chosen the different keys to symbolize a particular realm of musical expression (as in Beethoven's use of C minor to express the tragic); in Christian liturgical music the polarity between C major and C minor often represents the relationship between death,

FIGURE 4.1. Moritz Deutsch, *Vorbeterschule* (1871), no. 452, p. 113.
Oh may the Almighty shelter me, the presence of His shield protect me. When provably
He sees through the heart's delusiveness, His favor may serve us as support! Rise, oh
God! A servant of all the world, lend me strength, and listen to my pleading.

resurrection, and redemption. The prayers Yaḥbi'enu and Selaḥ Na are, however, not antithetical but complementary in content.

The piece follows the tradition of the chorale prelude, in which the synagogue melodies usually appear in the upper part. An exception is the motive
on "yaḥbi'enu" [shelter] and "ḥon yaḥon" [to salvage], which appear in unison in the bass, thus using the technique of word painting. For use in the

FIGURE 4.2. Moritz Deutsch, *Vorbeterschule* (1871), no. 379, p. 96.
Please forgive the people's guilt with the greatness of Your love and as You have forgiven
this nation from Egyptian times until now!

FIGURE 4.3. Moritz Deutsch, *Zwölf Präludien* (1864), no. 12, measures 19–25.

prelude, Deutsch modified the motive on "selaḥ na la'avon" [O pardon the iniquity] in its intervals and rhythm (see figure 4.3).

The changes applied to Selaḥ Na in the prelude are considerable. Deutsch omits upbeat and pitch repetitions, thus melodizing it. Consequently, the recitative character of the vocal version is lost in the prelude. The octave leap in measures 21–22, which is also different from the version in the *Vorbeter-schule*, helps to articulate the melody into two phases. Furthermore, Deutsch augments large segments of the vocal version and uses only keynotes in the melismas, apparently to facilitate performance on the organ. Before Deutsch introduces the full melody of Selaḥ Na, he begins by presenting only its initial motive in different pitches. Beginning with measure 23, the musical motive on "kegodel" [unto the greatness] is imitated by the tenor in stretto; more motivic play follows. The upbeat eighth notes (measure 22) reappear on the downbeat in the two middle parts (measure 25). In measure 27, the musical motive on "kegodel" is repeated in the upper part in C and is followed by its recurring appearance on "ḥasdekha" [Your love] in the middle parts (measure 29, an ascending rather than a descending line), the upper part (measures 30 and 33), and lower part (measure 33). Measure 35 presents the head motive of "selaḥ na la'avon" in the tenor, which is imitated one measure later by the middle voice in the octave. Throughout the prelude the initial motive on "selaḥ na" reappears with significant variations in pitch and key (see table 4.2).

Another motive prevalent in different variations throughout the prelude is that on "ḥasdekha" (table 4.3).

Later in the piece, another motive of the Selaḥ Na melody, "mimiẓrayim ve'ad hena" [from Egyptian times until now], is used, but again its rhythm deviates widely from that of the vocal version. It is first presented in measures 84–86 and then is repeated with and without variations through measure 101.

The last part of the prelude begins in measure 102 and combines the essential motives of Yaḥbi'enu and Selaḥ Na. The motive on "yaḥbi'enu" is reintroduced in measure 102, with a D-sharp accidental that serves to fill in the third and, at the same time, creates an augmented second to C—a feature commonly regarded as a characteristic element of Jewish music. The theme appears on an unprepared dissonance (C major four-two chord with D sharp). Measures 103–104 play with the core pitches of the motive on "ḥasdekha,"

TABLE 4.2. Introduction of the Motive on "Selaḥ Na"

Voice	Measure	Key/Comments
Upper part	19–26	C major, to "ḥasdekha"
Middle part	35–36	G major
Middle part	36–37	G major
Upper part	43–49	E minor
Lower part	49–53	E minor
Upper part	61–64	A minor; the suppressed measure is followed by a sequence based on the last motive
Lower part	72–75	D minor
Lower part	77–79	B major, ending in a pedal tone
Lower part	83–85	F major
Upper part	84–86	F major
Upper part	105–107	C major
Upper part	112–114	C major

followed by the beginning measures of the Selaḥ Na, which repeat and then lead into the final cadence.

The simple harmony that still predominates in the *Introduction zur Thodenfeier* has to some extent been overcome in Deutsch's Prelude no. 12. The first part (C minor) remains in the tonic for only the first eight measures and is followed by an increasing play with sharp accidentals (measure 8) and flat accidentals (measures 10–11) as passing notes, thus creating chromaticism in the middle voices. These harmonic turns intensify in the second part of the prelude. Modulations are rare, however, perhaps because of the inherently strong tonal character of the Selaḥ Na, which offers no opportunity for harmonic change at the beginning of a measure. This provides a clear instance of the problem Deutsch had to struggle with: transforming a modal melody into a harmonic construction. Deutsch's awareness of this difficulty and his method of coping with it are evident in a series of harmonic deviations that do not amount to modulations: In measure 24 Deutsch moves to a Phrygian cadence via C major, A major, D major, and finally to G major (measure 35; introduction of Selaḥ Na). Then he passes through A minor, D minor, E minor, and

TABLE 4.3. Introduction of the Motive on "Ḥasdekha"

Voice	Measure	Key/Comments
Upper part	25	C major
Middle voices	26	E major, reversed direction (ascending)
Upper part	28	part of a sequence
Middle voices	29	C major, reversed direction (ascending)
Upper part	30	shortened, C major
Upper part	31	shortened, A major
Middle voice	32	shortened, G major
Upper part	33	part of a sequence
Upper part	41	A minor
Middle voice	42	B major
Upper part	48	A minor
Upper part	53–54	augmented; minor second replaces major second; varied rhythm
Middle voice	54	minor second replaces major second
Upper part	55	augmented; varied rhythm
Middle voice	56–57	minor second replaces major second
Upper part	58	G major

F-sharp major to B major. The latter, as the dominant of E minor, serves as the upbeat for a new appearance of the Selaḥ Na theme in E minor (measure 43). In measure 54, new temporary modulations begin leading from B major, E major, A minor, C minor (sixte ajoutée), D major, A major, D major, G major, and E major to A minor, which serves as the key on which Selaḥ Na reappears in measure 61. Similar key successions follow, such as the temporary modulations passing through D minor (measures 65–71, followed by "selaḥ" in D minor), F major (measures 77–82, followed by "selaḥ" in F major), and returning to C major (measures 88–93). These harmonic progressions, however, have no specific function and represent only temporary changes of key, not full modulations. The prelude never fully leaves C major, and the

FIGURE 4.4. Adonai Malakh shtayger (skeleton).

tonal center remains clear throughout. All of the keys are related to C major, thus emphasizing the prelude's ritornello principle. The increased use of accidentals and the resulting chromaticism in the middle voice (elements typical of nineteenth-century music) are reminiscent of the Adonai Malakh shtayger (figure 4.4).

Other sections in the second part (most notably measures 30–35 and 73–74) and the increased use of accidentals suggest the Adonai Malakh shtayger as well. Whether Deutsch was intentionally alluding to this common traditional shtayger is a matter of conjecture. It is well known, however, that in nineteenth-century Ashkenazic synagogues, professional cantors often combined the traditional Adonai Malakh shtayger with its Western counterpart (the major mode) or even set the shtayger as major.[30]

Regarding rhythm and meter, Deutsch's *Zwölf Präludien für Orgel* features neither irregular rhythms nor recitative-like moments. The change of meter that separates the two parts of Prelude no. 12 does not affect the general rhythmic outline. The whole piece is conceived with a strong sense of meter in which the free rhythm often found in traditional Jewish vocal music is absent.

The relationship between text and music is prevalent not only in word painting but also in the repetition of particular motives. The second part of the prelude repeatedly plays with the motives of "selah na" [pardon] and "hasdekha" [Your love], thus emphasizing keywords of the prayer, which are also central for the feast of Yom Kippur. "Yahbi'enu" [shelter] and "hon yahon" [to salvage] are among the few motives that never appear in the upper part and are almost hidden in the lower parts—an excellent example of word painting.

Although Deutsch integrates musical elements into the prelude that can be easily identified as traditionally Jewish (particularly the two prayer melodies and their musical interpretation), these are combined with a harmony and a structure that were as yet foreign to synagogue music, especially the principles of auxiliary and passing notes. In the prelude, the already adapted and Westernized Jewish prayer melodies collide with elements of the Christian chorale prelude and the functional harmony of Western music.

Deutsch's style shows parallels to the organ repertoire of the Caecilianists,[31] a nineteenth-century group that was centered in Germany and advocated the reform of Catholic church music. Not always original and individualistic with regard to rhythm, harmony, and form, Caecilian style is always clean and correct with a primarily homophonic texture that at times uses imitative polyphony; it is not generally influenced by the style of contemporary nonliturgical compositions.[32] Additional characteristics are the vocal conception of the themes and the orientation toward the *stile antico*.[33] Composers who were committed to Caecilianism created organ works chiefly for practical use; their oeuvre stands in stark contrast to the historically significant compositions of Felix Mendelssohn-Bartholdy, Julius Reubke, and Joseph Rheinberger.[34] It is important to note that these composers also focused on a very different genre in their organ compositions: the sonata.

After Adolf Friedrich Hesse and August Gottfried Ritter, Johann Gottlob Töpfer (1791–1870) was one of the most important representatives of Caecilianism.[35] He left behind a substantial oeuvre of short free-style and chorale-based preludes, all of which display a transparent syntactic construction based on classical periodicity and a nearly omnipresent motive that is used in imitation, thus leading to a mix of homophony and polyphony.[36] Most of his preludes unequivocally present a cantus firmus, in contrast to the practice of avoiding direct melodic quotation, which was prevalent until the mid-nineteenth century.[37] In his shorter chorale preludes Töpfer quotes the cantus firmus in long note values (usually one or two lines) and extracts certain motives that become the basis of motivic work; colorations of the cantus firmus seldom occur.[38]

Moritz Deutsch's pieces are comparable in style with the Caecilian compositions, especially Töpfer's: The formal construction of the pieces, the treatment of the cantus firmus, and the structure show the same characteristics as the Caecilian organ music of the mid-nineteenth century. Despite these parallels the contemporary Jewish press praised the preludes as being products of "Jewish spirit":

> There pulses Jewish life, so warm and so youthfully fresh, that limbs stiffened by the icy-cold breath of the unhappy trends of the time are awakened to new, powerful life and bear witness to the unconquerable source of eternal truth and genuine efforts of art. These ten printed pages (a booklet that seems to have been unfortunately unnoticed by specialists up to now) of Deutsch's organ preludes testify not only to the proficiency and compositional maturity of its creator, but also in a negative respect—because they are undeservedly ignored—to the uncertainty, weakness of discernment, and the general ignorance and therefore arrogance of the masses, that nowadays sit in impertinent judgment on those who strive for and create art.[39]

Josef Singer (1841 or 1842–1911), an Austrian cantor who succeeded Sulzer as chief cantor of the Jewish community in Vienna, goes beyond merely reviewing the organ preludes to criticize the lack of enthusiasm with which they have been received in the synagogue:

> These 12 organ preludes for the synagogue represent the mature musician Deutsch in the clearest sunlight: not the maturity he has finally reached today through failed attempts and unremitting struggle, but the perfection of vision that Deutsch already possessed 25 years ago and has consciously expressed in these preludes. Why did he use old synagogue intonations as motives for these preludes? How can one possibly ask, if one has even a modest understanding of the task the organ in the synagogue has to fulfill as accompaniment and obbligato, and if one is forced even today to observe how the organ must fight and struggle for its right to exist in the synagogue, because of the limitless frivolity with which servants of no vocation use the sounds of the organ for criminal experiments which may well seem dazzling to the great majority, but fill the quietly observing connoisseur with unspeakable pain.[40]

Both excerpts from the *Oesterreichisch-ungarische Cantoren-Zeitung* emphasize the outstanding significance of Deutsch's preludes and at the same time bemoan most cantors' lack of interest in the creation of more organ music. Thus, Deutsch's compositions are rather an exception, a first attempt to create a specifically Jewish organ prelude, which had not yet fully developed.[41] Deutsch's preludes represent a counterpoint to the general situation of synagogue organ music in the mid-nineteenth century, which was still strongly oriented toward the models established by the Christian churches: "Thus, the synagogue organ prelude, ritornello etc. is left to the direction of the organist of a different religion, who no doubt capably learned the function and stylistically proper treatment of the organ for the church in his school, but hears not a word on the function and stylistically proper treatment of the organ in the synagogue from the cantor responsible for him, who is groping in the dark and anxiously looking for rescue; and so we have to be content if the musical work in the synagogue is done correctly to any degree at all."[42]

Since the synagogue organist in the early period was a trained church musician with a Christian background, while the cantor (aside from the almost unique cases of Sulzer and Deutsch) lacked the training to write organ music themselves, the development of organ music that integrated traditional Jewish melodies was a difficult, if not hopeless, undertaking. Cantor and teacher Ernst Rübenstein utters his discontent with the synagogue organ music of this time—especially with regard to its "Christianization": "In one synagogue, for example, the prelude consists of a mere cadence in the relevant key (first scale degree, second scale degree, fifth scale degree, tonic). In another synagogue the organist only knows two kinds of registration, 8′ and plenum, although the organ has many more combinations.—At best the player improvises ad libitum, or uses ecclesiastical preludes by Brixi, Seeger, Rinck, et al., masterful, in their own right, but which generally fit the subsequent [vocal] piece about as well as a fist in the face."[43]

Rübenstein's statement suggests that aesthetic aspirations and ideals for organ music played in the synagogue did exist but remained unfulfilled due to the absence of a suitable organ repertoire. Although the collection of synagogue music was increasing daily, as Rübenstein pointed out in the *Oesterreichisch-ungarische Cantoren-Zeitung*, there was nonetheless (with the exception of Sulzer's and Deutsch's works) a lack of "good organ preludes with Hebrew, synagogal character."[44]

The fact that the press was still reviewing Moritz Deutsch's organ compositions twenty-five years after their first publication testifies to their recognition in German-Jewish communities and indicates their relatively broad but perhaps slow circulation. With the compositions of Deutsch and Sulzer, traditional Jewish vocal music became, for the first time, the thematic basis of organ music. Both composers paved the way for the "Jewish chorale prelude," which was inspired by both synagogue music (especially ḥazzanut) and Western music (particularly the chorale prelude).

Louis Lewandowski continued the path begun by Moritz Deutsch and Salomon Sulzer. Because of his authority as cantor and composer, his work became the standard for synagogue music in German-speaking countries. His first opus for organ, the *Fünf Fest-Präludien*, op. 37, celebrated as "sensational music novelty," was groundbreaking in establishing the Jewish chorale prelude. One of the reasons for the success of his organ compositions may have been his creative environment: Working in a cosmopolitan area, Lewandowski may have found it much easier than Deutsch to distribute and popularize his works.

Most of Lewandowski's compositions were conceived during his time at the synagogue on Heidereuthergasse and the New Synagogue on Oranienburger Straße, both in Berlin. His style is generally described as a "synthesis between Western music culture and synagogue tradition"[45] and as following the oratorio style of Felix Mendelssohn-Bartholdy and the Gebrauchsmusik of the Caecilian tradition.[46] There is no doubt that the organ occupies a central position in his oeuvre; Lewandowski was among the first to convincingly and clearly define the organ's role in Jewish worship; he assigned it an autonomous part, however, without using it as a virtuoso instrument.[47]

Lewandowski's first compositions for solo organ were published without titles in the appendix of his collection of all-occasion synagogue songs for four-part choir, solo cantor, and organ ad libitum (*Toda W'simrah*, part two, [1883] 1921). Lewandowski composed these preludes and interludes on behalf of different Jewish communities with the intention (as he states in a short preface) of musically interpreting the time of silent prayer with works of varying lengths.[48]

The twenty-nine organ pieces are written for the silent prayers on Sabbath (Arvit and Shaḥarit), Shalosh Regalim (Arvit and Shaḥarit), Hallel service, Rosh Ha-Shanah, and Yom Kippur (Arvit and Shaḥarit) and are based on different musical motives related to Sabbath and Jewish holidays. The individual pieces range from four to forty-three measures and are to be played separately or together in any desired order. The first four works form a single unit, as do numbers 5–11, 12–15, 16–19, 20–24, and 25–29. The combination of individual preludes is left up to the organist. The option of putting different preludes together suggests that the flexible grouping was intended as an alternative to the musical improvisations that had previously been used during the time of individual prayer (unless it was silent). Lewandowski details his aspirations in the preface to the collection:

> On behalf of the Jewish communities of Nuremberg, Munich, Stettin et al., for whom I have written substantial scores, the appendix includes introductory pieces and interludes, preludes, and ritornellos. These are short movements, often consisting of six or eight measures, and more elaborate music pieces. All motives in these settings, taken from Sabbath and holiday melodies, are melodically, rhythmically, and harmonically arranged, and are meant to enliven through melody the often distressing quietness of the silent prayer! This task was by no means easy. To give a musical content to brief movements, while avoiding the alien [the "non-Jewish"], and to preserve and even enhance the given mood is highly awkward at best for a composer, for there is barely any time available between beginning and end. Whether this aspiration has been met I leave to the judgment of men of wisdom and knowledge; note, however, that a hasty criticism is not at all suited to do justice to these pieces.[49]

Lewandowski's second organ cycle, *Fünf Fest-Präludien*, was published in 1889 as his opus 37 by Berlin publisher Bote und Bock and celebrated as a "sensational music novelty." The five preludes are written for different Jewish holidays: The first was composed for Rosh Ha-Shanah, the second for Yom Kippur, the third for Sukkot, the fourth for Passover, and the last for Shavuot. All of the preludes integrate synagogue songs previously notated by Lewandowski in *Toda W'simrah*; each is characteristic of the respective feast, and its thematic material is taken from synagogue chants and songs quoted in full, in fragments, or in variation; Thus, the first prelude incorporates Barekhu (the call to worship and service to God on Rosh Ha-Shanah); the second prelude refers to Kol Nidrei; Prelude no. 3 is based on the Hallel; Prelude no. 4 uses Addir Hu and Al Ha-Rishonim; and the fifth prelude is based on the melody of Akdamut Millin and the recitative Ha'El. The works are similarly constructed, with introductions ranging from twenty-two to twenty-four measures, and infused with the vocal melodies, which are not simply inserted in the musical context but fragmented and deconstructed into tiny motives that are developed throughout the piece. A contemporary review by William Wolf, a Berlin-based composer and choir director known for his piano compositions, remarks that "the theme-melodies of the *Fünf Fest-Präludien* are subject to very interesting exploitations and interweavings."[50] However, the *Fünf Fest-Präludien* not only musically develop the synagogue song in the strict sense of the word but also underscore the interpretation of the underlying texts, as is shown by the following analysis of Prelude no. 5, composed for Shavuot.

In contrast to other festivals or Sabbath services, on Shavuot a unique prayer, usually chanted, is interpolated in the reading of the Torah. After the first verse of the Torah reading (Exodus 19:1), the scroll is closed and, in Ashkenazic synagogues,[51] the Aramaic prayer Akdamut Millin is recited, which praises the Creator, the Torah, and the people of Israel. With the first two verses of Akdamut Millin, the congregation asks permission to begin with the actual reading of the Torah.

Akdamut Millin is a piyyut, a religious poem that originated in psalms and songs for the pilgrim festivals of Passover, Shavuot, and Sukkot; it expresses individual feelings, the longing to be closer to God, the search for forgiveness, or thanks for blessings and is usually interspersed among the benedictions.[52] Today only the hymnlike poems, mostly songs of praise and thanks, are regarded as piyyutim, but this includes very different kinds of texts, designated according to their outer form, contents, or liturgical placement.[53]

Akdamut Millin was composed by Rabbi Meir ben Isaac Nehorai of Worms, whose son was murdered during the crusade of 1096. Forced to defend the Torah and his Jewish faith in a debate with local priests, Rabbi Meir successfully conveyed his certainty of God's power, His love for the Jewish people, and the excellence of Torah. Afterward Meir wrote Akdamut Millin, a ninety-line poem in Aramaic that stresses these themes.[54] The poem is written in a double acrostic pattern that spells out "Meir, son of Rabbi Isaac, may he grow in Torah and in good deeds. Amen, and may he be strong and have courage." In addition, each line ends with the syllable "ta," the last and first letters of the Hebrew alphabet, thereby alluding to the infinity of Torah. The first part of Akdamut Millin describes the Creator's omnipotence:

Of the One whose might is such that—
Even if all the heavens were parchment,
And all the reeds pens,
And all the oceans ink,
And all people were scribes,
It would be impossible to record
the greatness of the Creator,
Who created the world with a soft utterance,
And with a single letter, the letter "heh,"
The lightest of the letters.

This is followed by a description of the Torah's singularity and of the reward the pious will receive in the afterlife.

The melody for this poem underlines a sense of grandeur and triumph. Originally composed to be sung only on Shavuot, it continued to be used even after the texts of this and other piyyutim were largely forgotten. The melody was orally transmitted, however, with different texts, most of which were nonmetrical, such as the Kiddush, Hallel, and Mi-Kamoka.[55]

Many melodies originally composed for the piyyutim survived in this way and are still sung today; they generally serve as musical motto themes for different feasts.[56] A number of variants of the Akdamut Millin melody have emerged over the centuries; the best-known and most frequently used version, collected by Lewandowski in *Toda W'simrah* and the basis of the fifth prelude, is transmitted in the notation of southern German cantor Moses Levi (early nineteenth century), but its motivic elements can be traced to the mid-eighteenth century.[57] In Lewandowski's edition, the melody of Akdamut Millin (figure 4.5) is set to the text of Mi-Kamoka in a version for Shavuot.

FIGURE 4.5. Louis Lewandowski, *Toda W'simrah* (1921), no. 8, measures 1–8.
Who is like You among the heavenly powers, God,
Who is like You, mighty in holiness.

[Scho-] - - lom

FIGURE 4.6. Louis Lewandowski, *Toda W'simrah* (1921), no. 65, measures 46–48.

The closing of the Akdamut Millin version used in the prelude appears in a variant of the Akdamut Millin melody (figure 4.6) in Lewandowski.

With regard to the melodic construction of Akdamut Millin, first Aron Friedmann and later Eric Werner draw a parallel to the introitus for the fourth Sunday in Advent, *Rorate caeli* (figure 4.7).[58]

Given that non-Jewish melodies were used at times for the recitation of the piyyutim, that these "foreign melodies" began to play an important role in the genre,[59] and especially that chants used in Catholic liturgy influenced Jewish chants,[60] parallels between the traditional Advent chant and the Akdamut Millin melody noted by Lewandowski are easily explained.[61]

In addition to the Akdamut Millin melody, the fifth prelude also draws upon the Ha'El recitation (figure 4.8a), which commonly precedes the Akdamut Millin. The recitation serves as an introduction to other prayers as well (e.g., the Shokhen 'Ad in the Shaharit for holidays). The text of Ha'El recalls the exodus of the Israelites from Egypt and its proof of God's omnipotence.[62]

The brief coloraturas of the Ha'El recitation still hint at the originally rich melismas, which in modern times have been greatly moderated,[63] and thus attest to an early origin for this melody. In its tonal disposition, Lewandowski's arrangement of Ha'El exemplifies nineteenth-century synagogue song. If shtayger had once been a key element of synagogue music, in the nineteenth century it took on more of the character of a minor tonality "due to its sometimes soft and elegiac, sometimes austere character."[64]

TEMPORE ADVENTUS. *

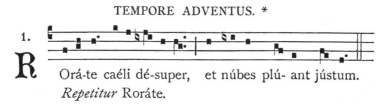

1. R

Orá-te caéli dé-super, et núbes plú- ant jústum.
Repetitur Roráte.

FIGURE 4.7. *Liber Usualis* (1934), p. 1868.
Drop down dew, ye heavens, from above, and let the clouds rain on the just.

FIGURE 4.8A. Louis Lewandowski, *Kol Rinnah U'T'fillah* (1954), no. 73, measures 1–11. God, in Your tremendous power, great in Your glorious name, mighty forever and revered for Your awe-inspiring acts; King seated upon a high and lofty throne.

Analysis of Prelude No. 5

The fifth prelude in D minor begins in unison with the first measures of Ha'El; however, the eighth-note triplet is diminished here to sixteenth notes followed by descending seconds.[65] Beginning with measure 3, the Ha'El theme is further developed by a distribution in fragments over various parts, and from measure 4 on (with the descending seconds augmented to fourths) it is used in sequence. Besides the triplet motive, another motive taken from Ha'El is of importance (see figure 4.8b).

This motive is introduced right after the sequence in measure 7 and appears in an A-major passage simultaneously with the prelude's opening motive, which is shortened by one measure and moved to the lower part (played in the pedal). After measure 7 is repeated once more, the rhythmic element of this motive finally breaks through in measure 9, modulating definitively to A major. Measure 11 introduces the opening theme in F major and continues similarly from measures 3 to 5 with the triplet motive used in original and retrograde motion.

FIGURE 4.8B.

A cadence leading to D minor ends on an incomplete cadence in A major, followed by a sequence that is based on the triplet motive (measures 16–19); this leads to a chordal passage that modulates to C major. In measure 23 the first four measures of the Akdamut Millin melody resonate in C major. After an eighth rest in all voices (marking a clear caesura), an interlude section begins, which is based on the sixteenth-note triplet of the opening, augmenting it from measure 31 by eighth-note triplets. This section serves as modulation, and in measure 35 the key definitively changes to D major. Despite the key change, a break is barely noticeable as the preceding motives and figures continue in the D-major section. Though the triplet motive has so far appeared twice in each measure, from measure 36 on, it is present on every beat.

Above the triplets rises the motive that is usually sung over "-moka" or "elim." From measure 42 on, the whole Akdamut Millin melody is presented in a true homophonic setting, ending in measure 49 on the dominant in an incomplete cadence. After a quarter-note rest in measure 50, it ends in the second closing formula (see figure 4.5) of Akdamut Millin. This is followed by the opening motive of Ha'El, now presented in D major instead of D minor and with its characteristic fifth reversed, thus ending the prelude.

The prelude's formal structure exhibits toccata-like elements: virtuoso figures and runs, short polyphonic passages based on Ha'El and combined with full chords that serve as a harmonic basis for Akdamut Millin, and dramatic dotted rhythms—basic compositional elements of the prelude.

Based on his choral writing and organ intonations in *Toda W'simrah*, Lewandowski's use of harmony has been compared, notably by Idelsohn, with Mendelssohn's.[66] This parallel is based, according to Idelsohn, on the frequent use of major chords or modulations to the major, as well as the general avoidance of minor keys.[67] Considering that Lewandowski composed these preludes in the 1880s, the "Mendelssohnian" harmonies and the absence of virtuoso elements reflect Lewandowski's rejection of the pull of late Romanticism. In these preludes Lewandowski had mostly recast the originally modal synagogue melodies, just as with the arrangements in *Toda W'simrah*, into major or minor tonality. The question whether the pieces belong to the "Mendelssohn school" in Idelsohn's sense is less clear and deserves a closer look.

Though the Barekhu melody of the first prelude is harmonized with both major and minor chords, major tonality prevails. The fugato (measures 24–42) appears in major; the play with motives derived from Barekhu (measures 75–80), however, occurs in the first church mode with the use of some minor chords. The second prelude draws upon the tonality of the Kol Nidrei melody as previously arranged by Lewandowski in G minor. The subsequent modulation, based on independent motives (measures 50–53), leads from G minor to

F major, only to let the continuation of the Kol Nidrei melody appear in B-flat major, the mediant; the modulation continues toward first C minor (measures 61–63) and then E-flat major (measure 63) and returns to G minor (measure 68). The introduction of the Hallel in the third prelude in E minor oscillates between minor and major (induced by an accidental third); later, the melody is harmonized in natural minor. In measure 47 Hallel appears first in D major and then in E major before a definitive change in key signature to E major for the last twenty measures. Prelude no. 4 shows best the tonal variability of a melody: Al Ha-Rishonim occurs in both major (measures 1–8) and minor (measures 15–29, 51–60). The tonality of the fifth prelude is defined by the harmonic relationship of D minor (tonic), A major (dominant), and D major (mediant). It also reveals Lewandowski's preference for harmonizing motives that have an inherent minor tonality with major chords (measures 10–13). The modulation in measure 29 with motives of Akdamut Millin, leading to C major, shows Lewandowski departing into more remote keys. As in Prelude no. 3, the fifth prelude also features a key signature change at the end—to the mediant D major.[68]

The tonality and harmony in the *Fünf Fest-Präludien* support Idelsohn's hypothesis with regard to Lewandowski's frequent use of major keys. This is especially evident in the preludes that begin in minor but change in their last twenty measures to a major key. The only exception is Kol Nidrei, whose tonal disposition, prominence, and key role in Jewish religion perhaps do not allow significant changes. To claim as Idelsohn does, however, that the use of major tonality is a sign of Mendelssohn's influence on Lewandowski may be overstating the case in view of the fact that Mendelssohn's own harmonies and style were in many ways far more progressive. Other influences in Lewandowski's oeuvre should not be underestimated, especially the musical traditions of his native Prussian and Polish cultures and the eastern European element resulting from his collaboration with Stettin-based cantor Abraham Jacob Lichtenstein.[69]

Lewandowski's *Fünf Fest-Präludien* are excellent examples of the treatment of synagogue songs in instrumental music. Each piece features the synagogue songs clearly, even emphasizing them through variations and contrasts in registration and performance indications. Barekhu serves as the first subject of a fugato and is thus very distinct, especially when first presented. Kol Nidrei, in the second prelude, appears in the bass and is marked "mezzoforte" with registration indications that, according to Lewandowski, should emphasize the melody "ben pronunziata." The first manual may support the bass line "con ottava bassa ad lib[itum]." Thus, the melody of Kol Nidrei, in spite of its somewhat hidden appearance in the bass, is reinforced. The introduction of Hodu in unison and later in the upper part beginning in measure 55 (Prelude no. 3), as well Al Ha-Rishonim and Addir Hu (both also in the upper part or "marcato" in the pedal [Prelude no. 4]), are as clearly exposed as the Ha'El and Akdamut Millin in the fifth prelude. The thematic character of the synagogue songs is underlined by dynamics, accentuations, and appearance in the outer voices.

An examination of the dynamic construction of the fifth prelude reveals the mood and meaning of the texts. Although Lewandowski's vocal version of the Ha'El recitation in *Toda W'simrah* is marked "piano," the lines at the beginning of Ha'El in the prelude are expressed in unison and forte, underlining the character of the text passage "God, in Your tremendous power." This expression is further increased in measure 11, when this exact theme appears in the mediant, F major. The imitations of the triplet motive on "beta'aẓumot" create the impression of increasing power. The final part of Akdamut Millin (in fortissimo) also emphasizes the text, which again expresses God's omnipotence. In this section Lewandowski uses specific techniques such as unison or presentation of the minor theme in major to convey the meaning of the content and to interpret it musically.

The polyphonic use and musical interpretation of synagogue melodies and their integration into major and minor tonality—quite innovative for Jewish liturgical music—are the main characteristics of the *Fünf Fest-Präludien* and the *Zwölf Präludien für Orgel oder Pianoforte zum gottesdienstlichen und häuslichen Gebrauch nach alten Synagogen-Intonationen*. Although these pieces are based on traditional Jewish liturgical music, their sonority reaches beyond the realm of what is commonly understood as "Jewish music." The use of the prelude form, contemporaneous compositional styles, and harmony in the tradition of Western music separates these works from the more traditional repertoire of Jewish worship to the extent that only those who are deeply familiar with synagogue music may recognize their tie to Jewish music and liturgy. Thus, the *Fünf Fest-Präludien* in particular represent "the essence of great majestic organ introductions of the kind that Christian worship has known for centuries and used to the most solemn effect on the gathering of the devout."[70]

After the *Fünf Fest-Präludien*, Lewandowski continued to write for keyboard instruments. Part of his oeuvre is the compilation *Augenblicke der Weihe: Consolations, Neun kleine Stücke für Harmonium, Orgel oder Klavier*, op. 44, published ca. 1892 by Carl Simon in Berlin. The nine pieces are intended for the bereaved at a funeral or at home during *shivah*, the seven-day mourning period which begins immediately after the funeral. During this period the mourners are not supposed to leave the house, not even to attend synagogue services. These pieces may be meant to be played during that time for consolation.

Lewandowski's last published collection of organ pieces—the *Synagogen-Melodieen für Harmonium, Orgel oder Klavier*, op. 47—was issued posthumously by Simon in 1895. The motives and themes used in these works derive from Ashkenazic songs such as Ya'aleh for Shemoneh Esreh on Rosh Ha-Shanah and Yom Kippur, Ya'aleh on Erev Yom Kippur, Zokharti Lokh as a hymnic song on Rosh Ha-Shanah and Yom Kippur, Veyatayu as a hymn on Rosh Ha-Shanah and Yom Kippur, and Onu Tovu for the confession of sins on Rosh Ha-Shanah and Yom Kippur.

With the exception of the *Fünf Fest-Präludien*, Lewandowski arranged his works so that they can be played on pipe organ, reed organ, or piano or—as with the *Synagogen-Melodieen* — sung by a chorus. This highlights the fact that the compositions were intended for use in the synagogue since they are adaptable to the different performance possibilities in individual communities.

With regard to their style, the *Fünf Fest-Präludien* have more in common with organ compositions intended exclusively for Christian liturgical use than with the concert music of Lewandowski's day: The styles of liturgical organ music that predominated in the early nineteenth century continued to do so in the latter part of the century, with only a few significant differences such as the development from a simple functional harmony toward typically Romantic harmony. Largely unaffected by new developments in organ music for secular performance, the liturgical organ music of the entire nineteenth century was influenced mainly by Caecilianism, with its many unoriginal chorale arrangements representing the main corpus of the repertoire.[71] Although not part of the Caecilian movement, Lewandowski's *Fünf Fest-Präludien* easily fit into the style of Caecilian organ music. In fact, Gotthold Frotscher includes Lewandowski's oeuvre in a highly critical description of different forms of Caecilian organ music, mentioning him in almost the same breath as Wilhelm Valentin Volckmar (1812–1887), whose Gebrauchsmusik for organ most notably includes the *Nachspiele für die Orgel* (5 vols., op. 137–41); *Sechs Tonstücke*, op. 94; and the Sonata in F-sharp Major from op. 50: "A more substantial type of setting is that of the *Festfantasie*, as established by the well-known Wilhelm Volckmar, which is a juxtaposition, succession, and intertwining of sequenced chords, passages, and imitative passages; or, in their absence, modulations; or a stereotypical alternation of figurations and melodic turns. Again, characteristics of this form are inconsequential and without the power of a personal style or typological significance, such as the presentation of one melodic formula in a variety of styles (Louis Lewandowski, Ludwig Hartmann)."[72]

The works of Deutsch, Sulzer, Lewandowski, and other cantors were written during a period of serious style change in organ music, one that aimed not at a homogenous language but rather at a previously unknown stylistic diversity that would incorporate Baroque and Romantic elements and style galant, which many organ composers utilized, in a general trend toward historicism, from the mid-nineteenth century on. However, as far as style is concerned, the cantors' pieces fall into the general category of liturgical music for actual use. Not having developed sufficiently to be part of contemporary concert repertory, organ music for the synagogue remained Gebrauchsmusik.

The quality of the cantors' compositions shows that they had no professional training as composers; thus, regarding counterpoint and harmony, their works were somewhat less accomplished than those of their contemporaries. Analysis of Deutsch's Prelude no. 12, for instance, often shows an incoherent use of harmony, imitations almost exclusively taking place within the ambitus of an octave, and the bass often being transposed to a higher octave (thus allowing for a performance on piano or reed organ). Louis Lewandowski's compositions for organ, however, seem to have been conceived with the intent of bringing the new repertoire of the synagogue to a standard equal to that of church music, especially Caecilian organ music.

The significance of Deutsch's and Lewandowski's organ works does not lie in their style and quality of writing. Moreover, they stand for more than a mere assimilationist expression in music. Rather, these works are the achievements of pioneers and represent their first attempts to find a new musical language in Judaism in tune with its time and environment. This ground-breaking effort was after all the very first attempt—with the much earlier exception of Salamone Rossi and his contemporaries—either to depart from the old traditions of Jewish music or to develop them further.

Early organ compositions reflect an apparent caution in their experimentation with elements of Jewish music. One reason for this may be that the organ had not yet been fully established as a synagogue instrument. When comparing the development of organ building in synagogues with the increase in the number of organ compositions for synagogues, it is evident that only with the rise of organ building in the 1880s did composers begin to compose original organ pieces. After the first attempts to create a new repertoire for Jewish worship, almost half a century had to elapse for a change to occur that would also affect organ music. Furthermore and perhaps more important, organ music became part of an adjustment process in Jewish society.

RENAISSANCE OF TRADITIONS

After a hundred years of increasing assimilation, around the turn of the twentieth century liberal Jews sought to reemphasize their distinct spirit of Judaism and to strengthen a collective Jewishness that was reinforced by anti-Semitic currents in society. Hannah Arendt has blamed the nineteenth-century Jews for sacrificing their Jewishness for the sake of "culture"; though remaining aware of their Jewish origin, they now identified with a secular culture without real-izing that they were inducing the secularization of their own heritage.[73]

These changes led to divergent developments in the Weimar Republic: On the one hand, conversion and intermarriage reached a peak, leading to the closest possible encounter of Jewish and non-Jewish society but not to the ex-tent of total assimilation; on the other hand, Jewish life flourished. Michael Brenner speaks of a "Renaissance of Jewish Culture,"[74] as almost all areas of Jewish life, such as activities in Jewish communities and publications of Jew-ish works and music, were inspired by different groups: religious and non-religious, Orthodox and liberals, Zionists, and those who sought to realize a synthesis of German and Jewish identity. The desire of some to detach them-selves altogether from the Jewish community coexisted with a strengthened Jewish identity of national and cultural nature. The majority, however, did not want to entirely give up either the German or the Jewish components of their identity.[75] As Brenner puts it, the Jewish sphere was no longer con-ceived as a spiritual ghetto, and whoever belonged to it had a plurality of identities and lived in many worlds.[76] One of these "many worlds" was the spiritual, intellectual, and cultural life of the Weimar Republic, in which the Jewish population participated.

That these developments also extended to Jewish liturgical music is not surprising. The compositions of Salomon Sulzer and Louis Lewandowski lost their original appeal among Weimar Jews, who regarded them as outdated. The new aspiration was to create a "distinctively Jewish" contemporary music for Jewish communities and associations.

Following the trend of the new nationalism in early twentieth-century music—as in the incorporation of folk song in the works of Igor Stravinsky and Béla Bartók—Jewish folk music gained popularity among Jewish com-posers and audiences in orchestral pieces, as well as chamber and vocal music. The ancient Jewish liturgical chant, to some extent neglected and replaced by new arrangements, experienced a revival, too, and began to play an important part in organ music. The combination of Western and liturgical music, which often derived from Eastern Jewry, led to a new style of art music that could be performed both in concert and in worship. The stylistic progression in twentieth-century music—especially atonality and expanded tonality—re-inforced this development, in which Arnold Schoenberg, according to Michael Brenner, played an important role: "Schoenberg's revolutionary use of ex-panded tonal and atonal music helped composers of Jewish liturgical music to solve a century-old dilemma. On one hand, they wanted to improve synagogue music along the lines of the general musical development, but on the other hand they did not want this improvement to blur the distinctiveness and authenticity of the music's Jewish setting."[77]

The tension between the aims of Jewish authenticity and participation in the wider cultural world of the Weimar periodicity is also evident in the organ music of Jewish communities. In addition, the new demands on the repertoire were reinforced by the changing function of organ music in Judaism at the turn of the century: For the first time organ music was part of the repertoire performed at synagogue concerts. At first glance, some of these performances might seem startling today, such as the organ concert that took place in the Dortmund synagogue on May 9, 1904, "for the benefit of the German troops in South West Africa" or a concert "for the benefit of the surviving dependents of the German corporals and crews of the First Army Corps" on April 2, 1916, in the Königsberg synagogue, with organ compositions by Joseph Rheinberger (Concerto in F Major) and Robert Franz (*Hebräische Melodie*). That such benefit performances—often featuring organ transcriptions of works by Wagner—took place in synagogues, of all places, expresses the dual identity of German Jews. Instead of performing organ music that conveys a specifically Jewish spirit, most of the Christian organists still working for synagogues played either the standard repertoire or rarities, as the *Dortmunder Zeitung* reported in its notice of the inauguration concert for a new echo manual built for the Dortmund synagogue by E. F. Walcker, which took place on October 9, 1907: "The new echo division in the local synagogue and its effects and capability were introduced to a number of music lovers yesterday evening. Using the echo division, Director Holtschneider played the Prelude and Fugue in B Minor by Joh. Seb. Bach, the prayer from *Rienzi* by Rich. Wagner, an *Invocation* by A. Guilmant, a free fantasy, and at the end, using an organola, the *Storm Fantasy* by Lemmens."

Carl Holtschneider (1872–1951), music director at the Reinoldikirche and conductor, only a few days later played an organ recital at the Dortmund synagogue, which was described as "very rich with organ novelties." The program included the *Fantaisie dialoguée* for organ and orchestra by Léon Boëllmann, *Marche héroique* by Marco Enrico Bossi, the same *Invocation* by Alexandre Guilmant, and the Organ Concerto op. 137 in F Major by Joseph Rheinberger, which had been performed only once six years earlier.[78] Christian organists often used a synagogue organ for concerts as a testing ground for their own compositions; Dutch organist Gerard Bunk, for example, performed his own organ concertos in the Bielefeld synagogue in 1906 and 1907.[79]

In the early twentieth century many composers of Jewish ancestry grew up without a close relationship to synagogue music; it was only in the 1920s and 1930s that a new generation of musicians, including Herbert Fromm and Heinrich Schalit, began composing Jewish liturgical music and even organ pieces for use in the synagogue. Many of these composers were especially inspired by Idelsohn's *HOM*. Thus began a breakthrough to a new type of liturgical music, according to musicologist Hugo Leichtentritt:

> The renewal of Jewish religious music is one of the most important tasks in the development of a liturgy tied to the life of the present-day. Temple worship in Germany may be amply furnished with music for the cantor, for the vocally trained prayer leader as soloist, and also for mixed or male chorus, and in many synagogues for organ as well. . . . What is needed today is a music that bears a strong Jewish character and religious dedication, but at the same time serves the demands of the listener whose ears have become attuned to more contemporary music. . . . In two words: The new Jewish music ought to be both Jewish and new—traditional and modern at the same time.[80]

Leichtentritt sees this development as a progression "from Lewandowski to Schalit." In the earliest years of the twentieth century, traditionalist cantor-composers still modeled their works on Louis Lewandowski, but in the course of time an alternative, progressive approach came into existence, one that sought to change the nature of organ music in the synagogue and found its fullest expression in the work of Heinrich Schalit. The history of synagogue organ music in the intervening years is best described in terms of this dialectic.

Leon Kornitzer (1875–1947), for one, followed in the steps of Lewandowski, cultivating and creating works built on his style. As the offspring of an old family of cantors, he was well versed in the Ashkenazic music tradition, especially synagogue song. With his appointment as chief cantor at the Hamburg Reform Temple in 1913, Kornitzer began composing vocal and instrumental music for worship. Although Kornitzer stated that he was far from regarding Lewandowski as the greatest master,[81] we find among his organ compositions a *Vorspiel zu "W'hogen baadenu"* (suggestive of Lewandowski)[82] and an *Interludium, nach K'wakkorass, als Überleitung zu "B'rosch haschanoh"* (evocative of Sulzer).[83]

Even as Kornitzer continued to follow older models of synagogue composition, a renewal in organ music was taking place. In his essay "Der Weg zur jüdischen Orgel," Hans Samuel describes a new direction in composition for the synagogue that developed in the 1920s. The new trend aimed at breaking away from the assimilated, church-oriented music that dominated the services of the time and moved toward a novel concept of what he calls *syna-*

gogale Orgelmusik [organ music for the synagogue], as opposed to *jüdische Orgel-musik* [Jewish organ music]. Samuel explains the former as follows:

> It is not the Baroque style of a Bach and Händel, which presents itself more in fixed forms derived from the instrumental realm, but rather one born out of a passionately moving *Sprechgesang* [speech-song], and thus much freer and more immediate. For this Baroque style in Jewish music is not a recent, but rather an ancient form. It is found in the oldest synagogue song—in the abundance of embellishments and ornaments, and the characteristically large interval leaps, so expressive in some piyyut melodies, reminiscent of the storm-tossed garments, the passionate movements of Baroque sculpture. . . . Today, the new music assumes the old Baroque element in instrumental music as well . . . [especially organ music], in place of compact harmonies . . . whether used on its own, or bringing out the cantorial recitative with its rich coloraturas, or in intensifying the effect of important motives in ornamental figuration through canonic imitation. . . . Thus, following the liturgy, a synagogal organ style could be created, reflecting in original form on the loveliest motives of the ḥazzan's recitative.[84]

Samuel's formulations reveal how assimilated his own thoughts on music were, with his use of terms such as "Baroque style"—a concept that had been introduced to musicology by Curt Sachs as recently as 1919—"embellishment," and "ornamentation," as well as "canonic imitation." Such concepts had never been used before in conjunction with traditional Jewish music. What were Samuel's intentions when speaking about Baroque style and its elements? He uses these terms, aware of their semantics, to create a contrast to the synagogue organ music of the nineteenth century and its orientation to Romantic ideals. At the same time, he refers to the common (as opposed to specifically Jewish) trend of the neo-Baroque inspired by the Orgelbewegung. He also uses these concepts to craft a musicologically adequate and generally comprehensible language for discussing a music whose native terminology was known to only a small number of specialists. The attempt to describe Jewish music with the concepts of Western art music not only is an expression of musicological assimilation but also provides a way of making this music accessible to a wider circle of musicians, Jewish and non-Jewish alike.

When Samuel speaks of revisiting the "old" Baroque style, he seems to have a double intention; he refers not only to the return of musical techniques and forms in combination with contemporary harmony and to the renaissance of

Western musical traditions but also to Jewish music, including organ music in particular.

The style Samuel envisioned had, in his view, been realized by only one composer, Hugo Chaim Adler (1896–1955). Born in Antwerp, Adler eventually made his way to Hamburg, Cologne, and Mannheim, where as a cantor and teacher at the local synagogue he became known as the "primary moving force in religious and musical activities."[85] Synagogue music above all provided an area of expression that allowed him to follow a new musical path. Philip Bohlman emphasizes that "Adler's means of reaching out to contemporary European compositional technique was the polyphonic treatment of liturgical melodies."[86] This technique is evident in Adler's organ compositions, among them the *Toccata und Fuge über ein hebräisches Thema für Orgel*, op. 11a,[87] and *Zwei Stücke für Orgel*, op. 11b (both in 1931). The first work was not composed for liturgical use only but was integrated into general musical life in Germany. It had its premiere with a performance of Adler's cantata *Licht und Volk* in Cologne's medieval Gürzenich Hall in 1931. The event was sponsored by the Jewish *Lehrhaus*, a center for Jewish adult education; the organist was well-known German church musician and composer Hermann Schroeder (1904–1984),[88] at the time still a student of church music at the Cologne Musikhochschule.

The reviews of the piece were highly mixed: According to the *Kölner Zeitung*, it was "a piece without its own musical face, whose fugue had a peculiar ending."[89] The *Generalanzeiger für Dortmund und das gesamte rheinisch-westfälische Industriegebiet* of December 15, 1931, referred to it as "a virtuous Toccata and Fugue by Hugo Adler, which, however, [Schroeder] played too loud and without subtle registration."[90] In contrast to these two critiques, the *Kölner Stadtanzeiger* of December 16, 1931, described the piece as "a musically complex work, which at the end lyrically dissolves the strict counterpoint and manifests the essential stylistic traits of the composer of the cantata [*Licht und Volk*]."[91] The *Kölner Tageblatt* wrote on December 17, 1931, that the work showcases "the composer as a sophisticated writer of counterpoint with a unique and interesting profile."[92]

A year later, the Toccata and Fugue was broadcast from the Cologne cathedral and thus reached a very broad audience. The same year, 1932, the *Israelitisches Gemeindeblatt Mannheim* published an article that gives important information about the composition: Josef Levi, organist at the Mannheim synagogue, describes Adler's compositions as a "symptomatic signal of the advent of an era of unique organ music for the synagogue."[93]

According to Levi's review—which constitutes the best description of the piece since no score is available[94]—Adler's achievement in this piece was not only his successful integration of traditional elements of Jewish music but also the creation of a new path. The work takes its thematic material from the first line of the piyyut A'apid Nezer, by one of the early and most prolific liturgical poets, Eleazar ben Kalir. (The piyyut A'apid Nezer was written for Shaḥarit on the first day of Rosh Ha-Shanah.) Rather than simply quoting the motive from its original vocal version, as Deutsch and Lewandowski had done, Levi says Adler appears to have fundamentally transformed it in rhythm and melody, focusing less on the theme itself than on its interpretation.

———

The development "from Lewandowski to Schalit" also found an advocate in the progressive chief cantor of Munich's Great Synagogue on Westernrieder-straße, Emanuel Kirschner. From the beginning of his appointment there in 1881, he focused on organ music in the synagogue and its evolution, as he relates in his memoirs: "Thus, I too felt the need for expansion and a deepening of the knowledge I had already acquired. For this purpose, the organist at our synagogue, Hans Hasselbeck (brother and teacher of the acclaimed Wagner singer Rosa Sucher-Hasselbeck) was warmly recommended."[95] Despite his efforts and progressive inclinations, Kirschner had an ambivalent relationship with the organ, as did most cantors who had grown up in musical traditions that did not utilize the organ. He did not, however, primarily criticize the instrument as a part of Jewish worship but rather the repertoire that was played on it; in his words, "the sounds [are] too marked with Christianity."

In a letter to Hans Samuel, Kirschner mentioned the compositions of David Nowakowsky (1848–1921), cantor at the Brody Synagogue in Odessa, as an example of "the most suitable music for organ."[96] Other composers, too, were, according to Kirschner, on the right path: "The art song in synagogue only attains a Jewish physiognomy when the motives for artistic elaboration derive from old Jewish traditional song, from the revered ḥazzanut. In the *Festpräludium* [italics added] of Lewandowski, the numbers by Birnbaum in today's program . . . the signs are happily multiplying that this not only justifiable but self-evident claim is on its way to general acceptance."[97]

Kirschner continued following in Lewandowski's path and having his works performed. A review of a synagogue concert on the occasion of the hundredth anniversary of the Great Synagogue on May 7, 1926, published in the *Bayerisch-israelitische Gemeindezeitung*, confirms this: "The organ was played by organist Robert Osenbrunner, who played a *Fest-Präludium* [italics added] for organ by Louis Lewandowski."[98] During the mid-1920s, however, he also created a number of new compositions for or with organ in public concerts at the Great Synagogue in Munich, often as an opening piece. Among them were the *Fantasie über Kol Nidrei in g-Moll* for organ solo by Austrian composer and conductor Joseph Ziegler (b. 1880), who worked as a conductor for the Jewish community in Munich, and vocal pieces composed by Kirschner himself, which featured an elaborate organ part.[99] Also in the 1920s the Munich congregation began to commission pieces for liturgical use from their own musicians, which were to be played along with the preludes of Louis Lewandowski and Moritz Deutsch. Kirschner contributed to this repertoire as well, with six preludes for organ.[100] He also commissioned liturgical organ compositions from Joseph Ziegler. This cooperation, in Kirschner's view, would ensure a unity of vocal and instrumental works that could be performed in the framework of liturgy and concerts alike. However, a few years later Kirschner decided to supplement Ziegler's organ compositions—besides the *Fantasie über Kol Nidrei*, he wrote an *Orgelpraeludium* and the *Praeludium (unter Verwendung der Motive Hoher Feiertage)* —and commissioned pieces from Hans Samuel:

> If I might make a request of you, it would be the following: I would like to commission, for our synagogue music program, suitable preludes and postludes coming out of practical knowledge and composed for practical use, employing traditional motives—the 5 *Festpräludien* [italics added] by Lewandowski seem too elaborate for the intended purpose. How would it be if you could make up your mind to commit your improvisations to paper? If I am not mistaken, our colleague Adler is planning an edition of such a compilation. Has he already spoken with you about this? I believe that such an edition would be gladly received in the admittedly small circle of interested persons.[101]

Kirschner was referring to Hugo Chaim Adler, whom Samuel greatly admired (as noted earlier) and who had already started to compile his own volume of organ music for Jewish worship, presumably at the request of his congregation in Mannheim or some other synagogue. After Samuel had sent his organ works to Kirschner, their correspondence continued; it reveals an awareness that organ music in the early twentieth-century synagogue still had the status of Gebrauchsmusik: "The point should never be disregarded that in our worship and for it the artist is mainly required to supply Gebrauchsmusik for well-defined purposes, a Gebrauchsmusik that must be comprehensible to the minds and ears of laypersons, since only in this way can the composer in the synagogue produce an educational effect."[102] In addition, Kirschner called for "simplicity, clarity, and clear exposition and development of motives to the degree . . . that even the laity will be in a position to follow the composer's artistic presentation."[103]

The turning point in Kirschner's engagement with organ music came, in fact, in 1927, when a new organist, Heinrich Schalit, was appointed at the

Great Synagogue. Kirschner initially saw Schalit's selection as a threat to his own position and, instead of collaborating, treated the new organist as a rival.[104] In the end, however, it was precisely because of Schalit, a well-versed musician, that the music at the Munich synagogue was to begin a new evolution.

On completing his studies in composition and voice at the Vienna Hochschule and experiencing his first successes as a composer of secular music, Schalit had moved to Munich in 1907 in search of new professional challenges. In 1910 he spent a semester studying organ at the Königliche Bayerische Akademie für Musik. Motivated by the political events of the time and the recognition that his options as a composer were limited, in the years between 1916 and 1920 he began feeling a call to compose Jewish music. He himself pinpointed the year 1916 as a defining moment, the "beginning of a creative period of music with Jewish content and Jewish character."[105] Schalit saw himself as a "Jewish composer" motivated by Zionism, as he stated in a letter to Anita Hepner: "Between 1928 and 1932, when there was no composer of Jewish birth who could have even thought of writing music with a consciously Jewish heartbeat, I was already a well-known composer of Jewish religious music. . . . As a conscientious Jewish musician and Zionist I considered it my duty to convince him [Paul Ben-Haim] of the necessity of devoting his talent to Jewish music and culture."[106]

One of the results of Schalit's preoccupation with Jewish music were the *Ostjüdische Volkslieder* (opp. 18–19). Then, in 1927, he applied for the position of music director and organist at the Munich synagogue. The appointment did not proceed without difficulties, however: "A talented non-Jewish organist had applied for the position and so did Heinrich. Dr. Elias Strauss championed Heinrich's cause and insisted that the congregation should hire a Jewish organist. A competition was held between the two musicians, and Heinrich won the contest."[107] Apparently issues of the organist's faith persisted well into the 1920s. Obviously, artistic excellence was an important factor as well.

With his appointment at the Great Synagogue, Schalit began to concentrate on Jewish liturgical music as a performer and a composer to the extent that liturgical composition became a sacred calling for him. He believed that the music of Lewandowski and Sulzer "gave Jewish music a Romantic and operatic sound rather than a spiritual one" and that the music of the service required a total change.[108]

His goal was to replace the "unorganic mixture of traditional cantorial chants with congregational and choral music in the German style of the nineteenth century" and to "create a new, unified liturgical music growing out of the soil of the old-new, significant and valuable source material"[109] that had become available through Idelsohn's *HOM*. In fact, Schalit was the first composer to draw on Idelsohn's collection of synagogue songs, focusing on the Eastern-Jewish material, though without neglecting the Ashkenazic repertoire.

Within only six weeks in the autumn of 1931, Schalit composed the *Freitagabend-Liturgie* (op. 29) for cantor, chorus, and organ. The conception of this work was reinforced by his meeting during the preceding summer with Alexander Weinbaum, music director at the Lützowstraße synagogue in Berlin, who also fiercely criticized the state of synagogue music.

On September 16, 1932, Schalit's *Freitagabend-Liturgie* received its premiere in the Lützowstraße synagogue with Max Janowski playing organ and Hanns John as soloist. Because it was too risky for a publisher to issue this work under the rising National Socialism, in 1933 Schalit published it himself. Many years later, upon settling in the United States, he revised the work for the American Reform Congregation as *Sabbath Eve Liturgy* (1951). This version contained two additional compositions for organ solo, a prelude and a piece titled "Silent Devotion."

The premiere of the *Freitagabend-Liturgie* was a complete success, as Oskar Guttmann reports:

> For the first time in decades, a music has been heard in the organ synagogue whose disposition and instinct can be characterized as liturgically Jewish. It was created not merely by a musician, but by a Jewish master—a Jewish human being, who tries to allow the inherent melos of the Hebrew language, its rhythm and meter, its accentuation, to resonate. Thus, for the first time, a fully correct intonation of the Hebrew text. The Hebrew meter as well, the symmetry and asymmetry of diction, is considered, so that the musical form does not senselessly destroy the word but rather grows out of it. Schalit borders on modernity. Through the use of church modes [shtayger] and their conforming harmonization, a unique and solemn atmosphere is created. . . . The house of worship was surprisingly full, as it is during the High Holidays, which is proof of a broad interest in the renewal of synagogue music.[110]

The last piece in the *Freitagabend-Liturgie* is titled "Nachspiel" [Postlude] for solo organ, with a musical treatment of motive and theme that is hard to classify. In a 1951 letter to Schalit, his colleague Herbert Fromm not only critiques the works but also gives insight into the thematic basis of the piece: "The potpourri character of the Nachspiel for organ does not conform to my ideals of a postlude. The fragmented form lets the piece appear short of breath. One only understands the piece if one has listened to the preceding service. However, a musical piece should be understandable in itself."[111]

Analysis of the "Nachspiel"

Formally, the postlude consists for the most part of different sections taken from the organ accompaniment of the *Freitagabend-Liturgie*. The different sections are either an exact quotation of the original accompaniment or are used in variation. The first five measures of the postlude provide a sort of introduction of the actual potpourri and a direct link without any break (*attacca*) between the preceding piece, "Wehojo Adonoj," and the postlude. Then measure 6 uses the organ accompaniment to "Schema" (no. 8, measures 7 and 14) with only minor alterations. The next eight measures take over the accompaniment to "Lechoh dodi" (no. 3, the last eight measures). Lekhah Dodi is a Hebrew liturgical song recited in synagogue on Fridays at dusk to welcome Sabbath prior to the evening services. It is part of the Kabbalat Shabbat [acceptance of the Sabbath]. During the singing of the last verse, the entire congregation rises and turns toward the open door to greet the "Sabbath bride" as "she" arrives. The text, based on the Song of Songs 7:12, goes back to the sixteenth century and is attributed to Rabbi Shlomo Halevi Alkabetz, a Kabbalist in Safed.[112] In his arrangement of Lekhah Dodi, Schalit draws on a melody from Idelsohn's *HOM* 4, "Gesänge der orientalischen Sefardim" [Songs of the Oriental Sephardim] (see figure 4.9a), which is preserved in the upper part of the organ accompaniment.

The melody is the Lekhah Dodi variant of the Syrian Jews, with Arabic-influenced quarter tones based on the maqām *rāst*:[113]

$$G^1 \ A^{3/4} \ \text{B-flat}^{3/4} \ C^1 \ D^{3/4} \ \text{E-flat}^{3/4} \ F^{\#3/4} \ G$$

Rhythm and meter reveal certain parallels to the *īqā'āt ayyūb* (figure 4.9b) (upward note stems indicate accented beats; downward note stems, unaccented beats).

As microtones can hardly be realized on organ, Schalit adapts Lekhah Dodi to Western tonality and meter. In the postlude it appears in C with accidentals B-flat and E-flat and in 4/4 time. The subsequent parts take up further sections of the *Freitagabend-Liturgie*, mostly those referring to Ashkenazic tradition: The broken triads over a pedal point in measures 16–21 are reminiscent of "Adonoj moloch" (no. 5, measures 9–12). Measures 22–29, however, are unrelated to any of the preceding parts of the music for the service, although Schalit uses similar motivic development techniques as before:

FIGURE 4.9A. Abraham Idelsohn, *HOM*, vol. 4, no. 3, measures 1–8.

Come, my beloved, to greet the Bride—the Sabbath let us welcome.

This short section plays with a motive (C–D–E-flat–F), which points to the modality of the Adonai Malakh shtayger. This is reinforced by the final cadence (a resumption of the final cadence of "Lechu nerananoh," no. 2): Instead of the progression subdominant–dominant–tonic, the cadence leads from the sixth degree (A minor with fourth) and the seventh degree (which, because it is common in Adonai Malakh, is harmonized with a major chord) to the tonic C major. If the different parts of the *Freitagabend-Liturgie* are clearly separated, they are united in the postlude; this, however, is accomplished by musical development.

Although the notation of the postlude indicates C major, Schalit uses every opportunity to break out of major-minor tonality. He achieves this by a modal harmonization of the shtayger (in this case, Adonai Malakh). With respect to the harmonization, he consciously avoids nineteenth-century harmonic idiom, forging instead his own, less conventional harmonic language that often incorporates moderate, controlled dissonance within a basically (if sometimes gently pungent) diatonic framework.

Although the postlude does not draw on traditional elements of ḥazzanut, the melodic-diatonic character is still prevalent. Five changes of meter and frequently shifting rhythms, accomplished by the composition of different sections within the piece, create the recitative character Schalit seeks.

In the postlude, the relationship between text and music is in the background: Since the excerpt from "Schema" (no. 8, measures 7 and 14) is not connected to any text passage, the organ accompaniment only imitates the

FIGURE 4.9B.

rich coloratura and melismatic-improvisational elements of ḥazzanut that are not found in the cantor's part of the model. The excerpts from "Adonoj moloch" (no. 5, measures 9–12) and "Lechu nerananoh" (no. 2) are not connected to concrete text either but likewise resemble cantorial improvisations, though it is the organ that performs them. Moreover, while the iambic-anapestic rhythm typical of the Hebrew language is prevalent in the vocal originals, the organ part, since it does not correspond to any text, does not convey the poetic meter.

Schalit's Nachspiel represents the ongoing changes in the organ music of Jewish communities in two respects. First, because it is as suitable for concert use as for worship, it goes beyond mere Gebrauchsmusik. Second, Schalit is the first organ music composer to make extensive use of Idelsohn's *HOM* by combining the music of the various Jewish ethnicities. He thus distanced himself from the adapted sources "normalized" to the scales and rhythms of common European practice that were created and further arranged by his predecessors (Deutsch, Sulzer, and Lewandowski) toward the creation of a new, authentically Jewish genre. In this he was following the trends of his day, for in the early twentieth century, music of the Middle Eastern and Yemenite Jews was regarded as especially "authentic."[114] The source of the piece's modernity is this quest for authenticity rather than any "modern invention."

It is not possible to compare the style and musical language of Schalit's postlude directly with other organ pieces of its time since it was not conceived as an autonomous work but rather as a collection of carefully selected fragments of organ accompaniments to the vocal parts of the *Freitagabend-Liturgie*, although its nonhomogenous character is completely intentional. There are, however, consistent style features in the rather elementary use of rhythm and the predominance of homophonic over contrapuntal texture. Dissonant diatonic chords alternate with open fifth and triads, often extended by a fourth or sixth. Here, Schalit shows a typically early twentieth-century renunciation of Romantic harmony in favor of freer, more modern structures.[115] At times Schalit departs from the tonal center, especially beginning with measure 12. The fluid formation of melody and the use of non-European, especially Eastern, musical material are also in accord with the taste of other early twentieth-century composers, especially Claude Debussy, Olivier Messiaen, and Giacomo Puccini. With regard to meter, it is evident that Schalit does not impose an artificial unity on the different sections extracted from the liturgical setting. Instead of working with an overall metric pattern and a single tonal center, he largely preserves the individual character of the various sections. The resulting changes of meter in the postlude lead to a certain asymmetry that composers have favored since around 1900.[116]

Schalit's tonal language and style take no inspiration from Romantic and Caecilian models, striving instead for a new style that marks the arrival of Jewish music into modernity. Nevertheless, the work arguably has a nineteenth-century antecedent in the potpourri compositions of the various nationalist schools, which strung together folkloristic elements, first in miniature forms and later in symphonies and other large-scale forms.

In the early twentieth century, different directions are prevalent in the organ music of Jewish composers, as the compositions of Hugo Adler and Heinrich Schalit evince. Analogous to nation-state building in the nineteenth and twentieth centuries, the Zionist, or national Jewish, movement also inspired composers. The concept of national musics corresponding to the developing nation-states of central and eastern Europe, from Smetana and Musorgsky in the mid-nineteenth century to Bartók and Kodály in the early twentieth century, also affected Jewish composers who were aware of the evolving Zionist movement. In Russia from 1908 to 1918 a Society for Jewish Folk Music, with branches in both Saint Petersburg and Moscow, began collecting traditional melodies with the intention of using them as material for art songs and chamber music; in the decade of its existence the organization presented more than twelve hundred concerts for an audience that overwhelmingly consisted of Zionists. Moreover, members of the society were among those who founded the Jewish School of composition in Russia in the 1920s.[117]

In German-speaking central Europe, too, Jewish composers (even if they were not in contact with Judaism as a religion) created art music that incorporated Jewish tradition and could be performed in both synagogues and concert halls. Jewish folk music or pieces from Idelsohn's compilation served as a resource for these compositions, which to some extent also infiltrated organ music.[118]

A revival of polyphony took place as well, as exemplified in Hugo Adler (and probably realized in his missing Toccata and Fugue). Heinrich Schalit, on the other hand, focused more on transparent melodic qualities in music, which had been neglected due to the Romantics' emphasis on harmony—the vertical-harmonic approach simplified and obscured the rich melismas of Eastern synagogue music. With the heightened interest in extra-European music and its new accessibility through Idelsohn's collection, more exotic colors were combined with modern compositional techniques to establish an "authentic" connection between modern composition and traditional Jewish music.

These tendencies could have been a starting point for the development of a modern Jewish music, including a new organ repertoire. However, the political developments that were beginning in Central Europe in 1933 gave organ music a different and quite unforeseeable position within the Jewish communities: Organ music would thus have to adapt to the altered conditions.

Departure and Destruction: Organ Music in the "Spiritual Ghetto"

When Arno Nadel, in his last letter before being deported to the Buchenwald concentration camp, invoked God's protection over "Holy Germany, the wise nation of poets and thinkers," he did not and probably could not foresee the consequences of his patriotism: his death in Auschwitz in 1943. Nadel was convinced that, after its "bloody detours and mistakes," Germany would eventually find its way back to "freedom of the spirit and the noble arts."[119] His apparently naive and, at the same time, tragic attitude toward Germany reflects the complexity of Jewish identity there in the early twentieth century, when German Jews sought to pursue and affirm Germanness and Jewishness as two autonomous and yet mutually stimulating intellectual and cultural realities.[120] This development took on different forms, one of which resulted in the conviction with which so many German Jews served in the First World War, only to end little more than a decade later in 1933, when Hitler came to power.

The Nazi seizure of power initiated a wave of forced conformity or *Gleichschaltung*, a process by which the regime successively established a system of totalitarian control over the individual and tight coordination over all aspects of society, commerce, and cultural life, eventually also affecting musical life. The independence of all associations, schools, universities, and theaters was curtailed, and art, education, and science henceforth had to conform to the principles of National Socialist ideology.

The *Entjudung* ["dejewification"] and destruction of Jewish culture in Nazi Germany was a gradual process conducted in five successive phases, beginning with a series of highly publicized acts to ostracize prominent Jewish figures and their friends through defamation, boycott, and cultural ghettoization between 1933 and 1935; legal dismemberment and dissimilation between 1935 and 1938; and the destruction of the economic basis of existence through the "bureaucratic exclusion" of all Jews;[121] the total disfranchisement of the Jüdischer Kulturbund between 1939 and 1941; and the "Final Solution" (1941–1945), the Nazis' plan to annihilate and exterminate the Jewish people.

The campaign against Jewish musicians began soon after the Nazi takeover, when organized mobs disrupted public concerts given by musicians deemed potentially hostile to the new regime. The first official step in the destruction of Jewish musical life and the elimination of Jewish musicians from public culture was undertaken on April 7, 1933, when the Nazi government promulgated the so-called Law for the Restoration of the Civil Service, which called for the dismissal of Jewish employees in the public realm, exempting at first only a very few, such as veterans of the First World War (by the fall of 1935 even these exemptions were by and large cancelled). The law applied to Jews who worked in cultural institutions and in the arts and extended to state-employed musicians of Jewish origin who, by the spring of 1933, began losing their tenured positions. Many private and semipublic institutions in the Third Reich took advantage of these regulations to rid themselves of unwanted Jewish members. Abruptly thousands of artists of Jewish origin were unemployed, and thus began the exodus of Jewish scholars, actors, writers, and musicians. Those who did not emigrate attempted to reorganize under the new regime.

Upon losing his position as professor at the Staatliche Akademische Hochschule für Musik and artistic director of the Berlin Städtische Oper in Charlottenburg, neurologist, musicologist, and conductor Kurt Singer (1885–1944), together with two employees, initiated a project to provide help and give his two thousand unemployed colleagues new opportunities. In May 1933 they presented a proposal for a Kulturbund deutscher Juden [Cultural League of German Jews] in Berlin to the National Socialist authorities. The plan called for a theater, an orchestra, an opera company, and further cultural activities for the benefit of unemployed artists of Jewish origin. Only two months later this concept was accepted on three conditions: that the word "German" be omitted from the league's name, that the organizers and the audience be exclusively Jewish, and that the events be closed to the general public. The National Socialists all too gladly approved the endeavor not only because it suited their own plan for the cultural ghettoization of the Jewish people but also because it would present the Jews as a sheltered minority, which would be useful for the purposes of propaganda abroad.[122]

In the fall of that year, the first so-called closed performances took place in Berlin. During its first six months the Kulturbund organized 313 events in Berlin alone and many more in the region around the capital. This example motivated the founding of similar organizations in the Rhineland (Westphalia), southwestern Germany (Bavaria), and elsewhere.[123]

After the emergency situation created by the Nazis, the events of the Kulturbund guaranteed Jewish artists and cultural figures an art scene, even if segregated, of their own. They initially carried on the existing German concert tradition and used the general repertoire of Western art music. Even though the performers and audiences were suddenly isolated, they continued with the repertoire they had known for decades and thus remained in contact with the Western musical culture of Europe. As the repertoire could be chosen freely, at least at first, the Kulturbund did not introduce a specifically "Jewish" program. However, this was to change when the censors banned them from performing the works of "German" composers. (Händel's music was permitted as one of a few exceptions, probably because of his affinity to England and preference for biblical subjects of the Old Testament.[124])

The isolation of Jews within German society inevitably led to an increased consciousness of Jewish identity and awoke the desire for "Jewish experiences" in the concert halls of the Kulturbund. Although the works of non-Jewish composers from outside the German-speaking world could still be played, works by Jewish musicians began to play a much greater role in the Kulturbund events, if in the end only for the survival of the organization. The question of "Jewishness" in art led to a crisis within the Kulturbund that threatened its very existence, which the leadership tried to avert by holding the 1936 conference on the subject of Jewish music (see chapter 1).[125] Even though the National Socialists had forced this development, it had unforeseen positive consequences on the arts by leading to a substantial enrichment of the repertoire (especially with regard to the rediscovered Jewish folk music, synagogue music, and the related works of contemporary Jewish composers). This development was reinforced by the music committee of the Reichsverband jüdischer Kulturbünde in Deutschland, which announced a competition for the advancement of contemporary Jewish music, open to all composers of Jewish heritage who lived in Germany and abroad.[126] At the same time, by inadvertently catering to the National Socialist *Judenpolitik*, which amounted to the suppression of all assimilatory endeavors, it also supported Zionist and national-Jewish activities.[127] The musicians were all too well aware of this dichotomy, as Herbert Fromm recalled in an interview with Eliott Kahn: "Like many German Jews I became more Jewish after 1933, when the Nazis came to power. I found that I belonged somewhere else—I was not German anymore. And I felt that there are two cultures, German and Jewish: my Jewish strings began to vibrate. . . . Very soon I adjusted to the new situation because every German became so disgusting to me. So I decided to come home to my own people."[128]

Fromm's experiences illustrate the way in which, after 1933, Jewish identity took on a double character, defined simultaneously as the Other and the self. For those Jews who considered themselves to be primarily German, the National Socialists' emphasis on the Jewish side of German-Jewish identity led them to reformulate their identity no longer as "Germans of Jewish faith" but rather as "Jews of German faith."[129] In the end, Jewish artists had no alternative to the Kulturbund, and although it provided at least prospect of employment and subsistence, the musicians in particular felt that they had been sent back into a new ghetto, "a spiritual ghetto of educated people."[130]

These musical developments under the Nazis also affected the role of the synagogue organ—although synagogue concerts rarely belonged to the framework of Kulturbund events but rather competed with them.[131] But from the early twentieth century, organ music had been an integral part of concerts organized by or held within Jewish communities, among them benefit events that took place in the synagogue. In the 1930s, concerts with organ music continued alongside the Kulturbund events, notably the benefits organized by the Jüdische Winterhilfe (a Jewish organization founded in the autumn of 1935 to help Jews in need get through the winter by providing them with food, medicine, and heating assistance) and the hybrid of religious service and musical presentation known as *Morgenfeier* [morning celebration],[132] a devotional and paraliturgical event that included hymns and other religious music, Bible readings, and spoken reflections on religious subjects.

In addition to these concerts, the Kulturbund organizations presented performances that featured organ music as well, in synagogues or more secular venues, including concert tours to distant and mostly nonurban communities. Ludwig Altman recounts his experiences as an active organist in the Kulturbund: "Several times I was sent to *Kulturfahrten* — that means tours, to smaller Jewish communities, usually with a singer or a recitant and an accompanist who would play the organ or the piano or the reed organ. I went on many of those, particularly in Prussia (the largest German state)."[133]

In this way, the competition between the Kulturbund and other concert-sponsoring organizations intensified the process by which the organ's function in the synagogue developed far beyond the provision of mere Gebrauchsmusik. If the repertoire initially consisted largely of classical pieces (e.g., preludes and toccatas by Bach and Buxtehude; compositions by Georg Friedrich Händel and Léon Boëllmann), it gradually grew to incorporate works by Jewish composers, often created specifically for these occasions. The list of concert performances (table 4.4) organized by the Kulturbund branches and other organizations in Berlin, Frankfurt am Main, and Hamburg as reported in the Jewish community's newspapers and journals between 1927 and 1941 is a representative selection of the numerous events that took place during the 1930s and provides insights into the rich and diverse repertoire of organ music played at the time.

In spite of the preponderance of classical organ music, a new repertoire was slowly emerging in consequence of a changing Jewish identity in music

TABLE 4.4.   Organ Concerts in Jewish Communities, 1927–1941

Concert Programs with Organ Solo	
Synagogue Concert May 1927 Munich Synagogue *Fantasie in g-Moll über Kol Nidrei* by Joseph Ziegler Robert Osenbrunner, organ (*Das Jüdische Echo*, May 15, 1927)	Concert for the Best of the Welfare Insti- tutions of the Jewish Community Dec. 7, 1931 Synagogue, Prinzregentenstraße, Berlin Erwin Jospe, organ (*Gemeindeblatt*, Dec. 6, 1931)
Lecture and Music Nov. 20,1932 Great Synagogue, Frankfurt am Main Rudolf Schucht, organ (*FIG* 11, no. 3 [November 1932])	Commemoration n.d. Jüdische Toynbee-Halle (Arnold Lazarus-Halle), Frankfurt am Main Siegfried Würzburger, organ (*FIG* 11, no. 4 [December 1932])
Benefit Concert Mar. 18, 1933 Venue unknown Siegfried Würzburger, organ (*FIG* 11, no. 7 [March 1933])	Concert for Artists in Need Sept. 11, 1933 Breslau Synagogue Prelude and Fugue in A Minor by Johann Sebastian Bach Erich Schäffer, organ (*CV-Ztg.*, Sept. 20, 1933)
Concert for Artists in Need n.d. Breslau Synagogue Organ Sonata in C Minor by Felix Mendelssohn-Bartholdy; Concerto for Organ and Orchestra in F Major by Georg Friedrich Händel Erich Schäffer, organ (*CV-Ztg.*, Nov. 30, 1933)	Consecration Hour for Funding of Improvements to the Synagogue's Facilities Dec. 14, 1933 Westend Synagogue, Frankfurt am Main Toccata and Fugue in D Minor by Johann Sebastian Bach Siegfried Würzburger, organ (*FIG* 12, no. 4 [December 1933])
Synagogue Concert n.d. Westend Synagogue, Frankfurt am Main Toccata and Fugue in D Minor by Johann Sebastian Bach Siegfried Würzburger, organ (*CV-Ztg.*, Dec. 21,1933)	Concert for the Winter Aid of the Jewish Community in Berlin January 1934 New Synagogue, Oranienburger Straße, Berlin Organ compositions by Johann Sebastian Bach, Georg Friedrich Händel, and Johann Mattheson Artur Zepke, organ (*Schild*, Feb. 2, 1934)

continued

TABLE 4.4. (Continued)

Concert Programs with Organ Solo

Concert for the Jewish Winter Aid
March 1934
Synagogue, Lindenstraße, Berlin
Prelude and Fugue in B-flat Major by
Johann Sebastian Bach; Organ Concerto
by Antonio Vivaldi
Ludwig Altmann, organ
(*CV-Ztg.*, Mar. 8, 1934)

Sacred Concert
n.d.
Great Synagogue, Wiesbaden
Passacaglia and Fugue for Organ by
Siegfried Würzburger (world premiere);
Prelude for Organ by Max Wolff
Erich Wolff, organ
(*FIG* 12, no. 8 [April 1934])

First Concert of a Series
November 1934
Synagogue, Lindenstraße, Berlin
Organ Sonata in C Minor by Felix
Mendelssohn-Bartholdy
Alexander Weinbaum, organ
(*CV-Ztg.*, Nov. 1, 1934)

First Event of "Freude im Winter"
December 1934
Synagogue, Fasanenstraße, Berlin
Organ compositions by Johann Sebastian
Bach
Ludwig Altmann, organ

Benefit Concert
Dec. 12, 1934
Saalbau, Frankfurt am Main
Variationen für Orgel über "Moaus-zur"
by Siegfried Würzburger; premieres
played from manuscript
Erika Schleyer and Siegfried
Würzburger, organ
(*FIG* 13, no. 4 [December 1934])

Sixth Orchestral Concert
Mar. 28, 1935
Westend Synagogue, Frankfurt am Main
Organ Concerto no. 4 in F Major by
Georg Friedrich Händel
Siegfried Würzburger, organ
(*FIG* 13, no. 7 [March 1935])

Musical Consecration Hour
Oct. 15, 1935
Westend Synagogue, Frankfurt am Main
Largo from the Trio Sonata in D Minor,
BWV 1036, by Johann Sebastian Bach;
Fugue for Organ by Herbert Fromm
Herbert Fromm, organ
(*FIG* 14, no. 1 [October 1935])

Concert on the Occasion of the 25th
Anniversary of the Westend Synagogue
in Frankfurt
n.d.
Westend Synagogue, Frankfurt am Main
Fugue in G Minor
Herbert Fromm, organ
(*Schild*, Oct. 25, 1935)

Concert of the Dresden Jewish
Community
n.d.
Synagogue, Dresden
"Jewish Preludes" by Hugo Leichtentritt
and Arno Nadel
Hermann Schwarz, organ
(*CV-Ztg.*, Feb. 6, 1936)

Chamber Music Evening (Winter Aid
of the Jewish Community)
February 1936
Synagogue, Prinzregentenstraße, Berlin
Prelude for Organ by Gustav Merkel
Alfred Mai, organ
(*CV-Ztg.*, Feb. 20, 1936)

14th Event, "Freude im Winter"
March 1936
Friedenstempel, Berlin
Orgelvorspiel über hebräische Motive by
Arno Nadel (world premiere)
Hermann Schwarz, organ
(*Gemeindeblatt*, Mar. 22, 1936)

"Ernst Wolff (baritone) and Herbert
Fromm (organ) successfully gave a con-
cert together in New York. The program
presented organ and vocal music by
Bach, Händel, and Herbert Fromm."
(*FIG* 14, no. 9 [June 1936])

Third Afternoon of Lights at the Jewish
Reform Congregation in Berlin
1936
Berlin
Organ compositions by Max Reger
Ludwig Altmann, organ
(*CV-Ztg.*, Feb. 6, 1936)

Fourth Afternoon of Lights at the Jewish
Reform Congregation in Berlin
February 1936
Berlin
Organ compositions by Max Reger
Ludwig Altmann, organ
(*CV-Ztg.*, Mar. 5, 1936)

Last Concert for the Winter Aid of the
Jewish Community in Berlin
April 1936
Synagogue, Fasanenstraße, Berlin
Organ compositions by Alexandre Guil-
mant and Ludwig Altmann
Ludwig Altmann, organ
(*CV-Ztg.*, Apr. 9, 1936)

Winter Aid of the Jewish Community in
Berlin (performance repeated on
Dec. 20, 1936, at Friedenstempel,
Halensee)
October 1936
New Synagogue, Oranienburger Straße,
Berlin
Freitagabend-Liturgie by Jakob Weinberg
(German premiere)
Erwin Jospe, organ
(*CV-Ztg.*, Oct. 29, 1936)

continued

TABLE 4.4. (Continued)

Concert Programs with Organ Solo

First Afternoon of Lights at the Jewish
Reform Congregation for the
Winter Aid
October 1936
Berlin
Organ preludes by Johann Sebastian
Bach
Carl Stabernack, organ
(*CV-Ztg.*, Nov. 5, 1936; *Gemeindeblatt*,
Nov. 15, 1936)

Festive Concert as Early Celebration of
Ḥanukkah
Nov. 11, 1936
Saalbau, Frankfurt am Main
Paraphrase zu "Kol nidre" und "Moaus zur"
by Siegfried Würzburger
Siegfried Würzburger, organ
(*FIG* 15, no. 2 [November 1936])

Sacred Consecration Hour on Ḥanukkah
Dec. 6, 1936
Westend Synagogue, Frankfurt am Main
Siegfried Würzburger, organ
(*FIG* 15, no. 3 [December 1936])

Concert of the Künstlerhilfe Orchestra
December 1936
Berlin
Organ Concerto in F Major by Georg
Friedrich Händel (two movements);
organ compositions by Felix
Mendelssohn-Bartholdy
Ludwig Altmann, organ
(*CV-Ztg.*, Dec. 24, 1936)

Third Afternoon of Lights at the Jewish
Reform Congregation
January 1937
Friedenstempel, Berlin
Chaconne by Dietrich Buxtehude
Hermann Schwarz, organ
(*CV-Ztg.*, Jan. 14, 1937; *Gemeindeblatt*,
Jan. 24, 1937)

Concert of the Jüdische Sängerknaben
January 1937
Berlin
Organ and choral music by Salamone
Rossi
Erwin Jospe, organ
(*CV-Ztg.*, Feb. 4, 1937)

Concert of the Temple Choir
Mar. 1, 1937
Tempel, Obernstraße, Hamburg
Organ compositions by Leon Kornitzer
and Max Reger
Herman Cerini, organ
(*MJKH* 2, no. 3 [March 1937])

Consecration Hour on Ḥanukkah
Nov. 28, 1937
Great Synagogue, Frankfurt am Main
Orgel-Variationen über "Moaus zur" by
Siegfried Würzburger
Martha Sommer, organ
(*FIG* 16, no. 2 [November 1937])

Commemoration of the Fallen
n.d.
Westend Synagogue, Frankfurt am Main
Siegfried Würzburger, organ
(*FIG* 16, no. 2 [November 1937])

Concert (Spiritual Winter Aid) of the
Künstlerhilfe Orchestra
Feb. 26, 1938
New Synagogue, Oranienburger Straße,
Berlin
Concerto for Organ and Orchestra no. 4
in F Minor by Georg Friedrich Händel
Paul Lichtenstern, organ

Afternoon of Lights at the Jewish
Reform Congregation
April 1938
Reform Congregation, Berlin
Suite gothique by Léon Boëllmann
Richard Altmann, organ
(*Gemeindeblatt*, Apr. 17, 1938)

Morning Celebration
September 1940
Synagogue, Lützowstraße, Berlin
Prelude by Girolamo Frescobaldi; Organ
Sonata by Felix Mendelssohn-Bartholdy
(two movements)
Erwin Rosenthal, organ
(Kulturbund)

Festive Hour (Welcoming of the New
Neighbors)
Feb. 8, 1936
Westend Synagogue, Frankfurt am Main
Siegfried Würzburger, organ
(*FIG* 16, no. 5 [February 1938])

Benefit Concert
Apr. 27, 1938
Westend Synagogue, Frankfurt am Main
Organ Sonata in C Minor by Felix
Mendelssohn-Bartholdy; Prelude by Max
Wolff; Fugue by Herbert Fromm
Siegfried Würzburger and Martha
Sommer, organ
(*FIG* 16, no. 7 [April 1938])

Orgel-Abend mit Orchester
Tempel, Obernstraße, Hamburg
May 24, 1938
Concerto for Organ in F Major by Georg
Friedrich Händel; organ compositions by
Léon Boëllmann, François Couperin,
Girolamo Frescobaldi,
and Jean-Philippe Rameau
Hermann Cerini, organ
(*MJKH* 3, no. 5 [May 1938])

Morning Celebration
1941
Synagogue, Lützowstraße, Berlin
Canzone for organ by Girolamo
Frescobaldi
Horst Faerber, organ
(*Jüd. Na.*, 1941)

and the constraints imposed on the playing of more familiar repertoire. The Jewish composers of organ music, confronted with their own heritage, created pieces based on Jewish subjects and themes that would unequivocally show a tie to Jewish musical tradition. Among these composers were Arno Nadel, Siegfried Würzburger, and Hans Samuel, each of whom chose a unique form and compositional technique to create Jewishness in organ music.

REINVENTION OF AUTHENTICITY

The musical development in organ music that began with Louis Lewandowski and his contemporaries and extended to the works of Heinrich Schalit in some ways continued in the work of Arno Nadel. Born in Vilna, Poland, Nadel began his musical education in Königsberg under Eduard Birnbaum and Robert Schwalm. In 1895 he enrolled in the Jüdische Lehrerbildungsanstalt [Jewish Teacher Training Institute] in Berlin and upon graduation settled there as educator and choirmaster at the Kottbuser Ufer synagogue. Nadel's talents were highly versatile: He became a collector of Jewish music and between 1923 and 1938 compiled an anthology of synagogue music, as well as eastern European Jewish folk music. Among his many other activities in the musical life of Berlin, Nadel was also an accomplished painter, poet, and playwright and was praised by art historian Max Osborn as a "gifted human being of blessed creativity."[134]

Nadel's organ compositions and their cultural and social impact attest to his artistic versatility. While the organ music of his time was generally composed for one function or another as Gebrauchsmusik or, with greater artistic ambitions in mind, for concert performance, his works fulfill several concurrent purposes: They have an educational dimension in having been written for *Gesprächskonzerte* [lecture-recitals] presented to various congregations, in which he introduced Jewish communities to organ music on a theoretical and practical level, thus contributing to its deeper integration in their shared Jewish life.

Nadel's music—for the most part, intricate arrangements of Jewish musical motives—is centered on traditional synagogue songs, biblical cantillations, and Jewish folk music, and all three aspects are manifested in his compositions for organ solo as well. He published most of his organ compositions as musical supplements to his scholarly articles in the *Gemeindeblatt der jüdischen Gemeinde zu Berlin* and introduced them (along with works composed by others and in other genres) and musicological commentary to wider audiences in his lecture-recitals. Together with Hans Samuel, Nadel advocated the public dissemination of organ music, as he details in a letter to Samuel from

1931: "How are you faring with the society for the cultivation of Jewish music that you discussed in your letter? Would it be possible for me to give a lecture in December, in Essen? Perhaps with your support? You would perform something by yourself and something by me, perhaps the organ piece[135] that I am sending along with this letter, and that I hope you will kindly assess in your next letter."[136]

A typical example of Nadel's concert commentaries appears in a manuscript in the collection of his papers held in the Gratz College Archives in Philadelphia. He then prepared for a performance in Berlin sometime in the 1920s, with Max Janowski at the organ and other performers, at which one of his own compositions, the *Orgelvorspiel (oder Zwischenspiel) für die Hohen Feiertage (Motive "Bor'chu" und "Hammelech")*, was played. He explains that the prelude has two main themes, "a kind of Ha-Malakh" of the High Holidays and a second, more general musical theme for the evening services of the High Holidays. According to Nadel, his goal will be accomplished if it fulfills two important tasks: to contribute to the aestheticization of Jewish liturgy and to legitimize the organ as a synagogue instrument.

Nadel achieved a deeper integration of organ music in the Jewish communities through not only lecture-recitals but also his articles on Jewish music, which were published with musical supplements. The *Orgelvorspiel (oder Zwischenspiel) für die drei Trauerwochen*, for example, served as a musical supplement to his article "Melodien um Tischah b'aw," published in the *Gemeindeblatt der jüdischen Gemeinde zu Berlin* 9 (August 1, 1924); the *Orgelvorspiel (oder Zwischenspiel) für die Hohen Feiertage (Motive "Bor'chu" und "Hammelech")* was the musical addendum to the article "Hauptmelodien der Hohen Feiertage"; and the *Orgelvorspiel (oder Zwischenspiel) für das Wochenfest* was published together with the short essay "Schowuos-Melodien" in the *Gemeindeblatt der jüdischen Gemeinde zu Berlin* 10 (September 5, 1924). However, a number of other compositions were never printed and remain only as manuscripts, among them the *Passacaglia für Orgel über "Wadonaj pakad es ssarah" (Toravorlesung am Neujahrsfest)*, which Nadel completed in February 1933, and the *Orgelvorspiel über hebräische Motive*, which premiered in 1936. In the following section I examine the former in greater detail.

"Ve-Adonai pakad et Sarah" [And God remembered Sarah] is the opening verse of the Torah reading for the first day of Rosh Ha-Shanah. While traditional congregations usually use a large portion of the text (Genesis 21:1–34), the German (and American) Reform congregations that have not abandoned the traditional Torah readings altogether substitute this passage with a shorter reading from the Torah (Genesis 22:1–19).[137] That Nadel uses the cantillation of the traditional reading as a basis for his organ composition is somewhat unusual: One would expect that he would follow the Reform customs, especially when composing organ music, but since the nineteenth century, the cantillation of the Torah has been practiced in only a very few Reform congregations in Germany. The Reformers believed that cantillation and biblical chant were no longer valid since both were a "post-biblical invention."[138] Besides, the Reform movement found cantillation to be antiquated and unattractive. The elimination of certain elements of Jewish music from worship was part of a larger movement in which the Reform Jews sought to aestheticize their service and make it more palatable to the younger generation. However, this did not happen without consequences, as Idelsohn points out: "The Reformers, and notably the rabbis, apart from their endeavor to emancipate the Jew and make him a modern European human being by stripping off all the medieval and Oriental elements still clinging to him, were deeply interested in retaining the youth which started to drift away from their people and culture and to become absorbed by the Christian environment. In their honest effort they wanted to reconstruct Judaism and to beautify it according to the model they had before them."[139]

Although Idelsohn's remarks simplify the complex relationship Reform congregations had with past (medieval) and Sephardic (Oriental) Jewish traditions, they provide one reason that cantillation was seldom practiced in some nineteenth-century Reform congregations: As an "authentic" Jewish cultural artifact, it was not in line with the current fashion of synagogue songs that followed the Protestant models. Chanting the Bible no longer corresponded to the aesthetics of "assimilated" Jews.

That Nadel and other composers reintroduced musical elements that had been abandoned less than a century earlier and even connected them with organ music suggests a new and different understanding of Jewish music oriented toward older traditions. In this context it is important to remember that, from the 1920s to the 1940s, the Middle Ages generally enjoyed a revival and played an important role in the general history of Western music.[140] If there is indeed a link between the reception of medieval music in Jewish and Western art music, it may be due to the ongoing process of assimilation; even in this instance, when turning toward their own musical traditions, Jewish musicians cannot deny structural assimilation.

The custom of chanting the Bible can be traced back to the first millennium of the Common Era, when the Masoretes introduced the te'amim (diacritic symbols that annotate the Hebrew Bible text for the purpose of cantillation). They serve as instructions for cantillation by depicting the syntactic structure of the underlying text and indicating the word stress. Thus cantillation emphasizes or enhances the Word to the benefit of its interpretation.[141]

The importance of the text in cantillation and its demarcation from other forms of vocal music making is expressed in the name itself—in the Hebrew, as well as the Arabic, linguistic usage. Cantillation—very different from any other vocal music presented in the synagogue—is not explicitly regarded as music or song but as reading. For this reason it did not have to be included in the Jewish prohibitions against instrumental and certain types of vocal music.

Each cantillation contains a series of typical melodic turns—a principle that can also be observed in the formalized melodic ordering of the maqām in Koranic chanting—that are related to the text in a specific way by being assigned to explicit places in the syntax and especially the main sections of sentences.[142] Neither the rhythm of cantillation nor the intervals used have led to a unified cantillation system; because rhythm is not fixed, it is subject to individual interpretation. The cantillation systems are orally transmitted; thus many different local variants are heard in Europe, North Africa, the Middle East, and Central Asia.[143] Only in some Ashkenazic communities were structures developed to assign each accent mark a distinct melodic formation.

The title of Nadel's Passacaglia suggests that the piece is based on the cantillation of the Torah on Rosh Ha-Shanah. Moreover, since it seems to be drawn from the Ashkenazic practices, the cantillation motives he uses as the main theme can be loosely determined. In view of the fact that Nadel belonged to different congregations in the course of his life (initially in Vilna [most likely Orthodox], then in Königsberg, and finally in Berlin), it is not possible to determine where he familiarized himself with cantillation and what particular style he knew. Nonetheless, the motives he used in the Passacaglia are identifiable as belonging to the Job cantillation.

At first it may appear surprising that on Rosh Ha-Shanah the Torah is associated with the book of Job rather than the general Pentateuch melody. For the Ashkenazim, the custom of having a unique cantillation for the Pentateuch on Rosh Ha-Shanah and Yom Kippur is in itself noteworthy, and the reason for this may lie in earlier historical developments.[144] The Job cantillation is so called because it is used in Sephardic practice only for the public reading of the book of Job, following the book of Lamentation, on Tishah Be-Av, the traditional day of mourning for the destruction of the temples in Jerusalem. This is how the cantillation of the book of Job has been transmitted up to the present day. Ashkenazic Jews, however, do not read the book of Job publicly and employ this cantillation for the Torah reading on the High Holidays.

The Job cantillation is based on the scale F–G–A–B-flat, which is almost identical to the Ionic or modified Mixolydian scale. The modality takes on the character of major, but its tetrachordal structure prevents a true feeling of major tonality. The following cantillation marks or accents (table 4.5) are characteristic for this Torah cantillation:[145]

The te'amim are not randomly joined but are subject to a specific order. Common combinations are as follows: merekha–tippeḥa–munaḥ–etnaḥta; merekha–tippeḥa–merekha–sof pasuk; and munaḥ–telishah ketanah.[146] The musical motives and themes in Nadel's Passacaglia are partly based on these common accent groupings.

Analysis of the Passacaglia für Orgel über "Wadonaj Pakad es Ssarah"

Although Nadel refers to his organ composition as a passacaglia, its form (with variations built on an ostinato bass line) is not stringently realized. In fact, the piece has neither a true basso ostinato nor a developing variation in the strict sense even though the first eight measures, which present five long, drawn-out notes (G–C–B-flat–G-flat–F–F-sharp solo; only in measures 4 and 7–8 do chords appear in the descant voices) in the pedal, evoke the impression of an ostinato. The ambitus of these eight measures is small, spanning only the interval of a fifth. During the next twelve measures (measures 9–21) this ambitus is expanded in the upper parts. The following short sixteenth-note runs, bundled into four-note increments in the range of a (diminished) fifth and later fourth (reminiscent of the very first interval of the piece, C–G), are presented without accompaniment. Then, in measure 12, a chromatically descending pedal line joins before (in measure 14) a quotation of the Job cantillation appears in the lowest part, played *manualiter*. Nadel chose the combination of accents shown in figure 4.10.

A comparison of the sequence of merekha–tippeḥa–munaḥ–etnaḥta (also known as the etnaḥta group) with the first eight introductory measures reveals their function: The etnaḥta group represents the core notes and intervals of the composition as a whole as a kind of base frame of the cantillation. Nadel continues in measure 16 with a rather unusual combination of accents (figure 4.11).

The common structure of the te'amim in the sof pasuk group is disturbed by the interpolation of munaḥ. Nadel may have had reasons for using such an accent combination, as the succession of the te'amim in the second motive creates a connection to the first motive. Moreover, through the insertion of munaḥ, the second motive becomes a variant of the first motive. The cantillation is accompanied by sixteenth-note passages whose individual motives have an ambitus mostly of a fifth. In measure 19 the motivic material changes: Scalar sextuplets accompany the cantillation melody. The next five measures (22–26) present another common accent combination (figure 4.12).

TABLE 4.5. Te'amim [Accents] Prevalent in Arno Nadel's *Passacaglia für Orgel über "Wadonaj Pakad es Ssarah" (Toravorlesung am Neujahrsfest)*

Ta'am	Name of Accent	Origin and Meaning	Associated Motive on High Holidays
\	*tippeḥa* (disjunctive)	Aramaic for descending	
⌐	*munaḥ* (conjunctive)	Hebrew for sustaining or resting	
		or	
'⌐	*munaḥ legarmeh* (disjunctive)	Indepedent munaḥ	
∧	*etnaḥta* (disjunctive)	Aramaic for resting point or pause	
⌣	*merekha* (conjunctive)	Aramaic for prolonging or lengthening	
|	*sof pasuk* or *siluk* (disjunctive)	Hebrew for end of verse	
.	*revia'* (disjunctive)	Aramaic for quarter (referring to four short notes)	
॰	*telishah ketanah* (conjunctive)	Hebrew for shorter protraction (postpositive accent)	

FIGURE 4.10. Arno Nadel, *Passacaglia für Orgel über "Wadonaj Pakad es Ssarah" (Toravorlesung am Neujahrsfest)*, MS (1933), measures 14–15 (first motive).

This motive appears four times successively: It is first introduced in unison (measure 22), followed by a sequence (measure 23), and then continuously ascends on higher pitches, accompanied by a chromatically descending pedal line—reminiscent of measure 12. In measure 27 the last ta'am combination is introduced by the pedal (figure 4.13).

These four musical examples show the importance of the intervals of fourth and fifth, which serve as the nucleus of all motives or accent combinations. In the further development of the organ piece all four of the ta'am combinations return. The third motive comes back in measures 32–36 with a concluding sof pasuk, followed by rhythmic variations of this motive from measure 37 on. After a short interlude that recalls the earlier chromatic passages, the first motive returns in measure 45, but with altered rhythm. After another homophonically set interlude, the third motive returns in measure 57, again with a different rhythm.

With regard to the tonal conception of the piece, Arno Nadel breaks with major-minor tonality. However, unlike his colleagues, he avoids speaking of shtayger or modality; instead, he prefers the term "principal motives," a concept that he realizes in the tonal and harmonic disposition of the Passacaglia: With reference to harmony, Nadel treats every single ta'am combination differently. Moreover, he avoids—with the exception of a very few measures—the impression of harmonic structures altogether by keeping the mostly two to three different musical lines independent from each other.

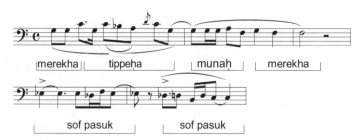

FIGURE 4.11. Arno Nadel, *Passacaglia für Orgel über "Wadonaj Pakad es Ssarah" (Toravorlesung am Neujahrsfest)*, MS (1933), measures 16–20 (core notes, second motive).

|munah| |telishah ketanah|

FIGURE 4.12. Arno Nadel, *Passacaglia für Orgel über "Wadonaj Pakad es
Ssarah" (Toravorlesung am Neujahrsfest)*,
MS (1933), measures 22–25 (core notes,
third motive).

The (for the most part) independent treatment of the musical lines extends also to the rhythmic conception of the piece. The use of polyrhythmic
passages (measures 18–21 and 32–34) and polymetric sections (measures
14–20), as well as the frequent change of rhythm (after measures 45, 46, 47,
48), creates a recitative character with a diatonically melodious form in general. Nadel follows the rhythmic experimentation prevalent in the early twentieth century, when a number of composers revolted against standard meters
and experimented with less symmetric patterns. In this, the composers of
Western art music were inspired by traditional music (Igor Stravinsky's and
Béla Bartók's rhythmic models were the most prominent examples).[147]

As the text-music relationship in cantillation generally has more to do
with the syntax of the text than with music, an examination of the relationship between text and music may not lead to any conclusive or important results. However, Nadel states that Jewish music had to follow the anapestic
rhythm of the Hebrew language,[148] a claim that he realizes in the Passacaglia.
With proper performance, its constant flow of sixteenth notes over many
measures blurs the feeling of alternation between strong and unaccented
beats, and the quotations of Bible cantillation motives are accented mostly on
the second or fourth beat of the measure (measures 14–20, 32–34).

Arno Nadel's Passacaglia continues the musical direction Schalit laid out
with his Nachspiel. The piece consists of older elements of Jewish music that
are generally considered traditional and authentic. Nadel, however, does not
submit them to major or minor tonality but instead focuses on the realization
of a subjective approach toward Jewish music, uniting theoretical and practical concepts.[149] In this organ piece he aims at recitativic expression combined
with diatonic-melodic form, polytonality, and constant change of rhythm—
elements that he regarded as authentically Jewish. Like Schalit, Nadel was in

|munah legarmeh| |munah| |revia'|

FIGURE 4.13. Arno Nadel, *Passacaglia für Orgel über
"Wadonaj Pakad es Ssarah" (Toravorlesung am Neujahrsfest)*,
MS (1933), measures 27–29 (core notes, fourth motive).

search of a new kind of Jewish music that would not be oriented toward or assimilate the organ music used in Christian tradition.

In large part Nadel accomplishes this, but he also draws upon forms, textures, and sometimes harmonies that are an integral part of Western music. Moreover, some of the characteristics of Nadel's Passacaglia follow a modern, more particularly neoclassicist approach. While composers of organ music continued the Romantic-symphonic tradition, which was in vogue from the late nineteenth century to the late 1920s, by 1930 a new development had set in and is visible in Nadel's works. Instead of chromaticism, his style is based on the free diatonicism that neoclassicists generally favored.[150] The recourse to a pre-Romantic tonal language is evident in contemporary organ music especially, alongside a turning toward absolute forms such as toccata, fugue, passacaglia, and variation.[151] Gotthold Frotscher draws attention to the passacaglia form in particular, noting that it had been revived as a genre for organ music after Max Reger's Introduction, Passacaglia and Fugue (op. 127, 1913) and Introduction and Passacaglia in D Minor.[152] The fact that a central form of Baroque music had again become popular is also a result of the Orgelbewegung: The building of organs in the style of Baroque models inspired a repertoire with numerous Baroque elements, a development that in the end affected Jewish composers as well.

FROM THE "SPIRITUAL GHETTO" TO EMIGRATION

While Arno Nadel, in spite of the increasingly dangerous situation for Jews in Germany, devoted himself to the development of an "authentically Jewish art," other composers withdrew more and more into an inner emigration or "spiritual ghetto." Among the organists and composers active in the Kulturbund was Siegfried Würzburger, who was born and educated in Frankfurt am Main, where he studied piano and theory at the Hoch'sches Konservatorium. He also took organ lessons from Carl Breidenstein, a teacher at the conservatory and choir director at the Great Synagogue in Frankfurt. With his wife, Gertrud, a professional pianist, Würzburger founded a private music school around 1907, and from the 1910s on he served Frankfurt's Westend Synagogue as organist. As a performer in Jewish worship services and a soloist in concerts at the synagogue, he showed his deep commitment to the organ. Almost blind from a congenital disability, Würzburger developed extremely good aural skills that defined his musicality. In the worship services he often improvised, especially before and after the liturgy, and most of his improvisations were based on musical themes taken from Jewish liturgical music. Two of his notated compositions have survived, the *Passacaglia über "Moaus-*

zur" (ca. 1933) and the *Passacaglia und Fuge über "Kol Nidre"* (ca. 1933). The latter premiered at the Wiesbaden synagogue in April 1934, as we know from a contemporary review: "In the course of the lecture and music events organized by the local Lodge and the Jewish Lehrhaus a 'sacred concert' took place as the last event of this winter, in the Great Synagogue, under the direction of cantor S[aul] Lilienthal.

It presented almost exclusively modern Jewish composers; of the nine offerings no less than six were premieres. The organ prelude by Max Wolff and the *Passacaglia und Fuge über 'Kol Nidre'* [italics added] are masterworks of counterpoint. (The former was masterfully played by Erich Wolff, the latter by the composer himself.)"[153] Würzburger's Passacaglia and Fugue is based on the central prayer of Yom Kippur, Kol Nidrei, which is recited at the beginning of the evening service right after the Torah scrolls are taken out of the ark. The Aramaic prayer is a kind of declaration in which all personal vows made to God are annulled.

The precise genesis of text and melody of Kol Nidrei is unknown and subject to much speculation. The melody is often associated with the New Christians of fourteenth- or fifteenth-century Spain but erroneously so.[154] The text is of much earlier date, being traceable back at least to the Gaonic period (seventh to eleventh centuries): Rabbi Yehudai Gaon around 740 CE formally introduced the Kol Nidrei prayer into the synagogue of the Babylonian city of Sura. His version lacked the preamble and triple repetition that is characteristic for the one used today, and thus suggests a different function.

Only the Ashkenazic Jews accepted the changes made by Rabbi Jacob ben Meir Tam (ca. 1100–1171), who changed the text (but not the wording) so drastically that the annulment no longer referred only to the past but also included the future.[155]

The custom of reciting Kol Nidrei exclusively on the evening of Yom Kippur was established by Rabbi Meir ben Baruch of Rothenburg (ca. 1215–1293), and with its becoming an integral part of Jewish tradition a wide musical reception began that resulted in numerous arrangements.

During the nineteenth century Kol Nidrei became a point of dispute of German Reform, instigated by the resolution of the First German Conference of Rabbis, which took place in 1844 in Braunschweig. The conference participants decided to remove Kol Nidrei as it no longer represented an essential prayer; moreover, the rabbis believed that its removal would prevent anti-Semitic suspicions.[156] Instead, the prayer was substituted by Psalm 130 or replaced with new texts that expressed the basic themes of Kol Nidrei through keywords and certain original phrases but without the controversial annulment of the vows. The congregations that abandoned Kol Nidrei during this period sang the new prayer to the old melody. Sulzer's *Schir Zion*, for example, provided the traditional melody for the new prayer and Kol Nidrei itself only in an appendix.

One of the first references to a Kol Nidrei melody goes back to Mordecai ben Abraham Jaffe (ca. 1530–1612), a rabbi in Prague, who was dissatisfied with the text variants of Kol Nidrei used during his day. As he recounts in his *Levush Malkhut*, a ten-volume codification of religious laws, he created a new version with a "correct text" but retained the melody that was commonly regarded as traditional.

The written transmission of the Kol Nidrei melody, in a version that is still known today, began in 1765, with the cantor's manual in manuscript by Aaron Beer (1739–1821), chief cantor of the Heidereutergasse synagogue in Berlin.[157]

Beer's version (figure 4.14) contains essential elements of the song, which have been copied and arranged by Jewish cantors and composers up to the present, in various versions, among which Louis Lewandowski's adaptation is important as it became the standard version used in Germany's Jewish Reform congregations. He arranged Kol Nidrei several times and incorporated minor variations in text and melody. Number 68 of his *Toda W'simrah* is based on the original Aramaic text, while numbers 70 and 71 use a German text of Psalm 130. The version I examine here (figure 4.15) is an arrangement of the Hebrew text used by most Reform congregations in Germany.

The Kol Nidrei melody as arranged by Lewandowski belongs to the group of Mi-Sinai songs, a Hebrew term for a traditional group of cantorial melodies sung in the Ashkenazic synagogues of both Eastern and Western European

FIGURE 4.14. Abraham Idelsohn, *HOM*, vol. 6, no. 1, measures 1–27.

FIGURE 4.15. Louis Lewandowski, *Toda W'simrah* (1921), no. 69, measures 3–33. All vows of the children of Israel, which they have sworn by our Father, when they lifted their eyes to You, who are in heaven, they regret with all their heart and soul, from this Day of Atonement until the next they are expecting.

rite. The melody consists of different parts, each containing a primary motive that relates to other Mi-Sinai songs, chants for Yom Kippur, or the te'amim (table 4.6).

In the rather artistically motivated editions of old synagogue songs, specifically those of Sulzer and Lewandowski, which still contain the structural influence of the migrating motives, many more of those motivic relationships appear.

Perhaps because of its deep expressiveness and its complex and emphatic motives, the melody of Kol Nidrei became one of the best-known melodies outside of the synagogue. It was arranged by Jewish and non-Jewish composers alike (e.g., Max Bruch, *Kol Nidrei* for violoncello and orchestra [op. 47, 1881]; Arnold Schoenberg, *Kol Nidre* for speaker, chorus, and orchestra [op. 39, 1938], a piece for the Yom Kippur liturgy with an English text revised by the composer).

TABLE 4.6. Motives in Kol Nidrei

Measures	Prayer Song on Yom Kippur	Cantillation
3–8; 19–23	Opening motive of the Ha-Malakh on High Holidays	
9–10; 24–25	Motives of different prayer songs on High Holidays[a]	
11–14	Be-Rosh Ha-Shanah ("mi vo'ash"),[b] Venislakh ("bish-gagah"),[c] and Aleinu	Ta'am: darga tevir (Prophets):
15–16; 17–18	Be-Rosh Ha-Shanah ("uve-yom zom kippur"),[d] Ki Keshimkha ("me'ofor")[e]	Ta'am: darga tevir (Esther):
26–27	Avodah and Aleinu	Ta'am etnaḥta (Prophets):

[a] See, for example, Lewandowski, *Toda W'simrah*, nos. 117–18.
[b] See Idelsohn, *HOM*, 7:73, no. 190b.
[c] See ibid., 7:80, no. 208 b.
[d] See ibid., 7:163, no. 155.
[e] See ibid., 7:164, no. 157.

Analysis of the Passacaglia und Fuge über "Kol Nidre"

Würzburger's Passacaglia consists of six parts: the introduction of the theme and five variations over the basso ostinato. The first four measures introduce the beginning of the Kol Nidrei melody solo in the pedal; each variation closes with a cadence ad libitum. After the last variation an interlude is inserted and is followed by the first four measures of the Kol Nidrei presented in the highest voice (measure 34); its last notes compose the beginning of a motive from the Kol Nidrei that is here used for the first time: "ha-yash ve bashamayim lo-shuv elekho bekhol levovom u-vekhol nafshom."

The variations over a bass are ostinato variations, which are considered additive forms. The first one moves almost exclusively in unison—in quarter notes; the two descant parts of the second variation go parallel in sixths—in eighth notes. The temporal structure of the third variation further accelerates in the fourth, where the parallel sixths now appear in sixteenth notes. The fourth variation also features arpeggios that always appear on the unaccented beat. In the fifth variation the tempo further accelerates with thirds appearing in thirty-second notes. With regard to the formal construction of the Passacaglia, Würzburger follows the traditional method. Also in terms of tonality he remains conservative and uses functional harmony.

However, the interludes and their melodic and tonal conception are notably different. All of the interludes are nonmetrical and consist of very fast, scalelike runs or broken chords. They only partially follow major or minor tonality, as occasionally Würzburger introduces the augmented second B–C-sharp (measures 8, 13, 19, and 24); F–G-sharp (measures 18 and 24), E-flat–F-sharp (measure 19), and so on. He thus evokes associations with the Ahavah Rabbah shtayger (figure 4.16). In spite of the tonal reminiscences of the shtayger, Würzburger never leaves the minor tonality but stays in the principal or related keys.

The subject of the four-part double fugue, which is introduced by the lower middle voice in measure 44, is based on the Kol Nidrei motive on "benotam eynehem eleykha." It comprises four measures and is followed by the real answer in the lower perfect fourth. After its respective appearance in the different parts, the theme is succeeded by the countersubject, which appears in each part. The exposition ends in measure 57 and is followed by an episode that uses the motive on "haba" in the descant voice. The first half of this motive, which is a scalelike run, is imitated by the other voices in the subsequent measures.

In measure 66 the subject reappears in the upper middle voice, this time in D minor (natural), followed by the tonal answer in the fourth on A (measure 69, highest voice). In measure 73 another episode begins with a new motive (ascending seconds with an ambitus of a sixth). Seven measures later a second subject in F major is introduced, based on the melody of "miyom kippurim zeh" and followed by the motive of "benotam eynehem." The tonal an-

FIGURE 4.16. Ahavah Rabbah shtayger (simplified skeleton).

swer occurs in the lowest part (measure 85) and appears again three measures later in the octave, after which a modulation to G minor ensues. In measure 90 the first subject returns in the bass part, in the deceptive cadence of E-flat major (relating to G minor), followed by a tonal answer in the lower middle voice in D major (measure 94). After a key change to D major, the second subject, "miyom kippurim zeh," appears three times: first, simultaneously with the opening of the Kol Nidrei in the bass (measure 100) and then with minor variations (measures 104 and 108). This threefold repetition leads into the fugue's final cadence.

That Würzburger does not strictly adhere to the melody of the Kol Nidrei but rather puts the subjects together on the basis of tonality (the first subject is minor; the second, major) suggests that he chose the motives for their textual meaning. The first subject relates to the text "when they lifted their eyes to You," while the second refers to "from this Day of Atonement until [the next]." Although the fugue provides little basis for textual interpretation, the musical realization of the prayer appears to some extent in the form itself. The infinity of the sky, toward which "the eyes are lifted," and the continuous guarantee of the forgiveness of sins is reflected in the form of the fugue, with its nearly "infinite" treatment of motives and themes.

Siegfried Würzburger's Passacaglia and Fugue is one of the few twentieth-century organ compositions that use a Jewish melody in combination with a strict retrospective-looking contrapuntal style. The fugue in particular shows how synagogue chant and counterpoint can be connected in organ music without intentionally creating a uniquely Jewish expression. In the end, the Jewish melody adheres to the compositional form. Thus, the piece represents a total assimilation to Western art music.

The Passacaglia and Fugue represents the repertoire that was available for use in early twentieth-century synagogues; indeed, the work sets itself apart from Jewish composers' new, unique compositions that were created for concert performance or various other functions. While Arno Nadel in his Passacaglia applied the contemporary compositional techniques of his time, Würzburger's style follows the many preludes, fugues, and variations for organ created by composers like Joseph Rheinberger, who presented solid work with a deliberate objectivity and individual traits.[158] Because of its (polyphonic) style, Würzburger's Fugue easily fits into the church music genre of the *Gebrauchsfuge*, in which the symmetrical use of the theme dominates over contemporary style.[159]

Although Siegfried Würzburger did not create a substantial and unique repertoire for organ, he was considerably more influential as an organ teacher. Indeed, his pedagogical work is of special importance, considering the many organists who studied under him. Some of them would continue the German-Jewish organ tradition, at least in part, in emigration, most notably the following three who also served as organ substitutes at the Westend Synagogue before emigration: Martha Sommer (b. 1918), who in 1939 left via Holland and England bound for the United States, where she worked for forty-four years as organist at the Congregation Habonim in New York City; Würzburger's son Walter (1914–1995), who emigrated in 1933 to France, continued his studies in composition from 1940 on in Australia, and settled in 1951 in England (although he never worked as an organist again, he composed two works for organ, a fugue in 1943 and a prelude and fugue in 1991, both dedicated to fellow emigrant and musician Uwe Radok); and especially Herbert Fromm (see also chapter 5), a talented organist who became one of the most prolific composers for the Reform Synagogue, leaving behind a vast oeuvre of works in different genres. Educated at the State Academy of Music in Munich, where he studied composition, conducting, piano, and organ, he, like Schalit, worked outside the Jewish communities as a conductor at the municipal theaters of Bielefeld and Würzburg. Like other Jewish musicians, when the National Socialists seized power, he was no longer allowed to work at these institutions, a fact that led to the painful realization that he could no longer continue his career: "This career ended abruptly early in 1933 when a Pharaoh arose in Germany who no longer knew Joseph. Being denied a career in the open society, I continued my musical activities in a Jewish Cultural Organization in Frankfurt, at the same time becoming assistant organist at the liberal synagogue."[160]

From 1933 until his emigration, Herbert Fromm was active as a composer, choir director, accompanist, and conductor in the Kulturbund of Frankfurt am Main, and from 1934 to 1936 he assisted Siegfried Würzburger at the Westend Synagogue. In addition, in 1935 he became the principal organist at the Great Synagogue in Wiesbaden. Hans Wilhelm (after his emigration, William) Steinberg, until 1933 principal conductor at the Frankfurt Opernhaus and thereafter artistic director of the Kulturbund there, describes in a 1936 letter of recommendation Fromm's enormous impact on the musical life of German Jews of the 1930s:

At these events primarily dedicated to the aims of Jewish music and to its demonstration, Herbert Fromm stood out as a composer who is highly familiar with the material of specifically Eastern art. His works for chorus, orchestra, and organ show the composer to be an artist who, in the much disputed field of Jewish music, knows how to convey new and highly individual ideas that he skillfully expresses using a mature compositional technique. Fromm is an organist of considerable style and highly advanced technique, which was often of decisive importance in synagogue events.

Besides the performance of his own Fugue for Organ, I would like to mention his particular qualifications for taking over the organ parts of oratorios. . . . Moreover I should add Fromm's special talent as a teacher of theory, particularly counterpoint and the usual subjects in composition.[161]

Fromm's teacher, Siegfried Würzburger, commended his student's "gift for free improvisation" and praised his compositions as a "valuable enrichment" of the repertoire.[162]

Fromm's early works for organ were composed shortly after he began working as synagogue organist. One of his first organ pieces is the Passacaglia and Triple Fugue of 1935, followed in 1936 by eight short chorale preludes for organ that are based on the German chorales *Wunderbarer König*; *Dies sind die heiligen zehn Gebot*; *Nun lasset uns den Leib begraben*; *Wächter ist die Nacht bald hin*; *Auf, auf mein Herz mit Freuden*; *Nun lasst uns Gott dem Herren Dank sagen und Ihn ehren*; *Oh Traurigkeit, oh Herzeleid*; and *Gelobt sei Gott im höchsten Thron*. Curiously, none of these works stand in any relation to Fromm's Jewish heritage and were perhaps composed only for the purpose of study.

Due to the increasingly dangerous political situation, Fromm's second career as organist and composer in Germany was of short duration. On January 9, 1937, he performed works by Bach, his own Triple Fugue in G Minor, and his eight organ chorales at a farewell concert in his home town, Bingen. Shortly thereafter he emigrated to the United States, where he continued his activities as composer and organist.

THE BREAKTHROUGH OF JEWISH MODERNITY

Like Herbert Fromm, Hans Samuel was one of the first Jewish musicians to dedicate himself almost exclusively to the organ as a synagogue instrument. Indeed, with a remarkable oeuvre of more than one hundred works, almost all including the organ in one way or another, he was perhaps the first to make a truly serious attempt to establish the genre of Jewish organ music in Germany, as he also did later in his "adopted" country—Israel. That he never achieved fame in either Germany or Israel and that his work remains little known today may be due to the difficulties he faced growing up in Germany of the 1930s and later living in Israel, where organ music of any sort was unfamiliar (these facts may also have been aggravated by claims that he had a somewhat odd personality). Indeed, his niece Rachel Thaller describes him as an unusually introverted and shy person to the extent that it added a certain strangeness to his behavior.[163]

Born the son of the liberal rabbi of Essen, Salomon Samuel, Hans grew up well educated in the Reform movement, its liturgy, and its music. By the time he took his first organ lessons from the local synagogue organist, in 1918, the organ was well established in Reform Judaism. Through his strong integration in the general musical life of his hometown, he also worked with cathedral organist Norbert Förster and music teacher Peter Hennes. During the 1920s Hans Samuel began his professional studies in music, first in piano at the Torshoff Conservatory in Essen, where he graduated as a piano teacher in 1925. He then resumed his organ lessons, initially with church music director Ebing at the Erlöserkirche in Essen and later at the Conservatory for Church Music in Dortmund with Peter Grunnemann. In Samuel's view, this period was of crucial importance for his further development as an organist and a composer:

> In the course of these studies he realized that synagogue organ music strongly imitated church music, while the character of the prayer leader's recitatives was altogether different. He investigated the origins of Jewish music and relentlessly sought new theories on the subject. And then, for the first time, it occurred to him that the modern organ, which in its malleability almost equaled the human voice, would encounter the essence of Jewish music in a completely different way, as he knew it from the prayers, table songs, and Torah reading, if it were played by a Jewish person filled with the spirit of the traditional melodies.[164]

These realizations would determine Samuel's development as a composer of organ music.

When Hans Samuel moved to Berlin in May 1933, he was a well-trained musician and thus assumed that he would easily find a position as an organist at one of the many city synagogues. However, finding employment turned out to be surprisingly difficult, leaving him at first with only substitute and other part-time work. Initially, Samuel played in Jewish prayer houses, sometimes helped out at the New Synagogue on Oranienburger Straße, and was engaged for the 1935 holy days by the Jewish congregation in Potsdam. Finally, in 1936 he found a permanent job at the Friedenstempel in Berlin-Halensee, a position he served in until the organ was destroyed in the pogroms of the Kristallnacht.

During his years in Berlin, Samuel established a good reputation as organist and composer by showing "full command of the instrument, exceptional musical abilities and knowledge of liturgy"[165] and "especially a great mastery of playing pedal."[166] While working in Berlin-Halensee, he was recognized as "an excellent musician and a talented composer."[167] The following report by music director Max Wachsmann further attests to Samuel's special and diverse talents:

> Mr. Samuel, who has regarded the organ as his primary instrument ab initio, fully mastered it and all its complicated facilities. He has not only fulfilled his duties most exactly but has always been available to me for preparations, meetings, rehearsals, etc.
>
> Furthermore, he was active as composer of preludes and interludes, as well as arrangements for organ, wherein his detailed knowledge of the liturgy was very useful. Outside of the synagogue, I got to know him as a very good piano accompanist and chamber music player. I have truly enjoyed working together with him during the two years of our collaboration, not only because of his musical competence, but also because I got to know him as a human being with exceptional character traits.[168]

Arno Nadel, too, praised Samuel as an "excellent organist and composer of organ music."[169] Among the works Samuel composed while still in Germany are the *Kleines Orgelpraeludium zu "Mah tauwu" am Vorabend des Neujahrsfestes* (1929), *Paraphrase über Abend-Rezitative der 3 Wallfahrtsfeste {Maarowaus-Rezitativ und Fuge}* (1930), *Fughetten über das Bor'chu-Motiv: C-H-D-C* (1930), *Trio-Paraphrase über das Bor'chu-Motiv an den hohen Feiertagen (Minhag Ashkenas)*, and a *Triovorspiel zum traditionellen "Borchu" am Vorabend des Pessachfestes*.

Besides his work as organist and composer, Samuel dedicated much time to theoretical writings on Jewish music. Organs and organ music played an important role in these discussions. Samuel developed theories on the compositional style of organ music for Jewish communities and offered criticism of compositions for Jewish worship in the traditional style. In his view, organ music performed in the framework of Jewish liturgy had been all too strongly influenced by the Christian repertoire and was "ecclesiastical, chorale-like, and homophonic-chordal." According to Samuel, the reason for this stylistic epigone has to do with the use of the instrument itself, which is commonly and erroneously regarded as inflexible, lifeless, and static, and he bemoans the total absence of an established organ tradition in the Jewish liberal service. Samuel explains that, because of the liturgical reforms instituted in the course of Jewish emancipation, traditional elements of Jewish music, such as ḥazzanut, were for the most part eliminated and destroyed by the organ. The ideal had been to follow the chorale-based style of Protestant church music and to imitate the techniques used by Mendelssohn-Bartholdy and his contemporaries. Here, Samuel is most likely alluding to the organ compositions of Louis Lewandowski and his contemporaries. Furthermore, Samuel believed that the strong orientation toward the musical models of church music is problematic since they are contrary to the core of synagogue music—the recitative. Thus, composers must endeavor to eliminate the foreign and church-like style associated with the organ and organ music in order to facilitate a "new, predominantly recitativic, Jewish-inspired organ style."[170]

According to Samuel's theory, organ music in Judaism should be strongly demarcated from the Christian and be characterized primarily by recitativic elements to serve as a mediator of deeply religious modes of expression. As a foundation for these compositions he recommends Abraham Baer's *Baal T'fillah oder "Der praktische Vorbeter"* (1883), a comprehensive collection of synagogue songs and chants according to the Polish and German rite (Ashkenazic), as well as the Portuguese (Sephardic); and Fabian Ogutsch's *Der Frankfurter Kantor* (1930), a compilation of traditional synagogue songs from Frankfurt am Main; both collections explain why one can speak only in a limited way about a common basis for Christian and Jewish organ music.[171] Samuel claims that if the core of organ in church music is the chorale prelude, the core of synagogue organ music is the free recitative, and the genres are opposites in their musical construction and expression.

With regard to style, Samuel favors a balance of Romantic harmony and polyphony with dynamic shadings and rhapsodic rhythm. More specifically, he says that the "preference for a one-sided harmonic (homophonic)-oriented music style" and the use of Western-style harmony weigh down the older traditional melodies, which are totally different in nature. The only sensible treatment of Jewish song is "a linear style, connected with elements of modern harmonic sounds embedded in melodic lines with 'flowing harmony.' Only in this fashion can the uniqueness of traditional synagogue melodies be used productively. In this way one could bring into being a modern development of the instrumental synagogue recitative."[172] A further distinguishing attribute of synagogue organ music is, according to Samuel, the augmented second; however this interval should not become the main component of synagogue music "as this would [not] correspond to its indubitably universalistic character."[173]

Further, the form of synagogue organ music should rely on the Western types often used in Christian worship—among them the chorale prelude and postlude, free imitation, canon and fugue, prelude and postlude, toccata, and fantasia—only insofar as the recitativic and rhapsodic elements of the Jewish liturgical melodies remain intact (as we have seen, this is evidently not the case in the nineteenth-century preludes and the Passacaglia and Fugue by Würzburger). Thus, at least for now, the only types of music chosen for organ compositions should be those that do not have to follow a strict form and structure. These are, according to Samuel, preludes, toccatas, and fantasias because these three have a specific connection to synagogue melodies: "It is in these free forms that an emphasis on the responsorial (parallelistic) elements in the Hebrew recitative is most easily attained, and it is of great importance. Within a responsorial style, it is possible to use different formal elements that can then be blended into an organic whole."[174] In spite of his preference for these forms, Samuel believes that, in the end, any form can be justified for the synagogue organ style as long as it is used freely.

In all of his attempts to find a distinctly Jewish voice in organ music, it is remarkable and somewhat contradictory that Samuel's musical vocabulary is oriented toward Western thought. Indeed, it is almost paradoxical that he describes his views on authentic Jewish music in terms of Western art music (most notable in the use of "rhapsody") and at the same time seeks a Jewish style—a kind of formal assimilation combined with the quest for dissimilation that gives linguistic expression to the transformation of Jewish life.

Besides publishing his ideas on organ music in different newspaper articles, Samuel simultaneously realized them in his compositions—he saw himself as a pioneer of a new style of organ works that are reminiscent of psalms or a "richly ornamented surface in Oriental architecture."[175] He composed an extraordinary quantity of organ pieces for Sabbath and holy days, all of which are based on motives of traditional synagogue music. If composers before him concentrated primarily on the search for authentic musical material to link with the genre of organ music, for Samuel, it was not enough merely to quote a Jewish melody. He focused on the specific and distinct use of the melodic material in the context of instrumental music. Samuel was one of the first composers who attempted to find a specifically Jewish style in organ music while making it an integral part of the contemporary repertoire.

His oeuvre shows some features that are remarkably different from those of the organ works of contemporary Jewish composers in that his personal style integrates elements of the rhapsodic, syncopation, and canonicity; he was the perhaps the first Jewish composer of organ music to use extended tonality. Most important, he established solid rules for the genre with its subdivisions into organ music for Jewish worship and concert music, which he differentiates with the terms "synagogue organ music" and "Jewish organ music": "Pure synagogue organ music for worship can coexist with a Jewish organ music for concert, which for the most part takes musical motives and moods from the best of ḥazzanut and develops them further—the neginot motives ought to be creatively used in the service of a stretched-out modern Hebrew melodic style, an old-new Hebrew musical language."[176]

Samuel followed this theory in his creative path as a composer, classifying his organ compositions into synagogue organ music and Jewish organ music in the catalogues of his works.[177] The table of contents of the first part of one catalogue, *Gesamt-Inhaltsangabe zur Sammlung "Synagogaler Orgelmusik" in 3 Teilen: Orgelstücke mit Verwertung von traditionellen Motiven sowie Neubearbeitungen von liturgischen Abschnitten des Schabats, der 3 Wallfahrtsfeste u. der Hohen Feiertage (des Neujahrs- und Versöhnungsfests)*, lists the works shown in table 4.7.

Table 4.8 lists other works that Samuel assigned to the category of Jewish organ music.

Samuel did not strictly follow his differentiation between synagogue and Jewish organ music; the compositions *Neilah-Klänge* and *Vier Fughetten über das Borchu-Rezitativ*, for instance, appear in both work lists, perhaps because the boundaries between Gebrauchsmusik and concert repertoire are sometimes not clearly delineated.

Among the compositions that Samuel lists under "Jewish organ music" is the variation cycle *Variationen über die jemenitische Weise "Achoth ketanah,"* also known by the English title *Variations in Canonic Style on a Hebrew-Oriental Prayer Cantillation ("Ahot Ketanah") for the New Years-Day acc. to the Yemenite Minhag*. The music paper (manufacturer's imprint: W. E. Fuchs, Frankfurt am Main) refers to a possible conception of the variations before Samuel's emigration. Dating and placing this work, however, are difficult in view of the fact that Samuel dated only five of his compositions; these works belong to his early period (composed between 1929 and 1931), and all employ prayer songs used in Ashkenazic liturgy.

The *Variations in Canonic Style* are Samuel's first attempt to integrate the tunes Idelsohn recorded, specifically the prayer Aḥot Ketannah [Little Sister], which Sephardic Jews sing on Rosh Ha-Shanah between the afternoon prayer service and the evening prayer. Aḥot Ketannah is a pizmon attributed to Abraham ben Isaac of Gerona (who is also known as "Gerondi"), a ḥazzan and writer of religious poetry who was active in Catalonia in the thirteenth century. The poem consists of eight metrical verses, each ending with the refrain "Tikhleh shanah ve-kiloteḥa" [May the year end, together with its curses]. The first words of the prayer stem from the Song of Solomon 8:8. After the last stanza, the refrain is replaced by the wish for the New Year and its blessings to begin. The text is calming, but it also evokes Israel's suffering in exile.

Although the prayer was initially only used in Sephardic liturgy, it was later adopted by Yemenite congregations (before the evening prayer) and Ashkenazic congregations (on the eve of Rosh Ha-Shanah). For the *Variations*

TABLE 4.7. Hans Samuel, Synagogue Organ Music

Synagogue Organ Music

Part I. Sabbath

1. *Kanonisches Vorspiel zu Mah tauwu in A-Dur*
2. *Gottesdienstliche Vorspiele zu Mah tauwu in A- und B-Dur*
3. *Rezitativisches Triovorspiel zum Maariw-Gebet des Sabbat*
3a. *Neubearbeitung des Bor'chu-Rezitativs und der Maariw-B'rochaus (nach Baers Baal t'filla)*
4. *W'schom'ru für den Monat Ellul u. Sabbat schuowoh (unter Verwendung des Pijut-Motivs Ono esaun) (Mussaf Jom Kippur)*
5. *Neubearbeitung des Kiddush (nach Lesart Lew. Kol rinna t'filla)*
6. *10 phrygische Vorspiele zum Morgengebet des Sabbat (10 Orgelstücke über den Ahawoh rabbo-Steiger)*
7. *Vorspiele zu En komaucho (bzw. Waj'hi binsoach)*
8–9. *2 Präludien in neu-phrygischem Stil (Zwei Praeludien in Fis phrygisch)*

Part II. Three Pilgrimage Festivals

1. *Paraphrase (Rezit. und Trio—Fuge) über die Maarowaus l'scholausch regolim (Abendrezitative der 3 Wallfahrtsfeste)*
2. *4 Fughetten über das Borchu-Motiv CHDC im Abendgebet*
2a. *Neubearbeitung des Borchu und der Maarowaus-Rezitative*
3. *Vorspiel zu Borchu am Vorabend des Pessachfestes*
4. *10 Niggunim, Orgelvorspiele für den Morgengottesdienst a. d. 3 Wallfahrtsfesten:*
   für Pessach: *Hoel besaazumaus usecho; B'rach daudi, z'ennoh urennoh*
   für Schowuaus: *Os schesch meaus; Akdomus-Volksweise*
   für Sukkaus: *Volksweise Chassidischer Niggun beim Lulow-Schütteln*
   für Schemini azeres: *Geschem-Weise; Af b'ri uttas schem*
   für Simchas tauroh: *Attoh hor' esso lodaas u. Ono hauschionoh (Umzugsgesänge)*

Part III. High Holidays (New Year and Day of Atonement)

A. Longer Preludes (or Solo Pieces)

1. *Improvisation über Hohefesttags-Motive (Vorspiel z. 1. Abend Roschhaschana)*
2. *Vorspiel zu Jaaleh tachanunenu*

B. Shorter Preludes and New Arrangements of Liturgical Sections

1. *Vorspiel zu Mahtauwu in F (unter Verwertung von Hohefesttagsmotiven)*
2. *Vorspiel zu den Maarowaus für den 2. Abend Roschhaschana (in D)*
3. *Fughette über das Kol Nidrei-Motiv in g-Moll*
4. *2 kurze Vorspiele zu Jaaleh tachanunenu*
5. *Kanonisches Triovorspiel in h-Moll*
5a. *Neubearbeitung von Dark'cho*
6. *Vorspiel zu Owinu malkenu in f-Moll*

7. *Zwischenspiel und Neubearbeitung von Aschre n. d. Schofarblasen*
8. *Neubearbeitung von Mussaf-Kaddish und Owaus*
9. *Fughette über Apid neser ojaum*
10. *W'hakohanim-Rezitativ*
11. *Paraphrase über Birkas kauhanim an hohen Feiertagen*
12. *Zwischenspiel zur Seelenfeier (Paraphrase üb. m'chalkel chajim)*
13. *Vorspiele zu den Neilahgesängen*

C. Series of Recitativic Organ Pieces

1. *Pentatonische Toccata, Variationen und Finale*
2. *Rezitativisches Triovorspiel zu Borchu-Maarowaus (3 Versionen)*
3. *Rezitativische Paraphrase über die Maarowaus (Mixolyd./C)*
4. *Triovorspiel über Selichot-Motiv*
5. *Paraphrase über die Tora-Neginoth an hohen Festen*
6. *Fuge über Achas w'achas (Awaudoh-Motiv d. Jom Kippur)*
7. *W'hakohanim-Rezitativ*
8. *Neilah-Klänge*

in Canonic Style, Hans Samuel draws on Idelsohn's transcription (figure 4.17a) of the Yemenite musical tradition.

Idelsohn's transcription respects the different pronunciation of the Yemenite Jews, whose song is significantly different from that of Ashkenazic Jews not only on the linguistic level. According to Idelsohn, synagogue songs of Yemenite Jews do not represent fixed melodies in the common sense but rather modes or motive groups that the prayer leader and the congregation recite in unison. The present melody of Aḥot Ketannah is based on a variant of the Seliḥa tune, also known as niggun neḥamah [consoling tune], which is recited in conjunction with soothing prayers of atonement and penance.[178] The tune consists of a motive group with three modes (see figures 4.17b–d) that each relate to Idelsohn's transcription of Aḥot Ketannah: The first is equivalent to the initial motive presented by the prayer leader; the second relates to the end of his section by preparing the closing and transition to the congregational section; and the third marks the end of the verse.

Analysis of the Variations in Canonic Style on a Hebrew-Oriental Prayer Cantillation

The theme Samuel borrows as a foundation for the variations is based on the prayer leader's part, with the exception of the motive on "el na refana." It is written in alla-breve time, as andante al recitativo, and departs markedly

TABLE 4.8. Hans Samuel, Jewish Organ Music

Jewish Organ Music

Part I. Sabbath

1. *Trio-Paraphrase über Abend-Rezitative*
2. *Suite im neu-phrygischen Stil (Ahava Rabba Mode) zum Morgengebet*
3. *Präludium und Fuge im neu-phrygischen Stil*
4. *Fantasie im neu-phrygischen Stil*
5. *Passacaglia im neu-phrygischen Stil*
6. *Sephardische Suite über Sabbatweise "Adonaj melech, Adonaj malach, Adonaj jimloch, leo-lam waed"*
6a. *Sephardische Kantate für Solo-Stimmen, Chor, und Orgel*
7. *Paraphrase über sephardische Haftara-Kantillationen "Im taschiw Mischabbat raglacha" (resp. Kiddusch le Schacharit)*

Part II. Three Pilgrimage Festivals (Passover, Shavuot, and Sukkot)

8. *Paraphrase über Abendrezitative (Maarowoth)*
9. *4 Fughetten über Bar'chu-Motiv*
10. *10 Niggunim zum Morgen- und Mussaphgebet (Neginoth-Paraphrasen)*

Part III. High Holidays (New Year and Day of Atonement)

11. *Paraphrase über die sephardische Neujahrsweise "Achoth ketanah"*
12. *Variationen über die jemenitische Weise "Achoth ketanah"*
13. *Trio-Paraphrase über das Bar'chu-Motiv (Minhag Aschkenas)*
14. *Fantasie im mixolydischen Stil, Abendklänge der Hohen Feiertage (Introduktion–Fugato–Rezitativ)*
15. *Fantasie über Abendmotive des Versöhnungstages (einschl. Kantorensolo "Jaaleh tacha-nunenu")*
16. *Kaddish-Weise (Minhag Sepharad Amsterdam, vor Bar'chu im Schacharit)*
17. *4 Paraphrasen zum Morgen- und Mussaphgebet (Kulam ahuvim; zur jissrael; misod chachamim; ochillah lael)*
18. *Fuge im hypodorischen Stil über einen Pijut (Ochillah lael), Minhag Aschkenaz maaravi*
18a. *Fuge über Abodah-Motiv "Achas w'achat"*
19. *2 Fugen (und Rezitativ) über sephardisches Schofar-Motiv "Adonaj bekol shofar" und "T'Kabel B'Razon"*
20. *Fuge über sephardische Weise "Schma jissrael"*
21. *Pentatonische Toccata, Variationen, und Finale (Sounds of the Selichot, Min hag Asch-kenaz maaravi)*
22. *Sephardische Selichoth-Weise "Kamti beaschmoret" (Ausgabe für Orgel-Solo)*
22a. *Fughetta on Sephardic Tune "Elohim, Eli Attah"*
23. *Wehakohanim-Rezitativ, Aboda-Tune (Ausgabe für Orgel-Solo)*
24. *Neilah-Klänge (Präludium zum Kaddish, Neilah und Schemone Esre des Schlußgebets des Versöhnungstags)*

FIGURE 4.17A. Abraham Idelsohn, *HOM*, vol. 1, no. 93.
The little sister [i.e., the Jewish people] prepares her prayers and sings her praise. God heal her sickness, and may her misfortunes cease.

from the rhythm of Idelsohn's transcription (the greatest change is the introduction of triplets). Two elements characterize the theme and become a central aspect of the following variations: Samuel's treatment of meter and syncopation.

At first it seems as if Samuel follows no particular system of musical order, especially in regard to meter. As early as the second measure of the theme's introduction, the measure in the lower part is incomplete. In this and many other compositions by Samuel, this is not an exception but the rule. Further instances of incomplete measures appear in the theme at the beginning (measures 3 and 5) and the first variation (measure 9). If this is not a mistake by the composer but an unusual and bold form of expression, one might well ask what it represents. Through the conscious violation of the time system, the meter is given a new and different role within the composition; it also leads to new considerations of performance practice since the only way to perform the piece is in an improvisatory-recitativic manner. The sound recording of

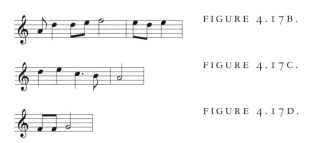

FIGURE 4.17B.

FIGURE 4.17C.

FIGURE 4.17D.

Hans Samuel's own performance of his compositions (held at the archive of Kol Israel in Jerusalem) confirms the inevitability of an improvisatory feeling evoked by the transgression of meter. A steady pulse is hardly noticeable, and the interpretation of the composition is very free. Thus, Samuel's treatment of meter creates the recitativic element in Jewish music that he desired, which until then had been practiced only by the ḥazzan in the long melismatic improvisations with rich coloratura.

Another key element of the variations is the use of syncopation (e.g., measures 2, 13, 14, 16, 18, 34). For Samuel, syncopation serves as a sort of principal rhythmic motive, partly because of the overall contrapuntal texture and partly because of Samuel's individual definition of Jewish music: The syncopations are an important means of attaining the independence of the voices in the polyphonic writing; the voices take their harmonic (and sometimes disharmonic) movement from the interplay of syncopated dissonance and resolution. Samuel's syncopated phrases seem to exist as such only as an artifact of the notation; in the reality of performance they reduce measure (and therefore meter) to absurdity. At the same time, the way in which syncopation pushes the accent away from the first beat evokes the anapestic rhythm of Hebrew speech. All of these features are prevalent in the theme and then modified in the fifteen variations and finale (table 4.9).

The other two voices that appear concurrently with the theme, Aḥot Ketannah, do not serve merely as accompaniment. As the texture is canonic and thus contrapuntal, the accompanying parts have their own function in the theme and the variations. Although Samuel describes his composition as canonic, strict imitation is not maintained. The canonic form serves rather as an auxiliary means derived from Western music that Samuel transforms into "Jewish music." Overall, the composition consists of three voices, each of which has a specific and alternating role:

Part I: theme on Aḥot Ketannah or Tikhleh part

Part II: imitation of the theme (very loose imitation)

Part III: inversion of the theme or head motive, which becomes the main motive of the third voice and later a theme with further variations

Both Aḥot Ketannah and the accompaniment in the introduction of the theme are subject to modification in the course of the piece. These microvariations are, in part, independent from the actual theme of the respective variation. The resulting texture raises the question of whether Samuel conceived the piece based on a theme melody in the classical sense or on a thematic complex with three voices. The continuous counterpoint and perpetual develop-

TABLE 4.9. Structure of the Variations in Canonic Style by Hans Samuel

Variation	Voice	Specifications
Var. I	Lower part	4/4 time
Var. II	Upper part	6/8 time; allegretto; with rich figurations
Var. III	Lower part	6/8 time; allegretto; with rich figurations, transposed from A to D
Var. IV	Upper part; lower part on "tikhleh"	4/4 time; "Responsione"; Andante; melody of congregation "tikhleh" appears for 2½ measures in the highest voice, then in the bass
Var. V	Upper part on "tikhleh"	4/4 time; allegretto; with rich figurations
Var. VI	Lower part on "tikhleh"	4/4 time, animato; with rich figurations
Var. VII	Upper part	6/8 time; allegro vivace; with rich figurations, in C
Var. VIII	Lower part	6/8 time; with rich figurations, in C
Var. IX	Upper part	3/4 time; andante; accompanying voices varied; richly ornamented
Var. X	Upper part	4/4 time; andante; with rich figurations; in E
Var. XI	Lower part	4/4 time; with rich figurations
Var. XII	Upper part	4/4 time; allegro; with rich figurations; in D
Var. XIII	Lower part	4/4 time; with rich figurations; in G
Var. XIV	Upper part	4/4 time; andante; accompanying voices varied; with rich figurations; in A-flat
Var. XV	Lower part	4/4 time; accompanying voices are varied; with rich figurations; in A-flat
Finale		in G

FIGURE 4.18. Hans Samuel, *Variations in Canonic Style*, MS (ca. 1930s), finale, measures 1–2.

ment of the theme(s) evokes the peculiar impression that Aḥot Ketannah, albeit audible, is running away and is barely graspable.

The final part of the composition is based on the head motive of Aḥot Ketannah (figure 4.18), ornamented to the utmost and changed beyond recognition.

The musical parameter that most distinguishes the variations from the finale is tonality. In what key or keys does the finale move? A close examination of the tonal progression gives no conclusive answer: The first three measures appear to be in B-flat major, not least because of their accidentals; however, a single tonal center or fundamental pitch does not exist, and neither does a cadence. After three measures, Samuel sets an enharmonic change by altering the accidentals of not only one chord but gradually voice by voice as well: First, the A-flat in the middle part is reinterpreted as G-sharp, followed by the D-flat in the top voice to C-sharp (measure 4). The following measures contain continuous changes of accidentals, first sharps and (from measure 10 on) flats.

An interesting twist occurs in measure 24, marked "quasi cadenza." With this descriptor Samuel refers to the old type of written-out passages for the soloist in a concerto or other works that became popular in the course of sixteenth- and seventeenth-century ornamentation practice. The solo passage is not restricted to one voice but is first taken up by the lowest part in the pedal, continued by the middle voice and the top part, and led in measure 31 once more into a virtuosic pedal solo. Thus the finale becomes a freely developing fantasia. In measure 34 it takes unexpected turns in its tonal construction. With the reintroduction of the entire prayer-leader part of Aḥot Ketannah— this occurs with striking rhythm changes while maintaining syncopation— the composition returns to monotonality: Aḥot Ketannah, originally in the Ahavah Rabbah mode, is now harmonized in A minor (natural). After five measures the congregation's part is introduced, transposed upward by a fourth. At this point the composition becomes a four-part work for the first time. Concurrently, the continuous imitations end, giving way to a harmonization of the Tikhleh part, which in its harmonic chiaroscuro and chromaticism is highly reminiscent of Max Reger's chorale preludes for organ. Unexpectedly but musically not unprepared, the finale ends in G major despite the fact that the tonal center of the congregation's part seems to be A minor. Thus the impression of a half cadence on the interdominant is evoked. With this unforeseen turn, does Samuel reinforce the meaning of the end of the poem ("may the year and its blessing begin"), which is both an end and a beginning at the same time?

The thematic construction and the tonality of Samuel's variation cycle are somewhat confusing. Its harmony, tonality, and rhythm are hardly classifiable, and there is no real development striving toward a climax. Instead, Samuel builds up a number of tensions that result in smaller climaxes, as is common in ḥazzanut or traditional music. Through these techniques Samuel achieves his compositional goal in organ music: dissociation from the functional harmony of Western music and particularly of the classic and Romantic era, which had never been part of the traditional music of Jewish liturgy, as well as the recitativic-improvisatory use of a Jewish theme in the style of traditional ḥazzanut.

Because of the virtuosic skill required in manual and pedal playing, which demands technical perfection of the organist, this piece goes far beyond mere Gebrauchsmusik for Jewish worship. It clearly belongs to the "Jewish organ music" (as opposed to "synagogue organ music") side of his oeuvre, intended for use in the concert hall.

In many ways the work is comparable to the organ compositions of Johann Nepomuk David (1895–1977), who was deemed a master of polyphony and contrapuntal style during the first half of the twentieth century, as is evident especially in his chorale preludes, partitas, and passacaglias written between 1932 and 1969.[179] An example of this affinity is the cycle *Christus, der ist mein Leben: Ein Lehrstück für Orgel* (1937), which uses different canonic forms ranging from simple canon to canon at the seventh, octave, fourth, and fifth and changes configurations throughout the canon at tenth by diminution and second in inversion, double counterpoint, and other forms such as the fugue. In *Jerusalem, du hochgebaute Stadt: Introduktion und Fuge* (1932) David works with a heavily figurated fugue subject.[180] His organ compositions follow the ideals of the Orgelbewegung, and his neo-Baroque style is the most obvious result. Some of David's most typical style characteristics include canonic structures, polymeter and polytonality, monothematic structures, counterpoint (as a means of expression), and thematic metamorphoses.[181]

David's chorale-based works composed after 1939 (in his second creative period) feature style characteristics similar to those of Samuel's organ pieces, especially in that the nature of the cantus firmus determines the composition's structure.[182] Both composers use an individualized approach to extended tonality that remains connected to a key note. In their polyphonic style they focus on horizontal lines instead of vertical chords, with the latter occurring only as a consequence of the contrapuntal texture. Thus any harmonic events are dependent on the polyphony and hence hold a secondary position in the overall composition; nonetheless, they are by no means arbitrary or irrelevant in auditory reception.

Samuel's and David's organ works are part of a larger development in organ music that departs from harmonically inspired figuration in the new direction of a widely drawn-out dissonant diatonicism, which culminates in a "synthesis of figuration and imitation, of fantasy and control."[183] Johann Nepomuk David continued his compositional style, especially the tonal emancipation, in the organ music of his third productive period—from 1950 on. Hans Samuel's attempts to further develop his theories of Jewish and synagogue organ music in Germany failed. The destruction of organs in the Kristallnacht of November 9–10, 1938, ended his career in Germany as organist and composer and any other future vocation there as well. The life-threatening situation for Jews in Central Europe forced him to emigrate as soon as possible, and in 1939 he departed for Palestine.

"AN OLD-NEW HEBREW MUSICAL LANGUAGE"

Over a period of a hundred years organ music evolved in Jewish culture partly along the same lines as the general repertoire of its time but always with the goal of representing the Jewish communities it was composed for. Its music-historical development is especially evident in its style, which changed from homophonic to complex polyphonic textures. With regard to thematic construction, the very early works evidently made no immediate reference to traditional Jewish music, while in the course of time some compositions began to incorporate Western Ashkenazic melodies and later introduced the music of other Jewish communities and geographic cultural areas of the Ashkenazim, Sephardim, and Yemenites. Connected to these thematic changes is the use of tonality and modality, which developed from a strong orientation toward major and minor tonality—from the harmonization of shtayger and other modal systems (maqām), often adapted to the tonality of Western art music, to the abandonment of functional and extended tonality. In rhythm, while the nineteenth-century repertoire is metrical (i.e., strictly adhering to a regular beat), early twentieth-century compositions utilized ametric or polymetric forms, in which the beat may be no more than a convenient "fiction."

That the organ repertoire of Jewish communities cannot be reduced to a single theme or style is evident in the *Introduction zur Thodenfeier* and the manifold arrangements of synagogue songs for organ by cantors of the nineteenth century, of which Louis Lewandowski's are perhaps the most significant, but Heinrich Schalit's Postlude, Arno Nadel's *Passacaglia über "Wadonaj pakad es ssarah" (Toravorlesung am Neujahrsfest)*, and Hans Samuel's *Variations in Canonic Style* are also important. They have distinct meanings within the Jewish communities and occupy different spaces in the field of Jewish music, and although most draw upon Jewish vocal music as a thematic foundation, they have little in common stylistically not only because they were composed in different periods but above all because of their gradually increasing distance from the norms of Christian-oriented organ literature.

The Jewish composers' overall objective was at first liturgical—to create a repertoire differentiated in form and style from church music, especially the Christian chorale prelude, which had served as a model for a number of earlier works. This goal expanded in the twentieth century with the development of an organ repertoire for concert use and included the creation of a uniquely Jewish organ music independent not only of music for Christian worship but also of the nonreligious Western repertoire. There was no longer a real model for composers of Jewish or synagogue organ music to follow, and thus began the detachment from the previous repertoires. In consequence, new developments in different musical directions occurred, one of which was the belief that "the core of synagogue organ music . . . in contrast to the Christian chorale prelude [can] only be the free recitative. The use of forms developed in the Christian and general organ repertoire is only allowed to the degree that the form absorbs the recitativic and rhapsodic elements of synagogue music as organic components."[184]

Thus, the use of Western music techniques became more and more a means to the end of creating a specific organ music in Jewish culture—an invention of a new authenticity or tradition. In this respect, the organ compositions of Arno Nadel, Heinrich Schalit, and Hans Samuel also form a sharp contrast to the organ music of Jewish congregations in the nineteenth century. Joseph Machlis confirms the differences in the use of musical elements from outside the common practice of Western European as they were adopted by composers of many different origins in the nineteenth and twentieth centuries: "Nineteenth-century Nationalism added a variety of idioms to the language of European music. . . . Twentieth-century Nationalism, understandably, took a different turn. The new Nationalists were determined to preserve the tunes of the folk singers in as accurate a form as possible."[185]

Indeed, the development of Jewish themes adapts to the general musical trends, especially those related to nationalism: Nineteenth-century organ music subordinates Jewish motives and themes to Western constraints, whereas twentieth-century composers tried to co-opt the compositional forms and techniques of early twentieth-century music in order to preserve and develop a new and unmistakably Jewish musical idiom.

Although between 1810 and 1938 organ music had unfailingly absorbed elements of Western art music, the consciousness of this assimilation was slowly changing. The wish for a modern but nonetheless uniquely Jewish expression was one of the foundations of the nineteenth- and early–twentieth-century search for Jewish identity, and it left its mark on organ music as well.

One of the key influences in this changing identity was the Law for the Restoration of the Civil Service, which inevitably led to the foundation of the Kulturbund, thereby isolating the Jewish population of Germany and its culture from its environment. Thus, in the 1930s and 1940s, organ music was performed exclusively by Jewish musicians, and only a Jewish audience was permitted to listen to the new compositions. The sharp division between "German" and "non-German" music, enforced by the Nazis, accompanied the outlawing of Jewish composers and their works. The new repertoire that emerged during this time was affected in that it became a symbol of forced demarcation and exclusion and developed its own dynamic. Instead of surrendering to outlaw status, Jewish composers created a repertoire that united two elements proscribed by the Nazis, Jewishness and modernity, to achieve an autonomous, both authentic and modern, Jewish art.[185] Musicians of the period adapted traditional Jewish melodies to the musical standards of the twentieth century by interweaving tonal and atonal motives, thus developing what was hailed as a distinctive and modern Jewish idiom.

The Kulturbund, even though exploited and abused by the Nazis in the program of cultural ghettoization and in propaganda, offered the only possibility for creating and performing this music. Before the Kulturbund, endeavors were already being undertaken in the Russian Empire, France, Italy, Poland, and Palestine toward a "national" Jewish music—a cultural- or community-specific repertoire that embodied Jewish identity.

The developing German-Jewish organ culture abruptly ended at its peak in 1938, when most of the instruments were destroyed in the Kristallnacht and with them the possibility of performing organ music. Although the Kristallnacht marks an end somehow, the extinction of this growing cultural tradition continued after 1938, when Jewish composers and musicians emigrated or were murdered. Thanks only to the mass exodus that began in 1933, the cultural Final Solution could not be completely consummated.

| The Aftermath of Emigration

With the National Socialists' 1933 seizure of power in Germany, a mass emigration[1] of German Jews began, a majority of whom headed for the United States, the British Mandate of Palestine, Great Britain, and South America. These events naturally had momentous consequences for the ways in which the Jewish musicians' identities were variously lost, reconstructed, or maintained. According to Reinhold Brinkmann, emigration as a profound personal experience influences identity in several ways: It introduces change, it is idealized in retrospect, and it is oriented toward the future.[2] One possible consequence of such experiences is an ambivalent attitude on the emigrants' part. Because of their need for social and professional integration, they had to balance preserving an identity that had been shaped by the European musical tradition and at the same time adjust to a new cultural situation.[3] Brinkmann's thoughts lead to the questions of whether the artists' cultural identity broadened in emigration, as many émigré musicians had to assimilate for a second time, and whether the process brought about a change in the place of German-Jewish identity in the hierarchy of their multiple identities.

The development of German-Jewish identity inevitably took different turns in diverse countries, for cultural identification with the "new home" varied from place to place.[4] Two elements, however, were common to all: their Jewish descent and the reason for their escape. Many of them showed a "remarkable attachment to German language and high culture (especially music and literature)."[5] Because German had become the mother tongue of German-Jewish composers, its loss affected the composition of vocal music more than instrumental music. For composers of religious music, this problem was perhaps less severe, as Hebrew was used beside vernacular languages in most synagogues.[6]

Unquestionably, forced relocation and new living conditions had an effect on composers' creative output, including their new organ works; by the same token, these émigrés had an important influence on the shaping of the musical life of their adopted countries.[7]

Two destinations were especially attractive for émigré musicians involved with the synagogue organ: the United States and the British Mandate of Palestine. Between 1825 and 1875 approximately 250,000 Jews (a majority of whom came from German-speaking countries) immigrated to the New World, which, by 1918, contained the largest Jewish community in the world.[8] Because of its splendid infrastructure, the United States was the ideal country for emigration. Large cities such as New York and Los Angeles promised a spectrum of possibilities and were especially attractive to artists inasmuch as the nation's economic and cultural life was highly concentrated in the metropolitan areas. In Baltimore, the German-Jewish Reform Society was founded in 1845 by a group of emigrants that applied the liturgical and musical reforms of the Hamburg Reform Temple. This movement spread throughout the United States and in the process introduced organs to many synagogues (both Reform and Conservative). Because of the nineteenth-century reforms following the German model, the United States became the ideal working place for émigré organists. Thus, the earlier wave of immigration paved the way for another influx, which reached its peak in the 1930s and 1940s.

After the Russian pogroms of 1881, Palestine became a refuge mainly for Zionists from Russia and eastern European countries,[9] while in the 1930s it was a safe haven for Jews fleeing Nazi Europe. Before 1930, the Jewish population of Palestine was less than a twentieth of its current size,[10] and with the increase in population the musical landscape steadily began to develop. The immigrants would have a considerable influence on the culture of the state of Israel and shape its musical landscape.[11] The conditions for a unique Jewish organ culture were unfavorable in view of the fact that no organ had ever been built in a synagogue in Palestine (nor has one yet been built in Israel). One can only speculate about the reasons for the absence of organs in Israeli synagogues and the fact that, in the Ashkenazic tradition, an *Orgelsynagoge* was never a priority in the creation of Jewish congregations in Israel. The first four Zionist aliyot (1882–1929) brought to Israel immigrants from the Ottoman Empire, the Russian Empire, Yemen, and Poland, in short, countries that had no (significant) tradition of the Reform movement, organ building, or organ music in the synagogue. Naturally, the development or continuation of an organ tradition was not foremost in the minds of these immigrants. Another cultural factor may have been (and probably still is) economic in nature. Given their difficult financial situation, the emigrants may have found it too costly an undertaking to import an instrument or finance the building of one by a manufacturer from abroad.

With regard to religious factors, the Ashkenazic Jews constitute less than half of all Israeli Jews, and only a fraction of them belong to Progressive Judaism,[12] which is more conservative in its approach than the German and American Reforms. Liberal branches of Judaism have always had a negligible presence in Israel. The Religious Affairs Ministry is Orthodox dominated, and the chief rabbinate has authority over a variety of issues, underlining the fact that Israel does not provide an easy ground for the continuation of the German-Jewish organ culture. Overall, the organ has never had a strong position in the Middle East, either in cultural institutions or in Christian churches.

Nonetheless, the creation and development of an Israeli music culture did include organ music, indirectly continuing the German-Jewish attempt at creating a uniquely Jewish repertoire. In this chapter I discuss the continuation of the German-Jewish culture in these two countries by drawing upon the lives and works of representative musicians.

Limitations in the "Land of Opportunity"

Among the countries of immigration, the United States was the preferred destination for German-Jewish artists, a fact that is reflected in the high number of musicians there. The majority were active as string players (34 percent), pianists (35.4 percent), and conductors (45.9 percent).[13] Although the statistics do not separately list cantors, organists, or other synagogue musicians, many of those who fled National Socialism to survive and to further their art in emigration worked in these fields as well. Organists and composers, including a number of historically important figures, transplanted the nascent Jewish organ culture to the United States to enable the continued development of musical traditions that had been born in Germany. Musicians who found employment at a synagogue influenced the Jewish-American service with their organ playing, as well as the construction of new organs; others became organ pedagogues. The frequently organized Refugees in Temple Concerts provided a forum in which excellent musicians could perform and thereby enrich the cultural life of the Jewish community. These concerts were in many ways reminiscent of events organized by the Kulturbund and may have been an unintended continuation.

Among the émigré musicians working at synagogues in the United States, a large number had been active as organists or composers before emigration. Others saw in synagogue music a new chance to find employment. While still in Europe, some musicians realized that synagogues in the United States could offer employment and that, other than in the secular music world, competition would be comparatively minor. Consequently, they prepared themselves before emigrating, as the example of Frank Rothschild demonstrates. As a music teacher at the secondary school Philanthropin in Frankfurt am Main, Rothschild sought a competitive edge and thus had one of his students, Martha Sommer, instruct him in organ playing before he left for the United States.[14] As a last resort to ensure some income, organists might also be able to find work playing for churches.

The career of Ludwig Altman illustrates the different paths musicians took for their survival: Although a trained organist, Altman first chose to teach piano after his arrival in New York on January 8, 1937, since a position as an organist was normally a poorly paid, part-time job that would not cover living expenses. Eager to work in his profession, however, he finally found a post as an organist at Beth Israel, a Conservative synagogue on Geary near Fillmore Street in San Francisco.[15] In his autobiography Altman shares details about being hired; although the following excerpt has a tinge of humor, it nonetheless reveals the important fact that church musicians were employed at synagogues as well, thus continuing the practice found in German synagogues:

> The organist at that time was a Christian—who could not play on the Passover, Pesach Service because it coincided with Easter. So the synagogue desperately needed an organist who could step in at the last moment. The Pesach service is not easy. It is like a Sabbath service, but with additions. So Cantor Rabinovich—a saintly man, a patriarch, a wonderful musician, but terribly hard of hearing—asked me to meet him. He was very anxious to know if I knew enough Hebrew to follow the service. I said "Yes, I am confident. I had, after all, four years of synagogue-playing in Berlin." He said, "Well, I'll give you one question. If you can answer it, then I'll give you the job." And what was the question? "Tell me the translation of the Hebrew word *chet*. What is *chet*?" I said to the cantor, "I know the translation in German, but I don't know the English word for it." "It's all right," he said. So I said, "*Chet* means *Suende*." *Suende* means in English, sin. And because I knew the equivalent to *chet*, I got the first organ job in America.[16]

Later Altman was hired as organist at the Second Church of Christ in Berkeley. He describes this step as exceptional and even unthinkable in Europe—a

Jew playing for the church. The hiring of Jewish musicians by various churches (or for that matter, that of Christian musicians by Jewish congregations) is not at all uncommon in the United States. The multiethnic and multireligious landscape of the United States has fed a genuine exchange on a purely professional level. These collaborations among denominations have been widespread in the course of interfaith dialogue from the mid-twentieth century on. Although Altman worked for Baptist, Episcopalian, and Presbyterian churches, he continued to play the organ for almost fifty years—albeit without a contract—at Temple Emanu-El in San Francisco. For him "it was just the place to be. It was just so overwhelming that there was no other within even a mile."[17]

The synagogue was not the only institution that provided a new artistic home for émigré musicians and composers. Jewish organ music was presented as an attractive repertoire to the Jewish-American secular music world, thus affording more performance opportunities for organists. A letter from the Lodz (Poland)-born organist and composer Joseph Yasser to Heinrich Schalit reads (in the original English): "It may interest you that I have been invited to play several organ recitals during this season at the newly opened Jewish Museum of New York City. As you may well understand, I am looking eagerly for worthy Jewish music to be presented at these recitals, and I would like very much to include your compositions, among others, into my programs."[18]

Yasser, already familiar with Schalit's compositions, regarded them as an enrichment of the American-Jewish repertoire, which had an insufficient number of adequate works. During the 1940s the Park Avenue Synagogue in New York annually commissioned compositions from resident composers and emigrants to fill this gap.

The lives and works of Herbert Fromm and Herman Berlinski trace different developments in the Jewish organ tradition from its beginning in Germany to its continuation in the United States. Fromm is representative of those reputable organists and composers of organ music who had been already established before their emigration and then continued in the same career; Berlinski, however, first discovered the potential of the synagogue organ after his emigration.

Even before Herbert Fromm emigrated, he ensured himself employment as an organist in the United States. In the summer of 1936 he had already been to New York to perform a concert of organ and vocal music together with baritone Ernst Wolff. But surprisingly and for some unknown reason, he returned to Germany after this first visit. Then, about six months later, a letter dated January 5, 1937, from Williard W. Saperston, counselor-at-law in Buffalo, New York, offers Fromm the position of organist at a synagogue in that city: "I am pleased to report to you that at a meeting of our Board of Directors held yesterday a resolution was adopted authorizing our music committee to engage you as an organist for Temple Beth Zion at a salary of $1000.00 a year, your term of service to begin July 1st, 1937, for a period of one year. . . . Kindly let me know at once whether you are in position to come to America to take up your duties with us on that date, giving us the name of the ship upon which you will sail and the date that you expect to arrive in the Port of New York."[19]

This offer encouraged Fromm to hasten his emigration to the United States. In 1937 he thus became organist and music director at Temple Beth Zion in Buffalo, and in 1939 he was hired as organist and choir director of the First Presbyterian Church in East Aurora, New York. He held both positions until June 1941. Shortly after his emigration he resumed giving organ concerts at Temple Beth Zion, presenting not only the works of Bach and Pachelbel but also his own compositions written during his years in Germany. On May 11, 1938, the *Buffalo News* reviewed his four short chorale preludes: "[They] stood out for their conciseness, their originality and their beauty of feeling. They should be more frequently heard. The program closed with his Passacaglia and Fugue, a scholarly and brilliant work."[20] Fromm quickly became known as an organist and a composer; an American newspaper reports only months after his arrival: "Something of a revolution in Jewish liturgical music originating here, which may have wide effect in American music circles, is predicted with the appointment of Herbert Fromm, youthful composer, as organist and choirmaster at Temple Beth Zion, Delaware Avenue. . . . His appointment to Temple Beth Zion is his first in the country. He has given recitals in Temple Israel in New York and he played his own compositions over the radio."[21]

Fromm's creativity impressed those who were active in the synagogue music scene in the United States, and his authority grew to the extent that news of his success reached the remaining Jewish communities in Germany, where he was celebrated as the "innovator of synagogue music."[22] Together with Heinrich Schalit and Hugo Adler, Fromm became a highly recognized reformer of synagogue music in the United States; he formulated his vision on the following objectives: "The assembly of service-music by choosing works by different composers is not yet the ideal. I entertain the idea of unity in music (not only a unified style, but the development of an underlying idea). This is my own goal and I aim at reaching it."[23]

Emigration offered Fromm possibilities in his development as a composer that he did not have in Germany. He was now able to pursue his vision of synagogue music unhindered, free from resentment by the congregation or the rabbinate, and, of course, free from persecution by the National Socialists. He continued his career as composer with two works: one for the synagogue, the other one for the church: *Partita for Organ: Let All Mortal Flesh Keep Silence*, which premiered on May 4, 1940, at Beth Zion in Buffalo, and *Veni Emmanuel* (1941), a work most likely related to his employment at the First Presbyterian Church in East Aurora.

The following years were decisive for Fromm in his professional development. By 1939 he had taken classes in counterpoint at the University of Buffalo, and from 1940 to 1941 he continued his studies with Paul Hindemith at the Berkshire Music Center in Tanglewood, Massachusetts. At the same time, Fromm was appointed music director and organist at Temple Israel in Boston, New England's largest Reform congregation, founded in 1854 by German members of Temple Ohabei Shalom. Fromm claimed that this position offered him many opportunities as a musician.[24] Indeed, the change of positions marked a turning point in his musical career as he further developed the ideas of synagogue organ music that he had first formulated in Buffalo and continued to compose on this basis. His review of Mario Castelnuovo-Tedesco's *Prayers My Grandfather Wrote* comments on the state of this music and expresses his own visions:[25]

New organ music for the synagogue will be eagerly seized upon by every temple organist who is tired of forever playing the established organ repertoire of the church. The last few decades have witnessed a renewal of vocal music for the synagogue and a modern liturgical style is clearly discernible in some of the new works. One should expect contemporary Jewish composers to parallel this development with music for organ. However, little has been done so far and it is disappointing to see that Castelnuovo-Tedesco's "Five Preludes" do not add weight to the literature of organ music for worship. . . . There is no room in a review to go into a lengthy discussion of what organ music for the synagogue should be. Only this: frugality of means would seem to be a desirable and honest start for an almost new branch of musical literature. Whether organ pieces for the synagogue should be based on Hebrew themes or freely conceived (as in the case of Castelnuovo-Tedesco) each composer must decide for himself. But one thing is sure: what we require is—to say it metaphorically—straight furniture; the curved and softly padded furniture of yesterday does not answer our needs. Castelnuovo-Tedesco's "Preludes," unfortunately, belong to the latter category.[26]

Motivated by the lack of repertoire and the inadequate quality of the few existing pieces, Fromm began writing a new composition in 1953: With *Organ Prelude (After a Chasidic Melody)*, he set the cornerstone for the *Suite of Organ Pieces on Hebraic Motifs*, which was completed in 1958.

The *Suite of Organ Pieces* was influenced by several different elements. As indicated in an article published in the *American Organist* (May 1959), it draws from Isadore Freed's book *Harmonizing the Jewish Modes*, which presents theories on shtayger.[27] In addition, aspects of Hindemith's compositional theory are noticeable. Further inspirations were drawn from different Jewish musical traditions: The first movement ("Cantillation"), the third ("Out of the Depths"), and the sixth ("Song of Praise") use the Sephardic melodies from Florence collected in Federico Consolo's *Sefer Shirei Yisrael Libro dei Canti d'Israele* (Florence, 1892). "Hassidic Interlude" (no. 2, intended as a wedding prelude) and "Pastorale" (no. 4) are inspired by hasidic and Israeli musical traditions, and the "Psalm" (no. 5) is based on a chant from the Ashkenazic *minhag* [custom] of eastern Europe. Fromm defines this work as "planned with the idea of bringing several traditions together under one roof, by which I mean the stylistic unity of consistent musical approach."[28]

Fromm wanted to create a work whose movements could either serve as independent pieces for prelude, interlude, or postlude within the Jewish liturgy or be performed as a cycle and thus become a concert piece. As he wrote to Isadore Freed, "It is my hope that my Suite will help further the cause of the organ music for the Synagogue."[29] Months later Fromm referred to the suite once again in a letter (in German) to Heinrich Schalit: "I am happy that you—as Hilde briefly informed me—like my organ suite. If your time allows, I'd be happy to have a more detailed discussion. Recently I saw Freudenthal in New York; the sale of the suite is going very well and seems to meet the requirements."[30] Joseph Freudenthal, president of Transcontinental Music Publications, anticipated the success of the *Suite of Organ Pieces*. Shortly after the publisher received the work, he acknowledged it as an important contribution to synagogue organ music: "First of all, let me tell you that I am very much impressed going over your Organ Suite. It will definitely be a valuable contribution not only to the music in the synagogue, but to organ literature in general. I have given much thought to the original idea of publishing the work in single pieces and now, having familiarized myself more with it, I feel that its Suite character would be served much better if it were published as a collection."[31]

Because of its character as a finale, Freudenthal proposed that the "Psalm" be the suite's concluding piece. Fromm, however, preferred the "Song of Praise," using audience reaction and the character of the movement as arguments:

"The quiet ending does not make much difference since applause is not ex-pected in organ recitals. Played as a postlude after the Service, the piece mirrors the natural decrescendo resulting from the commotion of a rising congrega-tion to the quietness of the dark sanctuary after the people have left."[32]

The *Suite of Organ Pieces* was well received by Fromm's fellow organists: On February 8, 1960, Ludwig Altman performed three movements at the Palace of the Legion of Honor in San Francisco, and the work was even played in church: On November 15, 1959, some of the movements were performed at Trinity Church in Boston, with George H. Faxon at the organ. A few years later Robert Noehren, organist and organ builder, confirmed another church performance: "I wanted to let you know that I will be playing your Pastorale (Suite on Hebraic Motifs) on the dedication recital of my new Organ at the First Unitarian Church, San Francisco (4m, 60 stops), Sunday evening Octo-ber 29th. I like it very much, and it should sound well on the new organ. I will use the Cromhorne (instead of a Clarinet) which is nicely located in the Rückpositiv division."[33]

With an arrangement commissioned by the California Woodwind Quin-tet in 1960, the *Suite of Organ Pieces* was arranged for flute, oboe, clarinet, horn, and bassoon. Thus, the work—with its universal Jewish concept—was transferred to the concert hall.

The success of the *Suite of Organ Pieces* may lie in the fact that it incorpo-rates various traditions that America's different Jewish cultures can identify with. Christians, at the same time, seemed to appreciate Fromm's new com-positional approach as well and did not shy away from adopting a Jewish piece for performance in church. That the work is based on Jewish themes did not seem to matter.

By using melodies from various Jewish cultures as a thematic basis for his composition, Fromm followed a trend that was already prevalent in the works of Jewish composers before emigration: the connection of musical material re-garded as authentically Jewish with contemporary compositional techniques. This approach continued to fascinate Jewish composers. Only in the United States did Herbert Fromm have an opportunity to introduce this style to a broader—non-Jewish—audience. This was also true for other émigré musi-cians and composers such as Ernest Bloch, Lazare Saminsky, Joseph Yasser, Jakob Weinberg, Oskar Guttmann, Hugo Adler, and Heinrich Schalit, who were no longer confined to the "spiritual ghetto" and took the opportunity to further develop as composers.[34] These representatives of Jewish organ music incorporated traditional motives of the Eastern Jews, the accents of the Torah, and melody and tonality based on the shtayger; they even searched for a Jew-ish idiom without including any explicitly Jewish material at all.

For Herman Berlinski, emigration meant choosing a new musical path. His career was initially unconnected to organ music; in fact, he had not intended to pursue an occupation in the world of synagogue music. Having grown up in a rather conservative Polish-Jewish family, the organ was for him a "symbol of abandoning Jewish culture—of absolute assimilation."[35] He began his studies at the Landeskonservatorium [State Conservatory] in Leipzig, where he studied theory with Sigfrid Karg-Elert between 1927 and 1932. As a composer, he was particularly interested in cabaret and musical theater. The Nazis' rise to power and subsequent adoption of anti-Jewish legislation, however, ended those opportunities. Having obtained the *Musiklehrerexamen* [teaching certificate in music] and the *Konzertexamen* [concert examination], Berlinski left the Leipzig conservatory and in March of 1933 emigrated to Paris:

> I was 23 years old when I left Leipzig to live in exile. The modest works left behind in the city of my birth have become, as Rabbi Leo Baeck said, "tombs of naïve, political, and cultural illusions." Freed from the superficial religious customs of my parents' house, a deeper analysis of my Jewish self-awareness became a self-sufficient necessity. This process was very difficult and slow, and eventually had a crippling effect on all my creative efforts. I knew that from an ideological perspective only one thing could remain, the fact that I was JEWISH.—I left Germany existentially as a Jew and not as a German any more. This situation finally became the central point in my musical development—as a Jewish composer.[36]

After concert tours as a pianist in Warsaw, Gdansk, Brussels, and Paris, Berlinski continued his education at the École Normale de Musique in Paris, where he studied composition and piano from 1934 to 1938 with Nadia Boulanger and, ironically, Alfred Cortot.[37] While studying at the Schola Cantorum in Paris from 1937 to 1939, he became acquainted with a group of composers known as La Jeune France,[38] who, albeit without a set program, were dedicated to fostering modern (national) French music. At this time, Berlinski was also music director of the Paris Avant-Garde Yiddish Theater. In 1938 he composed *Chazoth*, a suite for string quartet in five movements, which was premiered later that year in the Salle Erard. He composed the work upon learning of his father's death. In this piece Berlinski recalls the prayer chants and improvised melodies he had heard in his parents' home.

Berlinski began playing the organ while serving in the French Foreign Legion. At Christmas 1939 he was stationed in a village near Lyons, where, for a lack of an organist, he was asked to play the reed organ during Mass. After emigrating to the United States in 1941, he worked at first as a freelance composer and musician in New York. In 1948 he studied composition at Tanglewood with Olivier Messiaen, cofounder of La Jeune France. As Herbert Fromm in emigration had taken on the stamp of his teacher, Hindemith, so Berlinski's artistic development was dominated by Messiaen's influence. An organist and significant composer of organ music, Messiaen inspired Berlinski to devote himself to the organ as well: "I started writing major symphonic works when I worked with Messiaen in Tanglewood, but the organ seduced me and fulfilled all my symphonic aspirations. I could compose for it, play it, and I didn't have to go through a conductor. Most probably the eleven symphonies I wrote for organ by now would have been eleven symphonies for orchestra. That may or may not be a loss, I don't know."[39]

In 1953 Berlinski began studying organ performance with Joseph Yasser, a move that brought him closer to synagogue music. Realizing the synagogue offered him not only employment but also possibilities for expanding his creativity, he also resumed academic studies and earned a degree in sacred music at the Jewish Theological Seminary in New York: "There was a need for Jewish organists and there were possibilities to study, which I of course had benefited from."[40] Only a year later he was hired as organist by Temple Rodeph Sholom and worked as assistant organist at Temple Emanu-El, both in New York. It was his professional success as a synagogue performer that led him to making a career as the most successful Jewish composer of organ music.

One of Berlinski's key compositions for organ, *From the World of My Father*, had originated as a suite for piano, oboe, flute, and clarinet, titled *Chazoth*, in 1938, when Berlinski was in exile in Paris. Having lost the original manuscript, in 1957 he arranged the five-movement suite for organ from memory. Berlinski understood his composition as an expression of his Jewish heritage and identity. Musically, the work was inspired by Eastern European Jewish traditional culture, as well as the more urbane Yiddish culture, typified by the plays of Isaac Leib (Yitskhok Leybush) Peretz.[41] The thematic materials are, however, not merely folkloristic quotations. Both the melodic and harmonic materials are entirely original, though their affinity for and kinship with traditional Jewish musical elements is never denied. After a performance at Temple Emanu-El on February 26, 1961, Albert Weisser reviewed the piece as follows: "Written in memory of the composer's father, this work reflects the strange and fantastic world of eastern Jewry. Filled with folkloristic touches that convey a sense of nostalgia and deeply felt emotion for a world utterly destroyed—a world we will see no more—this is one of Berlinski's least complicated but nevertheless most persuasive creations."[42]

Seen as a whole, Berlinski's oeuvre was broadly influenced by the Jewish liturgical repertoire of eastern and central Europe. Those traditions he combined with Western art music and contemporary compositional techniques, particularly atonality, dodecaphony, and serial music.[43]

Eliyahu Schleifer believes that artists such as Herman Berlinski and Herbert Fromm, dislocated from Germany during the Holocaust, went to the United States to continue their former German-Jewish traditions in American synagogues, thus superimposing their heritage on the traditions that already existed there.[44] At that time the United States had become the center not only of Reform Judaism but also, alongside Israel, of a Judaism characterized above all by its enormous diversity. Given the circumstances, it is questionable whether it would have been possible to remain aloof from the multiplicity of influences offered by American life and to preserve the purity of the original German-Jewish identity and culture. Mark Slobin confirms this: "The synagogue itself was changing from the immigrant society, based on kinship and European town of origin, to an Americanized, symbolic institution. No longer the home just for immigrant men, it was now meant to serve families as a rallying point of identity: second generation Jews reconstructed the synagogue into an institutional bulwark of middle-class ethnicity, but no longer an ethnicity based on town of origin."[45]

Michael Meyer has observed that the immigrants' German-Jewish lifestyle, including their cultural and musical characteristics, has been disappearing since the 1970s; German-Jewish identity is still perceptible in the second generation of emigrants but is no longer a central aspect of their identity.[46] Rather, the German-Jewish descent has been transformed into a historical memory. This is also evident in the status of the organ and organ music in the synagogue. As of 1967, 80 percent of all Reform synagogues employed only one organist and a choir director; smaller congregations had only an organist and a cantor or a singer.[47] Most congregations had a single piano or organ, of which only 20 percent were pipe organs (the rest were electronic). Only 10 percent decided to purchase a second organ. These trends, however, are minor considering the efforts and aims of the generation that emigrated from Germany in the 1930s. Moreover, the fact that most congregations possessed an instrument is not a certain indicator that they actually used them. Once a congregation has installed an organ, it is unlikely to have it dismantled again— a costly undertaking.

Organists of Jewish descent have always been few and far between: In 1967, 85 percent of all organists playing in synagogues were not Jewish, a trend that would change little in the following decades.[48] In contrast to prewar Germany, the boundaries between organists of Jewish and Christian faith in the United States are permeable. Rather than being separately employed and organized, organists play in both churches and synagogues and belong to the same associations and societies (e.g., American Guild of Organists; American Conference of Cantors). The question of their ethnic origin or religious affiliation has become inconsequential.

These developments have had an impact on the choice of repertoire as well: In 75 percent of all congregations, the repertoire performed in synagogues is not necessarily Jewish music but rather a mix of works by composers of various religious traditions on the grounds that music is universal.[49] The composers' religious background and the proper use of repertoire have become irrelevant, as only 15 percent of all communities strive to play compositions by Jewish composers during the liturgy. About 10 percent accept a combination of works by Jewish composers and free improvisations on Jewish themes by the organist. In the late 1960s Herbert Fromm suggested that the influence of the émigrés was relatively slow to take hold:

> As a second category of the Synagogue composer's work, we listed organ music. It is customary for the organists of most Temples to play organ music for about 15 minutes before the Service and to end the Service with a postlude. Our organists use for the most part the rich organ literature of the church although a new literature of indigenous Jewish organ music is beginning to develop. Organ music based on Jewish themes or, in a wider sense, written in a Jewish idiom is needed and our composers should give more serious attention to this neglected aspect of our music. . . . In spite of what has been achieved so far, organ music for the synagogue is still a little known branch of Jewish music. It will grow in volume and stature and, at some future time, may well command the attention of the music world at large. In the works of Herman Berlinski I see the first steps in this direction.[50]

With few exceptions, liberal Jewish communities believe in the function and purpose of the organ during liturgy; Jewish Reform congregations even state that the organ plays an essential role.[51] Today the organ's function is to convey the atmosphere of the liturgy, accompany the singer and choir, and conclude the liturgy with preludes and postludes.

However, as in concerts, the extraliturgical use of the organ in American synagogues remains an exception. The Central Synagogue of New York, one of the oldest Reform Jewish congregations in the United States, is one of the very few synagogues to have elevated the organ to the status of a concert instrument. With the dedication of two large and interconnected instruments in September 2001, the synagogue created a place for organ music in a secular music program in addition to the congregation's worship services. Monthly master classes by prominent organists and the periodically organized Prism

Concerts present organ music to a wide audience. The concerts are frequented by people of all faiths and ethnicities who gather in an ecumenical effort to celebrate the organ in the sacred space of the synagogue. Even Orthodox Jews attend the concerts, a fact that demonstrates that the Central Synagogue provides a space for cultural appreciation of this instrument, thus reaching beyond its religious function. The reason for this may also lie in the choice of repertoire, which is generally secular and only occasionally has a religious overtone. Very few other congregations in the United States widen the spectrum of organ music in such a way.[52]

The developments and turns the German-Jewish organ tradition has taken in the United States illustrate the impact of the German-Jewish emigrants. Herman Berlinski, Herbert Fromm, Heinrich Schalit, Hugo Adler, and many other musicians who fled Europe tried to maintain their newly created tradition in emigration and even attempted to develop it further. To a certain extent they succeeded, as serious attempts were made to create a uniquely Jewish organ music repertoire based on European aesthetics but suited for synagogues in the United States. Yet these émigré composers were the last generation of German Jews involved in synagogue music. The following generation of synagogue musicians, despite all of the musical freedom and possibilities, was apparently not deeply concerned with the further development of the organ in Jewish worship.

This lack of interest in the traditions of German-Jewish culture is a surprising process, considering the strong ties of American Jewry to their European models. Steven Löwenstein affirms that in the 1980s German-Jewish culture dissolved into American culture: "All signs seem to point to the merging of the German-Jewish community into the larger American Jewish community within a generation. . . . Their sense of Jewishness has intensified though their sense of a specific German Jewishness seems to be on the wane."[53] The organ and its music, once so important and influential in German-Jewish communities, seemed to have met their end in contemporary America.

The Organ in Israeli Culture:
A Bridge between East and West

Following their escape from Nazism in the years after 1933, many musicians from German-speaking Europe began a new life in the British Mandate of Palestine. They transferred Western culture to their new home and began to shape—if not dominate—the musical life of the later state of Israel. If the musical landscape until then had been mainly influenced by Zionist emigrants from eastern Europe, the *aliyah germanit*, the emigration of German Jews, introduced radical changes. These immigrants, many of whom belonged to the contemporaneous European schools of composers, founded and supported musical institutions and thus brought the musical life to a level that nearly equaled that of the musical capitals of Europe. However, the experience of immigration was not an easy process for the émigré musicians since the Middle East exposed them to a new and complex reality. On the cultural level they had to come to terms with the different musical traditions, although (especially at first) Western concepts enjoyed some exclusivity.[54]

Having been a minority before emigration, the German-Jewish émigrés again became a minority in a new and different environment. Here, however, they were positively expected to integrate and acculturate: "During the Mandate and especially the early phase of statehood, the official attitude of the Zionist establishment toward ethnic cultural traditions advocated their disappearance in the 'melting pot' of a general 'Israeli society.'"[55] However, the wish for homogenization was more an ideal than a reality, as the German-Jewish music culture was reconstituted in Palestine and later played an important part in Israeli culture.[56] Over time, however, it was greatly transformed as the émigré musicians, inspired by their new environment, took interest in the music of Eastern Jewry and the Arabs. Composers used the Jewish music of the region as a basis for their new, mostly secular works. When the state of Israel was founded in 1948, concepts of "national Jewish" themes became prominent, though some composers rejected them.[57] Many composers in the new Israel sought a musical synthesis of East and West either by combining the harmonic and compositional techniques of Western music with rhythms, melodies, and instruments of Eastern music or by applying Eastern aesthetics without using the actual musical elements associated with Eastern music.[58] This syncretism led to the birth of an indigenous Israeli style.

Organ music was an integral part of these cultural and musical developments, although the organ remains one of the most neglected instruments in the Middle East. The modern history of the organ in Palestine/Israel can be traced from the mid-nineteenth century to an eventual accumulation of fifty-three instruments.[59] Because only a few local organ builders have been active—among them German-trained Gideon Shamir and Franciscan monk Delfin Fernandes Taboada, whose workshops are one-man businesses—most of the instruments were built by foreign firms. The styles of organs are a kaleidoscope of European (predominantly German, Austrian, and Italian) and American organ-building traditions. Besides Catholic monasteries and churches, organs were also built for music academies and private households of organ enthusiasts. However, the instrument has been largely absent in concert halls and public performance venues, thus not accessible to a broader audience: Only in 2001 was a three-manual concert instrument inaugurated at Clairmont Concert Hall at Tel Aviv University.[60] As the Jewish communities have had little contact with the musical life of Christian congregations there, the few organ concerts are frequented mostly by Christians.

Because of the position of the organ in the Middle East, organ music had not been a central part of the musical life of Palestine. However, many émigré musicians who were familiar with the organ from their youth in Europe revived their interest in this instrument; thus, an organ tradition slowly began to develop. Among the émigré composers and organists of the 1930s were those who continued the activities begun in Europe, as well as musicians for whom the organ became a melancholic reminder of the past.

In the 1930s the Palestine Conservatory of Music and Dramatic Art in Jerusalem (later renamed the Rubin Academy of Music) began offering organ lessons. Among the first organ teachers was Max Lampel, who emigrated from Austria and taught organ until his retirement in the 1970s. The organ as a specific subject in Western music pedagogy was thus transferred to Israel.

For the German-Jewish émigré musicians, the Jerusalem YMCA (Young Men's Christian Association), a worldwide, ecumenical, voluntary organization for young people, became a key venue for organ music. In 1932 the U.S. firm of Austin Organs built a four-manual organ with financial support from the Juilliard Foundation; the instrument, with its forty-seven stops, was for a long time the largest organ in the Middle East.[61] It was a typical concert organ of its time in the style of the cinema organ or orchestrion.

Although the YMCA was a Christian association, it became a meeting place for the Jewish population of Jerusalem and was thus initially the only location where a Jewish audience would enjoy the performance of organ music.[62] It was also one of the few sites where Jewish organists (e.g., Max Lampel, Hans Samuel, and, later in the 1970s, Valery Maisky, brother of cellist Mischa Maisky) were able to perform.

The Austin organ served as a source of inspiration for émigré composers from Germany, who became the first generation of Israeli composers. Karel Salomon (born Karl Salomon in Heidelberg) and Paul Ben-Haim (born Paul Frankenburger in Munich) composed organ music with this particular organ in mind, as registration instructions in their manuscripts and early printed scores (all held at the music department of the Jewish National and University Library in Jerusalem) indicate.

Utilizing Baroque elements, Salomon's *Invention*, written in 1954, is a short tonal triptych on a folkloristic melody fragment. His *Six Pieces for Organ*, written around the same time, draws upon traditional Jewish liturgical melodies such as chants of the Tunisian Jews of Djerba.

After two arias for soprano and organ written in 1929 and 1931, Ben-Haim composed only one more work for organ, his 1966 Prelude. In style and structure, this work is reminiscent of his German years. Ben-Haim makes use of a rich array of registers (all carefully marked) and the powerful sound of double stops in the pedals, typical of French organ music of the late Romantic period.[63] This short but complex work can be interpreted as a stylistic continuation of Ben-Haim's early work in that it uses the organ as a sound source and follows the European organ style. In this composition Ben-Haim turns away from the ornamental style he had developed as an "Israeli composer" to suit the harmonic and contrapuntal nature of organ music. The reversion to his European past is further evident in the piece's compositional technique and thematic approach, which recall the period when, under the influence of Heinrich Schalit, Ben-Haim was exploring the origins of Jewish music.

Two composers are representative of the main approaches of the émigré composers: Hans Samuel, who continued with the work as organist and organ composer that he had begun in Germany, and Haim Alexander, whose organ repertoire represents the expression of an inner return to the country of his birth. In the following, their lives and works are described in closer detail.

The preferred destination of Hans Samuel, a passionate organist and composer of organ music, was the United States, as he aimed at resuming his career as synagogue organist. Unable to obtain an affidavit, he had to change his plans quickly as the situation for Jews in Germany worsened considerably: In March 1939 Samuel was part of an illegal *Nottransport* to Palestine organized by the Zionistische Organisation [Zionist Federation]. Contacts he established before immigrating secured a smooth transition in Palestine. The Palestine Conservatory of Music and Dramatic Art in Jerusalem, which, in November 1938, had invited him to hold a series of lectures on European organ repertoire, offered him a place to practice, and the Conservatoire Michael Taube promised Samuel a position as piano and organ teacher for the following year.[64] Shortly after his arrival, Samuel began working as organist at the German Colony Church of St. Immanuel in Jaffa. He also played for services at the Presbyterian Church of Scotland in Jaffa, then a congregation of Romanian emigrants. In 1958 he became their main organist and played several concerts with a broad repertoire, ranging from classical and contemporary pieces to his own compositions.

Although these opportunities closely approximate Samuel's career in Germany, for him it was a bad compromise. He preferred to continue working as synagogue organist, a wish that had no prospect of fulfillment in Israel. Samuel was aware of the developments in Jewish music in the United States and initially was convinced that only there could he further his career as organist and composer, but in 1940 another attempt at immigrating to the United States failed.[65] Subsequently, France became another favored destination because Samuel believed his plans could also be realized there. After the Second World War he applied for different positions in Europe but was unsuccessful. The Jewish community in Hamburg justified its rejection by stating that "no *Orgelsynagoge* exists in Hamburg anymore."[66] Other congregations and institutions, among them the Union Libérale Israélite in Paris, did not even specify their reasons for rejection.

One would assume that after all of these failed attempts to gain a foothold outside of Israel, Samuel would have tried to adapt to the musical life in emigration. Although he used every opportunity to play the organ, even if this meant being outside the synagogue, his unfulfilled aspirations led him to withdraw into himself and dedicate the rest of his life to composing a "true Jewish organ music." He sought to establish a serious repertoire of works written specifically for the instrument.

A turning point in Samuel's life as a composer occurred in 1946, when he began living in the household of the Ricardo family, where he became a quasi-member. His friendship with David Ricardo would in time have a strong impact on his compositional approach and style.

In 1904 David Ricardo was born into an Orthodox Jewish family in Amsterdam. His father, Dr. Benjamin Ricardo, was the rabbi of the Portuguese community there, and his maternal grandfather, Elyakim ben Moshe Álvarez Vega (1846–1927), was a well-known ḥazzan and introduced David to ḥazzanut. David was well versed in the Sephardic musical tradition and at the age of eighteen became the conductor of an Amsterdam youth choir, which was part of the Mizrachi movement. This organization combined Zionist nationalism with more traditional or Orthodox Judaism, and David had joined shortly after his bar mitzvah. Later on he served as director of the Sephardic children's choir Santo Servizio, which regularly performed during the services at the Amsterdam Sephardic synagogue. In 1933 he emigrated to Palestine, though he never lost his strong ties to Amsterdam's Sephardic community. Fearing that, because of the German occupation of the Netherlands, Amsterdam's Sephardic musical tradition would be lost forever, in 1941 David began collecting and transcribing from memory all of the melodies he knew. It was his personal mission to preserve this legendary musical tradition. Samuel took part in the transcription process. According to Rachel Thaller, Ricardo's daughter, both men sat together at the piano for hours working on transcriptions of the Sephardic repertoire of Amsterdam.[67] Thus Samuel became acquainted with a musical world previously unknown to him. The wealth and beauty of the Sephardic chants and cantillations made such a deep impression on Samuel that he began using them as a basis for his own compositions. His sister Eva Samuel states that he "became in a sense a Sephardim, as he found the Sephardic world so much more beautiful."[68] Many of his subsequently composed works refer to these transcriptions.[69]

The oeuvre Samuel composed in immigration shows an unusual interplay of different Jewish musical traditions, thus going beyond Ashkenazic and Sephardic influences. Samuel also uses musical motives from Yemenite and Moroccan Jewish traditions (the latter are again closely linked to Amsterdam's Sephardic community).[70] In addition, Samuel's works present a stylistically novel approach that incorporates impressionistic sounds and an extreme use of polyphony, which makes it rather difficult to recognize the Jewish themes. By combining new themes in organ music with an unusual and even unique style, Samuel established a distinct organ music that goes beyond the Ashkenazic tradition.

As a musician Samuel found no home in Israel. His melancholy and shyness led to only rare performances of his vast oeuvre, which, with the exception of a few pieces, remained unpublished and undiscovered and was finally forgotten. Although socially and musically isolated within the emerging Israeli culture, he at least acculturated through music to Sephardic and Yemenite musical traditions.

Although unusual in itself, Samuel's evolution in emigration is paradigmatic of the experience of many other émigré composers from Europe, whose most immediate acculturative responses represent what Bohlman has called a "consolidation resulting from the composer absorbing new influences and expanding the technical vocabulary and aesthetic palette."[71]

This consolidation may also be found in a less "immediate" process, as seen in the world of Haim Alexander. Born in 1915 in Berlin as Heinz Alexander, he began his musical training at the age of five, when he began studying the piano. Alexander grew up in a Jewish orphanage, where he accompanied the school's worship services on a reed organ, thus becoming acquainted with the works of Louis Lewandowski. Although Alexander was familiar with the repertoire of the synagogue, liturgical pieces remained an exception in his work as composer. Pursuing a career as pianist and composer, he studied at the Sternsches Konservatorium in Berlin since he was denied entry to the Hochschule für Musik because of his Jewish ancestry. Upon his emigration to

Palestine in 1936, he resumed his studies, this time at the Palestine Conservatory, continuing classes in composition with Stefan Wolpe, with whom he had already worked in Berlin. At the same time, Alexander began to study serial music and Hindemith's theories with Hanoch Jacoby, an émigré composer from Königsberg. His first years as a composition student were heavily influenced and deepened by the discussions taking place between the two main schools of composition: "My first years in the country were an intensive intellectual debate on all levels, including music. First, two schools dominated: Wolpe, and Lavy and Ben-Haim. I personally was torn between my modal, Mediterranean tendency and Wolpe's aesthetic-dodecaphonic demands. Then, like today, symposia were held to deal with questions concerning the nature of new music, whether there was a Jewish music, an Israeli music, and so on."[72]

As a German Jew, Haim Alexander sought to maintain aspects of his origins such as the German language; however, he also aimed at integrating into his new intellectual and cultural environment: "There was a strong German clique, and we spoke German—even the Czechs among us. But we slowly learned Hebrew. This group was the standard bearer of music in the country. Later the Hungarians came, bringing with them new ideas and new material. Gradually new blood was added, from Eastern Europe, and the 'Yekke mafia' blended into new Israeli reality. The composers who had come from Germany had no interest in nationalistic trends, even scorned them. I was searching for a personal way, far from German culture which in the war years for me became [the] embodiment of evil."[73]

From 1945 on, he taught composition, harpsichord, and piano at the Rubin Academy of Music in Jerusalem and later became professor and director of its theory department. Although relieved at having escaped from the Nazis, he nonetheless remained connected to his German roots. Seminars in composition brought him, although hesitantly, back to Germany. At the Hochschule in Freiburg he studied with Wolfgang Fortner and in 1958, 1962, and 1964 participated in the Darmstädter Ferienkurse.

Alexander's creative period can be divided into three major periods: The first (until ca. 1960) produced works influenced by the music of the Middle East and the so-called Eastern-Mediterranean style; he describes the second period (ca. 1961–1972) as his serial and avant-garde days; the third period (after 1972) is a synthesis of the first two, although he took more liberties with form and material. His oeuvre is dominated by piano and chamber music, pedagogic works, and choral music and is generally defined as a bridge between Western and Eastern musical traditions.

Alexander's oeuvre contains two compositions for solo organ. The short choral fantasia *De profundis* originated in 1972 and was composed for an Arabic organist in Nazareth. Although a twelve-tone composition, it incorporates parts of the Lutheran chorale *In Deep Distress I Cry to Thee*. With *Die westöstliche Brücke: Geschichten aus Jerusalem* [The West-Eastern Bridge: Stories from Jerusalem], Alexander created a work that is very likely the last composition to come directly out of the German-Jewish organ tradition.

Commissioned by Oskar Gottlieb Blarr, who proposed the well-known Hanukkah song Maʻoz Zur for the theme, the organ piece was composed in 1998 for the festival Orgelpunkt Europa and premiered in the course of the concert series on June 24, 1998, in Düsseldorf. The creative process of this work shows its strong connection to German-Jewish culture. Conceiving this composition was a difficult endeavor for Haim Alexander, as he relates in a letter to Blarr (in German): "Regarding your commission of an organ composition, I have to tell you that I have undertaken many attempts but that I have thrown them all away. At the moment, I am attempting once more. . . . It seems that the organ is too great for me: I love this instrument and fear it at the same time."[74]

Die westöstliche Brücke is a mature, four-movement, eighteen-minute sonata. Although inspired by Maʻoz Zur, it is not intended as religious music. Rather, each movement refers to certain periods of Alexander's life: The first movement pays tribute to Johann Sebastian Bach by alluding to the Prelude no. 2 in C Minor from *Das wohltemperierte Clavier* I, BWV 847. With this musical dedication the composer intended to express his strong affinity for "his great master," Bach. The second movement, titled "Ostinato," is a trio based on a two-measure ostinato. It reflects upon Alexander's early years in immigration, his new home in Jerusalem, and the loss of his family, which was murdered by the National Socialists. The countermotive to the ostinato, so the composer claims, evokes his numerous attempts to hold his ground and adapt to a new and difficult environment. The third movement, "Betrachtungen über ein jemenitisches Volkslied" [Reflections on a Yemenite Folk Song], is a tonal chorale variation and refers to a later stage of Haim Alexander's life. The Yemenite melody is that of Psalm 118:4. Alexander sees this movement as the perfect synthesis of Eastern and Western elements in music: "Here now, my Western-influenced culture bridges the Eastern folk elements. Because of that I chose the title *Die westöstliche Brücke*, which is to reflect my gradual merging with Oriental art. Whether this also has something to do with *Geschichten aus Jerusalem* I leave up to the perception and judgment of the listener."[75]

The last movement on Maʻoz Zur is a toccata. When Blarr asked for this melody, he could not foresee the consequences. An excerpt of correspondence from Alexander to Blarr shows the role this prayer plays in his life by explaining the composition's melancholic and retrospective character:

Upon the completion of the Ma'oz Zur piece, I owe you an explanation: You commissioned a "merry toccata" on this melody. But you could not know that this melody is connected to an important part of my youth. I grew up in Berlin as "German citizen of Jewish faith" (perhaps also as a Jewish citizen of German faith). Our family was liberal; however, the Ma'oz Zur song was an integral part of the Hanukkah feast, it just belonged to it. Here in Israel our family continued the tradition of the Hanukkah blessing over the candles, however without my relatives, who had believed in their German citizenship altogether too blindly. It was just impossible for me to write a "merry toccata" on such a tragic fate. I either had to find another melody, or take a more serious course with Ma'oz Zur. So I did the latter and it emerged a reminiscence on bygone times.[76]

For Haim Alexander, the melody of Ma'oz Zur represents a leitmotif for his youth in Berlin; it awakened a longing for the lighting of the Hanukkah candles in the family circle. To set the tragic personal meaning of Ma'oz Zur to music, he decided to break up the melody into different parts, thus giving it a fragmented and blurred presentation. Only at the very end of the movement does the entire melody of Ma'oz Zur fully appear to give *Die westöstliche Brücke* a sense of completion.

Alexander's strategies to integrate himself into the musical life of Israel are very different from Hans Samuel's and manifest themselves musically even in a late work such as *Die westöstliche Brücke*. Alexander did not fuse directly with Israeli music culture but continued to live in a quasi German-Jewish Diaspora, thus at first separating himself from the multiethnic musical landscapes of his country of immigration. He is representative of a group of musicians who escaped Nazi persecution but, because of their forced emigration, sought to maintain—at least in the beginning—a German-Jewish identity. In the course of time the German-Jewish émigrés—like emigrants coming from other countries—slowly immersed themselves in the Israeli musical landscape. This process, as Gradenwitz points out, is evident in the numerous new works with titles like *Variations on a Palestine Tune* or *Rhapsody on Israeli Themes*. However, these pieces by the early immigrants were composed in German, Russian, or French late-Romantic or modern style. Only gradually did the composers lose these notions of musical expression and change their ways of musical thinking and feeling.[77]

Although Haim Alexander and his German-speaking colleagues isolated themselves upon immigration, in the end they could not withstand the influence of the different music cultures that were coming together in Israel:

I have a personal credo: war prevents artistic rootedness. I left Germany and came to Israel. I had high hopes and even moments of joy. . . . The world is marching towards the universal. In the arts, too, techniques are shared, and with the help of mass communication and mobility the world is becoming one unit. Against this background national expression may turn dissonant. Likeness of style began on the technical plane but is becoming quite natural: the same music is heard in Japan, Israel and Poland. Sometimes I think that what was a national Mediterranean expression now appears almost sinful. Almost fascist! The days are over, of the innocent Zionist idealism, that sincerely enabled the spontaneous growth of music drawn from the folk traditions and seeking national expression.[78]

Contemporary Israeli composers are a product of many different musical-cultural influences: Because of their geographic location in the Middle East, some of them tend to absorb the rhythmic and melodic characteristic of Arab music, as did their predecessors in the Middle Ages.[79] However, the Israeli composer, having studied in Europe or with teachers who had been educated there, is also a product of the European music culture.[80]

The later generations of Israeli musicians approached organ music with neither religious prejudices nor romantic feelings. Rather, they rediscovered the organ as a new medium of sound and celebrated it in various forums such as the First Israeli Organ Festival in 2003 and the Israeli Organists' Club, as well as in new compositions.

Many different aspects are integrated in Israeli organ music; in regard to compositional technique, for example, some composers created dodecaphonic works for the instrument. Following the model of Wolfgang Fortner, Giora Schuster's *Intrada—Passacaglia Piccola* (1966–1967) signals a change in style among the younger composers, who turned away from post-Romanticism and toward serial technique and structural thought. A composition related to Schuster's work is Artur Gelbrun's *Intrada and Passacaglia* (1981), which also uses dodecaphonic principles and is a transcription of the last movement of his six choreographic scenes for orchestra, *Hommage à Rodin* (1979–1981).

Zeev Steinberg, who owns a chamber organ built by Israeli organ builder Gideon Shamir, composed *Praeambulum, Fughetta canonica, Toccata and Imitatio I–III* (1967) for the International Schnitger Organ Competition in Zwolle, the Netherlands. The dodecaphonic work contains Middle Eastern melodies and melismatic passages and is based on traditional forms.

The integration of liturgical melodies, as well as Middle Eastern and Asian scales, in the organ works of Josef Tal and Gabriel Iranyi is approached in different ways: In *Kol hakavot: Salve venia* (1983), Tal paraphrases the cantus *Jerusalem, du liebe Stadt*, by Konrad Hagius from his book of psalms (Düsseldorf, 1589). Iranyi's first organ composition, *Song of Degrees: Shir Hamaalot*, is based on the series of numbers created by medieval Italian mathematician Leonardo Pisano (known as "Fibonacci," ca. 1170–1250)[81] and the series of intervals influenced by the Kabbalah. Similarly complex is Iranyi's second composition, *Tempora*, which in its aesthetics and compositional technique combines Near Eastern and Far Eastern traditions. Japanese and Indian modes dominate the first part; melodies of Ma'oz Zur appear twice in the second part, using the commonly known tune of West European Ashkenazic origin and an early Italian version first transcribed by Italian composer Benedetto Marcello in his *Estro poetico-armonico* (Venice, 1724). The third part again makes use of Far Eastern materials such as scales from Shinto practice and the Vietnamese *bac* mode.

A further characteristic of Israeli organ music is the use of word painting, depictions or imitations of optical and auditory events, as in Jacob Gilboa's triptych *Three Strange Visions of Hieronymus Bosch* (1987), inspired by the paintings *Haywain Triptych*, *Ship of Fools*, and *Paradise* by the Dutch Renaissance painter. Josef Dorfman's *Phantasie* (1984) is a musical projection of the mysterious Jewish predecessor of the organ, the magrepha. The composer endeavors to evoke the special atmosphere of Jerusalem: the sounds emanating from the city's hills, echoes, and nature. In concluding passages he imagines the sound of the ancient instrument. The magrepha also inspired Ari Ben-Shabetai in his program piece *Magrefa II: Intermezzo* (1998). In this composition, full-voice harmonies alternate with long-held chords and a hocketlike broken character. A periodic interruption of the wind supply underlines the intended unevenness.[82] That two contemporary Israeli composers are turning in their organ compositions to the magrepha is in itself an interesting phenomenon, as it musically continues the myth of being a predecessor of the organ.

The organ compositions of contemporary Israeli composers are as diverse as the origins of the composers themselves, most of whom are emigrants from Germany, Austria, Poland, Hungary, and the former Soviet Union; a substantial number are Israeli born. If there is no unified style or school of organ music in Israel, it is due to the lack of a long tradition of organ music and to the convergence of very different musical cultures—secular and religious, traditional and Western. A synthesis of Israel's music cultures may therefore not be possible after all.[83] As musicians and composers continue to immigrate, the culture of organ music may continue to diverge.

The German-Jewish émigré composers and organists in Israel and the United States were concerned about continuing their musical life begun in

Germany. This continuation, however, took different turns because of the dissimilar environments. Most of the emigrants perceived the new influences as positive and inspirational. Their new situation became the starting point for a fresh development in organ music. While organ music in Israel is still in a unique phase of development, in the United States it has almost disappeared with the passing of the émigré generation.

CHAPTER SIX | Between Assimilation
and Dissimilation
The Jewish Community in the Course of Modernity

The Jewish musical tradition of the German Jews in the nineteenth and early twentieth centuries is characterized by two simultaneous endeavors: the preservation of selected aspects of Jewish identity and tradition and the pursuit of modernization, which necessitates a degree of acculturation to the non-Jewish environment. The organ and organ music as an integral part of German-Jewish musical life in modernity played an important role in this dichotomous process.

The organ and organ music reflect the complexity and manifold implications of German-Jewish identity. Martin Stokes asserts that "musical styles can be made emblematic of national identities in complex and often contradictory ways;"[1] thus, the organ and organ music served as symbols chosen and reinterpreted by the liberal German Jews.

The organ symbolizes Reform identity, as well as the processes of assimilation and religious modernization; at the same time, it was introduced into the synagogue with the knowledge that it had long been considered a traditional "Christian" instrument. The potential for divergent interpretation is evident in the division of the Jewish people over the organ issue: Some considered it a Christian instrument and symbol, whereas others saw the organ within its new context, the synagogue, making it a symbol of emancipation, the dissolution of traditional structures of Jewish society, and the renewal of Jewish liturgy as an ideological revolution that subverted cultural values.

A specifically "Jewish" organ music, on the other hand, which would be received as such, had to be newly invented and developed. Indeed, development of the community's "own" repertoire to obviate its need to use organ music of the Christian tradition became an overriding goal. The newly created repertoire not only reflects changing Jewish identities but is at the same time the product of these redefined identities.

Thus, the organ and organ music are symbols of a different kind, having evolved from both preexisting symbols (church organ) and newly created ones (organ music). They also correspond in dissimilar ways to the dual identity of German Jews, with the organ standing for the rather external (German) identity and organ music expressing a more internal (Jewish) side of German-Jewish identity.

The introduction of the organ into the synagogue had an enormous impact on the Jewish liturgical and musical tradition, especially in the Reform branch. Moreover, it was one aspect of a number of dramatic changes that occurred over a period of 150 years, during which the German-Jewish people negotiated tradition, emancipation, assimilation, and dissimilation (the latter two concepts are also applicable to their lives in emigration). The organ music of the German Jews, on the other hand, mirrors the problems and changes in their religious, ethnic, and national-cultural identity, the structures of German-Jewish life, and the relationship between the Jewish minority and the non-Jewish majority of Western Europe. These changes involving organ and organ music have been traced in the course of four overlapping phases.

Before the eighteenth century, Jewish communities, with rare exceptions, constituted religiously and culturally self-contained units.[2] They identified themselves with a traditional Jewish music in which organs and organ music had no distinct roles.

In the course of the Haskalah, the Jewish Enlightenment of the late eighteenth century, which set off a series of reforms, Jewish identity began its transformation. When the Jews departed from the ghetto (thereby causing its dissolution), they gradually came into closer contact with their environment and integrated with it to varying degrees, thus creating new forms of identity. As a result of their exposure to the non-Jewish milieu, many Jewish people broke with certain aspects of (religious) tradition. The Orthodox, however, were perhaps an exception to this in that they continued to see Judaism as a closed, strict religious system that allows no negotiation with the surrounding Other.

According to cultural critic Kobena Mercer, "identity becomes an issue when it is in crisis, when something assumed to be fixed, coherent and stable is displaced by the experience of doubt and uncertainty."[3] The relative stability of Jewish tradition certainly reached a pivotal point during the Haskalah, especially when reorientation toward the Other resulted in breaking with thousand-year-old traditions and their attendant ideals. This break also led to a debate over the choice of Jewish, German, or German-Jewish identities with their various degrees of interconnection.

The introduction of the organ—the most Christian of all instruments— into the synagogue created boundaries and became a symbol of the break, alongside the less controversial introduction of vernacular language, sermons, and shared seating of men and women. Besides representing the division between Orthodoxy and Reform Judaism—linguistically this is evident in the term *Orgelsynagoge*, which is a synonym for Reform synagogue—the introduction of the organ illustrates the orientation of this new identity, which has turned toward Western culture and, on the religious level, toward Christianity. Michael Meyer sees in the religious and cultural borrowings an intention to make Judaism more acceptable to the outside world; at the same time, the nature of these borrowings reveals that German Jews were internalizing the values underlying them.[4]

During the process of assimilation in the nineteenth century, values that created new identities while preserving religious and cultural customs in the Jewish communities came under question. Because the religious and cultural borrowings were intended to sustain Judaism as an identifiable entity, a sharp division arose between assimilated forms and separative content.[5] In Judaism's search for a new self-understanding, music played an important part: The organ represented assimilation, and the newly composed organ music exemplified the search for separative content.

During the mid-nineteenth century, Jews defined the way in which they wished to acculturate to their environment. Within the rabbinical conferences and synods and in pamphlets, changes in Jewish life were extensively discussed. Advantages and disadvantages, as well as the degree of a possible assimilation between the Jewish community and overall society, were central subjects. The organ quarrels that took place within various communities illustrate the tensions generated by the disparate goals of adhering to Jewish traditions and giving in to the process of assimilation. In the end, the gradual adoption of the organ as a synagogue instrument and its increasing popularity in many Reform synagogues symbolize another "successful" step toward assimilation, while organ music represents the search for a new identity that lay somewhere between the Christian model of the chorale prelude and the use of Jewish melodies, most of which had already been adapted according to the rules of Western art music.

The compositions of Moritz Deutsch and Louis Lewandowski exemplify in their stylistic and cultural development the complex progression of assimilation—a development that in its far-reaching result leans toward Westernization or modernization: "Inevitably, therefore, if one wanted to be 'modern' one had in some way to be 'Western' culturally. If not Western religions, one had to adopt Western languages."[6] Most Jews in the German-speaking countries aimed at assimilation on social, religious, linguistic, and musical levels—an exemplary phenomenon of modernity. This process might have led to a total enculturation, even synthesis, if a number of developments that began in the nineteenth century had not triggered a change in direction.

At the turn of the century, assimilation was no longer a central point of contention; many Reform congregations accepted the organ as a synagogue instrument. Each community and each individual lived according to a personal model that shifted between adhering to traditions and pursuing modern concepts of life. Although assimilation was no longer the main concern, the actual full integration into larger society had yet to be achieved. This fact is reflected in works written for organ by Jewish composers influenced by two (political) movements of the time, Zionism and anti-Semitism, both of which—despite their different roles and consequences—played an important part in the dialectic process of dissimilation.[7] Dissimilation cannot be understood as assimilation in reverse as it is impossible to "deassimilate" culturally and socially in the sense of reverting to the "original" state. Rather, dissimilation implies a reorientation toward one's origins and a striving for new forms of difference, thus preventing a total assimilation. As such, dissimilation was instrumental in the creation of a new and modern Jewish tradition.

As anti-Semitism developed in German society, the Zionists became skeptical of what may have been only a perceived integration. In his article "Zionism under the Nazi Government," Joachim Prinz describes the general atmosphere among Zionists with regard to National Socialism and dissimilation:

> Everyone in Germany knew that only the Zionists could responsibly represent the Jews in dealings with the Nazi government. We all felt sure that one day the government would arrange a round table conference with the Jews, at which—after the riots and atrocities of the revolution had passed—the new status of German Jewry could be considered. The government announced very solemnly that there was no country in the world, which tried to solve the Jewish problem as seriously as did Germany. Solution of the Jewish question? It was our Zionist dream! We never denied the existence of the Jewish question! Dissimilation? It was our own appeal![8]

The dissimilation was a central part of the Zionist program to (re)create a distinct Jewish identity. Musically it expressed itself in the reintroduction of older elements of the Jewish music tradition, which were considered "authentic" (some of them had been partly abandoned in the nineteenth century). The organ works of Heinrich Schalit, Arno Nadel, and Hans Samuel are examples of the reorientation toward older traditions since their compositions are based on multicultural (Ashkenazic, Sephardic, Yemenite, and Western) and polystylistic concepts. These composers melded different cultural, stylistic, and socially determined musical models by applying forms used in Western art music. They were part of a larger trend in twentieth-century music that Peter Gradenwitz describes as a search for a synthesis between East and West.[9] In the end, much of the Jewish repertoire blended into Western music, a process that is also evident in secular organ compositions that have no relation to the synagogue or Jewish culture but were written by Jewish composers such as Karol Rathaus and Arnold Schoenberg. The development of Jewish organ music in the direction of Western music has a cultural equivalent in the Jewish minority's orientation toward the non-Jewish majority.

Under National Socialism, the meaning of dissimilation changed once and for all when the concept was adapted to Nazi ideology: Dissimilation (without a spatial exclusion of the community) was the first step in the three-point plan of the Final Solution—the second step was ghettoization, and step three was the removal of Jews from Europe. The German government began carrying out these official policies in 1941.[10]

Before 1933, German Jews could choose to either assimilate or dissimilate, and strictly Orthodox Jews decided against even the former. However, when the Nazis seized power, even these choices disappeared. Many Jewish citizens—especially musicians—were compelled to yield to their new status in German society. It is questionable whether Jewish musicians would have founded the Kulturbund, used Jewish themes in their compositions, and composed liturgical music for the synagogue if the political conditions had been different. It is almost as if Zionism and especially National Socialism jointly contributed—fatefully—to some kind of preservation of Jewish tradition.[11]

Monika Richarz suggests that the weakened liberalism and the anti-Semitic stance of the *Bildungsbürgertum* [middle-class intellectuals] pushed the Jews into a dangerous and conflicting role in politics and culture.[12] The Jews' success and influence, indeed power, in science and the arts (including music) led to controversies about the *Verjudung* of German culture as the society was unwilling to accept the Jewish people as the creators of German culture. These developments proved fatal for the Jewish minority in the Western Diaspora and for their identity: "When diasporic cultures accept the affirmative discourses of antiracism, there is the danger that they are also accepting the burden of representing themselves within categories which make their minority status more visible, without flushing out the invisible or that which secures the dominant culture in its place. The dominant culture has always defined its own identity through the racialized discourse of the Other. To repeat Sartre's famous dictum, if the Jew did not exist, he would have been invented.' "[13]

The Kulturbund, a forum in which Jewish organ music flourished, became the embodiment of the visible Otherness of Jews in the German Diaspora. For the Nazis it provided the "perfect" forum in which to distinguish between the Jewish and the German in Germany's musical life.

Richarz considers the special tie between politics, society, and Jewish culture as unfulfilled and the integration of Jews as incomplete. In her opinion, the social integration and the concurrent preservation of Jewry remained an unfulfilled hope.[14] Although their integration into central Europe's musical landscape, together with the preservation of Jewishness in the synagogue organ and organ music, was not fully accomplished, it had nonetheless begun.

One might, however, ask whether assimilation, as a concept that refers to social, cultural, and musical acculturation and integration had indeed failed. Sociology sees assimilation as a minority group's attempt to integrate into the society of the majority group with the ultimate goal of achieving a homogenous society.[15] A decisive factor in this process is the abandonment of characteristic traditions and identities of the minority as a consequence of assimilation: "In general, the assimilation model of racial and ethnic contact assumes that the unique and distinctive characteristics of a minority will be erased and that the minority's culture, social institutions, and identity will be replaced by those of the dominant group."[16]

The development of the organ repertoire shows that the musical assimilation of German Jews was a careful negotiation between Jewish and non-Jewish elements in order to create a new musical language, commonly perceived as modern or "progressive." As such it was never geared toward full integration into the musical landscape of Germany. Rather, the new organ repertoire reveals the way in which Jewish composers tried to integrate and to remain Jewish at the same time. A convincing implementation of Jewish elements in organ music was never fully accomplished. There were, however, continuous and more or less successful attempts to preserve, reintegrate, or reinvent Jewish elements.

As the example of synagogue organists makes clear, assimilation, at least to a certain extent, went both ways. Indeed, it shows that Jewish Kultus had an important impact on facets of German society in general. Thus the integration of German Jewry was as much a chapter in the history of the German bourgeoisie as it was an intrinsic aspect of Jewish history.

———

Between about 1810 and 1938 a new and liberal tradition of Jewish repertoire for organ and synagogue music with close ties to Reform Jewry developed. The Reform movement's invention of an organ tradition[17] played an important role in establishing this branch of Judaism in society and thereby became its symbol; it facilitated the establishment of Reform Judaism as an institution and helped to integrate and imprint new values. Liberal German Jews created an organ tradition that mirrors their reinvented identity. The formation of this identity was influenced by a continuous discourse with Judaism's history and traditions.

With its introduction as a synagogue instrument, the organ became a symbol of the restructuring of Jewish musical tradition and the manifestation of Reform Judaism. Moreover, it became a condition of the establishment and formation of the musical tradition of Reform Judaism. Organ music, on the other hand, shows the complexity of assimilation as an intercultural relationship (in sociology this is commonly referred to as *pluralism*[18]), which is a modern cultural phenomenon. The life of European Jews in the twentieth century certainly evinced elements of cultural pluralism. The path toward this particular relationship was instigated by the process of assimilation, but before assimilation could lead to symbiosis, dissimilationist tendencies reinforced already existing pluralistic tendencies.

Both the organ and its new repertoire reflect a seemingly contradictory process: On the one hand, they expressed the German Jews' wish for assimilation; on the other hand, many German Jews believed that these media ought to preserve Jewish identity. Concretely, the organ followed the Christian model as a well-tested accompanying instrument; at the same time, attempts were made to implement a specifically "Jewish" style—an endeavor that was never fully realized.

The processes of emancipation, assimilation, and dissimilation define the encounter between Jews and Gentiles in prewar Germany; they also invoked the pluralization of Jewish and German identities. The simultaneous processes of assimilation and dissimilation in Jewish music of the Western Diaspora is a phenomenon that has been little recognized and as such may well be unique.

Many modern societies and cultures are in a state of interaction that is leading to cultural transformations: "Cultures change; they are borrowed, blended, rediscovered, and reinterpreted."[19] This distinguishes them from the traditional societies of premodernity.[20] The complex encounter of Jew and Gentile in the German cultural orbit has undoubtedly been one of the fundamental experiences of modernity, and this is reflected in music as well. On the religious level, the German-Jewish relationship can be characterized as an encounter between Judaism and Christianity within which, for many Jews, a disturbing closeness coexists with an uttermost distance. Christian traditions served as inspiration, though simultaneously an explicitly Jewish rite was sought. Nonetheless, the musical encounter of Jews and non-Jews in Germany was mainly one sided and aimed at integration, a relationship of a minority to a majority. While this relationship stayed within a hegemonic power structure, it also had a lasting impact on German history and culture.

As a minority, the Jewish people were both inside and outside the general musical landscape so that no border should be drawn between Jewish and German. The common term *German-Jewish* indicates this relationship. This hyphenation of German-Jewish culture, music, and history is at once a separation and a connection. Since these concepts are applicable to other historical, ethnic, and cultural contexts as well, the German-Jewish encounter in music can be considered paradigmatic.

NOTES

Abbreviations

AZJ	*Allgemeine Zeitung des Judenthums: Ein unparteiisches Organ für alles jüdische Interesse in Betreff von Politik, Religion, Literatur, Geschichte, Sprachkunde, und Belletristik*
CV-Ztg.	*C.V.-Zeitung: Blätter für Deutschtum und Judentum: Organ des Central-Vereins deutscher Staatsbürger jüdischen Glaubens*
EJ	*Encyclopaedia Judaica*
FIG	*Frankfurter israelitisches Gemeindeblatt*
HmT	*Handwörterbuch der musikalischen Terminologie*
HOM	*Hebräisch-orientalischer Melodienschatz*
HUC	Hebrew Union College
JTS	Jewish Theological Seminary of America
LBI	Leo Baeck Institute
MJKH	*Monatsblätter des Jüdischen Kulturbunds*
OUCZ	*Oesterreichisch-ungarische Cantoren-Zeitung: Organ für die Gesammt-Interessen jüdischer Cantoren*
RISM	Répertoire International des Sources Musicales
Schild	*Der Schild: Zeitschrift des Reichsbundes jüdischer Frontsoldaten*
Urania	*Urania: Musik-Zeitschrift für Orgelbau, Orgel- und Harmoniumspiel: Organ für Orgelbauer, Organisten, Kantoren, und Freunde der Tonkunst*
ZfI	*Zeitschrift für Instrumentenbau*

Chapter 1

1. See Peter Williams, *The Organ in Western Culture, 750–1250*, Cambridge Studies in Medieval and Renaissance Music (New York: Cambridge University Press, 1993), 3–4. There may be significant parallels in the history of the organ as it was introduced to churches and synagogues, but the question is a problematic one. The story of how the organ became a church instrument has not been adequately studied: It is safe to say, how-

ever, that the process was prolonged and disputatious, but official documentation of that development is unavailable; see Williams, *Organ in Western Culture*, 14.

2. Ibid., 13–15.

3. See Bonnie C. Wade, "When West Met East: The Organ as an Instrument of Culture," in *Festschrift Christoph-Hellmut Mahling*, ed. Axel Beer, Kristina Pfarr, and Wolfgang Ruf, 2 vols. Mainzer Studien zur Musikwissenschaft 37 (Tutzing, Germany: Hans Schneider, 1997), vol. 2, 1479–84.

4. See Michael Brenner and Derek J. Penslar, eds., *In Search of Jewish Community: Jewish Identities in Germany and Austria 1918–1933* (Bloomington: Indiana University Press, 1998), x.

5. Milton Esman defines an ethnic group in diaspora as "a minority ethnic group of migrant origin which maintains sentimental or material links with its land of origin." Milton J. Esman, "Diasporas and International Relations," in *Ethnicity*, ed. John Hutchinson and Anthony D. Smith (New York: Oxford University Press, 1996), 316.

6. See John Armstrong, "Archetypal Diasporas," in *Ethnicity*, ed. John Hutchinson and Anthony D. Smith (New York: Oxford University Press, 1996), 126.

7. Richard Schermerhorn, "Ethnicity and Minority Groups," in *Ethnicity*, ed. John Hutchinson and Anthony D. Smith (New York: Oxford University Press, 1996), 17. Schermerhorn enumerates further factors such as kinship patterns, physical contiguity (as in localism or sectionalism), religious affiliation, nationality, and phenotypical features, as well as any combination of these.

8. David B. Coplan, "Ethnomusicology and the Meaning of Tradition," in *Ethnomusicology and Modern Music History*, ed. Stephen Blum, Philip V. Bohlman, and Daniel M. Neuman (Chicago: University of Illinois Press, 1993), 36.

9. See Manning Nash, "The Core Elements of Ethnicity," in *Ethnicity*, ed. John Hutchinson and Anthony D. Smith (New York: Oxford University Press, 1996), 27.

10. See Lawrence A. Hoffman and Janet R. Walton, eds., *Sacred Sound and Social Change: Liturgical Music in Jewish and Christian Experience*, Two Liturgical Traditions 3 (Notre Dame, Ind.: University of Notre Dame Press, 1992), 11.

11. Paul Mendes-Flohr, *German Jews: A Dual Identity* (New Haven, Conn.: Yale University Press, 1999), 12–13.

12. Martin Stokes, "Introduction: Ethnicity, Identity and Music," in *Ethnicity, Identity, and Music: The Musical Construction of Place*, ed. Martin Stokes (New York: Berg, 1994), 5.

13. See Arno Nadel, "Jüdische Musik," *Der Jude* 7 (1923): 227–36.

14. Jewish and non-Jewish scholars alike tackled the subject of "Hebraic music" from relatively early on; among them were Johann Nicolaus Forkel, "Litteratur der hebräischen Musik," in *Allgemeine Geschichte der Musik* (Leipzig: Schwickert, 1788–1801), 173–84, which provides a list of books on "Hebrew music" written before 1788; Joseph Gall, "Über hebräische Musik (Semiroth Israel)," *Neue Berliner Musik-Zeitung* 4 (1854): 289–91; Eduard Rosenberg, "Die Musik und der Gesang bei den Juden mit besonderer Rücksicht auf die nachbiblischen Zeiten," *Die Ungarische Kultusbeamten-Zeitung* (1887–1889). Especially noteworthy is a monograph by Joseph Levin Saalschütz, *Geschichte und Würdigung der Musik bei den Hebräern, im Verhältniss zur sonstigen Ausbildung dieser Kunst in alter und neuer Zeit, nebst einem Anhang über die Hebräische Orgel* (Berlin: G. Fincke, 1829); in an appendix, Saalschütz claims that "Hebraic organs" are a genuine phenomenon and not a mere curiosity; indeed, he believes that Jerome's epistle to Dardanus attests to their exis-

tence. Saalschütz further states that Hebraic organs inspired the church to introduce organs; see Saalschütz (1829, 133). Despite the interest in Hebraic music, the question and concept of "Jewish music" appear only very late in modern history.

15. See Erwin Felber, "Gibt es eine jüdische Musik?" *Anbruch* 10 (1928): 287.

16. Abraham Zvi Idelsohn, *Jewish Music in Its Historical Development* (1929; repr., New York: Dover, 1992), 24.

17. Ibid., 477.

18. Hermann Zivi, "Gibt es eine jüdische Musik?" *Programmheft des jüdischen Kulturbund Rhein-Ruhr* 5, no. 7 (1934): 1–2.

19. Hermann Zivi, "Jüdische Musik im Lichte des Verismus," in *Dem Andenken Eduard Birnbaums: Sammlung kantoral-wissenschaftlicher Aufsätze*, ed. Aron Friedmann (Berlin: C. Boas, 1922), 123.

20. Pamela Maxine Potter, *Most German of the Arts: Musicology and Society from the Weimar Republic to the End of Hitler's Reich* (New Haven, Conn.: Yale University Press, 1998), 22.

21. See Hans Samuel, "Der Weg zur jüdischen Orgel," ca. 1930, I.5.14, Hans Samuel Collection, Archive of Israeli Music, Tel Aviv University.

22. See chapter 4 for a detailed discourse.

23. Alfred Einstein was among the first to point out the problem of a "national" terminology, suggesting that we speak of the music (history) of Germany, France, and so on instead of German or French music. See Einstein, *Nationale und Universale Musik: Neue Essays* (Zurich: Pan, 1958), 232. However, since nation-states are always heterogeneous and ethnicities dispersed through migration, it may be more useful to speak of the music (history) of the Germans, French, and so on.

24. See David Sorkin, "Emancipation and Assimilation: Two Concepts and Their Application to German-Jewish History," *Leo Baeck Institute Yearbook* 35 (1990): 19–20. A general history of the terms appears in Zygmunt Bauman, "Modernity and Ambivalence," *Theory, Culture, and Society* 7 (1990): 143–69. Sorkin understands assimilation as a trap sprung on the Jews by non-Jewish Germans in order to deprive them of their self-respect.

25. See Bruno Nettl, *Theory and Method in Ethnomusicology* (London: Macmillan, 1964), 235.

26. Margaret J. Kartomi, "The Processes and Results of Musical Culture Contact: A Discussion of Terminology and Concepts," *Ethnomusicology* 25, no. 2 (1981): 230–32.

27. Ibid., 234–35.

28. Detailed discourses on the different positions on assimilation and acculturation appear in Bauman, "Modernity and Ambivalence," 143–69; and Michael A. Meyer, "German Jewry's Path to Normality and Assimilation: Complexities, Ironies, Paradoxes," in *Towards Normality? Acculturation and Modern German Jewry*, ed. Rainer Liedtke and David Rechter, Schriftenreihe wissenschaftlicher Abhandlungen des Leo Baeck Instituts 68 (Tübingen: Mohr Siebeck, 2003), 15–19. David Sorkin explores in detail the ideological and scholarly use of the terminology and concludes the following: "First and foremost, historians have restored assimilation by the Jews to its narrow acceptation, arguing that in the nineteenth century it was the equivalent of what contemporary parlance calls 'acculturation,' the adoption of some characteristics of the major group—language, education, manner, national identification—without renouncing other religious or cultural differences." Sorkin, "Emancipation and Assimilation," 27.

29. See Sorkin, "Emancipation and Assimilation," 20.

30. Ibid., 21.

31. See David Sorkin, "Religious Reforms and Secular Trends in German-Jewish Life: An Agenda for Research," *Leo Baeck Institute Yearbook* 48 (1995): 184.

32. See also Meyer, "German Jewry's Path to Normality and Assimilation," 13–15, 23.

Chapter 2

1. See the detailed source material presented in Erika Timm and Gustav Adolf Beckmann, *Historische jiddische Semantik: Die Bibelübersetzungssprache als Faktor der Auseinanderentwicklung des jiddischen und des deutschen Wortschatzes* (Tübingen: Niemeyer, 2005), 588.

2. *The New Grove Dictionary of Music and Musicians*, s.v. "Biblical instruments, §3: Old Testament instruments—(xii) 'Uġav" (by Joachim Braun), http://www.grovemusic.com (accessed Sept. 5, 2007).

3. More details on the magrepha appear in Alfred Sendrey, *Musik in Alt-Israel* (Leipzig: Deutscher Verlag für Musik, 1970), 365–76; *Encyclopaedia Judaica*, 1st ed., s.v. "Organ: Antiquity"; and Joseph Yasser, "The Magrepha of the Herodian Temple: A Fivefold Hypothesis," *Journal of the American Musicological Society* 13 (1960): 24–42. Yasser has reconstructed the instrument on the basis of several sources and concluded that it consisted of a cube-shaped chamber that housed the bellows, from which a long, shovel-like handle projected.

4. See Sendrey, *Musik in Alt-Israel*, 365–76.

5. MS Or.Qu.832 (Cat.St.143), Staatsbibliothek, Berlin; MS Ot.2854 (Cat.Marg.227), British Museum, London; MS 140, Ginzburg Collection, Gosudarstvennaja Biblioteka, Moscow; and MS Laud.103 (Cat.Neub.1535) (incomplete, with passages on music missing), Bodleian Library, Oxford; see Israel Adler, ed., *Hebrew Writings concerning Music in Manuscripts and Printed Books from Geonic Times up to 1800*, RISM 9(2) (Munich: G. Henle, 1975), 39–45, no. 060.

6. See Hanoch Avenary, "Ein hebräisches Zeugnis für den Aufenthalt Konrad Paumanns in Mantua (1470)," *Die Musikforschung* 16 (1963): 156–57.

7. MS héb.1037.2, Bibliothèque Nationale, Paris; see Adler, *Hebrew Writings*, 80–88, no. 140.

8. Hanoch Avenary, "The Mixture Principle in the Mediaeval Organ: An Early Evidence," *Musica Disciplina* 4 (1950): 51.

9. Avenary (ibid.) provides a detailed account.

10. The manuscript is no longer extant; see Adler, *Hebrew Writings*, 221–39, no. 530.

11. The kinnor, frequently mistranslated as "harp," is the instrument on which King David played. Musicological and archaeological documentation makes it clear that the reference is in fact to the Greek *lyra* [lyre]. Moscato here interprets it as an organ.

12. The source text is in Hebrew; it is translated here from the German version of the passages on music in Herzl Shmueli, *Higgajon Bechinnor: Betrachtungen zum Leierspiel des Jehudah ben Joseph Arjeh Moscato* (Tel Aviv: Neografika, 1953), 39.

13. See *The New Grove Dictionary of Music and Musicians*, s.v. "Organum: Etymology, early usage," http://www.grovemusic.com (accessed Sept. 5, 2007).

14. The manuscript is no longer extant; see Adler, *Hebrew Writings*, 243–83, no. 570. A German version is published in Gianfranco Miletto, *Die Heldenschilde des Abraham ben David Portaleone*, 2 vols. (Frankfurt am Main: Peter Lang, 2002).

15. See also the edition of the Hebrew source text with commentary in Adler, *Hebrew Writings*, 244, no. 570.

16. *The New Grove Dictionary of Music and Musicians*, s.v. "Biblical instruments, §3: Old Testament instruments—(xiv) Collective terms," http://www.grovemusic.com (accessed Sept. 5, 2007).

17. Accordingly, the Targum Jonathan (the official eastern—Babylonian—Aramaic translation of the Hebrew Bible) interprets minnim as *khalilin* [pipes, tubes]; in the second introduction to Moses Mendelssohn's translation of the Psalms, minnim is accepted as denoting the organ. *Jewish Encyclopedia*, s.v. "Organ," http://www.jewishencyclopedia.com (accessed Mar. 5, 2007).

18. See Timm and Beckmann, *Historische jiddische Semantik*, 590.

19. Ibid.

20. Joachim Braun, "The Iconography of the Organ: Change in Jewish Thought and Musical Life," *Music in Art: International Journal for Music Iconography* 28, nos. 1–2 (2003): 59.

21. Ibid.

22. Ibid.

23. MS Add.27210, fol. 15r, Bodleian Library, Oxford.

24. See Joachim Braun, "The Lute and Organ in Ancient Israeli and Jewish Iconography," in *Festschrift Christoph-Hellmut Mahling*, ed. Axel Beer, Kristina Pfarr, and Wolfgang Ruf, vol. 1, 174.

25. Braun, "Iconography of the Organ," 63.

26. Cod. 2761, fol. 69v, Österreichische Nationalbibliothek, Vienna.

27. Kaufmann Collection MS A387, fol. 343v, Magyar Tudományos Akadémia Könyvtár, Budapest. For depictions of organs and further comments see Zoltán Falvy, "Musical Instruments in the Kaufmann Manuscripts, Budapest," *Studia Musicologica Academiae Scientiarum Hungaricae* 37, nos. 2–4 (1996): 231–48.

28. MS I, 368 (6), fol. 186r, Sassoon Collection, Jerusalem.

29. Braun, "Lute and Organ," vol. 1, 170.

30. Kaufmann Collection MS A422, fol. 3v, Magyar Tudományos Akadémia Könyvtár, Budapest.

31. Ibid., fol. 60v.

32. Cod. Rossiana 555, fol. 292–93, Biblioteca Apostolica Vaticana, Vatican.

33. MS Opp.776, fol. 79v, Bodleian Library, Oxford. A reprint appears in Walter Salmen, *"Denn die Fiedel macht das Fest": Jüdische Musikanten und Tänzer vom 13. bis 20. Jahrhundert* (Innsbruck: Edition Helbling, 1991), 206, fig. 12.

34. The miniature accompanies a text excerpt from the Hoshanot sung during Sukkot, usually after the Shaḥarit or Musaf prayers. The unusual composition of musicians possibly relates to the theological concept that Sukkot is the messianic end of days for *every* nation; further, prayers for the peace of all nations (based on Isaiah 56:7) are recited.

35. MS XXIII F.202, National Library (Klementinum), Prague.

36. Braun, "Lute and Organ," 175.

37. Ibid., 176.

38. We know of the use of portatives in Jewish ceremonial life also from the following written source: *Judaeorum Morologia, oder jüdisches Affen-Spiel / Das ist: Der jüdischen Gemeinde zu Prage possir- und sehr lächerlicher Auffzug: Welchen Sie bey Celebrirung des Freuden-Festes über der höchst erfreulichen Geburt des Römischen Käiserl. Printzens in der Juden-Statt*

daselbst öffentlich gehalten / und nachgehends . . . zum Druck befördert worden (Leipzig: Justino Brandten, 1678). Hanoch Avenary quotes a passage that describes the use of three portative organs (one of which accompanied the *Spielleute*; the other two the choruses) during a procession in Prague on July 28, 1678, to celebrate the birth of Habsburg Prince Joseph. *Musik in Geschichte und Gegenwart*, 1st ed., s.v. "Jüdische Musik: A. Geschichte der jüdischen Musik—IV Wanderungen und Mischung der Stile (1500 bis 1750)," 249.

39. A reproduction of the engraving appears in David Ellenson, "A Disputed Precedent: The Prague Organ in Nineteenth-century Central-European Legal Literature and Polemics," *Leo Baeck Institute Yearbook* 40 (1995): 251–64.

40. The Israel Museum in Jerusalem holds another original print of the engraving.

41. Based on an analysis of eight manuscripts, Daniel S. Katz gives a detailed account of the eighteenth- and nineteenth-century meshorerim techniques; see "A Prolegomenon to the Study of the Performance Practice of Synagogue Music Involving M'shor'rim," *Journal of Synagogue Music* 24, no. 2 (1995): 35–79.

42. Leo Landman, "The Office of the Medieval 'Hazzan,'" *Jewish Quarterly Review* 62, no. 3 (1972): 157.

43. For further sources on the practice of meshorerim see Adler, *Hebrew Writings*, nos. 220, 240, 360, 560, and 570. On Abraham ben David Portaleone's description of the meshorerim see also Israel Adler, *La pratique musicale savante dans quelques communautés Juives en Europe aux XVIIe et XVIIIe siècle*, Etudes Juives 8 (Paris: Mouton, 1966), 192.

44. See Edith Gerson-Kiwi, "Vocal Folk Polyphonies of the Western Orient in Jewish Tradition," *Yuval: Studies of the Jewish Music Research Centre* 1 (1968): 192.

45. Ibid., 193.

46. Ibid., 192.

47. Eliezer Ehrenreich, "Der erste Synagogenchor in Berlin (aus alten Akten)," *Gemeindeblatt der jüdischen Gemeinde zu Berlin* 19 (February 1929): 67.

48. Heymann Steinthal, *AZJ* 12, no. 13 (1896), quoted in Heymann Steinthal, *Über Juden und Judentum: Vorträge und Aufsätze*, Schriften der Gesellschaft zur Förderung des Judentums 9 (Berlin: M. Poppelauer, 1906), 273.

49. More details are given in Salmen, *"Denn die Fiedel macht das Fest,"* 78–79.

50. See Idelsohn, *Jewish Music*, 205.

51. Translated from the Hebrew as given in Adler, *La pratique musicale*, 256.

52. Meijer Marcus Roest, ed., "Het verhaal van een reis door een groot gedeelte van Europa in het eerste vierde der 18e eeuw, door een Israëlit," *Israëlietische Letterbode* 10 (1884–85): 148–89, and *Israëlietische Letterbode* 11 (1885–1886): 21–38, 93–147; translated from the Yiddish as given in Adler, *La pratique musicale*, 252.

53. Idelsohn, *Jewish Music*, 205.

54. The life and work of this Jewish organ builder are discussed in a piece in the Jewish journal *Bikkurei ha-Ittim* 4 (1823): 257–58, which is based in turn on a Yiddish article in the *Naye Zaytung un yidischer Oyftsug* (Prague, 1716).

55. See Rudolph Quoika, *Der Orgelbau in Böhmen und Mähren*, Der Orgelbau in Europa 2 (Mainz: Rheingold, 1966), 68. Idelsohn (*Jewish Music*, 205) mentions a portative organ built by the same builder in 1716 and references this with an article from the journal *Bikkurei ha-Ittim* and with Paul Nettl, *Alte jüdische Spielleute und Musiker* (Prague: J. Flesch, 1923), 39. Quoika's account relies on Johann Jacob Schudt, *Juedisches Franckfurter und*

Prager Freuden-Fest: Wegen der höchst-glücklichen Geburth des durchläuchtigsten käyserlichen Erb-Prinzens, vorstellend mit was Solennitäten die Franckfurter Juden selbiges celebrirt, auch ein besonders Lied, mit Sinn-Bilder und Devisen, darauff verfertigt; So dann den Curieusen kostbahren, doch recht possirlichen Auffzug, so die Prager Juden gehalten (Frankfurt am Main: Mathias Andreä, 1716). Schudt mentions the building of the organ on page 69 but does not indicate the date: "Afterwards came a new organ, which was made by R. Maier Mahler / Cost above 400 [gulden] and six [with] musical instruments."

56. Johann Jacob Schudt, *Jüdische Merckwürdigkeiten: Vorstellende was sich Curieuses und Denckwürdiges in den neuern Zeiten bey einigen Jahrhunderten mit denen in alle IV. Theile der Welt, sonderlich durch Teutschland zerstreuten Juden zugetragen / mit historischer Feder in drey Theilen beschrieben* (1714–1718; repr., Berlin: Lamm, 1922), bk. VI, chap. 14, §3.

57. Ibid., chap. 34, §22.

58. Ibid.

59. In the playing of preludes, the organ supplied the celebrant and the choir with a reference pitch. It was also sometimes used within hymns, when it alternated with the choir, playing a verse after the choir had sung it (alternatim practice).

60. See Karl Honemeyer, *Thomas Müntzer und Martin Luther: Ihr Ringen um die Musik des Gottesdienstes; Untersuchungen zum "Deutzsch Kirchenampt" 1523* (Berlin: Merseburger, 1974); Johannes Rautenstrauch, *Luther und die Pflege der kirchlichen Musik in Sachsen (14.–19. Jahrhundert): Ein Beitr. zur Geschichte der katholischen Brüderschaften, der vor- u. nachreformator. Kurrenden, Schulchöre, u. Kantoreien Sachsens* (Hildesheim, Germany: Georg Olms, 1970); Otto Daube and Hans Joachim Moser, "Die Wittenbergisch Nachtigall" [Martin Luther und die Musik] (Dortmund: W. Crüwell, 1962); Karl Anton, *Luther und die Musik* (Berlin: Evangelische Verlagsanstalt, 1957).

61. In 1868 the Spanish Synagogue was built on the site of the Old Shul.

62. In the Diaspora communities, the playing of musical instruments is forbidden on the first day of the nine-day (eight in Israel) festival of Sukkot and on the last two days, Shemini Azeret and Simḥat Torah.

63. See Peter Gradenwitz, *The Music of Israel: From the Biblical Era to Modern Times*, 2d ed. (Portland, Ore.: Amadeus, 1996), 169. It is generally believed that the Scuola Tedesca, an Ashkenazic synagogue in Venice, also possessed an organ. Don Harrán gives detailed information on the ensemble; see "Dum Recordaremum Sion: Music in the Life and Thought of the Venetian Rabbi Leon Modena (1571–1648)," *AJS Review* 23, no. 1 (1998): 53–55.

64. Giulio Morosini, *Via delle fede mostrata a gli Ebrei: Divisa in tre parti* (Rome: Stamperia della Cong. de prop. Fide, 1683), vol. 2, 793. For a detailed history of the debates over the organ and the different rabbinical attitudes see Meir Benayahu, "Da'at ḥakhmey Italyah al ha-neginah be-'uġav ba-tefillah" [The Opinions of Italian Sages on Organ Playing in Prayer Service], *Asufot* 1 (1987): 265–318.

65. See Adler, *La pratique musicale*, 70–79.

66. See *Monatsschrift für Geschichte und Wissenschaft des Judentums* 39, no. 3 (1895): 350–57.

67. Ibid., 358.

68. Compiled before 1565 by Joseph ben Ephraim Caro, the *Shulḥan Arukh* [Set Table] is a codex of Jewish law in four extensive sections. The first part, *Oraḥ Ḥayyim* (rules

for every day, the Sabbath, and holy days), is today's standard halakhah codification for Orthodox Judaism.

69. See Adler, *La pratique musicale*, 263.

Chapter 3

1. On the complex and controversial relationship between Haskalah, Jewish emancipation, and Reform, see David Sorkin, "Religious Reforms and Secular Trends in German-Jewish Life: An Agenda for Research." *Leo Baeck Institute Yearbook* 48 (1995): 169–76.

2. Jewish families apparently began using the organ as a chamber instrument in private homes at a much earlier period. One of these is in the collection at the Musikinstrumentenmuseum of the University of Leipzig (no. 259; a late eighteenth-century cabinet organ by Gideon Thomas Bätz of Utrecht); see Klaus Gernhard, Hubert Henkel, and Winfried Schrammek, *Orgelinstrumente und Harmoniums*, Musikinstrumentenmuseum der Universität Leipzig: Katalog 6 (Wiesbaden: Breitkopf und Härtel, 1984), 36–38 (plates) and 51–54.

3. Caesar Seligmann, *Geschichte der jüdischen Reformbewegung von Mendelssohn bis zur Gegenwart* (Frankfurt am Main: Julius Kauffmann, 1922), 22.

4. The event is documented in an anonymous contemporary account; see "Feyerliche Einweihung des Jacobs-Tempels in Seesen," *Sulamith: Eine Zeitschrift zur Beförderung der Kultur und Humanität unter den Israeliten* 3, no. 4 (1810): 298–303.

5. See Abraham Zvi Idelsohn, *Jewish Music in Its Historical Development* (1929; repr., New York: Dover, 1992), 238.

6. See Rolf Ballof and Joachim Frassl, eds., *Die Jacobson-Schule: Festschrift zum 200-jährigen Bestehen der Jacobson-Schule in Seesen* (Seesen, Germany: Jacobson Gymnasium, 2001), 246.

7. Nahum Glatzer, ed., *Leopold Zunz: Jude—Deutscher—Europäer: Ein jüdisches Gelehrtenschicksal des 19. Jahrhunderts in Briefen an Freunde*, Schriftenreihe wissenschaftlicher Abhandlungen des Leo Baeck Instituts 11 (Tübingen: Mohr, 1964), 78.

8. See Michael A. Meyer, Michael Brenner, Mordechai Breuer, and Michael Graetz, eds., *German-Jewish History in Modern Times*, 4 vols. (New York: Columbia University Press, 1996), vol. 2, 126.

9. See Ismar Elbogen, *Der jüdische Gottesdienst in seiner geschichtlichen Entwicklung*, 3d ed. (Hildesheim, Germany: Georg Olms, 1967), 403.

10. See Moritz Henle, "Der gottesdienstliche Gesang im Israelitischen Tempel zu Hamburg," in *Festschrift zum hundertjährigen Bestehen des Israelitischen Tempels in Hamburg*, ed. David Leimdörfer (Hamburg: M. Glogau, 1918), 67–85.

11. Lois C. Dubin discusses the two collections, *Nogah ha-Zedek* and *Eleh Divrei ha-Berit*, in detail and focuses on the Italian involvement in the Reform controversy. Dubin, "The Rise and the Fall of the Italian Jewish Model in Germany: From Haskalah to Reform, 1780–1820," in *Jewish History and Jewish Memory: Essays in Honor of Yosef Hayim Yerushalmi*, ed. Elisheva Carlebach, John M. Efron, and David N. Myers, Tauber Institute for the Study of European Jewry Series 29 (Hanover, N.H.: University Press of New England, 1998), 271–95.

12. See ibid., 276–78.

13. From 1853 to 1854, after the demolition of the old main synagogue at Judengasse in Frankfurt am Main, congregational services were held in the Philantropin's prayer hall,

so the room was no longer normally available to the school. What effect these changes may have had on the use of the organ is not known; see Saldo Adler and Hermann Baerwald, *Geschichte der Realschule der israelitischen Gemeinde (Philantropin) zu Frankfurt am Main, 1804–1904* (Frankfurt am Main: Druck von Gebrüder Fey, 1904), 54.

14. Ibid., 50.

15. *Leipziger Zeitung*, Oct. 14, 1820, quoted in Glatzer, *Leopold Zunz*, 113–14.

16. See Eliezer Ehrenreich, "Der erste Synagogenchor in Berlin (aus alten Akten)," *Gemeindeblatt der jüdischen Gemeinde zu Berlin* 19 (February 1929): 66–67.

17. See Carsten Wilke, "Der Gießener Rabbiner Dr. Benedikt Levi (1806–1899)," *Ashkenas* 16, no. 1 (2006): 55.

18. See Benedikt Levi, *Beweis der Zuverlässigkeit des deutschen Choralgesanges mit Orgelbegleitung bei dem sabbathlichen Gottesdienste der Juden: Ein Beitrag zur jüdischen Liturgie* (Offenbach, Germany: Brede, 1833).

19. Anon., [untitled], *AZJ* 5, no. 25 (June 19, 1841): 368.

20. See Wilke, "Der Gießener Rabbiner Dr. Benedikt Levi," 53.

21. Anon., "Berichte über den Stand des Kultus, 13. Oktober 1841," *AZJ* 5, no. 45 (Nov. 6, 1841): 643.

22. Ibid.

23. See *Protokolle und Aktenstücke der zweiten Rabbinerversammlung* (Frankfurt am Main: E. Ullmann, 1845), 146.

24. Ibid., 326.

25. Ibid., 329.

26. Anon., "Aus Oberschlesien im Oktober: Privatmittheilung," *AZJ* 9, no. 45 (Nov. 3, 1845): 675. For further information on Frankel, who in spite of his early experiments eventually became a decided opponent of the instrumental accompaniment of synagogue music, see Andreas Brämer, *Rabbiner Zacharias Frankel: Wissenschaft des Judentums und konservative Reform im 19. Jahrhundert*, Netiva: Wege zur deutsch-jüdischen Geschichte und Kultur 3 (Hildesheim, Germany: Georg Olms, 2000).

27. The latter instrument was later purchased by the Catholic-Apostolic congregation of Berlin-Kreuzberg and rebuilt by Alexander Schuke at the beginning of the twentieth century. Disassembled in 1978, it now belongs, unrestored, to the private collection of a Berlin organist; see Berthold Schwarz, ed., *500 Jahre Orgeln in Berliner evangelischen Kirchen*, Veröffentlichung der Gesellschaft der Orgelfreunde 134 (Berlin: Pape, 1991), vol. 2, 491.

28. Michael Güldenstein, "Mitteilung, 25. November 1845," *AZJ* 10, no. 5 (Jan. 26, 1846): 68.

29. Monika Minniger, letter to the author, Jan. 5, 1999.

30. See Abraham Geiger, "Aktenstücke zur dritten Versammlung deutscher Rabbinen, 28. Mai 1846," *AZJ* 10, no. 24 (June 8, 1846): 346.

31. David Deutsch, "Die Orgel in der Synagoge: Eine Erörterung" (Wrocław, Poland: privately printed, 1863), 3.

32. See Abraham Berliner, ed., *Zur Lehr' und Wehr über und gegen die kirchliche Orgel im jüdischen Gottesdienste* (Berlin: Nathansen und Lamm, 1904), 48.

33. See Michael Sachs, "Gutachten gegen die Orgel (13.11.1861)," in ibid., 12–22.

34. See ibid., 48–54.

35. The year of Lewandowski's birth is disputed. Some scholars give it as 1821 (Aron Friedmann, Arno Nadel, and Eric Werner); others as 1823 (Eduard Birnbaum and Bern-

hard Jacobsohn). Geoffrey Goldberg suggests that Lewandowski, like Salomon Sulzer, falsified his birth date to make it easier to get a job; see Geoffrey Goldberg, "Neglected Sources for the Historical Study of Synagogue Music: The Prefaces to Louis Lewandowski's Kol Rinnah u'T'fillah and Toda W'simrah—Annotated Translations," *Musica Judaica* 11 (1989/1990): 30–31. Goldberg also raises the question of whether Lewandowski ever officiated as cantor or ḥazzan after he left the Heidereutergasse synagogue; see Geoffrey Goldberg, "The Training of ḥazzanim in Nineteenth-century Germany," *Yuval* 7 (2002): 305.

36. Louis Lewandowski, "Gutachten betr. den Antrag wegen Bewilligung der Geldmittel zur Herstellung eines Orgelwerkes in der neuen Synagoge," Jan. 13, 1862, Moritz Stern Collection P 17/585, leaves 57–59, Central Archives for the History of the Jewish People, Jerusalem.

37. Aron Ackermann "Die Orgel," in *Zur Lehr' und Wehr*, ed. Berliner, 9–10.

38. Ibid.

39. Anon., "Privatmittheilung, 11. Januar 1863," *AZJ* 27, no. 5 (Jan. 27, 1863): 70.

40. Deutsch, "Die Orgel in der Synagoge," iii.

41. Ibid., 44.

42. Anon., "Privatmittheilung, 18. Januar 1863," *AZJ* 27, no. 5 (Jan. 27, 1863): 70.

43. Anon., "Einweihung der Synagoge am 5. September 1866," *Berlinische Nachrichten von Staats- und gelehrten Sachen* 206 (Sept. 6, 1866): 3. The opening blessing was most likely an arrangement of Psalm 118.

44. Salomon Sulzer, "Antrag," abstracted in *Verhandlungen der ersten israelitischen Synode zu Leipzig* (Berlin: Gerschel, 1869), 250–51, quoted in Hanoch Avenary, ed., *Kantor Salomon Sulzer und seine Zeit: Eine Dokumentation* (Sigmaringen, Germany: Jan Thorbecke, 1985), 164.

45. On the controversies over the organ in the Viennese community, see Avenary, *Kantor Salomon Sulzer und seine Zeit*, 23–25, 166–70; and Tina Frühauf, "Jewish Liturgical Music in Vienna: A Mirror of Cultural Diversity," in *Vienna: Jews and the City of Music 1870–1938*, ed. Leon Botstein and Werner Hanak (Annandale-on-Hudson, N.Y.: Bard College, 2004), 78–82.

46. See *Die Beschlüsse der ersten und zweiten israelitischen Synode* (Mainz: J. Gottleben'sche Buchdruckerei, 1871), 8.

47. Salomon Sulzer, "Memorandum zur gottesdienstlichen Reform," draft, ca. Jan. 22, 1871, quoted in Avenary, *Kantor Salomon Sulzer und seine Zeit*, 166–67. The original manuscript is held in the library of the Hebrew Union College, Cincinnati, Birnbaum Collection, Arch. III (Correspondence).

48. Salomon Sulzer, "Denkschrift an die hochgeehrte Wiener israelitische Cultus-Gemeinde" (Vienna: Winter, 1876), quoted in Avenary, *Kantor Salomon Sulzer und seine Zeit*, 172–73.

49. It has been suggested that the Viennese congregation took its position against organ music as a way of differentiating itself from the Jewish community in Budapest, which had adopted the organ at a relatively early date; see Frühauf, "Jewish Liturgical Music in Vienna," 79.

50. Salomon Sulzer, *Schir Zion: Ein Cyclus religiöser Gesänge zum gottesdienstlichen Gebrauche der Israeliten* (Vienna: privately printed, 1840) (preface dated to 1838) and *Schir Zion: Gottesdienstliche Gesänge der Israeliten, zweiter Theil* (Vienna: J. Schlossberg, 1866) (preface dated to 1865).

51. See anon., *OUCZ* 7, no. 31 (Sept. 22, 1887), 4. The prelude may have been one of the *Vier Präludien für Orgel oder Harmonium*, op. 10 (Leipzig: Breitkopf und Härtel, n.d.).

52. See Edwin Seroussi, "Schir Hakawod and the Liturgical Music Reforms in the Sephardi Community in Vienna, ca. 1880–1925: A Study of Change in Religious Music" (PhD diss., University of California, 1988), 89–90.

53. The organ (III/16) was built by Henry Erben of New York. Moved to Columbia in 1865, it was replaced by a new two-manual instrument built by James M. Mandeville in March 1872. The case of this instrument is still in the rear gallery of the building today. Details on the Erben instrument appear in Sebastian Glück, "The American Synagogue Organ: A Brief Account," *Tracker* 50, nos. 3–4 (2006): 98–111. Glück surveys the early history of organs in the United States and describes selected instruments from the early period up to 1905.

54. About 40 percent of the older members of the congregation objected to the introduction of the organ and in 1844 took the matter to court. The decision went against the minority, who then appealed the case; however, the higher court affirmed the decision in 1846. The court held that, because it was unable to decide the merits of this religious controversy, it had no choice but to rely upon the judgment of the majority of the congregation. See in this connection Allan Tarshish's exhaustive study, "The Charleston Organ Case," *American Jewish Historical Quarterly* 54, no. 4 (1965): 411–49.

55. In the synagogue Shearith Israel (then located on Nineteenth Street), an organ was installed in 1881 but used at first only for weddings. Three years later instrumental playing was generally permitted, only to be again prohibited after eight months. From 1888 on, the organ was once more played at weddings. When George Gershwin moved from New York to California (ca. 1935), he donated his organ to the synagogue. See David De Sola Pool and Tamar Pool, *An Old Faith in the New World: Portrait of Shearith Israel, 1654–1954* (New York: Columbia University Press, 1955), 144.

56. In accordance with principles derived from Jewish law, the organ of the Sephardic synagogue in Bayonne was not played on the Sabbath or holy days; see Henry Léon, *Historie des Juifs de Bayonne* (Paris: Armand Durlacher, 1893), 302.

57. Johannes Wachten, "David Wolffsohn und die Kölner Judenschaft," in *Köln und das rheinische Judentum: Festschrift Germania Judaica, 1959–1984*, ed. Jutta Bohnke-Kollwitz (Cologne: J. P. Bachem, 1984), 304.

58. On the other hand, the debates on the introduction of an organ in the Rykestraße synagogue in Berlin, which took place at almost exactly the same time, went against the organ's advocates; see anon., "Die Gutachten des Berliner Rabbinats über die Orgel, 1. Februar 1904," *AZJ* 68, no. 6 (Feb. 5, 1904): 65–68.

59. See "Orgelakte: Opus 1525," Steinmeyer Company Archive, Oettingen, Germany.

60. See Michael Brocke, ed., *Feuer an Dein Heiligtum gelegt: Zerstörte Synagogen 1938 Nordrhein-Westfalen* (Bochum, Germany: Kamp, 1999).

61. Samuel Adler, letter to the author, Mar. 30, 2000.

62. Ibid.

63. David F. Kaelter, "Die 'Kristallnacht' in der Provinz," *MB: Wochenzeitung des Irgun Olej Merkas Europa*, nos. 42–43 (Oct. 18, 1963), quoted in Fred K. Prieberg, *Musik im NS-Staat* (Frankfurt am Main: Fischer Taschenbuch, 1982), 106.

64. Anon., "Es ist eine Schande! Die Judenorgel in der Sankt Korbinianskirche zu München," *Stürmer* 42 (Oct. 19, 1938).

65. The concept of the organ as "queen of the instruments" was in conformity with the National Socialists' ideas, and it is not surprising that Hitler made it his own and in 1935–1936 had the largest organ in Europe built for the Reichstag in Nuremberg. With sixteen thousand pipes and 220 stops in five manuals, the instrument was ironically the opposite of what the German organ revival meant by a "German sound ideal" (see the following section, "The Synagogue Organ in the Context of Organ-Building Traditions").

66. See Hermann Simon and Jochen Boberg, eds., *"Tuet auf die Pforten": Die Neue Synagoge 1866–1995, Begleitbuch zur ständigen Ausstellung der Stiftung "Neue Synagoge Berlin—Centrum Judaicum"* (Berlin: Stiftung Neue Synagoge Berlin–Centrum Judaicum, 1995), 245–46.

67. Siegmund Hirschberg to Hans Hirschberg, April 1939; formerly private collection of Hans Hirschberg (courtesy of the Feher Jewish Music Center, Beth Hatefutsoth, Tel Aviv).

68. See Alexander Lohe, "Orgeln in der Aachener Synagoge: Eine historische Spurenlese," in *Wer baut, will bleiben: Simon Schlachet zu Ehren*, ed. Wolfgang Krücken and Alexander Lohe (Aachen, Germany: Shaker, 1997), 170–72. The Israeli Organists' Club has made efforts to acquire this instrument and hopes to maintain it as a memorial.

69. For the effects of the *Gründerjahre* on the Jewish community see Meyer, Brenner, Breuer, and Graetz, *German-Jewish History*, vol. 2, 302.

70. See Jakob Thon, *Die jüdischen Gemeinden und Vereine in Deutschland*, Veröffentlichungen des Bureaus für Statistik der Juden 3 (Berlin: Verlag des Bureaus für die Statistik der Juden, 1906), 14–17.

71. *Grundtönigkeit* refers to tone quality that is based on fundamental or lower pitches. As a specific type of organ disposition, it was first used by the Baroque builders of southern Germany and then refined and systematized by the Walcker firm.

72. See Walter Kwasnik, *Die Orgel der Neuzeit* (Cologne: Staufen, 1948), 133–36.

73. Alfred Reichling, "Zur Frage des 'konfessionellen Orgelbaus' im 19. und 20. Jahrhundert," in *Die Orgel im Dienst der Kirche: Gespräch aus ökumenischer Sicht: Bericht über das sechste Colloquium der Walcker-Stiftung für orgelwissenschaftliche Forschung in Verbindung mit dem Pontificio Istituto die Musica Sacra 8.–14. Oktober 1984 in Rom*, ed. Hans Heinrich Eggebrecht (Murrhardt, Germany: Musikwissenschaftliche Verlags-Gesellschaft, 1985), 280.

74. Rafael Frank, "Der jüdische Organist," *AZJ* 72, no. 8 (Feb. 21, 1908): 91.

75. Anon., "Aus dem Badischen, im Juni: Privatmittheilung, 20. Mai 1846," *AZJ* 10, no. 31 (July 27, 1846): 450.

76. The dispositions of all of the organs discussed appear at http://www.oup.com/us/theorgananditsmusic.

77. See Emile Rupp, "Der Sachverständigenzwang: Eine Gefahr für den deutschen Orgelbau," *ZfI* 32 (1911–1912), 1241–43.

78. Even in the years to come, Jewish musicians remained heavily underrepresented in these commissions. At Berlin's New Synagogue on Oranienburger Straße (1909, E. F. Walcker et Cie.), the panel comprised Prof. Wolfgang Reimann and Prof. Carl August Haupt (probably for the disposition) and, later, organists Paul Rabe (disposition), Arthur Zepke, and Ludwig Altman (organ specialist). The commission that was to oversee the building of an organ in the synagogue on Herzog-Max-Straße in Munich (1929, Steinmeyer) consisted of Prof. Dr. Carl Emil von Schafhäutl (planning), Prof. Hermann Sagerer and Hans Steinmeyer (disposition), Domkapellmeister Ludwig Berberich, Kapellmeister Joseph Ziegler, and Heinrich Schalit (consultant).

79. The fact that the town and the new device had the same name suggests that the former influenced the designation; in accordance with other organ builders and theorists, Walcker nevertheless originally referred to this new type of windchest by the archaic term *Springlade*, or spring chest, as it would be called in the future.

80. Eberhard Kuhn, "Disposition über die vom Orgelbaumeister E. F. Walcker und Comp. in Ludwigsburg für die israelitische Gemeinde in Mannheim erbaute Orgel," *Urania* 13, no. 6 (1856): 82.

81. Walcker had in fact built a spring chest, but it was designed for an instrument meant to be played only occasionally: "In the year 1854, on the occasion of the Munich trade exposition, I . . . furnished proof of the superiority of the spring-chest to the slider-chest with a new instrument of 20 stops which is installed in the conservatory there. . . . As a consequence of this advancement in the art of organ building I was recognized with the Grand Medal for German Industry by the King of Bavaria, and the Grand Gold Medal for Art and Science by the King of Württemberg"; quoted in Emile Rupp, *Die Entwicklungs-geschichte der Orgelbaukunst* (1929; repr., Hildesheim, Germany: Georg Olms, 1981), 136.

82. Walcker describes the swell as follows: "A construction set up on the solidest basis, in my usual style, by means of which not only can both manuals be coupled together and, at will, the pedal, but also the player is enabled, by means of a single foot movement, to swell the sound from the feeblest and most delicate stop to the instrument's full strength, without needing to register it first with an inconvenient movement of the hand." Eberhard Friedrich Walcker, "Opusbuch," no. 4, p. 270, sec. 24, Walcker Company Archive, Kleinblittersdorf, Germany.

83. See the anonymous report "Die neue Synagoge zu Mannheim, 15. Juli 1855," *AZJ* 19, no. 36 (Sept. 3, 1855): 466.

84. See Ferdinand Moosmann and Rudi Schäfer, *Eberhard Friedrich Walcker (1794–1872): Zum Gedenken an seinen 200. Geburtstag am 3. Juli 1994* (Kleinblittersdorf, Germany: Musikwissenschaftliche Verlagsgesellschaft, 1994), 165.

85. Among the free-reed stops, the Physharmonika seems to be a specifically German phenomenon. Similar registers in French organs (such as the Euphone) were demonstrably less prevalent than in Germany. Free-reed stops were used still less often in British and American organs. A list of known Physharmonika stops appears in Christian Ahrens, " 'Mit Crescendo und Decrescendo zum Verwehen': Physharmonika-Register in Orgeln des 19. und 20. Jahrhunderts," *Ars Organi* 46, no. 3 (1998): 142–49. Of course, Ahrens was able to include only those examples whose existence can be verified today. Very few of the examples he enumerates are still extant (by my own count, roughly ten and more likely fewer rather than more). The Wanamaker organ in Philadelphia, built by Murray Harris in 1905, has two Euphones and a free-reed Musette imported from Germany. Another Euphone is stored in the basement of the Church of Saint Mary the Virgin in Manhattan. It is from the former Jardine instrument there and is perhaps a German import obtained by Jardine.

86. Compare the dispositions of the organs of St. Michael's, Schwäbisch Hall (1832–1837), the Protestant church in Hoffenheim (1846), and the cathedral in Frankfurt am Main (1856–1857); Moosman and Schäfer, *Eberhard Friedrich Walcker*.

87. Paul Smets, *Die Orgelregister: Ihr Klang und Gebrauch*, 2d ed. (Mainz: Rheingold, 1937), 332.

88. See Moosman and Schäfer, *Eberhard Friedrich Walcker*, 57–60.

89. The concept of additive Klangverschmelzung refers to the generation of an undertone that duplicates the sound of a 32′ pipe with the stop combination of 16′ and 10⅔′ or of an acoustic 16′ pipe with the combination of 8′ and 5⅓′; it may also refer in general to the reinforcing of the fundamental with mutation stops.

90. Hermann Ehrlich, "Die Orgel in unsern Synagogen," *Liturgische Zeitschrift zur Veredelung des Synagogengesangs mit Berücksichtigung des ganzen Synagogenwesens* 1, no. 12 (1848): 83.

91. See ibid., 84.

92. Josef Singer, "Chasonus: Die Orgel," *OUCZ* 3, no. 31 (Sept. 8, 1883), 1.

93. K. M., *Der Gottesdienst mit Orgel* (n.p., n.d.), section c.

94. Ibid., section e.

95. Ibid.

96. Moritz Tintner, "Die Orgel in der Synagoge," *OUCZ* 12, no. 2 (Jan. 11, 1892), 3.

97. Examples of smaller instruments include organs in Augsburg in 1865, builder unknown (I/8); Gießen, 1866, by Förster und Nicolaus, Lich/Hessen (I/11); Fürth, 1873, by Heinrich Buck, Bayreuth (I/10); Ludwigsburg, 1884, by E. F. Walcker et Cie., Ludwigsburg, op. 451 (I/4, without pedal); Benfeld, 1895, by Charles Wetzel, Strasbourg (I/7, without pedal); Fürth, 1909, by J. Strebel, Nuremberg (II/11); and Lippstadt, 1914, by Feith, Paderborn (I/6).

98. Larger instruments were built in the Berlin synagogue on Lützowstraße in 1898 by E. F. Walcker et Cie.; Ludwigsburg, op. 831 (III/44); Berlin, Oranienburger Straße, 1910, by E. F. Walcker et Cie., op. 1526 (IV/55); Berlin-Charlottenburg, Fasanenstraße, 1912, by E. F. Walcker et Cie., Ludwigsburg, op. 1658 (III/65); the consistorial synagogue in Strasbourg, 1925, by Roethinger, Strasbourg (III/62); and Berlin, Prinzregentenstraße, 1930, by G. F. Steinmeyer, Oettingen, op. 1525 (IV/68).

99. Wolfgang Adelung, *Einführung in den Orgelbau*, 3d ed. (Leipzig: Breitkopf und Härtel, 1974), 216.

100. Hans Hirschberg, "Die Orgelwerke der neuen Synagoge zu Berlin," *Ars Organi* 44, no. 3 (1996): 143.

101. Albert Schweitzer, *Deutsche und französische Orgelbaukunst* (1906; repr., Wiesbaden: Breitkopf und Härtel, 1976), 31–32.

102. See ibid., 14.

103. See ibid., 11.

104. Rolf Bothe, ed., *Synagogen in Berlin: Zur Geschichte einer zerstörten Architektur*, 2 vols. Stadtgeschichtliche Publikationen 1 (Berlin: Willmuth Arenhövel, 1983), vol. 1, 99.

105. Rupp, *Die Entwicklungsgeschichte der Orgelbaukunst*, 371.

106. Ibid., 118.

107. *Zfl* 30 (1909–1910), 461–63.

108. Rupp, *Die Entwicklungsgeschichte der Orgelbaukunst*, 345.

109. Rupp's aversion to these stops in particular, especially the high-pressure register, had to do with the fact that their obtrusive character does not allow them to be used in synthesis with other stops; see Walter Kwasnik, *Emile Rupp als Orgelreformer, Kirchenmusiker, und Mensch: Dem Begründer der Orgelreform zum Gedenken*, Das Musikinstrument 8 (Frankfurt am Main: Verlag das Musikinstrument, 1967), 20–21.

110. Rupp, *Die Entwicklungsgeschichte der Orgelbaukunst*, 346.

111. Ibid., 349.

112. Ibid.

113. This firm was founded in 1893. Roethinger, who served his apprenticeship with Koulen of Strasbourg and Maerz in Munich, took the specifics of Alsatian organ building into account from the beginning of his career and counts as one of those builders who followed the reform principles at a very early date. His three most significant works are the organs of the Catholic parish church of St-Pierre-le-Jeune, Strasbourg, with 40 stops; the Catholic parish church of the town of Erstein (Bas-Rhin, France), with 68; and the consistorial synagogue of Strasbourg, with 60 stops. Among other instruments, Roethinger also built a 23-stop organ for the synagogue of Metz, it is reported to have "employed all the innovations insofar as they have been proven" (*Zfl* 16 [1895–1896], 569).

114. See Kwasnik, *Emile Rupp*, 23–28.

115. Ibid., 26; see also the depictions there on pp. 24–28.

116. A further example of the installation of technical innovations is the synagogue organ in Bingen, built around 1875 by the firm of Johann Schlaad of Waldlaubersheim. Schlaad Senior had a patent for a knee-operated lever with which one could play the single-manual organ in a given registration first piano, then forte. The simple construction for this was the use of two windchests and two pallets for each key in a divided note channel. In the forte registers, the greater part of the channel could be opened or closed with a blocking valve (*Sperrventil*) for each windchest, thereby eliminating the need for a second manual. Teacher and organist Flory wrote, on the issuing of the patent for this device, "Therefore for this invention he has . . . received great acclaim, in that . . . five of these instruments have already been built, of which one . . . is in the synagogue at Bingen"; quoted in Manfred Wittelsberger, *Die Orgelbauerfamilien Engers und Schlaad in Waldlaubersheim bei Bingen: Ein Beitrag zur Orgelbaugeschichte am Mittelrhein*, Studien zur Landes- und Sozialgeschichte der Musik 12 (Munich: Katzbichler, 1994), 115. The organ of the Dortmund synagogue not only exemplifies technical innovation but is also a curiosity in the history of organ building inasmuch as it incorporates an organola, an automated instrument built into the organ (see figures 3.7a and 3.7b); for a detailed account see Frühauf, "'Jüdische Merckwürdigkeiten': Die Orgel in der Synagoge zu Dortmund," *Orgel International* 3, no. 1 (1999): 50–58.

117. Examples are the organs of St. Paul in Strasbourg (E. F. Walcker et Cie., 1907), St. Reinoldi in Dortmund (E. F. Walcker et Cie., 1909), Christuskirche in Mannheim (G. F. Steinmeyer, 1911), and St. Michaelis in Hamburg (E. F. Walcker et Cie., 1912).

118. See Harold Hammer-Schenk, *Synagogen in Deutschland: Geschichte einer Baugattung im 19. und 20. Jahrhundert (1780–1933)*, Hamburger Beiträge zur Geschichte der deutschen Juden 8 (Hamburg: Hans Christians Verlag, 1981), vol. 1, 311, 543.

119. See Theodor Wohnhaas, "Zur Geschichte der Orgeln in Berliner Synagogen," *Jahrbuch für die Geschichte Mittel- und Ostdeutschlands* 26 (1977): 199.

120. Memorandum, Nov. 26, 1912, Steinmeyer Company Archive.

121. At the turn of the century, synagogues were large in scale; they are described in the secondary literature as "powerful" and "monumental" buildings; see Hammer-Schenk, *Synagogen in Deutschland*, 445 ff.

122. Memorandum, Nov. 26, 1912, Steinmeyer Company Archive.

123. See in detail Hammer-Schenk, *Synagogen in Deutschland*.

124. The term was coined about 1930 as a simplified form of *Orgel-Erneuerungsbewegung*; in English it is often translated as "organ revival."

125. Historical research was backed up by the construction of the so-called Praetorius-Orgel in Freiburg im Breisgau, which was modeled on a disposition designed by Michael Praetorius. It began in 1921 with the building of the organ; destroyed during the Second World War, it was rebuilt in 1955.

126. See Michael Kater, *The Twisted Muse: Musicians and Their Music in the Third Reich* (New York: Oxford University Press, 1997), 171–76.

127. Hans Hirschberg, "Die Bedeutung der Orgel in Berliner Synagogen," in *Synagogen in Berlin*, ed. Bothe, vol. 1, 192. See also *Musik in Geschichte und Gegenwart*, 2d ed., s.v. "Orgel: IX. Gebrauchsgeschichte: 2. Die Orgel in der Synagoge" (by Alfred Reichling), 1024.

128. Werner Baer, "Meine Erinnerungen als Organist an der Synagoge Prinzregentenstraße," in *Synagogen in Berlin*, ed. Bothe, vol. 1, 195.

129. *Internationales Regulativ für Orgelbau entworfen und bearbeitet von der Sektion für Orgelbau auf dem 3. Kongreß der internationalen Musikgesellschaft, Vienna, 25. bis 29. Mai 1909* (Leipzig: Breitkopf und Härtel, 1909), 19.

130. Erwin Jospe, "Rückblick," in *Synagogen in Berlin*, ed. Bothe, vol. 1, 194.

131. Baer, "Meine Erinnerungen," 194.

132. Saskia Rhode, "Orgelprospekte in Synagogen: Skizzen zu einem bislang kaum bekannten Thema," in *"Niemand wollte mich hören . . .": Magrepha—Die Orgel in der Synagoge*, ed. Andor Izsák (Hannover: Freimann and Fuchs, 1999), 191. In the nineteenth century, Reform synagogues moved the bimah from the middle to the front of the temple, from which the rabbi faced the congregation.

133. Ibid.

134. See Meyer, Brenner, Breuer, and Graetz, *German-Jewish History*, vol. 2, 191.

135. See the detailed account in Rhode, "Orgelprospekte in Synagogen," 189–203.

136. Reinhard Rürup, "An Appraisal of German-Jewish Historiography," *Leo Baeck Institute Yearbook* 35 (1990): xxii.

137. Hans Samuel, "Der Weg zur jüdischen Orgel," n.d., Hans Samuel Collection, I.5.14.

138. Ibid.

139. Herman Berlinski, "Zur Frage der synagogalen Orgeldisposition," *Musik und Kirche* 46, no. 4 (1976): 182.

140. Ibid., 188.

141. See Sendrey, *Musik in Alt-Israel*, 266–78.

142. See ibid., 310–17.

143. See ibid.

144. See ibid., 307–310.

145. Reinhard Flender, *Hebrew Psalmody: A Structural Investigation*, Yuval Monograph Series 9 (Jerusalem: Magnes, 1992), 3.

146. The origin of the term *Mi-Sinai*, which means "from Mount Sinai," is subject to much speculation; in fact, various explanations have been suggested. Eric Werner claims that this concept, a sign of the reverence in which the melodies are held, goes back to the *Sefer ḥasidim* [Book of the Pious], which asserts that some of these chants were given to Moses along with God's law. See Eric Werner, *A Voice Still Heard: The Sacred Songs of the Ashkenazic Jews*, Leo Baeck Institute Series (University Park: Pennsylvania State University Press, 1976), 27.

147. Berlinski, "Zur Frage der synagogalen Orgeldisposition," 183.

148. Ibid.

149. Ibid., 184.

150. Ibid.

151. See *Musik in Geschichte und Gegenwart*, 2d ed., s.v. "Orgel: V. Geschichte der Orgel in einzelnen Ländern: 28. Vereinigte Staaten von Amerika," 1001.

Intermezzo

1. Heinrich Lemle, *Halachisches zur Orgelfrage* (Frankfurt am Main: Vereinigung jüdischer Kantoren, ca. 1933–1936), 32.

2. See the detailed discussion in ibid.

3. See *Protokolle und Aktenstücke der zweiten Rabbinerversammlung* (Frankfurt am Main: E. Ullmann, 1845), 326.

4. In *Or Nogah* Eliezer Liebermann justified permitting a non-Jewish organist to play the organ in divine services on the grounds that the act was a religious one and could not therefore be shevut and that this disposed of the objection based on the mourning for Jerusalem. Liebermann, *Or Nogah* (Dessau, Germany, 1818), 14–18.

5. *Protokolle und Aktenstücke*, 332.

6. See Oskar Guttmann, "Die Orgel in der Synagoge und wer sie spielen soll," *Jüdische Rundschau* 84, no. 37 (Oct. 21, 1932): 408.

7. Untitled and undated manuscript by Oskar Guttmann, Jacob Michael Collection, JMC 237, Jewish National and University Library, Jerusalem.

8. Rafael Frank, "Der jüdische Organist," *AZJ* 72, no. 8 (Feb. 21, 1908): 91.

9. Ibid.

10. The term *Kultus* is often rendered as "tradition"; however, it embraces Jewish life, as well as legacy, thus relating to both religious practice and culture.

11. See Till van Rahden, "Mingling, Marrying, and Distancing Jewish Integration in Wilhelminian Breslau and Its Erosion in Early Weimar Germany," in *Jüdisches Leben in der Weimarer Republik/Jews in Weimar Germany*, ed. Wolfgang Benz, Arnold Paucker, and Peter Pulzer, Schriftenreihe wissenschaftlicher Abhandlungen des Leo Baeck Instituts 57 (Tübingen: Mohr Siebeck, 1998), 197.

12. Israel Schwarz, "Ist die Einführung von Instrumental-Begleitung und speciell die der Orgel bei dem synagogalen Gottesdienst gestattet, und ist es erlaubt, an Sabbat- und Festtagen derartige Instrumente zu spielen, oder durch einen Nichtjuden spielen zu lassen?" *Der jüdische Kantor* 4, no. 36 (Sept. 26, 1882): 284–85.

13. See Michael Sachs, "Gutachten gegen die Orgel (13.11.1861)," in *Zur Lehr' und Wehr über und gegen die kirchliche Orgel im jüdischen Gottesdienste*, ed. Abraham Berliner (Berlin: Nathansen und Lamm, 1904), 20.

14. Anon., "Aus dem Badischen, im Juni: Privatmittheilung, 20. Mai 1846," *AZJ* 10, no. 31 (July 27, 1846): 450.

15. Music classes for cantors were offered at Jewish and non-Jewish *Lehrerseminare* [teachers' seminaries], particularly in Berlin, Hannover, Würzburg, Breslau, Münster, Hildburghausen, Karlsruhe, and Esslingen. In the late nineteenth century, cantors in Western Europe received structured musical training within an institutional framework. For a detailed account of the changes in cantorial instruction during the nineteenth century see

Geoffrey Goldberg, "The Training of *ḥazzanim* in Nineteenth-century Germany," *Yuval* 7 (2002): 299–367.

16. Alice Jacob-Loewensohn, "Keine Orgel im jüdischen Gottesdienst," *Jüdische Rundschau* 84, no. 37 (Oct. 21, 1932): 408.

17. Ludwig Altman, *A Well-tempered Musician's Unfinished Journey through Life* (Berkeley: Regional Oral History Office, 1990), 87.

18. Werner Baer, "Meine Erinnerungen als Organist der Synagoge Prinzregenten-straße," in *Synagogen in Berlin: Zur Geschichte einer zerstörten Architektur*, ed. Rolf Bothe, 2 vols. Stadtgeschichtliche Publikationen 1 (Berlin: Willmuth Arenhövel, 1983), vol. 1, 194.

19. David Deutsch, "Die Orgel in der Synagoge: Eine Erörterung" (Wrocław, Poland: privately printed, 1863), 43.

20. Louis Lewandowski, "Gutachten betr. den Antrag wegen Bewilligung der Geldmittel zur Herstellung eines Orgelwerkes in der neuen Synagoge," Moritz Stern Collection.

21. K. M., *Der Gottesdienst mit Orgel*, section e.

22. Erwin Jospe, "Rückblick," in *Synagogen in Berlin*, ed. Bothe, vol. 1, 194.

23. Ibid., 193.

24. Emile Rupp, *Die Entwicklungsgeschichte der Orgelbaukunst* (1929; repr., New York: Georg Olms, 1981), 347.

25. Rudolf Walter, "Die Orgelmusik der Caecilianer," *Der Caecilianismus: Anfänge—Grundlagen—Wirkungen*, ed. Hubert Unverricht, Eichstätter Abhandlungen zur Musikwissenschaft 5 (Tutzing, Germany: Schneider, 1988), 163.

26. Examples are Moritz Deutsch, *Zwölf Präludien für Orgel oder Pianoforte zum gottesdienstlichen und häuslichen Gebrauch nach alten Synagogen-Intonationen* (Wrocław, Poland: Julius Hainauer, 1864); and Jakob L. Weiss, *Musikalische Synagogenbibliothek . . . eingerichtet für Pianoforte, Harmonium und Orgel* (Vienna, 1881).

27. During the course of my research I found only one other organ composition by Schwantzer, the *Neun leichte Praeludien für die Orgel*, op. 21 (Berlin: T. Trautwein, n.d). I was unable to establish any relationship between these works and the Jewish community.

28. Hans Hirschberg, "Die Orgelwerke der neuen Synagoge," *Ars Organi* 44, no. 3 (1996): 146.

29. Ibid.

30. Ironically, on Aug. 27, 1935, the Reichskommissar of the Ministry for the People's Enlightenment and Propaganda, Hans Hinkel, ordered that organists of the Jewish faith were no longer allowed to play in churches: "I denounce this state of affairs as a bare-faced betrayal of Christianity against which we National Socialists are going to protect the Christian people"; quoted in Erik Levi, *Music in the Third Reich* (New York: St. Martin's, 1994), 273. Nevertheless, on rare occasions Jewish musicians performed in churches, as the following chapter shows. In contrast, as we have seen, church musicians often worked for synagogues.

31. Altman, *Well-tempered Musician's Unfinished Journey*, 7.

32. Ibid., 88.

33. See ibid.

34. See Ludwig Altmann, "Die Orgel der neuen Synagoge," *Gemeindeblatt der jüdischen Gemeinde zu Berlin* 24 (Nov. 17, 1934): 2.

35. "Zeugnis des Vorstands der jüdischen Gemeinde Berlin, 30.11.1936"; see Altman, *Well-tempered Musician's Unfinished Journey*.

36. Felix Saul, "Chor und Orgel im Gottesdienst der Zukunft," *Jüdische Rundschau* 77, no. 33 (Sept. 26, 1928): 546.

37. Lisel Lewin-Kassewitz, "Meine Zeit als Organistin und Gemeindesekretärin der jüdischen Gemeinde," in *Erinnertes Leben: Autobiographische Texte zur jüdischen Geschichte Heidelbergs*, ed. Norbert Giovannini and Frank Moraw (Heidelberg: Wunderhorn, 1998), 140.

38. Jacob Ostwald, *"Um Spott und Hohn der Wittener loszuwerden . . .": Erinnerungen des jüdischen Lehrers und Kantors Jacob Oswald 1863–1910* (Witten, Germany: Stadt Witten, 1994), 83.

Chapter 4

1. Interesting examples are the *Six Preludes for Organ* (Boston: G. Schirmer, 1948) and the *Four Wedding Marches* (Boston: G. Schirmer, 1951) by Ernest Bloch. Neither the title nor the theme of these pieces suggests a relation to Jewish culture. Only the manuscripts reveal their dedication for use in the synagogue. Next to the title—in the manuscripts the wedding marches are part of the preludes—appears this crossed-out text: "for use in the Synagogue." See David L. Sills, "Bloch Manuscripts at the University of California," *Notes* 42, no. 1 (1985): 13.

2. Amnon Shiloah, *Jewish Musical Traditions*, Jewish Folklore and Anthropology Series (Detroit: Wayne State University Press, 1992), 67.

3. See Eric Werner, *A Voice Still Heard: The Sacred Songs of the Ashkenazic Jews*, Leo Baeck Institute Series (University Park: Pennsylvania State University Press, 1976), 94.

4. See George List, "Distribution of a Melodic Formula: Diffusion or Polygenesis?" *Yearbook of the International Folk Music Council* 10 (1978): 46.

5. For a detailed description of this methodology see Zecharia Plavin, "Comparative Stylistic Analysis of Bloch's 'Jewish' and 'Non-Jewish' Works," in *Proceedings of the First International Conference on Jewish Music*, ed. Steve Stanton (London: City University, Department of Music, 1997), 97–99.

6. With regard to synagogue song, Hanoch Avenary states: "The most ancient heritage of synagogue music cannot be confined to measure lines or enclosed in a framework of symmetric phrases. Its rhythm is as free as that of Hebrew poetry of the time. It is worth noting that melodies in free rhythm have been preserved even in European communities as a body separate from Western music." *Encyclopaedia Judaica*, 1st ed., s.v. "Music."

7. See Bruno Nettl, *The Western Impact on World Music: Change, Adaptation, and Survival* (New York: Schirmer, 1985), 5.

8. Here, *modal* refers to a complex concept involving both scale type and melody type; see *The New Grove Dictionary of Music and Musicians*, s.v. "Mode: I. The term," http://www.grovemusic.com (accessed Sept. 5, 2007).

9. Examples of these organ books are in the Eduard Birnbaum Collection, Klau Library, Hebrew Union College, Cincinnati (Additional Collection and Blaue Hefte). In addition, this collection contains a number of separate organ compositions from the nineteenth century, composed mostly by church musicians, sometimes using a known Jewish melody. These works were never published.

10. Mus. Add. 16a, Eduard Birnbaum Collection; see also Israel Adler, *Hebrew Notated Manuscript Sources up to circa 1840: A Descriptive and Thematic Catalogue with a Checklist of*

Printed Sources, RISM 9(1) (Munich: G. Henle, 1989), 437. A copy by Carl Schauer, Berlin, dated 1831/1835, is available under the signature Mus. 93.13a.

11. See Johannes Heinrich, "Orgelmusik und Orgelspiel im evangelischen Gottesdienst," in *Zur deutschen Orgelmusik des 19. Jahrhunderts*, ed. Hermann Busch and Michael Heinemann (Sinzig, Germany: Studio Verlag, 1998), 15. Heinrich explains the concept of *Spielarten* in detail.

12. See Hermann J. Busch, " 'Hochgefeierter Veteran der geistlichen Tonkunst': Johann Christian Heinrich Rinck," in *Zur deutschen Orgelmusik des 19. Jahrhunderts*, ed. Busch and Heinemann, 175.

13. Ibid., 173–78.

14. See Heinrich, "Orgelmusik und Orgelspiel im evangelischen Gottesdienst," 18.

15. See ibid., 19.

16. Eduard Birnbaum Collection, Mus. Add. 14b. The preceding part of the manuscript, Mus. Add. 14a, a collection of traditional melodies of Portuguese-Jewish provenance arranged for keyboard or four voices to be used in the Hamburg Temple, is discussed by Edwin Seroussi, *Spanish-Portuguese Synagogue Music in Nineteenth-century Reform Sources from Hamburg: Ancient Tradition in the Dawn of Modernity*, Yuval Monograph Series 11 (Jerusalem: Magnes, 1996), 24. Seroussi also remarks that many of the eighteenth- and nineteenth-century music manuscripts from the Portuguese community of Amsterdam include choral compositions, sometimes with instrumental accompaniment. A possible involvement of the organ, however, cannot be confirmed.

17. Eduard Birnbaum Collection, Mus. 119b.

18. Eduard Birnbaum Collection, Mus. 199.a1. The presumption that the very popular Ḥanukkah melody called Ma'oz Ẓur serves as the main theme of this prelude cannot be confirmed.

19. Eduard Birnbaum Collection, Blaue Hefte 393. The journal *Der Jüdische Kantor* (33, no. 3) mentions Immanuel Faisst (1823–1894), together with Lewandowski, as a "coryphaeus," or choir leader in synagogue music. This is all the more remarkable as Faisst, in addition to his work as choir director at the Stuttgart synagogue and a composer of *Stuttgarter Synagogengesänge*, had a notably successful career as organist and choirmaster in Roman Catholic churches.

20. See David Sorkin, "Emancipation and Assimilation: Two Concepts and Their Application to German-Jewish History," *Leo Baeck Institute Yearbook* 35 (1990): 17–33.

21. Michael A. Meyer, "Jews as Jews versus Jews as German: Two Historical Perspectives," *Leo Baeck Institute Yearbook* 36 (1991): xix. See also Michael A. Meyer, Michael Brenner, Mordechai Breuer, and Michael Graetz, eds., *German-Jewish History*, 4 vols. (New York: Columbia University Press, 1996), vol. 3, 281–304.

22. See Reinhard Rürup, "An Appraisal of German-Jewish Historiography," *Leo Baeck Institute Yearbook* 35 (1990): xxii.

23. The precise date of this edition is unknown; Adolph Hofmeister's *Handbuch der musikalischen Literatur* (Leipzig: Friedrich Hofmeister, 1868) suggests only an approximate date. Josef Singer also provides clues on the date; see "Ueber die Entwicklung des Synagogengesanges: Zweite Serie XXVII," *OUCZ* 8, no. 36 (Nov. 5, 1888), 1. A few years later Deutsch composed two more short preludes, published in his collection *Breslauer Synagogengesänge: Liturgie der neuen Synagoge* (Leipzig: Breitkopf und Härtel, 1880): the

"Orgelpräludium am Neujahrstage" and the "Orgelpräludium an Festtagen." Both are most likely intended for the Torah procession.

24. Aron Friedmann, "Das Dreigestirn, Salomon Sulzer, Louis Lewandowski und Moritz Deutsch," *Jahrbuch für jüdische Geschichte und Literatur* 16 (1913): 224.

25. Josef Singer, "Chasonus: Die Orgel," *OUCZ* 3, no. 31 (Sept. 8, 1883), 2.

26. *Volkstümlichkeit* is difficult to render in a single English word. It embraces nationalism, popular appeal, and folksiness. It further merges an aesthetic category and a political one.

27. Moritz Deutsch, preface to *Zwölf Präludien für Orgel oder Pianoforte zum gottesdienstlichen und häuslichen Gebrauch nach alten Synagogen-Intonationen* (Wrocław, Poland: Julius Hainauer, 1864), 5.

28. In the *OUCZ*, Josef Singer criticizes the absence of a prelude for Purim and speculates that the reason for this may be that this feast has no characteristic melody or song: "Instead of the Prelude no. 8 for Tishah Be-Av, a colorful and fresh prelude for Purim, even general in character, would have been desirable, since in our view on Tishah Be-Av no instruments should be played." Singer, "Ueber die Entwicklung des Synagogengesanges," 2.

29. After the dispersion of Jews following the destruction of Judea, Jewish customs and rites (*minhagim*) developed further in the Diaspora. In central Europe two distinct groups developed: The Jews west of the Elbe River followed the German Ashkenazic rite, while those who migrated farther east during the Middle Ages cultivated the Polish Ashkenazic rite.

30. See Abraham Zvi Idelsohn, *Jewish Music in Its Historical Development* (1929; repr., New York: Dover, 1992), 285–86.

31. Caecilianism (after Saint Cecilia, the patroness of music) was a nineteenth-century reform movement in Roman Catholic church music that demanded the revival of the a-cappella repertoire of Palestrina and the church music principles of the Council of Trent; see Hubert Unverricht, ed., *Der Caecilianismus: Anfänge—Grundlagen—Wirkungen: Internationales Symposium zur Kirchenmusik des 19. Jahrhunderts*, Eichstätter Abhandlungen zur Musikwissenschaft 5 (Tutzing, Germany: Hans Schneider, 1988).

32. See Rudolf Walter, "Die Orgelmusik der Caecilianer," in *Der Caecilianismus: Anfänge—Grundlagen—Wirkungen: Internationales Symposium zur Kirchenmusik des 19. Jahrhunderts*, ed. Hubert Unverricht (Tutzing, Germany: Hans Schneider, 1988), 181.

33. See ibid.

34. In the nineteenth century, many volumes of organ music were published in the form of compilations such as Carl Schweich, ed., *Caecilia: 100 Kompositionen für Orgel* (Wiesbaden: Breitkopf und Härtel, n.d.), and August Reinhard, ed., *Caecilia: Sammlung von Choralvorspielen aus alter und neuerer Zeit für Orgel oder Harmonium* (Berlin: Carl Simon, 1894); see also Hermann Busch, "Neuausgabe deutscher Orgelmusik des 19. Jahrhunderts," in *Zur deutschen Orgelmusik des 19. Jahrhunderts*, ed. Hermann Busch and Michael Heinemann (Sinzig, Germany: Studio Verlag, 1998), 219–29.

35. Other early nineteenth-century composers and their organ compositions are presented in Gotthold Frotscher, *Geschichte des Orgelspiels und der Orgelkomposition*, 2d ed. (Berlin: Merseburger, 1959), vol. 2, 1122–95.

36. See Hans Peter Bähr, "Im Schatten Liszts: Johann Gottlob Töpfer," in *Zur deutschen Orgelmusik des 19. Jahrhunderts*, ed. Hermann Busch and Michael Heinemann (Sinzig, Germany: Studio Verlag, 1998), 210.

37. See ibid.

38. See ibid.

39. Singer, "Chasonus," 2.

40. Singer "Ueber die Entwicklung des Synagogengesanges," 1.

41. Ibid, 2.

42. Ibid.

43. Ernst Rübenstein, "Das Orgelpräludium in der Synagoge," *OUCZ* 6, no. 35 (Nov. 6, 1886), 1.

44. See ibid.

45. Andreas Nachama and Susanne Stähr, "Die vergessene Revolution: Der lange Weg des Louis Lewandowski," *Menora: Jahrbuch für deutsch-jüdische Geschichte* 3 (1992): 250.

46. See Artur Holde, *Jews in Music: From the Age of Enlightenment to the Mid-Twentieth Century*, new ed. prepared by Irene Heskes (New York: Bloch, 1974), 22; Idelsohn, *Jewish Music*, 277; Werner, *A Voice Still Heard*, 226–29.

47. See Nachama and Stähr, "Die vergessene Revolution," 252–53.

48. See Louis Lewandowski, *Toda W'simrah: Vierstimmige Chorgesänge für den Gottesdienst*. Part II: *Festgesänge* (1883; repr., Frankfurt am Main: Julius Kauffmann, 1921), 333.

49. Lewandowski, preface to *Toda W'simrah*.

50. William Wolf, "Zur Synagogen-Musik," *AZJ* 54, no. 29 (Aug. 1, 1890): 386.

51. Sephardim do not read Akdamut Millin, but before the evening service they sing *azharot*, poems that set out the 613 biblical commandments. The positive commandments are recited on the first day, and the negative commandments on the second day.

52. See Leo Trepp, *Der jüdische Gottesdienst: Gestalt und Entwicklung* (Stuttgart: Kohlhammer, 1992), 222–23.

53. See Ismar Elbogen, *Der jüdische Gottesdienst in seiner geschichtlichen Entwicklung*, 3d ed. (Hildesheim, Germany: Georg Olms, 1967), 208–209.

54. See Elijahu Kitov, *Das jüdische Jahr in Fest und Brauch*, 4 vols. (Zurich: Morascha, 1987–1990), vol. 3, 18.

55. See Werner, *A Voice Still Heard*, 89–90.

56. Ibid.

57. See ibid., 261, table 6.1.

58. See ibid. Also see Aron Friedmann, *Der synagogale Gesang: Eine Studie*, 2d ed. Musikwissenschaftliche Studienbibliothek Peters (1908; repr., Leipzig: Edition Peters, 1978), 105.

59. See Aron Ackermann, *Der synagogale Gesang in seiner historischen Entwicklung*, Literatur seit Abschluss des Kanons 3 (1896; repr., Hildesheim, Germany: Georg Olms, 1965), 510.

60. Ibid., 514.

61. A detailed analysis of the variants of Akdamut Millin and a comparison of the nonmetrical Akdamut Millin version with different plainchants appear in Daniel S. Katz, "From Mount Sinai to the Year 6000: A Study of the Interaction of Oral Tradition and Written Sources in the Transmission of an Ashkenazi Liturgical Chant ('Akdamut Millin')," *Rivista Internazionale di Musica Sacra* 20, no. 1 (1999): 175–206.

62. See Hans Samuel, "Die Melodien der drei Wallfahrtsfeste," *FIG* 10, no. 9 (May 1932): 194.

63. Ibid.

64. Ibid.

65. In the Ha'El version, *Toda W'simrah*, no. 17, measure 3, Lewandowski also uses sixteenth triplets instead of quarter triplets.

66. See Idelsohn, *Jewish Music*, 484.

67. See ibid., 484–85.

68. See ibid., 137.

69. See Sabine Lichtenstein, "Abraham Jacob Lichtenstein: Eine jüdische Quelle für Carl Loewe und Max Bruch," *Die Musikforschung* 49, no. 4 (1996): 349–67.

70. Wolf, "Zur Synagogen-Musik," 386.

71. See Frotscher, *Geschichte des Orgelspiels*, vol. 2, 1195–1204. He lists many exemplary compositions.

72. Ibid., vol. 2, 1203.

73. See Hannah Arendt, *The Jew as Pariah: Jewish Identity and Politics in the Modern Age* (New York: Grove, 1978), 92.

74. See Brenner's monograph by the same name, which features the different developments among German Jews in detail; Michael Brenner, *The Renaissance of Jewish Culture in Weimar Germany* (New Haven, Conn.: Yale University Press, 1996).

75. See Meyer, Brenner, Breuer, and Graetz, *German-Jewish History*, vol. 4, 71.

76. See Brenner, *Renaissance of Jewish Culture*, 4.

77. See ibid., 157.

78. See *Dortmunder Zeitung*, Oct. 14, 1907.

79. See Jan Böcker, "'Die Orgel störrisch, aber gemeistert . . .': Die Konzertauftritte des niederländischen Organisten, Pianisten, und Komponisten Gerard Bunk (1888–1958) in Deutschland in Kaiserreich, Weimarer Republik und 'Drittem Reich'" (PhD diss., Universität Münster, 1995). Interestingly, Bunk later served as organist at the Dortmund synagogue from 1930 to 1933.

80. Hugo Leichtentritt, "Über die Erneuerung der jüdischen Kultmusik," *Gemeindeblatt der jüdischen Gemeinde zu Köln* (Nov. 16, 1932): 211–13. A trained musicologist and critic, Leichtentritt was also a composer. Before his emigration to the United States in 1933, he wrote organ pieces that were performed in the synagogue on Prinzregentenstraße and the New Synagogue on Oranienburger Straße. Among his works are *Orgelvorspiel, Orgelspiel zum Einzug der Torarollen*, and *Orgelnachspiel* (see "Festordnung für die Einweihung der Synagoge Prinzregentenstraße am 16.09. 1930," in *Synagogen in Berlin: Zur Geschichte einer zerstörten Architektur*, ed. Rolf Bothe, 2 vols. (Berlin: Willmuth Arenhövel, 1983), vol. 1, 151), and the Toccata of ca. 1931 (see Hans Hirschberg, "Die Bedeutung der Orgel" [Appendix: Erwin Jospe, "Rückblick"; Werner Baer, "Meine Erinnerungen als Organist der Synagoge Prinzregentenstraße"], in *Synagogen in Berlin*, ed. Bothe, vol. 1, 190).

81. See Leon Kornitzer, "120 Jahre Kultmusik im Hamburger Tempel," in *Festschrift zum hundertzwanzigjährigen Bestehen des Israelitischen Tempels in Hamburg 1817–1937*, ed. Bruno Italiener (Hamburg, 1937), 28–29.

82. Leon Kornitzer, *Romemoss El: Jüdische gottesdienstliche Gesänge* (Frankfurt am Main: Julius Kauffmann, 1928), 66.

83. Ibid., 69.

84. Hans Samuel, "Der Weg zur jüdischen Orgel," Hans Samuel Collection, I.5.14.

85. Philip V. Bohlman, "Das Musikleben während der jüdischen kulturellen Renaissance in Mannheim vor dem zweiten Weltkrieg," *Mannheimer Hefte* 2 (1985): 117.

86. Ibid.

87. The organ compositions were published by K. F. Heckel of Mannheim; the then owner of the firm, Emil Heckel, had been a member of Wagner's inner circle, so it is noteworthy that he published the works of a Jewish composer.

88. Only a few years later, Herbert Gerigk, compiler of the *Lexikon der Juden in der Musik*, criticized a *Te Deum* by Schroeder as being too close to Jewish music in its musical style—though Schroeder was a church musician and the work was inspired by plainchant; see Erik Levi, *Musik in the Third Reich* (New York: St. Martin's, 1994), 91.

89. Clippings, box 4, folder 10, Hugo Chaim Adler Collection, Hebrew Union College, New York.

90. Ibid.

91. Ibid.

92. Ibid.

93. Josef Levi, "Hugo Adler: Toccata und Fuge über ein hebräisches Thema für Orgel, Op. 11," *Israelitisches Gemeindeblatt Mannheim* 10, no. 5 (May 24, 1932): 5–6.

94. The manuscript is neither in the holdings of the Hugo Chaim Adler Collection nor in Samuel Adler's possession; moreover, there are no known copies of the print version published by the Heckel firm.

95. Emanuel Kirschner, *Erinnerungen aus meinem Leben, Streben und Wirken* (Woerishofen, Germany: privately printed, 1933), 57.

96. See Emanuel Kirschner to Hans Samuel, Jan. 19, 1932, Hans Samuel Collection, I.3.1.3.; Emanuel Kirschner to Hans Samuel, Feb. 4, 1932, Hans Samuel Collection, I.3.1.4. In the last letter Kirschner confuses Nowakowsky with Minkowsky, who had never composed a piece for solo organ. In the Minkowsky collection, Mus. 16, Jewish National and University Library in Jerusalem, are thirty-two pieces for three voices and organ, which is used only as an accompaniment instrument.

97. Kirschner, *Erinnerungen*, 160.

98. Clippings, Emanuel Kirschner Collection, Klau Library, Hebrew Union College, Cincinnati.

99. See Emil Cahn, "Synagogenkonzert des jüdischen Gesangvereins," *Das Jüdische Echo* 12, no. 20 (May 15, 1925): 386; and Kirschner, *Erinnerungen*, 112.

100. All of the works remained unpublished; the manuscripts are held in the Emanuel Kirschner Collection.

101. Emanuel Kirschner to Hans Samuel, Jan. 19, 1932, Hans Samuel Collection, I.3.1.3.

102. Emanuel Kirschner to Hans Samuel, Feb. 4, 1932, Hans Samuel Collection, I.3.1.4.

103. Ibid.

104. See Michael Schalit, *Heinrich Schalit: The Man and His Music* (Livermore, Calif.: Author, 1979), 33.

105. List of works, 1936, Heinrich Schalit Collection, Series I, B (Subject Files), folder 14, JTS, New York.

106. Heinrich Schalit to Anita Hepner, 1971, Heinrich Schalit Collection, Series I, A (Correspondence), box 1, folder 26.

107. Schalit, *Heinrich Schalit*, 33.

108. Ibid.

109. Schalit, preface to *Eine Freitagabend-Liturgie für Kantor, einstimmigen und gemischten Chor und Orgel* (Munich: privately printed, 1933).

110. Oskar Guttmann, "Heinrich Schalits neue Komposition in Berlin," *Bayerische Israelitische Gemeindezeitung* 8, no. 21 (Nov. 1, 1932), 328.

111. Herbert Fromm to Heinrich Schalit, July 23, 1951, Herbert Fromm Collection, SHF 2800:2, box 8, folder 21, JTS, New York.

112. See Trepp, *Der jüdische Gottesdienst*, 57–59, 241.

113. Idelsohn erroneously believes that the undersecond and underthird (related to G) refer to the maqām *sikāh* and the quarter-tone accidental F refers to the maqām *nawā* (see *HOM*, vol. 4, 21–22). However, the quarter-tone accidental E-flat suggests that maqām *rāst* is a variant from Turkey or northern Syria (the geographic proximity of both countries led to shared musical elements). Thus the melody of Lekhah Dodi may be a variant found in northern Syria.

114. See Alice Jacob-Loewensohn, "Zur alten und neuen liturgischen Musik," *Jüdische Rundschau* 77, no. 76 (Sept. 28, 1928): 546.

115. See Joseph Machlis, *Introduction to Contemporary Music*, 2d ed. (New York: Norton, 1979), 20.

116. See ibid., 33.

117. Examples of their works include Joseph Achron, *Symphonic Variations and Sonata on a Palestinian Theme* for piano (1915); Aleksander Krein, *Tantseval'naya syuita* [Dance Suite] for piano (1928); Lazare Saminsky, *Hebrew Folk Songs and Folk Dances* for piano (1922), and Aleksander Veprik, *3 narodnïye plyaski* [3 Folk Dances] for piano (1928). A theoretical foundation was proposed in Leonid Leonidovich Sabaneev's 1927 essay "Die nationale jüdische Schule" (Vienna: Universal-Edition); see Irene Heskes, *Historic Contribution of Russian Jewry to Jewish Music* (New York: National Jewish Music Council, 1967).

118. See also several articles published in *Nationaler Stil und europäische Dimension in der Musik der Jahrhundertwende*, ed. Helga de La Motte-Haber (Darmstadt: Wissenschaftliche Buchgesellschaft, 1991).

119. Eric Werner, "Arno Nadel," n.d., MS 422, Eric Werner Collection, AR 2179, LBI Archives, New York.

120. See Meyer, Brenner, Breuer, and Graetz, *German-Jewish History*, vol. 4, 12.

121. See Bernd Sponheuer, "Musik auf einer 'kulturellen und physischen Insel': Musik als Überlebensmittel im jüdischen Kulturbund 1933–1941," in *Musik in der Emigration 1933–1945: Verfolgung, Vertreibung, Rückwirkung*, ed. Horst Weber (Stuttgart: J. B. Metzler, 1994), 108ff.

122. See Meyer, Brenner, Breuer, and Graetz, *German-Jewish History*, vol. 4, 286.

123. Singer eventually saw the Kulturbund as a basis for continuing German-Jewish culture outside of Nazi Germany and undertook efforts to transplant the Kulturbund first to Palestine and then to the United States but was unsuccessful. See Adam J. Sacks, "Kurt Singer's Shattered Hopes," *Leo Baeck Institute Yearbook* 48 (2003): 191–203.

124. See Meyer, Brenner, Breuer, and Graetz, *German-Jewish History*, vol. 4, 290. For example, in 1936 the performance of Beethoven's works was forbidden and in May 1938 was extended to Mozart's compositions; see Michael H. Kater, *The Twisted Muse: Musicians and Their Music in the Third Reich* (New York: Oxford University Press, 1997), 101.

125. See Sponheuer, "Musik auf einer 'kulturellen und physischen Insel,'" 118, 123, 125; see also chapter 1 of this volume.

126. Sponheuer, "Musik auf einer 'kulturellen und physischen Insel,' " 118.

127. Ibid.

128. Herbert Fromm, interview by Eliott Kahn, May 7–8, 1994.

129. Haim Alexander to Oskar Gottlieb Blarr, Feb. 8, 1998, private collection of Oskar Gottlieb Blarr.

130. Herbert Fromm, interview by Eliott Kahn, May 7–8, 1994.

131. It is important to note that organ music did not flourish in the Kulturbund context as other genres did if only because almost all of the organs available to Jewish musicians under the Nazi regime were housed in synagogues, whereas the Kulturbund events could be held in various other places.

132. The Nazis, too, held *Morgenfeiern*, but for them it had a different meaning. Their celebration was a morning assembly under the auspices of the party and substituted for religious services.

133. Ludwig Altman, *A Well-tempered Musician's Unfinished Journey through Life* (Berkeley: Regional Oral History Office, 1990), 60.

134. Quoted in Werner, "Arno Nadel," 1.

135. Here Arno Nadel is most likely referring to his organ composition on Ma'oz Zur; see Arno Nadel to Hans Samuel, n.d., Hans Samuel Collection, I.3.1.6.

136. Arno Nadel to Hans Samuel, Oct. 29, 1931, Hans Samuel Collection, I.3.1.5.

137. See Trepp, *Der jüdische Gottesdienst*, 260.

138. See *Protokolle und Aktenstücke der zweiten Rabbinerversammlung* (Frankfurt am Main: E. Ullmann),133.

139. See Idelsohn, *Jewish Music*, 242–43.

140. See Machlis, *Introduction to Contemporary Music*, 37.

141. See the detailed explanations of Daniel S. Katz, "Biblische Kantillation und Musik der Synagoge: Ein Rückblick auf die ältesten Quellen," *Musiktheorie* 15, no. 1 (2000): 57–78. Joshua R. Jacobson lists seven reasons for chanting the Bible in *Chanting the Hebrew Bible* (Philadelphia: Jewish Publication Society, 2002), 6–11.

142. For details, see Shiloah, *Jewish Musical Traditions*, 87–109; Werner, *A Voice Still Heard*, 64–87.

143. See Robert Lachmann, *Gesänge der Juden auf der Insel Djerba*, Yuval Monograph Series 7 (Jerusalem: Magnes, 1978), 42.

144. See Idelsohn, *Jewish Music*, 56–57; Werner, *A Voice Still Heard*, 77–78.

145. The accents are divided into two groups: The disjunctives usually end a phrase or sentence, while "servants" or conjunctives serve as connecting elements within a phrase. Each disjunctive may be preceded or "served" by its appropriate conjunctive. See also Jacobson, *Chanting the Hebrew Bible*, 23–24.

146. See Abraham Binder, *Biblical Chant* (New York: Philosophical Library, 1959), 85ff; and Katz, "Biblische Kantillation," 60.

147. On the experimentation with rhythm in the early twentieth century see Machlis, *Introduction to Contemporary Music*, 32–33.

148. See Arno Nadel, "Jüdische Musik," *Der Jude* 7 (1923): 227–36.

149. Chapter 1 of this volume discusses Nadel's definition of Jewish music.

150. On the stylistic developments of neoclassicism and Igor Stravinsky as its exemplary representative see Machlis, *Introduction to Contemporary Music*, 163–73.

151. Ibid.

152. Frotscher lists a representative number of works in *Geschichte des Orgelspiels*, vol. 2, 1247ff.

153. Clippings, 1932–1952, Heinrich Schalit Collection, Series I, B (Subject Files), folder 2.

154. During the Spanish Inquisition all Jews were forced to choose between conversion to Christianity or leaving the country forever without their possessions. While 150,000 Jews left the Iberian Peninsula, a small group of *conversos* met annually on Yom Kippur at a secret place and recited the Kol Nidrei three times, thus asking God to annul all unkept vows. On the text and music of Kol Nidrei, see the detailed article in *Encyclopaedia Judaica*, 2d ed., s.v. "Kol Nidrei." The article includes a detailed list of further references.

155. See Trepp, *Der jüdische Gottesdienst*, 129.

156. See Idelsohn, "The Kol Nidre Tune," *Hebrew Union College Annual* 8–9 (1931): 495.

157. The manuscript was published by Idelsohn in *HOM*, vol. 6; see also Idelsohn, *Jewish Music*, 154, 160.

158. Many organists created church music that is stylistically similar to Würzburger's works. Examples are *Postludium in Fugenform zu dem Choral "O daß ich tausend Zungen hätte,"* op. 22, by Camillo Schumann (1872–1946); *Christ ist erstanden: Vorspiel und Choralfuge,* op. 13 (1922), by Johannes Conze (1875–1946); *Präludium und Fuge über "Hüter, wird die Nacht der Sünden nicht verschwinden,"* by Bernhard Dreier (1879–1946); and *Fuge über Motive aus "Wachet auf,"* op. 32 (1910), by Reinhold Lichey (1880–1957). For more examples see Frotscher, *Geschichte des Orgelspiels*, vol. 2, 1211.

159. See ibid., vol. 2, 1212.

160. Herbert Fromm, *The Key of See: Travel Journals of a Composer* (Boston: Plowshare, 1967), 8.

161. Hans Wilhelm Steinberg, letter of recommendation, Jan. 9, 1936, Herbert Fromm Collection, SHF 2801:1, box 13, folder 3.

162. Siegfried Würzburger, letter of recommendation, Jan. 9, 1936, Herbert Fromm Collection, SHF 2801:1, box 13, folder 3.

163. Rachel Thaller, discussion with the author, May 5, 1998.

164. Hans Samuel, curriculum vitae, n.d., Hans Samuel Collection, I.5.24a.

165. S. Guttmann, letter of recommendation (copy), Oct. 21, 1935, Hans Samuel Collection, I.2.10.

166. Eliezer Ehrenreich, letter of recommendation (copy), Dec. 21, 1938, Hans Samuel Collection, I.2.14.

167. Karl Neumann, letter of recommendation (copy), December 1938, Hans Samuel Collection, I.2.12.

168. Max Wachsmann, letter of recommendation (copy), Dec. 19, 1938, Hans Samuel Collection, I.2.13.

169. Arno Nadel, letter of recommendation, December 1939, Hans Samuel Collection, I.2.15.

170. Hans Samuel, "Der Weg zur jüdischen Orgel," ca. 1930, Hans Samuel Collection, I.5.14.

171. See Hans Samuel, "Synagogale Orgelmusik," *Der jüdische Kantor: Zweimonatsschrift des Allgemeinen Deutschen Kantorenverbandes* 3 (June 1, 1931): 7.

172. Hans Samuel, Notebook, ca. 1932, Hans Samuel Collection, I.6.1.

173. Samuel, "Synagogale Orgelmusik," 8.

174. Ibid.

175. Hans Samuel, notebook, ca. 1932, Hans Samuel Collection, I.6.1.

176. Hans Samuel, fragment, Hans Samuel Collection, I.5.

177. Samuel created several different versions of his opus list, each of which is slightly different. Most of them are undated, and the choices for the lists in tables 4.7 and 4.8 are based on the fact that these are the most complete. Furthermore, each work itself existed in different versions, with German and sometimes English and Hebrew titles. These versions are at times quite dissimilar, reminiscent of the ḥazzan's improvisation of traditional prayers, which gives each "performance" a distinctly unique character in keeping with the uniqueness of ḥazzanut itself, which lies in the existence of a creative variance instead of absolute versions.

178. See Idelsohn, *HOM*, vol. 1, 1–18.

179. Johann Nepomuk David's oeuvre for organ consists of twenty freely composed pieces and fifty based on chorales (all in all, twenty-one books) of different forms and lengths; the chorale preludes range from short two-minute pieces and longer chorale partitas of twenty minutes to lengthy cycles of ninety minutes' duration (*Zwölf Orgelfugen*, op. 66). On the chorale-based works see Wolfgang Dallmann, *Johann Nepomuk David: Das Choralwerk für Orgel* (New York: Peter Lang, 1994).

180. See ibid., 32–36.

181. See ibid., 17.

182. See ibid.

183. Frotscher, *Geschichte des Orgelspiels*, vol. 2, 1246.

184. Hans Samuel, "Zur Entwicklung synagogaler Orgelmusik," *Jüdische Rundschau* 84, no. 21 (Oct. 21, 1932): 408.

185. See Machlis, *Introduction to Contemporary Music*, 126.

186. See Meyer, Brenner, Breuer, and Graetz, *German-Jewish History*, vol. 4, 155.

Chapter 5

1. In this chapter I use the concepts "exile" and "emigration" with the understanding that exile implies a return, whereas emigration is a definitive escape from one's home country. The term *exile* is valid only during time of war, whereas *emigration* goes beyond this timeframe; see Reinhold Brinkmann and Christoph Wolff, eds., *Driven into Paradise: The Musical Migration from Nazi Germany to the United States* (Berkeley: University of California Press, 1999; and Horst Weber, "Betroffenheit und Aufklärung," in *Musik in der Emigration 1933–1945: Verfolgung, Vertreibung, Rückwirkung*, ed. Horst Weber (Stuttgart: J. B. Metzler, 1994.). This is not to ignore the fact that some emigrants (of whom Bertolt Brecht is the most prominent example; see Brecht's poems "Über die Bezeichnung Emigranten" and "Gedanken über die Dauer des Exils") used different terms. As the present study concentrates on organs and organ music in German-speaking lands, the concept of "exile" is hardly adequate. As long as National Socialists retained control of the country, musicians and composers could not hope to return to Germany as artists; moreover, all of the synagogue organs had been destroyed.

2. See Brinkmann and Wolff, *Driven into Paradise*, 165.

3. See ibid., 9.

4. See Michael A. Meyer, Michael Brenner, Mordechai Breuer, and Michael Graetz, eds., *German-Jewish History in Modern Times*, 4 vols. (New York: Columbia University Press, 1996), vol. 4, 397.

5. Ibid., 396.

6. See also Ludwig Altman's anecdote, *A Well-tempered Musician's Unfinished Journey through Life* (Berkeley: Regional Oral History Office, 1990), 197.

7. Jarell C. Jackmann and Carla M. Borden, for example, conclude that the high concentration of central European emigrants Europeanized American music; see *The Muses Flee Hitler: Cultural Transfer and Adaptation 1930–1945* (Washington, D.C.: Smithsonian Institution Press, 1983).

8. See Meyer, Brenner, Breuer, and Graetz, *German-Jewish History*, vol. 4, 234.

9. See Philip V. Bohlman, "The Musical Culture of Central European Jewish Immigrants to Israel" (PhD diss., University of Chicago, 1984), 91.

10. In 1914 Palestine had 85,000 inhabitants, while in 2001 Israel had 6.5 million, a number that increases from 2.2 to 3 percent annually.

11. See Philip V. Bohlman, *"The Land Where Two Streams Flow": Music in the German-Jewish Community of Israel* (Chicago: University of Illinois Press, 1989), 139.

12. *Progressive Judaism*, a term used by Israeli Jews, corresponds to *Reform Judaism* in Europe and the United States.

13. Many musicians were active in more than one category. For detailed statistics see Peter Gradenwitz, *Die Musikgeschichte Israels* (Kassel, Germany: Bärenreiter, 1961), 131.

14. Martha Sommer Hirsch, interviews by and correspondence with the author, New York, 1998–2000.

15. Altman, *Well-tempered Musician's Unfinished Journey*, 40.

16. Ibid., 41.

17. Ibid., 112.

18. Joseph Yasser to Heinrich Schalit, Nov. 13, 1947, Heinrich Schalit Collection, Series I, A (Correspondence), box 1, folder 50.

19. Williard W. Saperston to Herbert Fromm, Jan. 5, 1937, Herbert Fromm Collection, SHF 2802:1, box 19.

20. *Buffalo News*, May 11, 1938, Herbert Fromm Collection, SHF 2802:1, box 19.

21. Newspaper clipping, ca. 1940, Herbert Fromm Collection, SHF 2802:1, box 19.

22. Oskar Guttmann, "Erneuerung der Synagogenmusik in Amerika," *Jüdische Rundschau* (May 13, 1938): 15, Herbert Fromm Collection, SHF 2802:1, box 19.

23. Ibid.

24. Herbert Fromm to Williard W. Saperston, May 25, 1941, Herbert Fromm Collection, SHF 2802:1, box 19. He recommended Dr. Nathan Ehrenreich as his successor at Temple Beth Zion in Buffalo. Ehrenreich had been choir director at the synagogue on Boernestraße in Frankfurt am Main before his emigration.

25. Castelnuovo-Tedesco, an assimilated, nonobservant Jew, composed his organ work in 1962 in homage to his maternal grandfather, Bruto Senigaglia. The composition consists of a theme and five variations based on a liturgical piece for three voices written by Senigaglia in 1882. In the introduction to *Prayers My Grandfather Wrote* Castelnuovo-Tedesco said, "In 1925 . . . I discovered in a bookcase, hidden under many books, a tiny little book of musical manuscripts. It was in the handwriting of my grandfather; there were some Hebrew prayers set to music by himself. No one, even in the family, knew that

he was able to compose. I found there a source of my whole life, both in music and in faith; it was the revelation, the symbol perhaps, of my destiny."

26. Herbert Fromm, "Review of Five Preludes," *Jewish Music Notes* (April 1952): 2, Herbert Fromm Collection, SHF 2802:1, box 19.

27. "It is interesting that this small volume should appear so soon after the little manual on harmonization of the Jewish modes, by Dr. Isadore Freed. The music is welcome since the pieces can be performed by organists of any denomination. Backgrounds of the pieces are drawn from Hebraic sources, but the sources themselves are rather widely separated, leading to greater probable interest in the music." Herbert Fromm, *American Organist* (May 1959), Herbert Fromm Collection, SHF 2803:4, box 28.

28. Herbert Fromm, *On Jewish Music: A Composer's View* (New York: Bloch, 1978), 57.

29. Herbert Fromm to Isadore Freed, Oct. 10, 1958, Herbert Fromm Collection, SHF 2799, box 5, folder 7.

30. Herbert Fromm to Heinrich Schalit, Mar. 1, 1959, Herbert Fromm Collection, SHF 2799, box 5, folder 7.

31. Joseph Freudenthal to Herbert Fromm, Aug. 7, 1958, Herbert Fromm Collection, SHF 2799, box 5, folder 7.

32. Herbert Fromm to Joseph Freudenthal, Aug. 11, 1958, Herbert Fromm Collection, SHF 2799, box 5, folder 7.

33. Robert Noehren to Herbert Fromm, Sept. 15, 1967, Herbert Fromm Collection, SHF 2800:2, box 8, folder 17.

34. See Albert Weisser, introduction to *On Jewish Music: A Composer's View*, by Herbert Fromm (New York: Bloch, 1978), vi.

35. Herman Berlinski, discussion with the author, Nov. 13, 1999.

36. Herman Berlinski, "Memories," in *Jüdische Musiker in Leipzig 1855–1945*, ed. Thomas Schinköth (Altenburg, Germany: Klaus-Jürgen Kamprad, 1994), 282.

37. Cortot supported the Vichy regime and played in Nazi-sponsored concerts in France during the Second World War and was consequently declared persona non grata after the war. His motivations have been disputed, but he was banned from performing publicly for a year. Although his public image in France suffered greatly, he continued to be well received as a recitalist in other countries, notably England.

38. The group was founded in 1936 and consisted of Yves Baudrier, Jean Yves Daniel-Lesur, André Jolivet, and Olivier Messiaen. Jehan Alain was also invited to join but declined. These composers had the common spiritual goals of promoting and encouraging the values of emotional expression and sincerity in music, in opposition to neoclassicism, which was prevalent at the time. The group's manifesto allowed for a wide range of musical styles.

39. Quoted in Louise Craig Wilson, "Herman Berlinski at 85," *American Organist* 29, no. 9 (1995): 67.

40. Berlinski, "Memories," 285.

41. Herman Berlinski, discussion with the author, Nov. 13, 1999.

42. Recital program notes, Hermann Berlinski, private collection.

43. See Achim Seip, "Die Orgel im Leben und Werk von Herman Berlinski," *Orgel International* 3, no. 1 (1999): 28.

44. Eliyahu Schleifer, "Jewish Liturgical Music from the Bible to Hasidim," in *Sacred Sound and Social Change: Liturgical Music in Jewish and Christian Experience*, ed. Lawrence

A. Hoffman and Janet R. Walton (Notre Dame, Ind.: University of Notre Dame Press, 1992, 28.

45. Mark Slobin, *Chosen Voices: The Story of the American Cantorate*, Music in American Life (Chicago: University of Illinois Press, 1989), 68.

46. See Meyer, Brenner, Breuer, and Graetz, *German-Jewish History*, vol. 4, 402.

47. For detailed statistics see Bess Estelle Hieronymus, "Organ Music in the Worship Service of American Synagogues in the Twentieth Century" (DMA diss., University of Texas–Austin, 1969).

48. For a list of Christian organists who served synagogues as of 1997 see Tina Frühauf, *Orgel und Orgelmusik in deutsch-jüdischer Kultur* (Hildesheim, Germany: Georg Olms, 2005), 197, or *Membership Directory* (New York: American Conference of Cantors, 1997).

49. See Hieronymus, "Organ Music," 79.

50. Fromm, *On Jewish Music*, 12, 60.

51. See Hieronymus, "Organ Music," 79.

52. One such congregation is that of the Plum Street Temple in Cincinnati, which in March 2006 held a symposium to celebrate the restoration of the 1866 Koehnken and Company pipe organ. The Noack Organ Company, which undertook the restoration, continues the German tradition of organ building in Ohio. The Plum Street Temple hosts many concerts and has commissioned a few compositions, among them William Bolcom's *Four Preludes on Jewish Melodies* for organ in 2006.

53. Steven M. Löwenstein, *Frankfurt on the Hudson: The German-Jewish Community of Washington Heights, 1933–1983, Its Structure and Culture* (Detroit: Wayne State University Press, 1989), 237, 248.

54. See Amnon Shiloah and Eric Cohen, "The Dynamics of Change in Jewish Oriental Ethnic Music in Israel," *Ethnomusicology* 27, no. 2 (1983): 234.

55. Ibid.

56. See Bohlman, "Musical Culture," 90.

57. Zvi Keren describes the antinationalist trend among some composers as follows:

> There are those composers in Israel who claim that self-conscious nationalism in art is not creative, and therefore do not "try" to write Israeli music. This group includes Joseph Tal, Yitzhak Sadai, Jonel Patin, Eric W. Sternberg, Haim Alexander and Arthur Gelbrun. Although these composers allow themselves to be influenced by musical folklore, they do not feel compelled to use either the style or the specific melodies of musical folklore as the basis of every composition. Haim Alexander, for example, in a recent radio interview said among other things, "I don't try to achieve an Israeli style. I try to write lovely music, and if it turns out to sound Israeli, so much the better." (*Contemporary Israeli Music: Its Sources and Stylistic Development* [Bar Ilan, Israel: Bar Ilan University Press, 1980], 75)

58. See ibid.

59. For an overview of instruments see Gerard Levi and Sabin Levi, *Organ Culture in Israel and Palestine* (Charleston, S.C.: BookSurge, 2005).

60. Ami Maayani, an Israel composer and architect, not only designed the hall but, as head of the Music Academy of Tel Aviv University, was also involved in the realization of the organ project. He had to counter some resistance from university officials, who did not

believe in the importance of building an organ of this caliber. Constructed by Hermann Eule of Bauzen, a well-known German builder of high-quality organs, the organ sports thirty-nine stops with mechanical (manual) action and electric stop action.

61. In the 1970s the organ was disassembled and stored. Several attempts to rebuild it in a different location failed, and today most of the pipework has been lost.

62. See Bohlman, "Musical Culture," 270.

63. Jehoash Hirshberg, *Paul Ben-Haim: His Life and Works* (Jerusalem: Israeli Music Press, 1990), 340.

64. See the Palestine Conservatoire of Music and Dramatic Art in Jerusalem to Hans Samuel, Nov. 24, 1938, Hans Samuel Collection, I.3.1.9; Conservatoire Michael Taube to Hans Samuel, Nov. 29, 1938, Hans Samuel Collection, I.3.1.10.

65. Hans Samuel to the U.S. Consulate General, Nov. 4, 1940, Hans Samuel Collection, I.3.2.2.

66. The Jewish community to Hans Samuel (with reference to Samuel's letter dated Nov. 1, 1951), Dec. 3, 1951, Hans Samuel Collection, I.3.1.16.

67. Rachel Thaller, discussion with the author, May 5, 1998.

68. Eva Samuel, interview by Angela Genger, Monika Josten, and Jutta Dick, Sept. 26, 1986, Archiv, Alte Synagoge, Essen, Germany.

69. Among the Sephardic-inspired compositions are *Sephardische Suite über Sabbatweise "Adonaj melech, Adonaj malach, Adonaj jimloch, leolam waed"*; *Sephardische Kantate für Solo-Stimmen, Chor, und Orgel*; *Paraphrase über sephardische Haftara-Kantillationen "Im taschiw Mischabbat raglacha" (resp. Kiddusch le Schacharit)*; *Paraphrase über die sephardische Neujahrsweise "Achoth ketanah"*; *Kaddish-Weise (Minhag Sepharad Amsterdam, vor Bar'chu im Schacharit)*; *2 Fugen (und Rezitativ) über sephardisches Schofar-Motiv "Adonaj bekol shofar" und "T'Kabel B'Razon"*; *Fuge über sephardische Weise "Schma jissrael"*; *Sephardische Selichoth-Weise "Kamti beaschmoret" (Ausgabe für Orgel-Solo)*; and *Fughetta on Sephardic Tune "Elohim, Eli Attah."*

70. In 1473, the secret Jews of Andalusia, fleeing persecution during the Reconquista, sought permission to settle in Gibraltar, where the Sephardic tradition has been continued ever since. Among them were cantors who later settled in Amsterdam or were invited to resettle in Holland. See Israel Adler, *Musical Life and Traditions of the Portuguese Jewish Community of Amsterdam in the XVIIIth Century*, Yuval Monograph Series 1 (Jerusalem: Magnes, 1974), 11, 93.

71. See Bohlman, *"Land Where Two Streams Flow,"* 183.

72. Robert Fleisher, *Twenty Israeli Composers: Voices of a Culture* (Detroit: Wayne State University Press, 1997), 84–85.

73. Ibid.

74. Haim Alexander to Oskar Gottlieb Blarr, December 1997, in the author's possession.

75. Haim Alexander, discussion with the author, June 24, 1998.

76. Haim Alexander to Oskar Gottlieb Blarr, December 1997, in the author's possession.

77. See Peter Gradenwitz, *Musik zwischen Orient und Okzident: Eine Kulturgeschichte der Wechselbeziehungen* (Wilhelmshaven, Germany: Heinrichshofen, 1977), 17–18.

78. Fleisher, *Twenty Israeli Composers*, 92.

79. See Keren, *Contemporary Israeli Music*, 11–12.

80. See ibid., 12.

81. The Fibonacci series assimilates a variety of cultural modes of thought. It may be traced back to the position-based system of decimal places, one of the most significant cultural accomplishments of the peoples of India. The Indian system was known in Baghdad as early as the eighth century; having been adopted by the Arabs at a time when they ruled most of the Iberian peninsula, the Indian idea reached Europe's medieval Latin scholars. The number sequence for which Fibonacci is still remembered is 0, 1, 1, 2, 3, 5, 8, 13, 21, 34 . . . or, in general, $x_{n+2} = x_{n+1} + x_1$. See *The Dictionary of Scientific Biography*, s.v. "Fibonacci, Leonardo."

82. A list of compositions by Israeli composers appears in Peter Gradenwitz, "Musik israelischer Komponisten für die Orgel," in *"Niemand wollte mich hören . . ."*: *Magrepha—Die Orgel in der Synagoge*, ed. Andor Izsák (Hannover: Freimann and Fuchs, 1999), 210–14, and Levi and Levi, *Organ Culture*, 139–42.

83. Keren, *Contemporary Israeli Music*, 107.

Chapter 6

1. Martin Stokes, "Introduction: Ethnicity, Identity and Music," in *Ethnicity, Identity, and Music: The Musical Construction of Place*, ed. Martin Stokes (New York: Berg, 1994), 13.

2. See Michael A. Meyer, "Jews as Jews versus Jews as German: Two Historical Perspectives," *Leo Baeck Institute Yearbook* 36 (1991): xv.

3. Kobena Mercer, "Welcome to the Jungle: Identity and Diversity in Postmodern Politics," in *Identity*, ed. Jonathan Rutherford (London: Lawrence and Wishart, 1990), 43.

4. See Michael A. Meyer, "German Jewry's Path to Normality and Assimilation: Complexities, Ironies, Paradoxes," in *Towards Normality? Acculturation and Modern German Jewry*, ed. Rainer Liedtke and David Rechter, Schriftenreihe wissenschaftlicher Abhandlungen des Leo Baeck Instituts 68 (Tübingen: Mohr Siebeck, 2003), 24.

5. See ibid.

6. Immanuel Wallerstein, "Culture as Ideological Battleground," *Theory, Culture, and Society* 7 (1990): 45.

7. On the different usages of the term *dissimilation* see Shulamit Volkov, "Jüdische Assimilation und jüdische Eigenart im deutschen Kaiserreich: Ein Versuch," *Geschichte und Gesellschaft* 9, no. 3 (1983): 331–48; and Jonathan Skolnik, "Dissimilation and the Historical Novel: Hermann Sinsheimer's Maria Nunnez," *Leo Baeck Institute Yearbook* 43 (1998): 228–30.

8. Joachim Prinz, "Zionism under the Nazi Government," *Young Zionist* (November 1937): 18.

9. See Peter Gradenwitz, *Musik zwischen Orient und Okzident: Eine Kulturgeschichte der Wechselbeziehungen* (Wilhelmshaven, Germany: Heinrichshofen, 1977), 14.

10. See Steffen Werner, *Die 2. babylonische Gefangenschaft: Das Schicksal der Juden im europäischen Osten seit 1941* (Pfullingen, Germany: privately printed, 1990), 29.

11. Besides Zionism and anti-Semitism, other developments were instrumental in creating dissimilatory tendencies. The counterassimilation doctrine developed by religious leadership took place long before Zionism; see Meyer, "German Jewry's Path to Normality and Assimilation," 24. The immigration of Eastern European Jews and a certain liberalism may have had a dissimilatory effect as well; see Stefanie Schüler-Springorum,

"Assimilation and Community Reconsidered: The Jewish Community in Königsberg, 1871–1914," *Jewish Social Studies* 5, no. 3 (1999): 122.

12. See Michael A. Meyer, Michael Brenner, Mordechai Breuer, and Michael Graetz, eds., *German-Jewish History in Modern Times*, 4 vols. (New York: Columbia University Press, 1996), vol. 3, 388.

13. Nikos Papastergiadis, *The Turbulence of Migration: Globalization, Deterritorialization, and Hybridity* (Cambridge, UK: Polity, 2000), 157.

14. See Meyer, Brenner, Breuer, and Graetz, *German-Jewish History*, vol. 3, 388.

15. See John E. Farley, *Majority-minority Relations*, 4th ed. (Upper Saddle River, N.J.: Prentice-Hall, 2000), 81; and Norman R. Yetman, ed., *Majority and Minority: The Dynamics of Race and Ethnicity in American Life* (Boston: Allyn and Bacon, 1999), 229.

16. See Yetman, *Majority and Minority*, 229.

17. For the concept of "invention of tradition" see Eric Hobsbawm and Terence Ranger, eds., *The Invention of Tradition* (New York: Cambridge University Press, 1983), 9.

18. In *Majority-minority Relations* Farley states:

> In pluralism, some aspects of culture and social structure are shared in common throughout society; other elements remain distinct in each racial or ethnic group. There is a common culture and set of institutions such as churches [and synagogues], clubs, businesses, and media; and a distinct set of *primary group* relations such as friendship networks and families. Thus, under pluralism there exists one society made up of a number of distinct parts. In contrast to the melting pot, the pluralist model is often compared to a *mosaic*: one unit made up of many distinct parts. . . . Cultural pluralism occurs when each group in society retains certain sets of attitudes, beliefs, and lifestyles while sharing others." (2000, 183)

The term *pluralism* should not be confused with the concept of plural societies, which has strong political connotations.

19. Joanne Nagel, "Constructing Ethnicity: Creating and Recreating Ethnic Identity and Culture," in *Majority and Minority*, ed. Norman R. Yetman (Boston: Allyn and Bacon, 1999), 64.

20. See Stuart Hall, "Identity in Question," in *Modernity: An Introduction to Modern Societies*, ed. Stuart Hall, David Held, and Don Hubert (Cambridge, UK: Polity, 1995), 599.

Music

The music bibliography provides only a selection of works. For a comprehensive list of organ compositions (manuscripts and prints) see Tina Frühauf, *Orgel und Orgelmusik in deutsch-jüdischer Kultur* (Hildesheim, Germany: Georg Olms, 2005).

MANUSCRIPT COLLECTIONS

Berlinski, Herman. Jewish Theological Seminary of America, New York.

Birnbaum, Eduard. Hebrew Union College, Klau Library, Cincinnati.

Fromm, Herbert. Jewish Theological Seminary of America, New York.

Idelsohn, Abraham Zvi. Jewish National and University Library, Jerusalem.

Kirschner, Emanuel. Hebrew Union College, Klau Library, Cincinnati.

Levy, Ernst. Universitätsbibliothek Basel, Basel.

Mandell, Eric. Gratz College Archives, Philadelphia.

Nadel, Arno. Gratz College Archives, Philadelphia.

Ricardo, David. Bar Ilan University Archives, Bar Ilan.

Samuel, Hans (Yohanan). Archive of Israeli Music, Tel Aviv University, Tel Aviv.

Schalit, Heinrich. Jewish Theological Seminary of America, New York.

Werner, Eric. Leo Baeck Institute Archives, New York.

PUBLISHED SOURCES

Adler, Hugo. *Organ Prelude*. In *Nachlat Israel: Sabbath Eve Service Based on Traditional Chanting*. New York: Transcontinental Music, 1951.

Adler, Samuel, ed. *Organ Music for Worship*. New York: Wallan Music, 1964.

———. *Two Meditations for Organ*. New York: Mercury Music, 1965.

Altman, Ludwig. *Avinu, Malkenu (Our Father, Our King): Based on a Traditional Melody*. New York: Transcontinental Music, 1980.

———. *Festive Prelude or Postlude for a Pilgrimage Festival*. New York: Transcontinental Music, 1973.

———. *Meditation Song*. New York: World Library, 1972.

———. *Organ Music for the Synagogue and Church*. Dalton: Sacred Music Press, 1986.

———. *Prelude on Leoni*. New York: Transcontinental Music, 1977.

Beimel, Jacob. *Organ Music for Jewish Worship*. New York: Transcontinental Music, 1951.

Berlinski, Herman. *Avodat Shabbat: Friday Evening Service*. New York: Mercury Music, 1958.

———. *The Burning Bush*. Melville, N.Y.: H. W. Gray, 1957.

———. *From the World of My Father*. New York: Mercury Music, 1956.

———. *In Memoriam: Prelude for Organ*. New York: Associated Music Publishers, 1959.

———. *Passacaglia on the Melody "Kol Nidre."* Bryn Mawr, Penn.: Mercury Music, 1962.

———. *Processional Music*. New York: Mercury Music, 1965.

———. *Shovas vayeenofash: Prelude for the Sabbath*. New York: Transcontinental Music, 1968.

———. *Three Preludes for the Festivals*. Bryn Mawr, Penn.: Mercury Music, 1961.

Bloch, Ernest. *Four Wedding Marches*. Boston: G. Schirmer, 1951.

———. *Processional*. Boston: G. Schirmer, 1961.

———. *Six Preludes for Organ*. Boston: G. Schirmer, 1948.

Chajes, Julius. *Prayer for Organ*. New York: Transcontinental Music, 1979.

Deutsch, Moritz. "Orgelpräludium am Neujahrstage." In *Breslauer Synagogengesänge: Liturgie der neuen Synagoge*. Leipzig: Breitkopf and Härtel, 1880.

———. "Orgelpräludium an Festtagen." In *Breslauer Synagogengesänge: Liturgie der neuen Synagoge*. Leipzig: Breitkopf and Härtel, 1880.

———. *Vorbeterschule: Vollständige Sammlung der alten Synagogen-Intonationen*. Wrocław, Poland: Julius Hainauer, 1871.

———. *Zwölf Präludien für Orgel oder Pianoforte zum gottesdienstlichen und häuslichen Gebrauch nach alten Synagogen-Intonationen*. Wroclaw, Poland: Julius Hainauer, 1864.

Fromm, Herbert. *Days of Awe: Organ Sonata in Four Movements*. New York: Transcontinental Music, 1968.

———. *In Memoriam*. New York: Transcontinental Music, 1963.

———. *Organ Prelude Based on High Holiday Motifs*. New York: Transcontinental Music, 1965.

———. *Partita on Baruch haba*. Boston: Schirmer, 1958.

———. *Processional Based on Israeli Motifs for Organ Solo*. New York: Transcontinental Music, 1990.

———. *Silent Devotion*. New York: Transcontinental Music, 1963.

———. *Suite of Organ Pieces on Hebraic Motifs*. New York: Transcontinental Music, 1987.

———. *Ten Studies for Organ (Based on Hymns and Chants of the Synagogue)*. New York: Transcontinental Music, 1982.

Gratitude and Praise: Organ Works by Jewish-American Composers. Pullman, Wash.: Vivace, 1994.

Idelsohn, Abraham Zvi. *Hebräisch-orientalischer Melodienschatz*. 10 vols. Leipzig: Breitkopf and Härtel, 1914–1933.

———. *Synagogue Service for Friday Evening in E-flat Major: Based upon the Ancient Pentateuch Mode, Utilizing the Mode of Mogen Ovos*. New York: National Council of Jewish Women, 1924.

———. *Synagogue Service for Sabbath Morning in E-flat: Based upon Psalm Mode in Major, Utilizing the Mode of Ahava Rabba*. Cincinnati: Zimmermann Print, 1924.

Jadassohn, Salomon. *Phantasie {Praeludium (Kanon); Aria; Fuge} für Orgel*, op. 95. Leipzig: Fr. Kistner, 1888.

Helfmann, Max. *Silent Devotion*. New York: Transcontinental Music, 1942–1956.

Janowski, Max. *Organ Prelude for Shabbat: Based in Part on the Sabbath Mode*. New York: Transcontinental Music, 1973.

Kellermann, Albert. *Hebräische Gesänge für Harmonium*, op. 54 and 55. Leipzig: Breitkopf and Härtel, 1902.

Kornitzer, Leon. *Romemoss El: Jüdische gottesdienstliche Gesänge*. Frankfurt am Main: Julius Kauffmann, 1928.

Lewandowski, Louis. *Augenblicke der Weihe: Consolations, Neun kleine Stücke für Harmonium, Orgel, oder Klavier*, op. 44. Berlin: Carl Simon, 1891.

———. *Fünf Fest-Präludien für die Orgel*, op. 37. Berlin: Bote and Bock, 1889.

———. *Kol Rinnah U'T'fillah: Ein- und zweistimmige Gesänge für den israelitischen Gottesdienst*. 1921. Reprint, New York: Sacred Music Press, 1954.

———. *Synagogen-Melodieen für Harmonium, Orgel oder Klavier*, op. 47. Berlin: Carl Simon, 1895.

———. *Toda W'simrah: Vierstimmige Chorgesänge für den Gottesdienst*. Part II: *Festgesänge*. Frankfurt am Main: Julius Kauffmann, 1921.

Liber Usualis. Paris: Society of St. John the Evangelist, 1934.

Mendelssohn, Ludwig. *Kol Nidre (Hebräische Melodie) für Harmonium oder Orgel*. Leipzig: Breitkopf and Härtel, 1899.

Nadel, Arno. *Orgelvorspiel (oder Zwischenspiel) für die drei Trauerwochen*. Printed in *Gemeindeblatt der jüdischen Gemeinde zu Berlin* 9 (August 1, 1924).

———. *Orgelvorspiel (oder Zwischenspiel) für die hohen Feiertage (Motive "Bor'chu" und "Hammelech")*. Printed in *Gemeindeblatt der jüdischen Gemeinde zu Berlin* 10 (September 5, 1924).

Rathaus, Karol. *Präludium und Toccata*, op. 32. Vienna: Universal-Edition, 1933.

Samuel, Hans. *Paraphrase on Sephardic New Year's Evening Tune "Achot Ketanah" (Minhag Sepharad Amsterdam)*. Tel Aviv: Israel Composers League, n.d.

———. *Sephardic Cantata on Traditional Sabbath Cantillations "Ad. Melech, Ad. Malach, Ad. Jimloch l'eolam Waed."* Tel Aviv: Israeli Composers League, ca. 1960.

———. *Trio-paraphrase über Bor'chu-Motiv an den hohen Feiertagen (Minhag Ashkenas)*. Printed in *Der jüdische Kantor: Zweimonatsschrift des allgemeinen deutschen Kantorenverbandes* 3 (June 1, 1931), appendix.

———. *Triovorspiel zu{m traditionellen} "Borchu" am Vorabend des Pessachfestes (in D)*. Printed in *Der jüdische Kantor: Zweimonatsschrift des Allgemeinen deutschen Kantorenverbandes* 3 (June 1, 1931), appendix.

Schalit, Heinrich. "Nachspiel." In *Eine Freitagabend Liturgie für Kantor, einstimmigen und gemischten Chor und Orgel*, op. 29. Munich: privately printed, 1933.

Sinzheimer, Max. *Twelve Hymn Prelude and Improvisations*. St. Louis: Concordia, 1967.

Starer, Robert. *Festive Prelude: From "Sabbath Service."* New York: MCA and Mills, 1971.

———. *Three Quiet Interludes: Benediction—In Memoriam—Silent Prayer*. New York: MCA and Mills, 1971.

Sulzer, Joseph. *Vier Präludien für Orgel oder Harmonium*, op. 10. Leipzig: Breitkopf and Härtel, n.d.

Sulzer, Salomon. *Schir Zion: Ein Cyclus religiöser Gesänge zum gottesdienstlichen Gebrauche der Israeliten.* Vienna: privately printed, 1840.

———. "Drei Präludien für Orgel." In *Schir Zion: Gottesdienstliche Gesänge der Israeliten, zweiter Theil.* Vienna: J. Schlossberg, 1866).

Union of American Hebrew Congregations, ed. *Meditations and Memorials.* Organ Music for Jewish Worship and Celebration 4. New York: Transcontinental Music, 1996.

Weintraub, Max. *Agende für Trauungen: Vorspiel, Duo f. 2 Bariton, 2 Zwischenspiele, 1 Nachspiel.* Frankfurt am Main: E. H. Schuncke, ca. 1880.

Weiss, Jakob L. *Musikalische Synagogenbibliothek . . . eingerichtet für Pianoforte, Harmonium, und Orgel.* Vienna, 1881.

Werner, Eric. *Fantasy and Fugue on Motifs of Hebrew Cantillation.* New York: Transcontinental Music, 1987.

———. *Musical Worship for the High Holydays: According to the Newly Revised Union Prayer Book.* Part I: *Rosh Hashono.* New York: Bloch, 1952.

Yamim noraim / Days of Awe. New York: Transcontinental Music, 1991.

Zivi, Hermann. *Abend-Gottesdienst für Scholosch-Regolim*, op. 20. Frankfurt am Main: Julius Kauffmann, 1909.

———. "Praeludium." In *Freitag-Abend-Gottesdienst unter spezieller Berücksichtigung des aschkenasischen Chasonus*, op. 11. Leipzig: M. W. Kaufmann, 1906.

———. *Praeludium für das Chanukkahfest.* Printed in *Jüdisch-liberale Zeitung* (special issue) (September 19, 1924).

Written Materials

ARCHIVES AND MANUSCRIPT COLLECTIONS

Adler, Hugo Chaim. Papers. Hebrew Union College, New York.

Fromm, Herbert. Papers. Jewish Theological Seminary of America, New York.

Lewandowski, Manfred. Papers. Leo Baeck Institute, New York.

Michael, Jacob Collection. Jewish National and University Library, Jerusalem.

Phonoteca. National Sound Archives. Jewish National and University Library, Jerusalem.

Samuel, Hans (Yohanan). Papers. Archive of Israeli Music, Tel Aviv University, Tel Aviv.

Schalit, Heinrich. Papers. Jewish Theological Seminary of America, New York.

Steinmeyer, G. F. Dispositions and Drawings. Company Archive, Oettingen, Germany.

Stern, Moritz, Papers. Archives for the History of the Jewish People, Jerusalem.

Walcker, E. F., et Cie. Dispositions and Drawings. Company Archive, Kleinblittersdorf, Germany (company dissolved in 2000).

Werner, Eric. Papers. Leo Baeck Institute, New York.

ORAL HISTORIES

Adler, Samuel. Interviews and correspondence with the author, 1998–2000.

Alexander, Haim. Interview with the author, June 24, 1998.

Berlinski, Herman. Interview with the author, November 13, 1999.

Fromm, Herbert. Interview by Eliott Kahn, May 7–8, 1994.

Hirsch, Martha Sommer. Interviews by and correspondence with the author, 1998–2000.

Hirschberg, Hans. Interviews and correspondence with the author, 1998–2000.

Kochba, Hagit. Interview with the author, May 1, 1998.

Maayani, Ami. Interviews and correspondence with the author, April and May 1998.

Samuel, Eva. Interview by Angela Genger, Monika Josten, and Jutta Dick, September 26, 1986 (recording from the archives at the Alte Synagoge in Essen, signature IN, 176).

Thaller, Rachel. Interview with the author, May 5, 1998.

Ward, Kenneth. Interviews and correspondence with the author, 1998–2000.

PRIMARY AND SECONDARY SOURCES

This section does not precisely conform to the *Chicago Manual of Style* as it provides additional information on newpaper sources to serve as an aid in finding a combination of the journal, magazine, and newspaper format. Without these additions (volume, issue, and page numbers) many of the sources would be difficult to locate.

Altmann, Ludwig. "Die Orgel der neuen Synagoge." *Gemeindeblatt der jüdischen Gemeinde zu Berlin* 24 (November 17, 1934): 2–3.

———. *A Well-tempered Musician's Unfinished Journey through Life*. Berkeley: Regional Oral History Office, 1990.

Anonymous. "Aus dem Badischen, im Juni: Privatmittheilung, 20. Mai 1846." *Allgemeine Zeitung des Judenthums (AZJ)* 10, no. 31 (July 27, 1846): 449–51.

———. "Aus Oberschlesien im Oktober: Privatmittheilung." *AZJ* 9, no. 45 (November 3, 1845): 675.

———. "Berichte über den Stand des Kultus, 13. Oktober 1841." *AZJ* 5, no. 45 (November 6, 1841): 643–44.

———. "Die Gutachten des Berliner Rabbinats über die Orgel, 1. Februar 1904." *AZJ* 68, no. 6 (February 5, 1904): 65–68.

———. "Die neue Synagoge zu Mannheim, 15. Juli 1855." *AZJ* 19, no. 36 (September 3, 1855): 465–67.

———. "Einweihung der Synagoge am 5. September 1866." *Berlinische Nachrichten von Staats- und gelehrten Sachen* 206 (September 6, 1866): 3.

———. "Es ist eine Schande! Die Judenorgel in der Sankt Korbinianskirche zu München." *Stürmer* 42 (October 19, 1938).

———. "Feyerliche Einweihung des Jacobs-Tempels in Seesen." *Sulamith: Eine Zeitschrift zur Beförderung der Kultur und Humanität unter den Israeliten* 3, no. 4 (1810): 298–303.

———. "Musikalisches." *Der jüdische Kantor* 14 (March 4, 1892): 70.

———. "Orgona német zsinagógákban." *Magyar-zsidó szemle* 3 (1886): 506–507.

———. "Privatmittheilung, 11. Januar 1863." *AZJ* 27, no. 5 (January 27, 1863): 70.

———. "Privatmittheilung, 18. Januar 1863." *AZJ* 27, no. 5 (January 27, 1863): 70.

———. [untitled]. *AZJ* 5, no. 25 (June 19, 1841): 368.

Berliner, Abraham, ed. *Zur Lehr' und Wehr über und gegen die kirchliche Orgel im jüdischen Gottesdienste*. Berlin: Nathansen und Lamm, 1904.

Berlinski, Herman. "Die Aufgabe der Orgel in der Synagoge." *Musik und Kirche* 45, no. 3 (1975): 109–15.

———. "Zur Frage der synagogalen Orgeldisposition." *Musik und Kirche* 46, no. 4 (1976): 182–88.

Die Beschlüsse der ersten und zweiten israelitischen Synode. Mainz: J. Gottleben'sche Buchdruckerei, 1871.

Bunk, Gerard. *Liebe zur Orgel: Erinnerungen aus einem Musikerleben*, 2d ed. Dortmund: Ardey, 1958.

Cahn, Emil. "Synagogenkonzert des jüdischen Gesangvereins." *Das Jüdische Echo* 12, no. 20 (May 15, 1925): 386.

Cavaillé-Coll. *Maison A. Cavaillé-Coll, Paris 1889*. Documenta organologica 2/ Veröffentlichung der Gesellschaft der Orgelfreunde 55. 1889. Reprint, Berlin: Merseburger, 1977.

Deutsch, David. "Die Orgel in der Synagoge: Eine Erörterung." Wrocław, Poland: privately printed, 1863.

Deutsch-israelitischer Gemeindebund. *Statistisches Jahrbuch des deutsch-israelitischen Gemeindebundes*. Berlin, 1898–1901.

Ehrlich, Hermann. "Die Orgel in unsern Synagogen." *Liturgische Zeitschrift zur Veredelung des Synagogengesangs mit Berücksichtigung des ganzen Synagogenwesens*, 1–2, nos. 10–12; no. 4 (1848–1862): 77–90.

Eleh Divrei ha-Berit. 1819. Reprint, Westmead, Farnborough, UK: Gregg, 1969.

Felber, Erwin. "Gibt es eine jüdische Musik?" *Anbruch* 10 (1928): 282–87.

Frank, Rafael. "Der jüdische Organist." *AZJ* 72, no. 8 (February 21, 1908): 91–92.

Fromm, Herbert. *The Key of See: Travel Journals of a Composer*. Boston: Plowshare, 1967.

———. *On Jewish Music: A Composer's View*. New York: Bloch, 1978.

Geiger, Abraham. "Aktenstücke zur dritten Versammlung deutscher Rabbinen, 28. Mai 1846." *AZJ* 10, no. 24 (June 8, 1846): 345–46.

Güldenstein, Michael. "Mitteilung, 25. November 1845." *AZJ* 10, no. 5 (January 26, 1846): 68.

Guttmann, Oskar. "Heinrich Schalits neue Komposition in Berlin." *Bayerische israelitische Gemeindezeitung* 8, no. 21 (November 1, 1932): 328.

———. "Die Orgel in der Synagoge und wer sie spielen soll." *Jüdische Rundschau* 84, no. 37 (October 21, 1932): 408.

Henle, Moritz. "Der gottesdienstliche Gesang im Israelitischen Tempel zu Hamburg." In *Festschrift zum hundertjährigen Bestehen des Israelitischen Tempels in Hamburg*, ed. David Leimdörfer, 67–85.

Internationales Regulativ für Orgelbau entworfen und bearbeitet von der Sektion für Orgelbau auf dem 3. Kongreß der internationalen Musikgesellschaft, Vienna, 25. bis 29. Mai 1909. Leipzig: Breitkopf and Härtel, 1909.

Italiener, Bruno. *Festschrift zum hundertzwangigjährigen Bestehen des Israelitischen Tempels in Hamburg 1817–1937*. Hamburg, 1937.

Jacob-Loewensohn, Alice. "Keine Orgel im jüdischen Gottesdienst." *Jüdische Rundschau* 84, no. 37 (October 21, 1932): 408.

———. "Zur alten und neuen liturgischen Musik." *Jüdische Rundschau* 77, no. 76 (September 28, 1928): 546.

K. M. *Der Gottesdienst mit Orgel*. n.p., n.d.

Kirschner, Emanuel. *Erinnerungen aus meinem Leben, Streben und Wirken*. Woerishofen, Germany: privately printed, 1933.

Kornitzer, Leon. "120 Jahre Kultmusik im Hamburger Tempel." In *Festschrift zum hundertzwanzigjährigen Bestehen des Israelitischen Tempels in Hamburg 1817–1937*, ed. Bruno Italiener, 25–31.

Kuhn, Eberhard. "Disposition über die vom Orgelbaumeister E. F. Walcker und Comp. in Ludwigsburg für die israelitische Gemeinde in Mannheim erbaute Orgel." *Urania* 13, no. 6 (1856): 81–83.

Leichtentritt, Hugo. "Über die Erneuerung der jüdischen Kultmusik." *Gemeindeblatt der jüdischen Gemeinde zu Köln* (November 16, 1932): 211–14.

Leimdörfer, David, ed. *Festschrift zum hundertjährigen Bestehen des Israelitischen Tempels in Hamburg*. Hamburg: M. Glogau, 1918.

Lemle, Heinrich. *Halachisches zur Orgelfrage*. Frankfurt am Main: Vereinigung jüdischer Kantoren, ca. 1933–1936.

Levi, Benedikt. *Beweis der Zuverlässigkeit des deutschen Choralgesanges mit Orgelbegleitung bei dem sabbathlichen Gottesdienste der Juden: Ein Beitrag zur jüdischen Liturgie*. Offenbach, Germany: Brede, 1833.

Levi, Josef. "Hugo Adler: Toccata und Fuge über ein hebräisches Thema für Orgel, Op. 11." *Israelitisches Gemeindeblatt Mannheim* 10, no. 5 (May 24, 1932): 5–6.

Lewin-Kassewitz, Lisel. "Meine Zeit als Organistin und Gemeindesekretärin der jüdischen Gemeinde." In *Erinnertes Leben: Autobiographische Texte zur jüdischen Geschichte Heidelbergs*, ed. Norbert Giovannini and Frank Moraw, 138–43.

Liebermann, Eliezer. *Or Nogah*. Dessau, Germany, 1818.

Morosini, Giulio. *Via delle fede mostrata a gli Ebrei: Divisa in tre parti*. Rome: Stamperia della Cong. de prop. Fide, 1683.

Nadel, Arno. "Jüdische Musik." *Der Jude* 7 (1923): 227–36.

Orgel-Katalog: Hof-Orgel-Fabrik Gebrüder Rieger, 4th ed. Krnov, Czech Republic: Gebrüder Rieger, 1890.

Orgona-Katalogus Angster József és Fia, Orgona- és Harmonium-Gyárából Pécsett / Orgel-Catalog aus der Orgel- und Harmonium-Fabrik Josef Angster and Sohn in Fünfkirchen. Pécs, Hungary, 1896.

Prinz, Joachim. "Zionism under the Nazi Government." *Young Zionist* (November 1937): 18ff.

Protokolle und Aktenstücke der zweiten Rabbinerversammlung. Frankfurt am Main: E. Ullmann, 1845.

Rock, Christa Maria, and Hans Brückner, eds. *Judentum und Musik mit dem ABC jüdischer und nichtarischer Musikbeflissener*, 2d ed. Munich: Hans Brückner, 1936.

Rübenstein, Ernst. "Das Orgelpräludium in der Synagoge." *Oesterreichisch-ungarische Cantoren-Zeitung: Organ für die Gesammt-Interessen jüdischer Cantoren (OUCZ)* 6, no. 35 (November 6, 1886): 1–2.

Rupp, Emile. *Die Entwicklungsgeschichte der Orgelbaukunst*. 1929. Reprint, New York: Georg Olms, 1981.

———. "Der Sachverständigenzwang: Eine Gefahr für den deutschen Orgelbau." *Zeitschrift für Instrumentenbau (ZfI)* 32 (1911/1912): 1241–43.

Sachs, Michael. "Gutachten gegen die Orgel (13.11.1861)." In *Zur Lehr' und Wehr über und gegen die kirchliche Orgel im jüdischen Gottesdienste*, ed. Abraham Berliner. 12–22. Berlin: Nathansen und Lamm, 1904.

Samuel, Hans. "Die Melodien der drei Wallfahrtsfeste." *Frankfurter israelitisches Gemeindeblatt (FIG)* 10, no. 9 (May 1932): 193–94.

———. "Synagogale Orgelmusik." *Der jüdische Kantor: Zweimonatsschrift des Allgemeinen deutschen Kantorenverbandes* 3 (June 1, 1931): 7–8.

————. "Zur Entwicklung synagogaler Orgelmusik." *Jüdische Rundschau* 84, no. 21 (October 21, 1932): 408.

Saul, Felix. "Chor und Orgel im Gottesdienst der Zukunft." *Jüdische Rundschau* 77, no. 33 (September 26, 1928): 546.

Schudt, Johann Jacob. *Jüdische Merckwürdigkeiten: Vorstellende was sich Curieuses und Denckwürdiges in den neuern Zeiten bey einigen Jahrhunderten mit denen in alle IV. Theile der Welt, sonderlich durch Teutschland zerstreuten Juden zugetragen, mit historischer Feder in drey Theilen beschrieben.* Frankfurt: Samuel Tobias Hocker, 1714–1718. Reprint, Berlin: Lamm, 1922.

————. *Jüdisches Franckfurter und Prager Freuden-Fest: Wegen der höchst-glücklichen Geburth des durchläuchtigsten käyserlichen Erb-Prinzens, vorstellend mit was Solennitäten die Franckfurter Juden selbiges celebrirt, auch ein besonders Lied, mit Sinn-Bilder und Devisen, darauff verfertigt; So dann den Curieusen kostbahren, doch recht possirlichen Auffzug, so die Prager Juden gehalten.* Frankfurt am Main: Mathias Andreä, 1716.

Schwarz, Israel. "Ist die Einführung von Instrumental-Begleitung und speciell die der Orgel bei dem synagogalen Gottesdienst gestattet, und ist es erlaubt, an Sabbat- und Festtagen derartige Instrumente zu spielen, oder durch einen Nichtjuden spielen zu lassen?" *Der jüdische Kantor* 4, no. 36 (September 26, 1882): 284–85.

Schweitzer, Albert. *Deutsche und französische Orgelbaukunst.* 1906. A facsimile of the first edition. Wiesbaden: Breitkopf and Härtel, 1976.

Singer, Josef. "Chasonus: Die Orgel." *OUCZ* 3, no. 31 (September 8, 1883): 1–3.

————. "Ueber die Entwicklung des Synagogengesanges: Zweite Serie XXVII." *OUCZ* 8, no. 36 (November 5, 1888): 1–2.

Steinthal, Heymann. *Über Juden und Judentum: Vorträge und Aufsätze.* Schriften der Gesellschaft zur Förderung des Judentums 9. Berlin: M. Poppelauer, 1906.

Stengel, Theo, and Herbert Gerigk. *Lexikon der Juden in der Musik: Mit einem Titelver- zeichnis jüdischer Werke.* Veröffentlichungen des Instituts der NSDAP zur Er- forschung der Judenfrage 2. Berlin: Bernhard Hahnefeld, 1940.

Thon, Jakob. *Die jüdischen Gemeinden und Vereine in Deutschland.* Veröffentlichungen des Bureaus für Statistik der Juden 3. Berlin: Verlag des Bureaus für die Statistik der Juden, 1906.

Tintner, Moritz. "Die Orgel in der Synagoge." *OUCZ* 12, no. 2 (January 11, 1892): 2–3.

Wolf, William. "Zur Synagogen-Musik." *AZJ* 54, no. 29 (August 1, 1890): 385–86.

Zivi, Hermann. "Gibt es eine jüdische Musik?" *Programmheft des jüdischen Kulturbund Rhein-Ruhr* 5, no. 7 (1934): 1–2.

————. "Jüdische Musik im Lichte des Verismus." In *Dem Andenken Eduard Birnbaums: Sammlung kantoral-wissenschaftlicher Aufsätze,* ed. Aron Friedmann, 121–25.

LITERATURE

Ackermann, Aron. *Der synagogale Gesang in seiner historischen Entwicklung.* 1896. Die jüdische Literatur seit Abschluss des Kanons 3. Reprint, Hildesheim, Germany: Georg Olms, 1965.

Adelung, Wolfgang. *Einführung in den Orgelbau,* 3d ed. Leipzig: Breitkopf and Härtel, 1974.

Adler, Israel, ed. *Hebrew Notated Manuscript Sources up to circa 1840: A Descriptive and*

Thematic Catalogue with a Checklist of Printed Sources. 2 vols. Répertoire International des Sources Musicales (RISM) 9(1). Munich: G. Henle, 1989.

———, ed. *Hebrew Writings concerning Music in Manuscripts and Printed Books from Geonic Times up to 1800.* RISM 9(2). Munich: G. Henle, 1975.

———. *Musical Life and Traditions of the Portuguese Jewish Community of Amsterdam in the XVIIIth Century.* Yuval Monograph Series 1. Jerusalem: Magnes, 1974.

———. *La pratique musicale savante dans quelques communautés Juives en Europe aux XVIIe et XVIIIe siècle.* Etudes Juives 8. Paris: Mouton, 1966.

———, ed. *Yuval: Studies of the Jewish Music Research.* Jerusalem: Magnes, 1968.

Adler, Saldo, and Hermann Baerwald. *Geschichte der Realschule der israelitischen Gemeinde (Philantropin) zu Frankfurt am Main, 1804–1904.* Frankfurt am Main: Druck von Gebrüder Fey, 1904.

Ahrens, Christian. " 'Mit Crescendo und Decrescendo zum Verwehen': Physharmonika-Register in Orgeln des 19. und 20. Jahrhunderts." *Ars Organi* 46, no. 3 (1998): 142–49.

Akademie der Künste. *Geschlossene Vorstellung: Der jüdische Kulturbund in Deutschland 1933–1941—Begleitheft zur Ausstellung in der Akademie der Künste vom 27. Januar bis zum 26. April 1992.* Reihe deutsche Vergangenheit 60. Berlin: Edition Heinrich, 1992.

Alte Synagoge Wuppertal. *Hier wohnte Frau Antonie Giese: Die Geschichte der Juden im Bergischen Land.* Wuppertal, Germany: Trägerverein Begegnungsstätte Alte Synagoge, 1997.

Anton, Karl. *Luther und die Musik.* Berlin: Evangelische Verlagsanstalt, 1957.

Arbeitskreis Jüdische Geschichte Hannover. *Die jüdischen Ladenburger: Ein Beitrag zur Stadtgeschichte.* Jüdische Bibliothek 2. Mannheim: VWM-Verlag Wagener, 1991.

Arendt, Hannah. *Eichmann in Jerusalem: A Report on the Banality of Evil.* Rev. and expanded ed. New York: Viking, 1964.

———. *The Jew as Pariah: Jewish Identity and Politics in the Modern Age.* New York: Grove, 1978.

Armstrong, John. "Archetypal Diasporas." In *Ethnicity*, ed. John Hutchinson and Anthony D. Smith, 120–27.

Arnsberg, Paul. *Die jüdische Gemeinde in Hessen: Anfang, Untergang, Neubeginn.* Frankfurt am Main: Societäts-Verlag, 1971.

Avenary, Hanoch. "Ein hebräisches Zeugnis für den Aufenthalt Konrad Paumanns in Mantua (1470)." *Die Musikforschung* 16 (1963): 156–57.

———, ed. *Kantor Salomon Sulzer und seine Zeit: Eine Dokumentation.* Sigmaringen, Germany: Jan Thorbecke, 1985.

———. "The Mixture Principle in the Mediaeval Organ: An Early Evidence." *Musica Disciplina* 4 (1950): 51–57.

Bähr, Hans Peter. "Im Schatten Liszts: Johann Gottlob Töpfer." In *Zur deutschen Orgelmusik des 19. Jahrhunderts*, ed. Hermann Busch and Michael Heinemann, 209–17. Sinzig, Germany: Studio Verlag, 1998.

Ballin, Gerhard. *Geschichte der Juden in Seesen.* Seesen: Stadt Seesen, 1979.

Ballof, Rolf, and Joachim Frassl, eds. *Die Jacobson-Schule: Festschrift zum 200-jährigen Bestehen der Jacobson-Schule in Seesen.* Seesen, Germany: Jacobson Gymnasium, 2001.

Barnard, Leslie S. "The Restored Organ in the Liberal Jewish Synagogue." *Organ* 33 (1953): 122–26.

Bauman, Zygmunt. "Modernity and Ambivalence." *Theory, Culture, and Society* 7 (1990): 143–69.

Beckmann, Volker. *Die jüdische Bevölkerung der Landkreise Lübbecke und Halle i.W.: Vom Vormärz bis zur Befreiung vom Faschismus (1815–1945)*. Lage, Germany: Jacobs, 2001.

Beer, Axel, Kristina Pfarr, and Wolfgang Ruf, eds. *Festschrift Christoph-Hellmut Mahling zum 65. Geburtstag*. 2 vols. Mainzer Studien zur Musikwissenschaft 37. Tutzing, Germany: Hans Schneider, 1997.

Beer, Gisela. *Orgelbau Ibach, Barmen 1794–1904*. Beiträge zur rheinischen Musikgeschichte 107. Cologne: Volk, 1975.

Benayahu, Meir. "Da'at ḥakhmey Italyah al ha-neginah be'ugav ba-tefillah" [The Opinions of Italian Sages on Organ Playing in Prayer Service]. *Asufot* 1 (1987): 265–318.

Bendt, Veronika, Eike Geisel, and Carolin Hilker-Siebenhaar. *Wegweiser durch das jüdische Berlin: Geschichte und Gegenwart*. Berlin: Nicolai, 1987.

Benham, Gilbert. "The Organ in the West London Synagogue, Upper Berkeley Street, W." *Organ* 18 (1938): 45–50.

Binder, Abraham. *Biblical Chant*. New York: Philosophical Library, 1959.

Birkmann, Günter, and Hartmut Stratmann. *Bedenke vor wem du stehst: 300 Synagogen und ihre Geschichte in Westfalen und Lippe*. Essen: Klartext, 1998.

Blum, Stephen, Philip V. Bohlman, and Daniel M. Neuman, eds. *Ethnomusicology and Modern Music History*. Chicago: University of Illinois Press, 1993.

Blumesberger, Susanne, Michael Doppelhofer, and Gabriele Mauthe, eds. *Handbuch österreichischer Autorinnen und Autoren jüdischer Herkunft 18. bis 20. Jahrhundert*. 3 vols. Munich: K. G. Saur, 2002.

Böcker, Jan. "'Die Orgel störrisch, aber gemeistert . . . ': Die Konzertauftritte des niederländischen Organisten, Pianisten, und Komponisten Gerard Bunk (1888–1958) in Deutschland in Kaiserreich, Weimarer Republik und 'Drittem Reich.'" PhD diss., Universität Münster, 1995.

Bohlman, Philip V. *"The Land Where Two Streams Flow": Music in the German-Jewish Community of Israel*. Chicago: University of Illinois Press, 1989.

———. "The Musical Culture of Central European Jewish Immigrants to Israel." PhD diss., University of Chicago, 1984.

———. "Das Musikleben während der jüdischen kulturellen Renaissance in Mannheim vor dem zweiten Weltkrieg." *Mannheimer Hefte* 2 (1985): 111–19.

———. *The World Centre for Jewish Music in Palestine 1936–1940: Jewish Musical Life on the Eve of World War II*. Oxford: Clarendon, 1992.

Bösken, Franz. *Quellen und Forschungen zur Orgelgeschichte des Mittelrheins*. Mainz: Schott, 1967.

Bothe, Rolf, ed. *Synagogen in Berlin: Zur Geschichte einer zerstörten Architektur*. 2 vols. Stadtgeschichtliche Publikationen 1. Berlin: Willmuth Arenhövel, 1983.

Brämer, Andreas. *Judentum und religiöse Reform: Der Hamburger Israelitische Tempel 1817–1938*. Hamburg: Dölling und Galitz, 2000.

———. *Rabbiner Zacharias Frankel: Wissenschaft des Judentums und konservative Reform im 19. Jahrhundert*. Netiva: Wege zur deutsch-jüdischen Geschichte und Kultur 3. Hildesheim, Germany: Georg Olms, 2000.

Brändle, Gerhard. *Jüdische Gotteshäuser in Pforzheim*. Pforzheim, Germany: Druckerei Adolf Klingel, 1990.

Braun, Joachim. "Aspekte der Musiksoziologie in Israel." In *Studien zur Systematischen Musikwissenschaft*, ed. Constantin Floros, 85–103.

———. "The Iconography of the Organ: Change in Jewish Thought and Musical Life." *Music in Art: International Journal for Music Iconography* 28, nos. 1–2 (2003): 55–69.

———. "The Lute and Organ in Ancient Israeli and Jewish Iconography." In *Festschrift Christoph-Hellmut Mahling*, ed. Axel Beer, Kristina Pfarr, and Wolfgang Ruf, vol. 1, 163–89.

Brenner, Michael. *The Renaissance of Jewish Culture in Weimar Germany*. New Haven, Conn.: Yale University Press, 1996.

———, and Derek J. Penslar, eds. *In Search of Jewish Community: Jewish Identities in Germany and Austria 1918–1933*. Bloomington: Indiana University Press, 1998.

Brinkmann, Reinhold, and Christoph Wolff, eds. *Driven into Paradise: The Musical Migration from Nazi Germany to the United States*. Berkeley: University of California Press, 1999.

Brocke, Michael, ed. *Feuer an Dein Heiligtum gelegt: Zerstörte Synagogen 1938 Nordrhein-Westfalen*. Bochum, Germany: Kamp, 1999.

Brod, Max, and Yehuda Walter Cohen. *Die Musik Israels*. Rev. ed. Kassel, Germany: Bärenreiter, 1976.

Brülls, Holger. *Synagogen in Sachsen-Anhalt*. Berlin: Verlag für Bauwesen, 1998.

Busch, Hermann J. "'Hochgefeierter Veteran der geistlichen Tonkunst': Johann Christian Heinrich Rinck." In *Zur deutschen Orgelmusik des 19. Jahrhunderts*, ed. Hermann Busch and Michael Heinemann, 173–78. Sinzig, Germany: Studio Verlag, 1998.

Carspecken, Ferdinand. *Fünfhundert Jahre Kasseler Orgeln: Ein Beitrag zur Kultur- und Kunstgeschichte der Stadt Kassel*. Kassel, Germany: Bärenreiter, 1968.

Cirsovius, Leopold Iwan. *Orgel-Dispositionen aus Schleswig-Holstein: 194 Dispositionen und Beschreibungen (1868–1895)*. 1872. Documenta organologica 10. Reprint, Kassel, Germany: Merseburger, 1986.

Coplan, David B. "Ethnomusicology and the Meaning of Tradition." In *Ethnomusicology and Modern Music History*, ed. Stephen Blum, Philip V. Bohlman, and Daniel M. Neuman, 35–49.

Dallmann, Wolfgang. *Johann Nepomuk David: Das Choralwerk für Orgel*. New York: Peter Lang, 1994.

Daube, Otto, and Hans Joachim Moser. *Die Wittenbergisch Nachtigall* [Martin Luther und die Musik]. Dortmund, Germany: W. Crüwell, 1962.

De Sola Pool, David, and Tamar Pool. *An Old Faith in the New World: Portrait of Shearith Israel, 1654–1954*. New York: Columbia University Press, 1955.

Diekmann, Irene, and Julius H. Schoeps. *Wegweiser durch das jüdische Brandenburg*. Berlin: Edition Hentrich, 1995.

Dubin, Lois C. "The Rise and the Fall of the Italian Jewish Model in Germany: From Haskalah to Reform, 1780–1820." In *Jewish History and Jewish Memory: Essays in Honor of Yosef Hayim Yerushalmi*, ed. Elisheva Carlebach, John M. Efron, and David N. Myers, 271–95. Tauber Institute for the Study of European Jewry Series 29. Hanover, N.H.: University Press of New England, 1998.

Eggebrecht, Hans Heinrich, ed. *Die Orgel im Dienst der Kirche: Gespräch aus ökumenischer Sicht—Bericht über das sechste Colloquium der Walcker-Stiftung für orgelwissenschaftliche*

Forschung in Verbindung mit dem Pontificio Istituto die Musica Sacra, 8.–14. Oktober 1984 in Rom. Veröffentlichungen der Walcker-Stiftung für Orgelwissenschaftliche Forschung 10. Murrhardt, Germany: Musikwissenschaftliche Verlags-Gesellschaft, 1985.

Ehrenreich, Eliezer. "Der erste Synagogenchor in Berlin (aus alten Akten)." *Gemeindeblatt der jüdischen Gemeinde zu Berlin* 19 (February 1929): 66–67, 107–11.

Einstein, Alfred. *Nationale und Universale Musik: Neue Essays.* Zurich: Pan, 1958.

Elbogen, Ismar. *Der jüdische Gottesdienst in seiner geschichtlichen Entwicklung,* 3d ed. Hildesheim, Germany: Georg Olms, 1967.

Ellenson, David. "A Disputed Precedent: The Prague Organ in Nineteenth-century Central European Legal Literature and Polemics." *Leo Baeck Institute Yearbook* 40 (1995): 251–64.

Esman, Milton J. "Diasporas and International Relations." In *Ethnicity,* ed. John Hutchinson and Anthony D. Smith, 316–20.

Falkenberg, Hans-Joachim. *Der Orgelbauer Wilhelm Sauer 1831–1916: Leben und Werk.* Veröffentlichung der Gesellschaft der Orgelfreunde 124. Lauffen am Neckar: Rensch, 1990.

Falvy, Zoltán. "Musical Instruments in the Kaufmann Manuscripts, Budapest." *Studia Musicologica Academiae Scientiarum Hungaricae* 37, nos. 2–4 (1996): 231–48.

Farley, John E. *Majority-minority Relations,* 4th ed. Upper Saddle River, N.J.: Prentice-Hall, 2000.

Fischer, Hermann, and Theodor Wohnhaas. *Lexikon süddeutscher Orgelbauer.* Taschenbücher zur Musikwissenschaft 116. Wilhelmshaven: Florian Noetzel, 1994.

———. "Der Liturgiestreit und die Orgel in der Fürther Synagoge." *Fürther Heimatblätter* 24, no. 1 (1974): 3–7.

———. "Miszelle: Nachrichten über Synagogenorgeln." *Jahrbuch des Instituts für deutsche Geschichte* 6 (1977): 531–38.

———. "Miszelle: Quellen zur Geschichte der Orgeln in westdeutschen Synagogen." *Jahrbuch des Instituts für deutsche Geschichte* 5 (1976): 467–81.

———. "Die Orgel in bayerischen Synagogen im späten 19. Jahrhundert." *Jahrbuch für fränkische Landesforschung* 33 (1973): 1–12.

———. "Zur Geschichte der Münchner Synagogenorgeln." *Oberbayerisches Achiv* 100 (1975): 309–13.

Fleisher, Robert. *Twenty Israeli Composers: Voices of a Culture.* Detroit: Wayne State University Press, 1997.

Flender, Reinhard. *Hebrew Psalmody: A Structural Investigation.* Yuval Monograph Series 9. Jerusalem: Magnes, 1992.

Floros, Constantin, ed. *Studien zur systematischen Musikwissenschaft.* Hamburger Jahrbuch für Musikwissenschaft 9. Hamburg: Laaber, 1986.

Freie Universität Berlin, Zentralinstitut für sozialwissenschaftliche Forschung. *Gedenkbuch Berlins der jüdischen Opfer des Nationalsozialismus.* Berlin: Druckhaus Hentrich, 1995.

Freise, Judith, and Joachim Martini. *Jüdische Musikerinnen und Musiker in Frankfurt 1933–1942: Musik als Form geistigen Widerstands.* Frankfurt am Main: Otto Lembeck, 1990.

Friedmann, Aron. "Das Dreigestirn, Salomon Sulzer, Louis Lewandowski und Moritz Deutsch." *Jahrbuch für jüdische Geschichte und Literatur* 16 (1913): 191–227.

————, ed. *Dem Andenken Eduard Birnbaums: Sammlung kantoral-wissenschaftlicher Aufsätze*. Berlin: C. Boas, 1922.

————. *Der synagogale Gesang: Eine Studie*, 2d ed. Musikwissenschaftliche Studienbibliothek Peters. 1908. Reprint, Leipzig: Edition Peters, 1978.

Frotscher, Gotthold. *Geschichte des Orgelspiels und der Orgelkomposition*, 2d ed. 2 vols. Berlin: Merseburger, 1959.

Frühauf, Tina. "Jewish Liturgical Music in Vienna: A Mirror of Cultural Diversity." In *Vienna: Jews and the City of Music 1870–1938*, ed. Leon Botstein and Werner Hanak, 77–91. Annandale-on-Hudson, N.Y.: Bard College, 2004.

————. " 'Jüdische Merckwürdigkeiten': Die Orgel in der Synagoge zu Dortmund." *Orgel International* 3, no. 1 (1999): 50–58.

————. "Louis Lewandowski's Five Festival Preludes Opus 37 for Organ." *Journal of Jewish Music and Liturgy* 21 (1998–1999): 20–41.

————. *Orgel und Orgelmusik in deutsch-jüdischer Kultur*. Netiva: Wege zur deutsch-jüdischen Geschichte und Kultur 6. Hildesheim, Germany: Georg Olms, 2005.

Gernhardt, Klaus, Hubert Henkel, and Winfried Schrammek. *Orgelinstrumente und Harmoniums*. Musikinstrumentenmuseum der Universität Leipzig: Katalog 6. Wiesbaden: Breitkopf and Härtel, 1984.

Gerson-Kiwi, Edith. "Vocal Folk Polyphonies of the Western Orient in Jewish Tradition." *Yuval: Studies of the Jewish Music Research Centre* 1 (1968): 169–93.

Giovannini, Nobert, and Frank Moraw, eds. *Erinnertes Leben: Autobiographische Texte zur jüdischen Geschichte Heidelbergs*. Heidelberg: Wunderhorn, 1998.

Glatzer, Nahum, ed. *Leopold Zunz: Jude—Deutscher—Europäer: Ein jüdisches Gelehrtenschicksal des 19. Jahrhunderts in Briefen an Freunde*. Schriftenreihe wissenschaftlicher Abhandlungen des Leo Baeck Instituts 11. Tübingen: Mohr, 1964.

Glück, Sebastian. "The American Synagogue Organ: A Brief Account—The Jacksonian Period to the Progressive Era." *Tracker* 50, nos. 3–4 (2006): 98–110.

Goldberg, Geoffrey. "Neglected Sources for the Historical Study of Synagogue Music: The Prefaces to Louis Lewandowski's Kol Rinnah u'T'fillah and Toda W'simrah—Annotated Translations." *Musica Judaica* 11 (1989–1990): 28–57.

————. "The Training of *ḥazzanim* in Nineteenth-century Germany." *Yuval* 7 (2002): 299–367.

Gradenwitz, Peter. *The Music of Israel: From the Biblical Era to Modern Times*, 2d ed. Portland, Ore.: Amadeus, 1996.

————. "Musik israelischer Komponisten für die Orgel." In *"Niemand wollte mich hören,"* ed. Andor Izsák, 210–14.

————. *Musik zwischen Orient und Okzident: Eine Kulturgeschichte der Wechselbeziehungen*. Wilhelmshaven, Germany: Heinrichshofen, 1977.

Grellert, Mark, and Manfred Koob, eds. "Synagogen in Deutschland: Eine virtuelle Rekonstruktion," 2000. http://www.cad.architektur.tu-darmstadt.de/synagogen/inter/menu.html (accessed April 22, 2008).

Guttmann, Hermann Zvi. *Vom Tempel zum Gemeindezentrum: Synagogen im Nachkriegsdeutschland*. Frankfurt am Main: Athenäum, 1989.

Hahn, Joachim. *Erinnerungen und Zeugnisse jüdischer Geschichte in Baden-Württemberg*. Stuttgart: Theiss, 1988.

Hall, Stuart, David Held, and Don Hubert, eds. *Modernity: An Introduction to Modern Societies*. Cambridge, UK: Polity, 1995.

Hammer-Schenk, Harold. *Synagogen in Deutschland: Geschichte einer Baugattung im 19. und 20. Jahrhundert (1780–1933)*. Hamburger Beiträge zur Geschichte der deutschen Juden 8. 2 vols. Hamburg: Hans Christians Verlag, 1981.

Harrán, Don. "Dum Recordaremum Sion: Music in the Life and Thought of the Venetian Rabbi Leon Modena (1571–1648). *AJS Review* 23, no. 1 (1998): 17–62.

Heinrich, Johannes. "Orgelmusik und Orgelspiel im evangelischen Gottesdienst." In *Zur deutschen Orgelmusik des 19. Jahrhunderts*, ed. Hermann Busch and Michael Heinemann, 11–42. Sinzig, Germany: Studio, 1998.

Heskes, Irene. *Historic Contribution of Russian Jewry to Jewish Music*. New York: National Jewish Music Council, 1967.

Hieronymus, Bess Estelle. "Organ Music in the Worship Service of American Synagogues in the Twentieth Century." DMA diss., University of Texas–Austin, 1969.

Hilfrich-Kunjappo, Carola, and Stéphane Mosès, eds. *Zwischen den Kulturen: Theorie und Praxis des interkulturellen Dialogs*. Conditio Judaica: Studien und Quellen zur deutsch-jüdischen Literatur- und Kulturgeschichte 20. Tübingen: Max Niemeyer, 1997.

Hillsman, Walter. "Organs and Organ Music in Victorian Synagogues: Christian Intrusions or Symbols of Cultural Assimilation?" In *Christianity and Judaism*, ed. Diana Wood, 419–33.

Hirschberg, Hans. "Die Bedeutung der Orgel in Berliner Synagogen" (Appendix: Erwin Jospe, "Rückblick"; Werner Baer, "Meine Erinnerungen als Organist der Synagoge Prinzregentenstraße"). In *Synagogen in Berlin: Zur Geschichte einer zerstörten Architektur*, ed. Rolf Bothe, vol. 1, 184–95.

———. "Die Orgelwerke der neuen Synagoge zu Berlin." *Ars Organi* 44, no. 3 (1996): 139–47.

Hirshberg, Jehoash. "Heinrich Schalit and Paul-Ben-Haim in Munich." *Yuval: Studies of the Jewish Music Research Centre* 4 (1982): 131–50.

———. *Paul Ben-Haim: His Life and Works*. Jerusalem: Israeli Music Press, 1990.

Hobsbawm, Eric, and Terence Ranger, eds. *The Invention of Tradition*. New York: Cambridge University Press, 1983.

Hoffman, Lawrence A., and Janet R. Walton, eds. *Sacred Sound and Social Change: Liturgical Music in Jewish and Christian Experience*. Two Liturgical Traditions 3. Notre Dame, Ind.: University of Notre Dame Press, 1992.

Hofmeister, Adolph, ed. *Handbuch der musikalischen Literatur oder allgemeines systematisch geordnetes Verzeichnis der in Deutschland und in den angrenzenden Ländern erschienenen Musikalien und musikalischen Schriften, Abbildungen, und plastischen Darstellungen mit Anzeige der Verleger und Preise: Die von Anfang 1860 bis Ende 1867 erschienenen und neuaufgelegten musikalischen Werke enthaltend*. Leipzig: Friedrich Hofmeister, 1868.

Holde, Artur. *Jews in Music: From the Age of Enlightenment to the Mid-Twentieth Century*. New ed. prepared by Irene Heskes. New York: Bloch, 1974.

Honemeyer, Karl. *Thomas Müntzer und Martin Luther: Ihr Ringen um die Musik des Gottesdienstes; Untersuchungen zum "Deutzsch Kirchenampt" 1523*. Berlin: Merseburger, 1974.

Hutchinson, John, and Anthony D. Smith, eds. *Ethnicity*. New York: Oxford University Press, 1996.

Idelsohn, Abraham Zvi. *Jewish Music in Its Historical Development.* 1929. Reprint, New York: Dover, 1992.

———. "The Kol Nidre Tune." *Hebrew Union College Annual* 8–9 (1931): 493–509.

Izsák, Andor, ed. *"Niemand wollte mich hören . . .": Magrepha—Die Orgel in der Synagoge.* Schriftenreihe des europäischen Zentrums für jüdische Musik 5. Hannover: Freimann and Fuchs, 1999.

Jackman, Jarrell C., and Carla M. Borden, eds. *The Muses Flee Hitler: Cultural Transfer and Adaptation 1930–1945.* Washington, D.C.: Smithsonian Institution Press, 1983.

Jacobson, Joshua R. *Chanting the Hebrew Bible.* Philadelphia: Jewish Publication Society, 2002.

Jerke, Birgit. "Personen an der neuen Synagoge: Kurzbiographien." In *"Tuet auf die Pforten,"* ed. Hermann Simon and Jochen Boberg, 100–29.

Kartomi, Margaret J. "The Processes and Results of Musical Culture Contact: A Discussion of Terminology and Concepts." *Ethnomusicology* 25, no. 2 (1981): 227–49.

Kater, Michael H. *The Twisted Muse: Musicians and Their Music in the Third Reich.* New York: Oxford University Press, 1997.

Katz, Daniel S. "Biblische Kantillation und Musik der Synagoge: Ein Rückblick auf die ältesten Quellen." *Musiktheorie* 15, no. 1 (2000): 57–78.

———. "From Mount Sinai to the Year 6000: A Study of the Interaction of Oral Tradition and Written Sources in the Transmission of an Ashkenazi Liturgical Chant ('Akdamut')." *Rivista Internazionale di Musica Sacra* 20, no. 1 (1999): 175–206.

———. "A Prolegomenon to the Study of the Performance Practice of Synagogue Music Involving M'shor'rim." *Journal of Synagogue Music* 24, no. 2 (1995): 35–79.

Keren, Zvi. *Contemporary Israeli Music: Its Sources and Stylistic Development.* Bar Ilan, Israel: Bar Ilan University Press, 1980.

Kitov, Elijahu. *Das jüdische Jahr in Fest und Brauch.* 4 vols. Zurich: Morascha, 1987–1990.

Kleemann, Gotthilf. "Orgelbauer in Württemberg vom Ende des 18. bis zur Mitte des 19. Jahrhunderts." *Acta Organologica* 12 (1978): 148–95.

Krenek, Ernst. "Amerikas Einfluß auf eingewanderte Komponisten." In *Verdrängte Musik: Berliner Komponisten im Exil,* ed. Habakuk Traber and Elmar Weingarten, 99–109.

Krinsky, Carol Herselle. *Synagogues of Europe: Architecture, History, Meaning.* Cambridge, Mass.: MIT Press, 1985.

Krücken, Wolfgang, and Alexander Lohe, eds. *Wer baut, will bleiben: Simon Schlachet zu Ehren.* Aachen, Germany: Shaker, 1997.

Kwasnik, Walter. *Emile Rupp als Orgelreformer, Kirchenmusiker, und Mensch: Dem Begründer der Orgelreform zum Gedenken.* Das Musikinstrument 8. Frankfurt am Main: Verlag das Musikinstrument, 1967.

———. *Die Orgel der Neuzeit.* Cologne: Staufen, 1948.

La Motte-Haber, Helga de, ed. *Nationaler Stil und europäische Dimension in der Musik der Jahrhundertwende.* Darmstadt: Wissenschaftliche Buchgesellschaft, 1991.

Lachmann, Robert. *Gesänge der Juden auf der Insel Djerba.* Yuval Monograph Series 7. Jerusalem: Magnes, 1978.

Landesarchivverwaltung Rheinland-Pfalz and Landesarchiv Saarbrücken. *Dokumentation zur Geschichte der jüdischen Bevölkerung in Rheinland-Pfalz und im Saarland von 1800 bis 1945,* vol. 4. Koblenz, Germany: Landesarchivverwaltung Rheinland-Pfalz, 1974.

Landman, Leo. "The Office of the Medieval 'Hazzan.' " *Jewish Quarterly Review* 62, no. 3 (January 1972): 156–87.

Leach, Brenda Lynne. "Organ Music by Israeli Composers: A Tradition of Diversity." *Diapason* 1028 (1995): 12–13.

———. "Organs of Israel." *American Organist* 25, no. 4 (1991): 62–65.

Léon, Henry. *Historie des Juifs de Bayonne*. Paris: Armand Durlacher, 1893.

Lepper, Herbert. *Von der Emanzipation zum Holocaust: Die israelitische Synagogengemeinde zu Aachen 1801–1942*. Aachen: Verlag der Mayer'schen Buchhandlung, 1994.

Levi, Erik. *Musik in the Third Reich*. New York: St. Martin's, 1994.

Levi, Gerard, and Sabin Levi, *Organ Culture in Israel and Palestine*. Charleston, S.C.: BookSurge, 2005.

Lichtenstein, Sabine. "Abraham Jacob Lichtenstein: Eine jüdische Quelle für Carl Loewe und Max Bruch." *Die Musikforschung* 49, no. 4 (1996): 349–67.

List, George. "Distribution of a Melodic Formula: Diffusion or Polygenesis?" *Yearbook of the International Folk Music Council* 10 (1978): 33–53.

Lohe, Alexander. "Orgeln in der Aachener Synagoge: Eine historische Spurenlese." In *Wer baut, will bleiben: Simon Schlachet zu Ehren*, ed. Wolfgang Krücken and Alexander Lohe, 161–79.

Löwenstein, Steven M. "The 1840s and the Creation of the German-Jewish Religious Reform Movement." In *Revolution and Evolution 1848 in German-Jewish History*, ed. Werner E. Mosse, Arnold Paucker, and Reinhard Rürup, 255–99.

———. *Frankfurt on the Hudson: The German-Jewish Community of Washington Heights, 1933–1983, Its Structure and Culture*. Detroit: Wayne State University Press, 1989.

Lucas, Franz D., and Margret Heitmann. *Stadt des Glaubens: Geschichte und Kultur der Juden in Glogau*, 2d ed. Hildesheim, Germany: Georg Olms, 1991.

Machlis, Joseph. *Introduction to Contemporary Music*, 2d ed. New York: Norton, 1979.

Martini, Joachim, and Thomas Schinköth. *Jüdische Musikerinnen und Musiker in Leipzig und Frankfurt a.M. 1933–1945*. Leipzig: Klaus-Jürgen Kamprad, 1996.

Mendes-Flohr, Paul. *German Jews: A Dual Identity*. New Haven, Conn.: Yale University Press, 1999.

Mercer, Kobena. "Welcome to the Jungle: Identity and Diversity in Postmodern Politics." In *Identity: Community, Culture, Difference*, ed. Jonathan Rutherford, 43–71. London: Lawrence and Wishart, 1990.

Metz, Franz. "Orgelbau im Banat." *Ars Organi* 45, no. 3 (1997): 150–71.

Meyer, Hans, and Gerd Mentgen. *Sie sind mitten unter uns: Zur Geschichte der Juden in Ingelheim*. Ingelheim, Germany: Kügler, 1998.

Meyer, Herbert. "Max Sinzheimer: Ein Beitrag zur Mannheimer Musikgeschichte." *Mannheimer Hefte* 1 (1979): 14–15.

Meyer, Michael A. "German Jewry's Path to Normality and Assimilation: Complexities, Ironies, Paradoxes." In *Towards Normality? Acculturation and Modern German Jewry*, ed. Rainer Liedtke and David Rechter, 13–25. Schriftenreihe wissenschaftlicher Abhandlungen des Leo Baeck Instituts 68. Tübingen: Mohr Siebeck, 2003.

———. "Jews as Jews versus Jews as German: Two Historical Perspectives." *Leo Baeck Institute Yearbook* 36 (1991): xv–xxii.

———, Michael Brenner, Mordechai Breuer, and Michael Graetz, eds. *German-Jewish History in Modern Times*. 4 vols. New York: Columbia University Press, 1996.

Meyer-Siat, Pié. "Les orgues Wetzel dans les synagogues d'Alsace." *Saisons d'alsace* 55 (1975): 245–50.

Miletto, Gianfranco. *Die Heldenschilde des Abraham ben David Portaleone.* 2 vols. Frankfurt am Main: Peter Lang, 2002.

Molkenbur, Norbert, ed. *Jüdisches Musikschaffen und europäische Musikkultur: Bericht des Kolloquiums am 1. Oktober 1988 in Leipzig.* Leipzig: Edition Peters, 1989.

Moosmann, Ferdinand, and Rudi Schäfer. *Eberhard Friedrich Walcker (1794–1872): Zum Gedenken an seinen 200. Geburtstag am 3. Juli 1994.* Kleinblittersdorf, Germany: Musikwissenschaftliche Verlagsgesellschaft, 1994.

Mosse, Werner E., Arnold Paucker, and Reinhard Rürup, eds. *Revolution and Evolution 1848 in German-Jewish History.* Schriftenreihe wissenschaftlicher Abhandlungen des Leo Baeck Instituts 39. Tübingen: Mohr, 1981.

Nachama, Andreas, and Susanne Stähr. "Die vergessene Revolution: Der lange Weg des Louis Lewandowski." *Menora: Jahrbuch für deutsch-jüdische Geschichte* 3 (1992): 241–55.

Nagel, Joane. "Constructing Ethnicity: Creating and Recreating Ethnic Identity and Culture." In *Majority and Minority,* ed. Norman R. Yetman, 57–85.

Nash, Manning. "The Core Elements of Ethnicity." In *Ethnicity,* ed. John Hutchinson and Anthony D. Smith, 24–28.

Nettl, Bruno. *Theory and Method in Ethnomusicology.* London: Macmillan, 1964.

———. *The Western Impact on World Music: Change, Adaptation, and Survival.* New York: Schirmer, 1985.

Nettl, Paul. *Alte jüdische Spielleute und Musiker.* Prague: J. Flesch, 1923.

Obenaus, Herbert. "Orgeln in Synagogen." In *"Niemand wollte mich hören,"* ed. Andor Izsák, 156–60.

Oehme, Fritz. *Handbuch über ältere, neuere, und neueste Orgelwerke im Koenigreiche Sachsen.* 1889–1897. Reprint, Leipzig: Edition Peters, 1978.

Ostwald, Jacob. *"Um Spott und Hohn der Wittener loszuwerden . . .": Erinnerungen des jüdischen Lehrers und Kantors Jacob Ostwald 1863–1910.* Witten, Germany: Stadt Witten, 1994.

Papastergiadis, Nikos. *The Turbulence of Migration: Globalization, Deterritorialization, and Hybridity.* Cambridge, UK: Polity, 2000.

Pape, Uwe. *Die Orgelnde Stadt Braunschweig,* Norddeutsche Orgeln 2. n.p., 1966.

Peiser, Jacob. *Die Geschichte der Synagogen-Gemeinde zu Stettin: Eine Studie zur Geschichte des pommerschen Judentums,* 2d ed. Göttinger Arbeitskreis 37. Würzburg: Holzner, 1965.

Plavin, Zecharia. "Comparative Stylistic Analysis of Bloch's 'Jewish' and 'non-Jewish' Works." In *Proceedings of the First International Conference on Jewish Music,* ed. Steve Stanton, 95–101. London: City University, Department of Music, 1997.

Potter, Pamela Maxine. *Most German of the Arts: Musicology and Society from the Weimar Republic to the End of Hitler's Reich.* New Haven, Conn.: Yale University Press, 1998.

Prieberg, Fred K. *Musik im NS-Staat.* Frankfurt am Main: Fischer Taschenbuch, 1982.

Quoika, Rudolph. *Der Orgelbau in Böhmen und Mähren.* Der Orgelbau in Europa 2. Mainz: Rheingold, 1966.

Rahden, Till van. "Mingling, Marrying, and Distancing Jewish Integration in Wilhelminian Breslau and Its Erosion in Early Weimar Germany." In *Jüdisches Leben in der Weimarer Republik/Jews in Weimar Germany,* ed. Wolfgang Benz, Arnold Paucker, and Peter Pulzer, 197–222. Schriftenreihe wissenschaftlicher Abhandlungen des Leo Baeck Instituts 57. Tübingen: Mohr Siebeck, 1998.

Rautenstrauch, Johannes. *Luther und die Pflege der kirchlichen Musik in Sachsen (14.–19. Jahrhundert): Ein Beitr. zur Geschichte der katholischen Brüderschaften, der vor- u. nachreformator. Kurrenden, Schulchöre, u. Kantoreien Sachsens.* Hildesheim, Germany: Georg Olms, 1970.

Reichling, Alfred. "Zur Frage des 'konfessionellen Orgelbaus' im 19. und 20. Jahrhundert." In *Die Orgel im Dienst der Kirche: Gespräch aus ökumenischer Sicht: Bericht über das sechste Colloquium der Walcker-Stiftung für orgelwissenschaftliche Forschung in Verbindung mit dem Pontificio Istituto die Musica Sacra 8.–14. Oktober 1984 in Rom,* ed. Hans Heinrich Eggebrecht, 253–82. Murrhardt, Germany: Musikwissenschaftliche Verlags-Gesellschaft, 1985.

Rhode, Saskia. "Orgelprospekte in Synagogen: Skizzen zu einem bislang kaum bekannten Thema." In *"Niemand wollte mich hören,"* ed. Andor Izsák, 189–203.

Riedel, Friedrich W. "Die Ästhetik des Orgelklanges im 19. Jahrhundert." In *Zur Orgelmusik im 19. Jahrhundert: Tagungsbericht 3. Orgelsymposium Innsbruck, 9. bis 11.10.1981,* ed. Walter Salmen, 19–27.

Roden, Günter von, and Rita Vogedes. *Geschichte der Duisburger Juden.* Duisburger Forschungen: Schriftenreihe für Geschichte und Heimatkunde Duisburgs 34. 2 vols. Duisburg, Germany: Walter Braun, 1986.

Röder, Werner, and Herbert A. Strauss, eds. *Biographisches Handbuch der deutschsprachigen Emigration nach 1933.* New York: K. G. Saur, 1983.

Rothmüller, Aron Marko. *Die Musik der Juden: Versuch einer geschichtlichen Darstellung ihrer Entwicklung und ihres Wesens.* Zurich: Pan, 1951.

Rothschild, Lothar. *Im Strom der Zeit: Hundert Jahre israelitische Gemeinde St. Gallen.* St. Gallen, Switzerland: Volksstimme, 1963.

Rozenblit, Marsha L. "Jewish Ethnicity in a New Nation-State: The Crisis of Identity in the Austrian Republic." In *In Search of Jewish Community: Jewish Identities in Germany and Austria 1918–1933,* ed. Michael Brenner and Derek J. Penslar, 134–54.

Rürup, Reinhard. "An Appraisal of German-Jewish Historiography." *Leo Baeck Institute Yearbook* 35 (1990): xv–xxiv.

Saalschütz, Joseph Levin. *Geschichte und Würdigung der Musik bei den Hebräern, im Verhältniss zur sonstigen Ausbildung dieser Kunst in alter und neuer Zeit, nebst einem Anhang über die Hebräische Orgel.* Berlin: G. Fincke, 1829.

Sabaneev, Leonid Leonidovich. "Die nationale jüdische Schule in der Musik." [Essay.] Vienna: Universal-Edition, 1927.

Sacks, Adama J. "Kurt Singer's Shattered Hopes." *Leo Baeck Institute Yearbook* 48 (2003): 191–203.

Salmen, Walter. *"Denn die Fiedel macht das Fest": Jüdische Musikanten und Tänzer vom 13. bis 20. Jahrhundert.* Innsbruck: Edition Helbling, 1991.

———. "Die Orgelsynagoge 1810–1900." In *"Niemand wollte mich hören,"* ed. Andor Izsák, 134–46.

———, ed. *Zur Orgelmusik im 19. Jahrhundert: Tagungsbericht 3. Orgelsymposium Innsbruck, 9. bis 11.10.1981.* Innsbrucker Beiträge zur Musikwissenschaft 9. Innsbruck: Musikverlag Helbling, 1983.

Schaeffer, Stephen Gleim. "The Organ Works of Darius Milhaud." DMA thesis, University of Cincinnati, 1977.

Schalit, Michael. *Heinrich Schalit: The Man and His Music.* Livermore, Calif.: Author, 1979.

Schermerhorn, Richard. "Ethnicity and Minority Groups." In *Ethnicity*, ed. John Hutchinson and Anthony D. Smith, 17–18.

Schinköth, Thomas. *Jüdische Musiker in Leipzig 1855–1945*. Altenburg, Germany: Klaus-Jürgen Kamprad, 1994.

Schleifer, Eliyahu. "Jewish Liturgical Music from the Bible to Hasidim." In *Sacred Sound and Social Change: Liturgical Music in Jewish and Christian Experience*, ed. Lawrence A. Hoffman and Janet R. Walton, 13–59.

Schüler-Springorum, Stefanie. "Assimilation and Community Reconsidered: The Jewish Community in Königsberg, 1871–1914." *Jewish Social Studies* 5, no. 3 (1999): 104–31.

Schwarz, Berthold, ed. *500 Jahre Orgeln in Berliner evangelischen Kirchen*. Veröffentlichung der Gesellschaft der Orgelfreunde 134. Berlin: Pape, 1991.

Seip, Achim. "Die Orgel im Leben und Werk von Herman Berlinski." *Orgel International* 3, no. 1 (1999): 26–31.

———. *Die Orgelbauwerkstatt Dreymann in Mainz*. Lauffen am Neckar: Rensch, 1993.

Seligmann, Caesar. *Geschichte der jüdischen Reformbewegung von Mendelssohn bis zur Gegenwart*. Frankfurt am Main: Julius Kauffmann, 1922.

Sendrey, Alfred. *Bibliography of Jewish Music*. 1951. Reprint, New York: Kraus, 1969.

———. *Musik in Alt-Israel*. Leipzig: Deutscher Verlag für Musik, 1970.

Seroussi, Edwin. "Schir Hakawod and the Liturgical Music Reforms in the Sephardi Community in Vienna, ca. 1880–1925: A Study of Change in Religious Music." PhD diss., University of California, 1988.

———. *Spanish-Portuguese Synagogue Music in Nineteenth-century Reform Sources from Hamburg: Ancient Tradition in the Dawn of Modernity*. Yuval Monograph Series 11. Jerusalem: Magnes, 1996.

Shiloah, Amnon. *Jewish Musical Traditions*. Jewish Folklore and Anthropology Series. Detroit: Wayne State University Press, 1992.

———, and Eric Cohen. "The Dynamics of Change in Jewish Oriental Ethnic Music in Israel." *Ethnomusicology* 27, no. 2 (1983): 227–51.

Shmueli, Herzl. *Higgajon Bechinnor: Betrachtungen zum Leierspiel des Jehudah ben Joseph Arjeh Moscato*. Tel Aviv: Neografika, 1953.

Sills, David L. "Bloch Manuscripts at the University of California." *Notes* 42, no. 1 (1985): 7–21.

Simon, Hermann, and Jochen Boberg, eds. *"Tuet auf die Pforten": Die Neue Synagoge 1866–1995: Begleitbuch zur ständigen Ausstellung der Stiftung "Neue Synagoge Berlin—Centrum Judaicum."* Berlin: Stiftung Neue Synagoge Berlin–Centrum Judaicum, 1995.

Skolnik, Jonathan. "Dissimilation and the Historical Novel: Hermann Sinsheimer's Maria Nunnez." *Leo Baeck Institute Yearbook* 43 (1998): 225–37.

Slobin, Mark. *Chosen Voices: The Story of the American Cantorate*. Music in American Life. Chicago: University of Illinois Press, 1989.

———. *Subcultural Sounds: Micromusics of the West*. Music/Culture. Hanover, N.H.: University Press of New England, 1993.

Smets, Paul. *Die Orgelregister: Ihr Klang und Gebrauch*, 2d ed. Mainz: Rheingold, 1937.

Sorkin, David. "Emancipation and Assimilation: Two Concepts and Their Application to German-Jewish History." *Leo Baeck Institute Yearbook* 35 (1990): 17–33.

———. "Religious Reforms and Secular Trends in German-Jewish Life: An Agenda for Research." *Leo Baeck Institute Yearbook* 48 (1995): 169–84.

Sponheuer, Bernd: "Musik auf einer 'kulturellen und physischen Insel': Musik als Über-lebensmittel im jüdischen Kulturbund 1933–1941." In *Musik in der Emigration 1933–1945: Verfolgung, Vertreibung, Rückwirkung*, ed. Horst Weber, 108–35.

Stokes, Martin. "Introduction: Ethnicity, Identity, and Music." In *Ethnicity, Identity, and Music: The Musical Construction of Place*, ed. Martin Stokes, 1–27. New York: Berg, 1994.

Summereder, Roman. *Aufbruch der Klänge: Materialen, Bilder, Dokumente zur Orgelreform und Orgelkultur im 20. Jahrhundert*. Innsbruck: Edition Helbling, 1995.

Tarshish, Allan. "The Charleston Organ Case." *American Jewish Historical Quarterly* 54, no. 4 (1965): 411–49.

Theobald, Hans-Wolfgang. *Der Ostheimer Orgelbauer Johann Georg Markert und sein Werk: Ein Beitrag zur Geschichte des Orgelbaus in Thüringen im 19. Jahrhundert*. Würzburger musikhistorische Beiträge 12. Tutzing, Germany: Hans Schneider, 1990.

Timm, Erika, and Gustav Adolf Beckmann. *Historische jiddische Semantik: Die Bibelüber-setzungssprache als Faktor der Auseinanderentwicklung des jiddischen und des deutschen Wortschatzes*. Tübingen: Niemeyer, 2005.

Traber, Habakuk, and Elmar Weingarten, eds. *Verdrängte Musik: Berliner Komponisten im Exil*. Berlin: Argon, 1987.

Tremmel, Erich. "Jüdisches Musikleben in Waldeck im 19. und frühen 20. Jahrhun-dert: Versuch einer Rekonstruktion am Beispiel Korbach." *Geschichtsblätter für Waldeck* 77 (1989): 209–16.

Trepp, Leo. *Der jüdische Gottesdienst: Gestalt und Entwicklung*. Stuttgart: Kohlhammer, 1992.

Unverricht, Hubert, ed. *Der Caecilianismus: Anfänge—Grundlagen—Wirkungen: Interna-tionales Symposium zur Kirchenmusik des 19. Jahrhunderts*. Eichstätter Abhandlungen zur Musikwissenschaft 5. Tutzing, Germany: Hans Schneider, 1988.

Viktora, Adam. "Tschechische Synagogenorgeln." In *"Niemand wollte mich hören,"* ed. Andor Izsák, 172–79.

Voigt, Lore M. I. "Christian Friedrich Voigt (1803–1868) und Karl Heinrich Voigt (1845–1906): Leben und Werk." *Acta Organologica* 24 (1994): 59–96.

Volkov, Shulamit. "Jüdische Assimilation und jüdische Eigenart im deutschen Kaiser-reich: Ein Versuch." *Geschichte und Gesellschaft* 9, no. 3 (1983): 331–48.

Wachten, Johannes. "David Wolffsohn und die Kölner Judenschaft." In *Köln und das rheinische Judentum: Festschrift Germania Judaica, 1959–1984*, ed. Jutta Bohnke-Kollwitz, 300–307. Cologne: J. P. Bachem, 1984.

Wade, Bonnie C. "When West Met East: The Organ as an Instrument of Culture." In *Festschrift Christoph-Hellmut Mahling*, ed. Axel Beer, Kristina Pfarr, and Wolfgang Ruf, vol. 2, 1479–84.

Waldhoff, Johannes. *Die Geschichte der Juden in Steinheim*. Paderborn, Germany: Heimatverein Steinheim, 1980.

Walk, Joseph. *Kurzbiographien zur Geschichte der Juden 1918–1945*. New York: K. G. Saur, 1988.

Wallerstein, Immanuel. "Culture as Ideological Battleground." *Theory, Culture, and Soci-ety* 7 (1990): 31–55.

Walter, Rudolf: "Die Orgelmusik der Caecilianer." In *Der Caecilianismus*, ed. Hubert Unverricht, 163–82.

Weber, Horst, ed. *Musik in der Emigration 1933–1945: Verfolgung, Vertreibung, Rückwirkung*. Stuttgart: J. B. Metzler, 1994.

Werner, Eric. *The Sacred Bridge: The Interdependence of Liturgy and Music in Synagogue and Church during the First Millenium*. New York: D. Dobson/Columbia University Press, 1959.

———. *A Voice Still Heard: The Sacred Songs of the Ashkenazic Jews*. Leo Baeck Institute Series. University Park: Pennsylvania State University Press, 1976.

Werner, Steffen. *Die 2. babylonische Gefangenschaft: Das Schicksal der Juden im europäischen Osten seit 1941*. Pfullingen, Germany: privately printed, 1990.

Wilhelmus, Wolfgang. *Juden in Vorpommern*. Schwerin, Germany: Ingo Koch, 1996.

Wilke, Carsten. "Der Gießener Rabbiner Dr. Benedikt Levi (1806–1899)." *Ashkenas* 16, no. 1 (2006): 37–75.

Williams, Peter. *The Organ in Western Culture, 750–1250*. Cambridge Studies in Medieval and Renaissance Music. New York: Cambridge University Press, 1993.

Wilson, Louise Craig. "Herman Berlinski at 85." *American Organist* 29, no. 9 (1995): 66–67.

Wininger, Salomon, ed. *Grosse jüdische national-Biographie mit mehr als 8000 Lebensbeschreibungen namhafter jüdischer Männer und Frauen aller Zeiten und Länder: Ein Nachschlagewerk für das jüdische Volk und dessen Freunde*. 7 vols. Cernauti, Ukraine: Druck Orient, 1925–1936.

Wittelsberger, Manfred. *Die Orgelbauerfamilien Engers und Schlaad in Waldlaubersheim bei Bingen: Ein Beitrag zur Orgelbaugeschichte am Mittelrhein*. Studien zur Landes- und Sozialgeschichte der Musik 12. Munich: Katzbichler, 1994.

Wohnhaas, Theodor. "Zur Geschichte der Orgeln in Berliner Synagogen." *Jahrbuch für die Geschichte Mittel- und Ostdeutschlands* 26 (1977): 195–201.

Wood, Diana, ed. *Christianity and Judaism: Papers Read at the 1991 Summer Meeting and the 1992 Winter Meeting of the Ecclesiastical History Society*. Studies in Church History 29. Cambridge, Mass.: Published for the Ecclesiastical History Society by Blackwell, 1992.

Yasser, Joseph. "The Magrepha of the Herodian Temple: A Five-fold Hypothesis." *Journal of the American Musicological Society* 13 (1960): 24–42.

Yetman, Norman R., ed. *Majority and Minority: The Dynamics of Race and Ethnicity in American Life*. Boston: Allyn and Bacon, 1999.

INDEX

Abraham ben Isaac of Gerona, 175
abuv, 84
acculturation, 80, 103, 201, 205,
    214–215
  concept of, 8–9, 223*n*28
  See also assimilation
Ackermann, Aron, 36
Adler, Hugo Chaim, 44–45, 192, 195, 200
  organ works, 136–138, 144
Adler, Samuel, 44–45
Ahot Ketannah, 102, 175, 177, 180, 182
Akdamut Millin, 102, 111, 123–125,
    127–129, 242*n*52
Alain, Jehan, 110, 250*n*38
Alemanno, Johanan ben Isaac, 12
Alexander, Haim, 203, 205–207, 209,
    251*n*57
  Die westöstliche Brücke, 207–208
Alkabetz, Shlomo Halevi, 141
Alsatian organ reform movement, 55–59,
    63–64
Altman, Ludwig, 44, 93, 96, 150–151
  as organist, 97–98, 148, 195
  in emigration, 190–191
Altmann, Richard, 153
Alzey, 34
Amsterdam, 18, 204–205
Angster, Josef, 74, 82
anti-Semitism, 216, 253*n*11
Arendt, Hannah, 132
Asher, Jacob ben, 17

assimilation, 25, 43, 91, 132, 147, 196, 218
  concept of, 8–9, 100, 216, 218–219,
    223*n*24, 223*n*28
  of German-Jews, 9, 74, 214–217
  Haskalah and, 27
  linguistic, 27, 174, 216
  musical 91, 104, 131, 134–135, 156,
    162, 168, 186–187, 213, 218
Augsburg, 234*n*97
Auschwitz, 145
Austin Organs, 202

Bach, Johann Sebastian, 57, 91, 109, 135, 207
  organ works, 94, 95, 103, 133, 148–152,
    170, 192
Bad Buchau, 34
Baeck, Leo, 196
Baer, Werner, 69–70, 93
Barekhu, 113, 123, 127, 128
Bartók, Béla, 132, 144, 161
Bass, Shabbetai ben Joseph, 23
bassoon (instrument), 19, 195
Bayonne, 43, 231*n*56
Bayreuth, 51
Beer, Aaron, 164
Beer, Jacob Herz, 29–30
Beethoven, Ludwig van, 109, 113, 245*n*124
Benfeld, 74, 234*n*97
Ben-Haim, Paul, 139, 202–203, 206
Ben-Shabetai, Ari, 210
Berkeley, California, 190

Berlin, 29, 44, 47, 59, 68, 93, 171, 205, 208, 234*n*98
  Fasanenstraße synagogue in, 73, 150, 151
  Friedenstempel in, 151, 152, 171–172
  Heidereuthergasse synagogue in, 31, 35
  Kulturbund in, 146, 148
  New Synagogue in, 34–38, 46, 58–60, 92, 96–99, 150–152
  prayer rooms in, 33
  Prinzregentenstraße synagogue in, 43–44, 69–70, 72, 94, 149, 151
  Reform Congregation (Johannisstraße) in, 33, 51, 65
Berlinski, Herman, 80, 83–88, 191, 199
  in emigration, 196–198, 200
  From the World of My Father, 197–198
Beuthen, 33
Bible, 11, 14, 15, 16, 84, 156, 225*n*17
  Genesis, 11, 155
  Job, 11, 157
  Lamentations, 157
  Numbers, 113
  Psalms, 11, 23, 111, 123, 163, 164, 207
  Song of Solomon, 175
  Song of Songs, 12, 141
Bielefeld, 34, 133, 169
Binder (organist), 50
Bingen, 32, 170, 235*n*116
Birnbaum, Eduard, 110, 137, 154
Blarr, Oskar Gottlieb, 207
Bloch, Ernest, 104–105, 195, 239*n*1
Boëllmann, Léon, 133, 148, 153
Bohlman, Philip, 136, 205
Bossi, Marco Enrico, 133
Boston, Massachusetts, 55, 193, 195
Braunschweig, 48, 110, 163,
Breil firm, 47
Breslau. *See* Wrocław
Brussels, 196
Buchau. *See* Bad Buchau
Buchholz firm, 51
Buck, Heinrich, 234*n*97
Budapest, 74–75
Buffalo, New York, 192–193
Bunk, Gerard, 133, 243*n*79
Buxtehude, Dietrich, 95, 103, 148, 152

Caecilianism, 118–119, 121, 130–131, 144
cantillation, 7, 102, 103, 105, 154, 156–157, 205, 246*n*145

and organ music, 155–159, 161, 166, 175, 177, 194
and Reform Judaism, 28, 156
Castelnuovo-Tedesco, Mario, 193, 249*n*25
Cavaillé-Coll, Aristide, 64
Cerini, Hermann, 152, 153
Charleston, South Carolina, 42, 231*n*54
chorale prelude, 110, 114, 118, 121, 173, 185, 215
Christian-Jewish relations. *See* Jewish-Christian relations
Cincinnati, Ohio, 100, 251*n*52
clarinet (instrument), 19
clavicordo, 14
Cologne, 43, 91, 136
Conservative Judaism, 188, 190
Consolo, Federico, 194
Conze, Johannes, 247*n*158
Corcos, Samuel ben Abraham, 24
Cosel, 33
cymbal (instrument), 13, 15, 23

Danzig, 63
Darmstadt, 35, 206
David, Johann Nepomuk, 183–184, 248*n*179
Deutsch, David, 37
Deutsch, Moritz, 111, 130, 137, 138, 143, 216
  Zwölf Präludien für Orgel oder Pianoforte, 102, 112–121, 131
dissimilation, 9, 145, 174, 214, 216–219, 253*n*7
Dorfman, Josef, 210
Dortmund, 58, 171
  St. Gertrudis in, 46–47
  synagogue in 46, 79–80, 133
Dreier, Bernhard, 247*n*158
Dresden, 33, 47, 151

East Aurora, New York, 192, 193
Ebing (organist), 171
Ehrenberg, Samuel Meyer, 29
Ehrenreich, Eliezer, 19
Ehrenreich, Nathan, 249*n*24
Ehrlich, Hermann, 55–56
Eleazar ben Kalir, 137
Elias, Abraham M., 42
emancipation, 9, 25, 27–29, 110, 172, 213, 214, 219

emigration, 162, 169, 175
concept of, 187–188
Palestine, 188, 200–202
United States of America, 188, 189–191
Erben, Henry, 231n53
Essen, 76, 155, 171
Eßlingen, 59
ethnicity, 5, 198, 222n5

Faerber, Horst, 153
Faisst, Immanuel Gottlieb, 109, 110,
240n19
Faxon, George H., 195
Feith firm, 234n97
Felber, Erwin, 6
Fibonacci. *See* Pisano, Leonardi
fiddle, 15, 17
Fischer, Michael Gotthard, 109
Fischer (organist), 50
flute (instrument), 11, 19, 84, 195, 197
Förster und Nicolaus firm, 234n97
Fortner, Wolfgang, 206, 209
Franckel, Simon, 18
Frankel, Zacharias, 33
Frankfurt am Main, 23, 149, 150, 152,
153, 173
activities of Würzburger in, 162
Great Synagogue in, 52–55
Kulturbund in, 148, 169
Philantropin in, 31, 190
Second Rabbinical Conference in, 32, 90
Westend Synagogue in, 47, 169
Franz, Robert, 133
Frauenzimmern, 52
Freed, Isadore, 194, 250n27
Freiburg im Breisgau, 206, 236n125
Freudenthal, Joseph, 194
Friedmann, Aron, 125
Fromm, Herbert, 96, 134, 140, 147,
169–170
activities in Kulturbund, 169
in emigration, 191–193
as organist, 150, 151, 153
Suite of Organ Pieces on Hebraic Motifs,
194–195
Frotscher, Gotthold, 130, 162
Fürth, 234n97

Geiger, Abraham, 35
Gelbrun, Artur, 209, 251n57

Gerson-Kiwi, Edith, 19
Gießen, 32, 234n97
Gilboa, Jacob, 210
Gliwice (Gleiwitz), 33
Głogów (Głogau), 33
Gniezno (Gnesen), 96
Gonzaga, Ludovico III, 13
Gradenwitz, Peter, 208, 217
Graziano, Abraham Joseph Solomon, 25
Grunnemann, Peter, 171
Guilmant, Alexandre, 133, 151
Gurlitt, Wilibald, 69
Guttmann, Oskar, 90, 140, 195

halakhah, 4, 17, 23, 35, 42, 89–92
halil, 84
Hallel, 56, 94, 111, 122, 123, 124, 128
Hama, 15
Hamburg, 18, 31, 58, 107, 148, 204
First Temple, 29–30, 188
New Israelite Temple Association,
29–30
Obernstraße synagogue, 43, 152, 153
Händel, Georg Friedrich, 135, 147, 148,
149, 150, 151, 152, 153
harp (instrument), 11, 14, 42, 84,
224n11
Hartmann, Ludwig, 130
Haskalah, 27, 214, 215, 228n1
Hasselbeck, Hans, 137
Haydn, Joseph, 19
ḥazzanut, 90, 106, 121, 137, 142, 143,
172, 174, 183, 204
Heidelberg, 33, 99, 202
Heine, Salomon, 30
Hepner, Anita, 139
Herzl, Theodor, 43
Hesse, Adolf Friedrich, 109, 119
Hildesheim, 33, 51
Hindemith, Paul, 193, 194, 197, 206
Hirsch, Martha Sommer, 94, 152, 153,
169, 190
Hirschberg, Siegmund, 46
Hirschberg, Hans, 46, 68, 69, 97
Hlučín, 33
Hohenems, 42
Holtschneider, Carl, 133
Hrádec Králové, 83
Hultschin. *See* Hlučín
hydraulis, 11

Ibn Gaon, Joshua ben Abraham, 15
iconography, 12, 14–17
Idelsohn, Abraham Zvi, 6, 127, 128, 156
  Hebräisch-orientalischer Melodienschatz, 104,
    134, 140, 142, 143, 144, 164, 166,
    177, 179
identity, 25, 27, 31, 74, 99, 104, 105, 148,
    186, 217, 218
  concept of, 5
  emigration and, 187, 197
  German-Jewish, 5–9, 110, 111, 132,
    133, 145, 147, 187, 198, 208,
    213–215, 219
improvisation (organ), 25, 49, 92, 94, 95,
    121, 122, 138, 162, 170, 180, 199
instruments. *See abuv*; bassoon; clarinet;
    clavicordo; cymbal; fiddle; flute; *halil*;
    harp; hydraulis; kettledrums; *kinnor*;
    lute; lyre; *ma't*; *magrepha*; *minim*; *nāy*;
    nebel; *neqqāra*; organ; *organum*; *Rausch-
    pfeife*; reed organ; *shofar*; *'uğav*; viola
    da gamba
Introduction zur Thodenfeier, 102, 107–110,
    116, 184
Iranyi, Gabriel, 209–210
Isaac ben Samuel of Dampierre, 113

Jacobson, Israel, 28–29
Jacoby, Hanoch, 206
Jaffa, 203
Jaffe, Mordecai ben Abraham, 164
Jahnn, Hans Henny, 69
Janowski, Max, 140, 155
Jerusalem, 3, 30, 73, 157, 180, 202, 207, 210
Jewish-Christian relations, 31, 32, 33, 56,
    74, 83–84, 89–93, 95, 98–100, 104,
    110, 112, 133, 191, 195, 198, 202,
    219–220
Jewish Enlightenment. See *Haskalah*
Jewish music, 5, 86–87, 101, 103–106
  definitions of, 6–8
Jews and Christianity, 3, 7, 17, 18, 24, 25,
    28, 30, 43, 73, 96, 120, 137, 156,
    162, 172, 173, 185, 214, 215
John, Hanns, 140
Joseph II (emperor), 20
Jospe, Erwin, 69, 94, 149, 151, 152
Judah ben Isaac, 13
Jüdischer Kulturbund, 4, 65, 145–148,
    153, 186, 189, 217–218, 245n123,
    246n131

Kabbalah, 85–86, 210
Kaliningrad, 45, 133, 154, 157, 206
Kaltschmidt firm, 77
Karg-Elert, Sigfrid, 196
Karlsruhe, 47, 99, 237n15
Kartomi, Margaret, 8
Keila (Kegel), 52
Keller (organist), 59
kettledrums, 17
kinnor, 13, 14, 84, 224n11
Kirschner, Emanuel, 63, 137–139
Kley, Eduard, 29, 107
Koblenz, 33
Koehnken firm, 251n52
Kol Nidrei, 102, 113, 123, 127–128, 137,
    138, 149, 152, 163–168, 176,
    247n154
Königgrätz. *See* Hradec Králové
Königsberg. *See* Kalinigrad
Kornitzer, Leon, 134, 152
Kosel. *See* Cosel
Kotykiewicz, T. (reed organ builder), 39
Krapkowice (Krappitz), 33
Kristallnacht, 4, 44–46, 171, 184, 186
Krützfeld, Wilhelm, 46
Kuhn, Eberhard, 52–53
Kulturbund Deutscher Juden. *See* Jüdischer
    Kulturbund
Kwasnik, Walter, 49, 64

Lambsheim, 55
Lampel, Max, 202
Landsberger, Julius, 35
Leichtentritt, Hugo, 134, 151, 243n80
Leipzig, 31, 34, 196
  First Jewish Synod in, 38, 41, 47, 111
Lemle, Heinrich, 89
Levi, Benedikt, 32
Levi, Josef, 136, 137
Levi, Moses, 124
Lewandowski, Louis, 38, 63, 126, 131, 132,
    134, 137, 139, 143, 154, 185, 205,
    216, 229–230n35
  Fünf Fest-Präludien, 102, 121, 122,
    126–130, 137, 138
  Toda W'simrah, 122, 124, 125, 127, 129,
    164, 165, 166
  views on organ in synagogue, 35–37, 41
Lewin-Kassewitz, Johanne-Lise, 99
Liber Usualis, 125
Liebermann, Eliezer, 30, 237n4

Lichey, Reinhold, 247*n*158
Lichtenstern, Paul, 98, 153
Liszt, Franz, 75
Lobkowicz family, 17
London, 18, 43, 73
Löwe, S. G., 35
Ludwigsburg, 52, 234*n*97
lute, 11, 14, 15, 17, 19
Luther, Martin, 24, 207
Lyons, 34, 196
lyre, 13, 84, 224*n*11

Maerz firm, 52
Magdeburg, 35, 112
magrepha, 12, 14, 15, 33, 210
Mahler, Gustav, 7
Mahler, Meir, 23, 227*n*55
Mahrenholz, Christhard, 69
Mai, Alfred, 151
Mainz, 33
Maisky, Valery, 202
Mandeville, James M., 231*n*53
Mannheim, 44, 52–53, 55, 136, 138
Mantua, 12, 13, 14, 17
Maria Theresia (empress), 24
Mariamin, 15
ma't, 11
Meir ben Baruch of Rothenburg, 163
Meir ben Isaac Nehorai of Worms, 123
Meisel, Mordecai ben Samuel, 23
Melzer, Josef, 78
Mendelssohn, Moses, 27, 28, 225*n*17
Mendelssohn-Bartholdy, Felix, 7, 121, 127, 128
    organ works of, 119, 149, 150, 152, 153, 173
meshorer, 18–19, 22, 23, 32
Messiaen, Olivier, 143, 197, 250*n*38
Meyerbeer, Giacomo 7, 29
Mikulov, 111
minim, 14, 225*n*17
Mishnah, 11, 12
mode, 85, 105, 116, 127, 157, 160, 177, 184, 210
    Ahavah Rabbah (shtayger), 85, 167, 182
    Adonai Malakh (shtayger), 85, 118, 142
    Magen Avot (shtayger), 85
    maqām , 141, 157, 184, 245*n*113
    shtayger, 85, 106, 125, 140, 160, 184, 194, 195

Modena, Leon, 19, 24, 25, 30
Morosini, Giulio, 19, 24
Moscato, Judah ben Joseph, 13–14, 224*n*11
Moscow, 144
Munich, 45–46, 47, 52, 122, 137–139, 149, 169
Murray Harris firm, 233*n*85

Nadel, Arno, 96, 145, 151, 154–155
    Passacaglia für Orgel, 102, 155–162
National Socialism, 4, 6, 64, 93, 97, 140, 145–147, 169, 187
    dissimilation and, 216, 217
    organ and, 45, 46, 69, 232*n*65
Naumbourg, Samuel, 63
nāy, 11
nebel, 14
Neisse. *See* Nysa
neqqāra. *See* kettledrums
Nettl, Bruno, 8, 106
Neustadt. *See* Prudnik
New York, 43, 141, 169, 188, 190, 191, 192, 194, 197, 199
Nikolsburg. *See* Mikulov
Noack firm, 251*n*52
Noehren, Robert, 195
Norzi, Samuel Isaac, 24–25
Nowakowsky, David, 137, 244*n*96
Nysa, 33

Odessa, 34, 137
Oesterreichisch-ungarische Cantoren-Zeitung, 57, 120, 121
Offenbach, Jacques, 7
Opole, 33
Oppeln. *See* Opole
organ. *See also* organ stops
    Barker lever, 55
    bellows, 12, 13, 15, 33, 99, 100, 224*n*3
    casing, 46, 69, 78, 87–88, 231*n*53
    combination actions (couplers, pistons, *Walze*, etc.), 58, 63, 64
    cone chest, 52, 53, 55,
    console, 45, 58, 64, 80
    disposition, 9, 43, 44, 49–55, 57–60, 62–66, 68–70, 72, 80, 83–88, 232*n*71
    electric action, 69, 252*n*60
    electropneumatic action, 59, 83–84
    façade, 9, 53, 65, 73, 74, 79
    Grundtönigkeit, 49, 55, 57, 63, 232*n*71

organ (*continued*)
  mechanical action, 59, 69, 87–88,
    252*n*60
  pouch chest, 69
  placement of, 39, 44, 49, 73–74
  portative, 14, 15, 17, 18, 23,
    225–226*n*38, 226*n*55
  positive, 16, 17, 22
  registration, 49, 50, 57, 85, 86, 90, 97,
    98, 212, 128, 136, 202, 235*n*116
  registration aids, 52, 54, 58, 63, 64
  spring chest, 53, 233*n*79, 233*n*81
  Werkprinzip, 69
  windchest system, 52, 79, 233*n*79,
    235*n*116
  wind pressure, 63
organ revival, 68, 69, 72, 135, 162, 183,
    235*n*124
organ stops, 44, 49, 50, 51, 52, 54, 57, 58,
    59, 64, 65, 68, 69, 72, 74, 86, 87, 97,
    195, 202, 203
  Aeoline, 54, 60, 62, 69
  Bifra, 62, 63
  Bourdon, 17, 51, 54, 60, 62, 64, 66
  Clarinet, 53, 54, 57, 61, 62, 67, 86, 195
  Cromhorne, 195
  Doppelflöte, 60, 62, 63
  flutes, 51, 53, 54, 60, 62, 63, 64, 66, 70
  free reeds, 55, 57, 233*n*85
  Gamba, 53, 53, 54, 60, 62, 69, 70
  Gedackts, 51, 53, 54, 60, 62, 63, 69, 70
  Harp, 66, 87
  Ḥazozerah , 87
  Konzertflöte, 60, 62, 70, 86
  mixtures, 13, 58, 64, 69, 72, 79, 85–86,
    87
  Oboe, 61, 71, 86
  Physharmonika, 53–55, 233*n*85
  principals, 51, 53, 55, 60, 62, 66, 70, 86,
    87
  reeds, 12, 64, 69, 87,
  Salicional, 51, 53, 60, 62, 66, 69, 70
  Shofar, 87
  Spanish Trumpets, 86
  Stentor Flute, 63
  Stentor Gamba, 63
  Synthematophon, 59, 60, 68
  Trombone, 57
  Trumpet, 57, 64
  Unda Maris, 66, 69, 70, 87

  Violon, 51, 53, 54, 60, 62, 63, 66, 70
  Vox Humana, 61, 69, 70
  woodwinds, 63
  Zartgedeckt, 69, 70
organum, 13
Orgelbewegung. See organ revival
Orthodoxy, 28, 111, 132, 189, 204, 214,
    217
  organ and, 37, 42, 43, 47, 200, 215
Osborn, Max, 154
Osenbrunner, Robert, 137, 149
Ostwald, Jacob, 100

Pachelbel, Johann, 192
Palestine, 4, 11, 15, 186, 201–204, 206,
    245*n*123, 249*n*10
  emigration to, 46, 184, 187–188
paraliturgy, 34, 95, 103, 148,
Paris, 196–197, 204
Paumann, Konrad, 13
Pels, Samuel, 100
Peretz, Isaac Leib (Yitskhok Leybush), 197
Phillipson, Ludwig, 35
Pico della Mirandola, Giovanni, 12
Pisano, Leonardi, 210, 253*n*81
piyyut, 104, 123-25, 135–137
pizmon, 103, 113, 175
pluralism, 219, 254*n*18
Portaleone, Abraham ben David, 14
Prague, 18, 20–25, 78, 225–226*n*38
Prinz, Joachim, 216
Prudnik, 33
Prussia, 29, 48, 57, 99, 128, 148
psalmody, 85, 103, 105

Rabe, Paul, 59, 232*n*78
Racibórz, 33, 35
Rathaus, Karol , 217
Ratibor. *See* Racibórz
Rauschpfeife (instrument), 17
recitation, 23, 93, 94, 125, 129
recitative, 41, 55, 56, 83–84, 85–86, 93,
    106, 115, 118, 123, 135, 142, 161,
    172–174, 185
reed organ, 33, 34, 39, 42, 43, 47, 48, 107,
    130, 131, 148, 196, 205
Reform Judaism, 27–34, 39, 86, 198, 215,
    219
Reger, Max, 151, 152, 162, 182
Reimann, Wolfgang, 44, 94, 232*n*78

Reubke, Julius, 119
Rheinberger, Joseph, 52, 119, 133, 168,
Ricardo, Benjamin, 204
Ricardo, David, 204–205
Rieger firm, 40, 75, 81
Rinck, Johann Christian Heinrich, 109, 121
Ritter, August Gottfried, 112, 119
Roethinger, Edmond Alexandre, 64, 66,
    234n98, 235n113
Rosenstein, Elkan, 34
Rosenstein, Gerson, 28–29
Rosenthal, Erwin, 153
Rossi, Salamone, 131, 152
Rothschild, Frank, 190
Rübenstein, Ernst, 120–121
Rupp, Emile, 58–59, 62–64, 94–95
Russo, Marco, 42
Rybnik, 33

Sachs, Curt, 12, 135
Sachs, Michael, 34–35, 92
Safed, 141
Saint Petersburg, 55, 144
Saint-Saëns, Camille, 75
Salomon, Karel, 202–203
Saminsky, Lazare, 195, 245n117
Samuel, Hans, 7, 80, 83, 134–136, 137, 138,
    154, 170–175, 176, 177, 178, 217
  in emigration, 202, 203–205, 208
  Variations in Canonic Style, 102, 175,
    177–184, 185
San Francisco, California, 190, 191, 195
Saperston, Williard W., 191–192
Saul, Felix, 98–99
Schäffer, Erich, 149
Schalit, Heinrich, 134, 138–140, 144, 154,
    161, 169, 203, 217
  Freitagabend-Liturgie, 102, 140–143, 185
  in emigration, 191, 192, 194, 195, 200
Schaper firm, 51
Schicht, Johann Gottfried, 107
Schiffner, Karl, 78
Schlaad firm, 235n116
Schleyer, Erika, 150
Schnitger, Arp, 97
Schoenberg, Arnold, 86–87, 132, 165, 217
Schroeder, Hermann, 136, 244n88
Schucht, Rudolf, 149
Schudt, Johann Jacob, 23–24,
    226–227n55

Schumann, Camillo, 247n158
Schuster, Giora, 209
Schwäbisch Hall, 55
Schwantzer, Hugo, 38, 96, 238n27
Schwarz, Hermann, 151, 152
Schweitzer, Albert, 58
Second Temple, 12, 14, 30, 31, 33
Seesen, 28–30
Sephardi Jewry, 102, 113, 156, 157, 173,
    242n51
  musical tradition, 103, 141, 175, 184,
    194, 204–205, 217
  use of organs, 39, 42–43, 231n56
Shamir, Gideon, 201, 209
shofar, 15, 84
Shulḥan Arukh, 25, 30, 227–228n68
Silbermann, Gottfried, 64
Singer, Joseph, 56, 119
Singer, Kurt, 146, 245n123
Sommer, Martha. *See* Hirsch, Martha Sommer
Sorge, Georg Andreas, 55
Spain, 15, 17, 18, 163
Stabernack, Carl, 152
Steinberg, Hans Wilhelm (William),
    169–170
Steinberg, Zeev, 209
Steinmeyer firm, 234n98
Steinthal, Hermann Heymann, 22
Stern, Julius, 35, 37
Stettin. *See* Szczecin
Strasbourg, 34, 59, 62–64, 66, 234n97,
    234n98, 235n113
Strauss, Elias, 139
Stravinsky, Igor, 132, 161
Strebel firm, 234n97
Stuttgart, 52, 59, 100, 240n19
Sucher-Hasselbeck, Rosa, 137
Sulzer, Joseph, 42
Sulzer, Salomon, 63, 119, 120, 121, 130,
    132, 134, 139, 143, 165, 230n35
  Schir Zion, 42, 111–112, 164
  views on organ in synagogue, 35, 38, 41
Szczecin, 77, 122, 128
Szekszárd, 74

ta'am. See *cantillation*
Taboada, Delfin Fernandes, 201
Tal, Josef, 109–110, 251n57
Tall, Abraham Levi ben Menahem, 23
Talmud, 11, 12, 32, 90